# Parmenides, Venerable and Awesome

(Plato, *Theaetetus* 183e)

# Parmenides, Venerable and Awesome

(Plato, *Theaetetus* 183e)

Proceedings
of the International Symposium
Buenos Aires, October 29–November 2, 2007

Edited by
Néstor-Luis Cordero

PARMENIDES
PUBLISHING
Las Vegas | Zurich | Athens

PARMENIDES PUBLISHING
Las Vegas | Zurich | Athens



This edition published in 2011 by Parmenides Publishing
in the United States of America

ISBN soft cover: 978-1-930972-33-9
ISBN e-Book: 978-1-930972-62-9

**Library of Congress Cataloging-in-Publication Data**

Parmenides, venerable and awesome (Plato, Theaetetus 183e) : proceedings of the international symposium (Buenos Aires, October 29/November 2, 2007) / edited by Néstor-Luis Cordero.
p. cm.
Includes bibliographical references and index.
ISBN 978-1-930972-33-9 (softcover : alk. paper)
ISBN 978-1-930972-62-9 (e-book)
1. Parmenides—Congresses. 2. Parmenides. Nature—Congresses. I. Cordero, Nestor-Luis. II. Title.

B235.P24P37 2011
182'.3—dc22

2011013496

Typeset in Adobe Caslon Pro and OdysseaUBSU (Greek)
by 1106 Design | www.1106design.com
Printed and lay-flat bound by USBookPrint | www.usbookprint.com

Cover Image: Parmenides. Detail from *The School of Athens* by Raffaello Sanzio, ca. 1510-1512. Stanza della Segnatura, Stanze di Raffaello, Vatican Palace, Vatican State. Image Source: Scala / Art Resource, NY. Rendering of the image by Arnold Hermann | lightandnight.com

1-888-PARMENIDES
www.parmenides.com

# Contents

## Part II: Parmenides in the Tradition and Cognate Themes

# Foreword

Although Parmenides probably wrote as early as the beginning of the 5th century BCE, his work was still in circulation some eleven centuries later, even if it was considered "a rarity" (σπάνιν) by then according to Simplicius (6th century AD).[1] Since then, the text of Parmenides, like most of the treatises written in ancient times, has been on the list of works irredeemably lost. For several centuries, the only access to Parmenides' philosophy lay in the rare references to his work preserved in those of other philosophers or ancient authors, references that were sometimes accompanied by textual quotations (which lets us assume that these authors had a copy of the original text of Parmenides' Poem at hand).

The practice was eventually abandoned when, by the end of the 16th century, philologists like Henri Estienne and Julius Caesar Scaliger began to reconstruct the lost text through a meticulous search and compilation of the quotations spread throughout classical treatises. This process arguably culminated in 1835, when Simon Karsten succeeded in gathering nineteen passages (one of them in Latin) from the lost original to publish the most complete reconstruction. We now call this set of 152 verses "Parmenides' Poem." Thanks to the efforts of these scholars, researchers now have an approximate (given its fragmentary nature) but faithful (given its literal character backed-up by the work of philologists and codicologists) version of the original poem.

[1] Simplicius, *Comments on Aristotle's* Physics, p. 144.

Since then, we've been able to confirm that the adjectives "venerable and awesome," used by Plato (*Theaetetus*, 183e) to describe Parmenides' personality, were fully justified. "Venerable," without doubt, since the four or five pages that constitute the "complete work" of Parmenides today are a relic that inspires great respect and admiration, but also "awesome," because any conscientious researcher must approach the fragments with precaution and astuteness, keeping in mind the force and the power of those pieces of the text that will most likely never be known in their integrity.

Thousands of works have been dedicated to the study of the Poem since the publication of Henri Estienne's *Poesis Philosophica* in 1573. From a formal point of view, significant progress has been made in "cleansing" the text of impurities and erroneous readings by the original sources, errors which were passed down and repeated until the arrival of Hermann Diels's version in 1897, which has been considered "orthodox" ever since. However, even Diels' cleverness did not prevent him from introducing new anomalies to the misreadings transmitted by tradition.[2]

Some questions certainly remain concerning the formal structure of the text, such as what position certain "fragments" may have occupied in the original. The present arrangement, which arbitrarily establishes fragment 19 as the end of the Poem, may not correspond with the original. As the purification of the text continues, studies about the ideas conveyed by Parmenides find increasingly strong and clear grounds. Proof of this lies in the remarkably high level of discourse reached by Parmenidean studies over the last few years. Some titles may have escaped us, but there have been at least thirteen books on Parmenides

[2] In the last forty years it was possible to free verse 1.3 from the uncomfortable "ἄστη" (incompatible with a trip carried out through "a way *separate* from the human path"), which had no manuscript authority (cf. A. H. Coxon, "The Text of *Parmenides* fr. 1.3," *Classical Quarterly* 18 [1968], 69). The authenticity of πάντων (and not πάντα) in 12.4 has been confirmed (cf. David Sider, "Confirmation of Two 'Conjectures' in the Presocratics: Parmenides B12 and Anaxagoras B15," *Phoenix* 33, 1 [1979], 68). At the same time, it was possible to restore the original second τὸ (instead of τε) in 6.1, present in all the manuscript traditions of Simplicius: τὸ λέγειν τό νοεῖν (cf. Néstor-Luis Cordero, "Les Deux Chemins de Parménide dans les fr. 6 et 7," *Phronesis* 24 [1979], 1).

published between 2005 and 2008.[3] In addition, beginning in 2004, an annual philosophical conference has been held in Ascea-Velia, where Parmenides holds a privileged place.[4] Moreover, since 2000, a prestigious publishing house (which is honoring us with the publication of these *Proceedings*) has been dedicating its efforts to the dissemination of classical thought by invoking the great Elean: Parmenides Publishing.

Worldwide interest in Parmenidean studies has also touched the austral end of the Southern hemisphere, and in November 2007, the "Centro de Estudios de Filosofía Antigua" (CEFA) of the National University of San Martín (Buenos Aires, Argentina), decided to dedicate an International Symposium to the philosophy of Parmenides. Invited to participate in the event were those main scholars who had published *at least* one book on Parmenides.[5] Sixteen authors confirmed their participation (two who were unable to attend nevertheless sent their contributions).

Part I of the present volume gathers together the set of papers presented at the Symposium, whose topics were divided up based on the "traditional" structure of the Poem: one section dedicated to the exposition of the way of truth, and the other to the description of the "opinions (δόξαι) of mortals." This

---

[3] Arnold Hermann, *To Think Like God: Pythagoras and Parmenides* (Las Vegas: Parmenides Publishing, 2004); Cordero, *By Being, It Is* (Las Vegas: Parmenides Publishing, 2004); Massimo Pulpito, *Parmenide e la negazione del tempo* (Milano: LED Edizioni Universitarie, 2005); Chiara Robbiano, *Becoming Being: On Parmenides' Transformative Philosophy* (Sankt Augustin: Akademia Verlag, 2006); Fernando Santoro, *Poema de Parmênides: Da Natureza* (Rio de Janeiro: Azougue Editorial, 2009); Jean Bollack, *Parménide: de l'étant au monde* (Paris: Verdier, 2006); José Solana Dueso, *De Logos a Physis: Estudio sobre el Poema de Parménides* (Zaragoza: Mira, 2006); Panagiotis Thanassas, *Parmenides, Cosmos and Being* (Milwaukee: Marquette University Press, 2007); Parménides, *Poema: Fragentos y tradición textual,* edited and translated by A. Bernabé; introduction, notes and commentary by J. Pérez de Tudela; epilogue by N.-L. Cordero (Madrid: Istmo, 2007); Scott Austin, *Parmenides and the History of Dialectic: Three Essays* (Las Vegas: Parmenides Publishing, 2007); Walter Fratticci *Il bivio di Parmenide* (Siena: Cantagalli, 2008); Giuseppe Scuto, *Parmenides' Weg* (Sankt Augustin: Akademia Verlag, 2008); Néstor-Luis Cordero et al., *Parmenide scienziato?*, ed. L. Rossetti and F. Marcacci (Sankt Augustin: Akademia Verlag, 2008).

[4] The conference is titled ELEATICA and is organized by Livio Rossetti (Perugia University).

[5] See "About the Contributors," pp. xiii–xvi.

rigorous partition was nevertheless an object of criticism and the source of much debate as to its meaning. Panagiotis Thanassas, for instance, discusses the dual structure of the Poem and its impact on the traditional perception of Parmenides as a rigorous "monist." Jean Bollack found that the most satisfactory solution to explaining the two parts of the Poem lies in considering the whole and to show that one part, the definition of Being, actually refers to the other as the projection of an organization of the world, and that both terms correspond perfectly to each other.

Other papers went deeply into the part of the Poem concerning the "opinions of mortals." Jean Frère proposed to restrict the "mortals" to just certain people who were part of particular philosophical schools, specifically the Pythagoreans. But most presentations examined the value of "Parmenidean Physics" as shown in this part of the poem. Giovanni Casertano discussed the special status of Parmenides in the history of scientific thought, while Massimo Pulpito proposed to limit correct physical theories to certain passages of the Poem, which would be a development of the formula "τὰ δοκοῦντα." Alexander P. D. Mourelatos, on his part, was interested in some astronomical theories that he considers to be "breakthroughs." More radically, my own paper read all fragments referring to the physics as part of the speech on truth, because, given the not-true and deceptive character that Parmenides attributes to δόξαι, "Parmenidean physics" cannot belong to the "opinions of mortals." This proposition therefore suggests a new rearrangement of the fragments.

The section of the Poem concerning the fact of being and its characteristics was the subject of Robbiano's, Solana Dueso's, Santoro's, and Austin's papers. Chiara Robbiano, answering the question "What is Parmenides' Being?" found that Being is the fundamental unity of what-is and what-understands, the unity that is also the condition for the possibility of human understanding. José Solana Dueso analyzed the relationship between logic and ontology, and proposed different arguments for a primarily logical and only secondarily ontological interpretation of the ἀλήθεια of Parmenides (fr. 2–fr. 8.50). Fernando Santoro found in the "σήματα" of fragment 8 a genealogy of the idea of ontological categories. And Scott Austin affirmed that Parmenides' absolute monism puts existence and essence into an absolutely monistic Being as it joins levels in an ontological hierarchy that other philosophers were later to separate.

Two further contributions dealt an analysis of the notion of "thought." For José Trindade Santos the identity of thought and Being dominates Parmenides' argument in the Way of Truth and persists in later relevant conceptions as Platonic ἐπιστήμη and Aristotelian "active intellect." Patricia Curd on her part analyzed the relation between thought and body, as suggested by fragment 16, and saw that the mortal's error is to mistake the passive experiences of sense perception for genuine thought about what-is, and hence fail to understand the true nature of what-is.

Arnold Hermann was interested in Parmenides' heritage in Plato's *Parmenides,* and considers that the so-called "parricide" of the *Sophist* is only an heir. Finally, Barbara Cassin asked the question that every scholar silently asks himself: Is it possible to translate Parmenides? The eventual conclusion is that "Parmenides is lost in translation."

The organizers of the meeting, which was open to the public, offered eight young and high-level Argentine researchers (graduate students, professors, or advanced students) the opportunity to present a short paper in front of the prestigious assembly of foreign authors. The exchange of ideas between them and their "teachers" was a very enriching experience. These eight papers are included in Part II of the present volume.

The International Symposium's success would have been impossible without the support of two prestigious institutions: Parmenides Publishing (United States), and the HYELE Institute for Comparative Studies (Switzerland), an institution whose name alludes to the *polis* of Parmenides. The CEFA is greatly and deeply thankful to both institutions for their support.

—Néstor-Luis Cordero

## About the Contributors

The principal speakers invited to the Symposium "Parmenides, Venerable and Awesome" shared the distinction of having published at least one, if not several books on Parmenides. To honor these works, the notes below focus on the contributors' books on Parmenides exclusively.

**Scott Austin** is Associate Professor of Philosophy at Texas A&M University. He is the author of *Parmenides: Being, Bounds, and Logic* and *Parmenides and the History of Dialectic.*

**Jean Bollack** is Professor Honorarium at Charles de Gaulle University–Lille3. He is the author of *Parménide. De l'étant au monde.*

**Giovanni Casertano** is retired Professor of the History of Ancient Philosophy at the University of Naples Federico II. He is the author of *Parmenide. Il metodo, la scienza, l'esperienza.*

**Barbara Cassin** is Director of Research at the National Center for Scientific Research (CNRS), Léon Robin Research Center on Ancient Thought. She is the author of *Si Parménide*, *L'Effet Sophistique*, and *Parmenides, Sur La nature ou sur L'étant: la langue de l'être?*

**Giovanni Cerri** is Professor of Greek Literature at Roma Tre University. He is the author of *Parmenide di Elea: Poema sulla natura.*

**Néstor-Luis Cordero** is Emeritus Professor at the University of Rennes I. He is the author of *Les deux chemins de Parménide* and *By Being, It Is: The Thesis of Parmenides.*

**Patricia Curd** is Professor of Philosophy at Purdue University. She is the author of *The Legacy of Parmenides: Eleatic Monism and Later Presocratic Thought.*

**Jean Frére** is Professor of Philosophy at the Léon Robin Research Center on Ancient Thought, Paris-Sorbonne University (Paris IV). He is the co-author, with Denis O'Brien, of *Le poème de Parménide: texte, traduction, essai critique.*

**Arnold Hermann** is the founder and director of the Hyele Institute for Comparative Studies. He is the author of *To Think Like God: Pythagoras and Parmenides. The Origins of Philosophy.*

**Alexander P. D. Mourelatos** is Professor Emeritus of Philosophy and Classics at the University of Texas at Austin. He is the author of *The Route of Parmenides: A Study of Word, Image, and Argument in the Fragments.*

**Massimo Pulpito** holds a PhD in the History of Philosophy and is a tenured Teacher of Philosophy at the Liceo Classico Statale "Quinto Ennio," Taranto. He is the author of *Parmenide e la negazione del tempo.*

**Chiara Robbiano** is Assistant Professor of Philosophy and Tutor at University College Utrecht. She is the author of *Becoming Being: On Parmenides' Transformative Philosophy.*

**Fernando Santoro** is Professor of Philosophy at the Federal University of Rio de Janeiro. He is the author of *Poema de Parmênides da Natureza.*

**José Trindade Santos** is Associate Professor of Philosophy at the Federal University of Paraíba and retired Professor of Philosophy at the University of Lisbon. He is the author of *Da Natureza Parmênides.*

**José Solana Dueso** is Professor of Philosophy at the University of Zaragoza. He is the author of *De Logos a Physis. Estudio sobre el poema de Parménides.*

**Panagiotis Thanassas** is Assistant Professor of Philosophy at the Aristotle University of Thessaloniki. He is the author of *Die erste "zweite Fahrt": Sein des Seienden und Erscheinen der Welt bei Parmenides* and *Parmenides, Cosmos and Being: A Philosophical Interpretation.*

***Additional Contributors***

**Esteban Bieda** is Assistant Professor of Philosophy at the University of Buenos Aires.

**María Elena Díaz** is Assistant Professor of Philosophy at the University of Buenos Aires.

**Gabriel Livov** is Assistant Professor of Political Philosophy at the University of Buenos Aires.

**Ezequiel Ludueña** is Assistant Professor of the History of Medieval Philosophy at the University of Buenos Aires.

**Claudia T. Mársico** is Professor of Philosophy at the University of Buenos Aires and at the National University of San Martín, as well as Researcher at the National Council of Scientific and Technical Research (CONICET).

**Fabián Mié** is Associate Professor of Ancient Philosophy at the National University of Córdoba and Associate Researcher at the Argentinian National Council of Scientific and Technical Research (CONICET).

**Lucas Soares** is Assistant Professor of Philosophy at the University of Buenos Aires.

**Pilar Spangenberg** is Assistant Professor of Ancient Philosophy at the University of Buenos Aires.

**A Note on the Translations:** Most of the papers collected in this volume were originally presented in Spanish, Portuguese, Italian, and French. Contributors subsequently submitted English translations of their papers for publication. While these were edited for clarity and consistency, the principal goal has been to preserve the original voice of each scholar.

# Part I: On Parmenides

# Existence and Essence in Parmenides

Scott Austin

**Summary**

Parmenides' absolute monism puts existence and essence into an absolutely monistic Being as it joins levels in an ontological hierarchy that other philosophers, from the Neoplatonists through Hegel, were later to separate. The result is a fusion of presentation and representation, a fusion not teased apart until the twentieth century.

In this offering, I would like to suggest that Parmenides' philosophy and methodology already contain, in a focused way, many crucial elements which later philosophers merely set out and distinguish from one another. I shall concentrate on the question of existence and essence; the questions of negation and necessity; and on features of Eleatic methodology which become features of later ontology. First, a comparison between Parmenides and Aquinas on the question of necessity.

In Aquinas, the distinction between contingent and necessary beings can be phrased in terms of the distinction between existence and essence. In a contingent being, we have existence separate from essence, a kind of boundary. In a necessary being, we have no separation between existence and essence, together with unboundedness. And Aquinas reads Exodus, "I Am Who Am," as meaning that God is the being which is What Is, i.e., the being in Whom existence and essence are one: I am the One Who Is. Parmenidean Being is also a being which is its essence. Its essence, as logical subject, is simply what is: it is the ἐόν: for it to be is for it to be ungenerable, unperishing, whole, and so on. This is why the subject is a participialized version of the copula.

Being is; it has no other essence than to be in certain ways, ways expressive of complete being outside of time, in uniformity and completeness. Being as essence is simply what it is to be what is. This is why we do not find the copula directly negated in a description of Being in fragment 8 of Parmenides' poem, although we do find negated predicates; to negate the copula would be to destroy the essence, to make it impossible to introduce a transcendental predicate, to bring it about that what is is not, either globally or in some particular respect.

Another way to approach Parmenidean Being is to notice that, in it, source and archetype coincide. In a contingent hierarchical series, the cause of the series, the reason for its being, is not necessarily the same as the archetypal member of the series, the embodiment of its essence. The prototype is not necessarily its own cause. But Aquinas' God is both prototype, the essence in which all beings participate, and cause, the only being which is unlimited being. Similarly with Parmenides: there is no difference between Being, as a proper name, and What-Is, since for it to be is for it to be what it is.

Finally—and this is a difference between Parmenides and Aquinas—Parmenidean Being is also the only member of the series, the only thing that participates in being, whereas, for Aquinas, the whole order of created natures consists in beings which, deriving their being from God, are nevertheless distinct from God. Thus Parmenidean Being is the only embodiment, the only particularization, of the essence which it is.

Parmenidean Being is, then, what Aquinas' God would be if it were the only being in existence. It collapses metaphysical distinctions within itself just as Aquinas' God does, and also collapses the distinction between God and creation. The result is a being which, as logical subject, simply is a participialized version of the copula, and whose predicates all express totality in Being's possession of its own essence. And all of this follows from Being's necessity—in Aquinas, expressed by Being's infinity, in Parmenides by its finitude or boundedness.

Parmenidean Being is also a collapsed version of the three hypostases of Neoplatonism. For, I take it, the One, the first hypostasis, is the source in the series of realities; Mind, the second, is the archetype which has all the intelligibles, all the Platonic Forms, within it; and Soul, expressing the relationship between Mind and the One as Mind returns to the One, is the participant in the archetype as caused by the source, the hypostasis which puts the many intelligibles into time one by one. Collapse these three principles into an ontological monism, and you have Parmenidean Being as I have just described it. It is the reason why it is, the source; it is the ultimate essence, the archetype; and it is the only being which has being, the only being which particularizes the archetype. This, again, is simply a consequence of monism, for when I say, for example, "What-is is whole," I name a subject which is the participialization of the copula; I connect it, using the copula, with a predicate; and I also express its essence using that predicate—and yet all three of these roles are one.

There are also other distinctions that are collapsed in the absolute monism of fragment 8. The universe of the goddess, besides being a universe with only one member, is also a universe without contingency: Being is necessary, but it is also the only being which is possible, so, in a sense, whatever is possible is also necessary, if one leaves out of consideration for a moment the haphazard universe of mortal opinion. Thus there are only four possible modal propositions, propositions which I take to be expressed by the modal metaphors in the poem, and also by the pervasive metaphors of fetters, chains, and boundedness. First, it is not possible for Being to alter in time: Justice does not allow it to come to be or to perish. Second, it is necessary that it not alter in time: True Trust drove off coming-to-be and perishing. Third, it is necessary that it occupy space uniformly: Necessity held it in bonds. Finally, it is not right for it to be incomplete, a double-negation. The four faces of necessity, the necessity in the modal relationship of Being to the road-markers expressive of its essence, all coincide at the bound, which does not allow itself to be transgressed either from inside or from outside, and which does not weaken its grip or relax its hold on Being.

Negative and positive modal propositions coincide in these four faces of necessity.

There is also a coincidence of negativity and positivity in the essence itself. Positive predicates are asserted ("whole," "perfect") and denied ("bigger," "divisible"), and this is also true of privative predicates ("incomplete" is denied while "unperishing" is asserted). But no predicate is introduced with a negated copula. The point seems to be that Being can tolerate denials, especially where contraries are concerned, as well as affirmations, especially where uniformity is concerned, either where positive predicates are concerned or where privative predicates are concerned. Instead of denying something of Being with a negated copula, Parmenides seems to prefer modal paraphrase: Justice does not allow Being to fail to be at any time, either by way of coming-to-be or by way of perishing, and Doom does not allow anything besides Being to come to be, either now or in the future, which would make it fail to be whole and immovable. The spectrum of possible types of predications is thus represented at every point. Thus the essence of Being, as expressed by these affirmations and denials, is such that it necessarily is globally and in every way, and cannot be otherwise—i.e., existence and essence coincide: to be identical with what completely is, essentially, is to be What Is, denominatively. All four faces of modality and of predication are, then, represented in fragment 8.

There is also a group of variations on the theme of unity and plurality. Being in lines 6–15 is defined negatively with regard to the line of time, a line which is full of contrariety at every point: it does not come to be or perish, but just is now, a one which excludes a many and which, as we saw, receives negative modal treatment. But Being in lines 22–25 is, metaphorically at least, occupying a plurality in space, which has no gaps or inhomogeneities. It is a one (Being itself, metaphorically represented as a mass) distributed through a many (the points in space) rather than in opposition to a many, as was the case with time. Thus it is a one in relation to itself, "the same, and in the same place, it stays within itself," a one which, instead of being described merely negatively, can also be described positively, by affirming its self-identity. Finally, in the section comparing Being to a ball (lines 42–49), we have not just one relation between Being and itself, but many, as the center relates to each point on the surface of the ball equally. Here we have many relations between one and one, or, alternatively, a one (the center) in relation to itself (a point on the surface) taken many times, not just once. This is, then, not just one relation to self, but many relations to self, a relation of relations, depicted as the ball itself. And the ball can then be described not only positively, with "perfect," but double-negatively, with "not . . . imperfect." The sequence in these three passages is thus:

6–15 one versus many
22–25 one in many
42–49 many in many

or

6–15 no relations allowed
22–25 relation to self
42–49 relation of relations

or

6–15 negative
22–25 positive
42–49 double-negative

The relational complexity continues to grow as the logical alternatives of positivity and negativity continue to be filled out.

Here the title of Plato's *Parmenides* becomes relevant. For there are comparisons between the sequence of alternatives just outlined in the poem and the sequence of sections presented in the second half of the dialogue. Leaving out of consideration the section of text that Proclus calls the third hypothesis and that Cornford calls Hypothesis 2A, the first four hypotheses consider, respectively, what happens if the One is, first, for the One in relation to itself (and here the consequences are all negative); second, for the One in relation to the Others (positive consequences); third, for the Others in relation to the One (again, positive consequences); and fourth, for the Others in relation to each other (negative consequences). Where the One relates only to itself, or the Others relate only to each other, the consequences are negative; where the One relates to the Others, or vice versa, the consequences are positive. Thus:

I. One-One —

II. One-Others ++

III. Others-One ++

IV. Others-Others —

Here there is, indeed, I would suggest, a parallel with Parmenides' own poem. For the first section of the poem (lines 6–15) does consider Being as unrelated to time, or related only negatively to coming-to-be and perishing; lines 22–25 consider Being positively as related to a manifold of places within itself; and lines 42–49 consider the relations among those relations as the ball's many surface-points relate to each other, double-negatively. What shows up in the poem as differences in methodology, as different road-markers are treated, shows up in the dialogue in the differences among hypotheses. Proclus, indeed, thought that each hypothesis represented a new descending level in an elaborate triadic ontology. I do not think that it is necessary to go that far; but, for example, the first three hypostases in Plotinus are, respectively, an isolated One, knowable only negatively; Mind as a one-in-many as it presents the unity in one consciousness of all the Platonic intelligibles; and Soul, presenting the many, now in time, as they relate to each other one after the other. Here we have the same kind of radiation from a separate One down to an immanent Many through a series of stages. In Parmenides, the progression is methodological only, since the three successive contexts are, after all, only different ways of looking at one Being; but in Plotinus and Proclus, the progression is a descent down the upper levels of an ontological hierarchy. Plato's dialogue is, perhaps, the point of transition between the monistic and the pluralistic approach here, as the successive hypotheses move from the isolated One down to a set of comparisons among the Many.

Here, again, the roles played by different principles, or different metaphysical constituents, in later thinkers, are all played by Being in the Parmenidean approach. But even Parmenides has a triadic methodology, three different ways of taking Being as it may relate to itself, as it may be described negatively, positively, or double-negatively. Thus the historical Parmenides is the result of a retroactive collapse of Neoplatonic Ontology and methodology into an absolute monism.

Hegel, of course, is Proclus set into motion, and the connection is clear between Neoplatonic One (=Hegelian Being-in-Itself), Neoplatonic Mind (=Hegelian Being-for-Itself), and Neoplatonic Soul (=Being-in-and-for-Itself). Somewhere in between would be the Christian Trinitarian filiation and spiration, as well as the positives and negatives of, for example, Pseudo-Dionysian negative theology. The basic triad in all these cases comprises 1) a pure presence, knowable only as a plenum and keeping strictly to itself; 2) the outward representation of that presence, its irradiation into plurality and distinction; 3) the return back to the first level, a plurality reorganizing itself into a unity, knowable both negatively and positively. The tradition after Parmenides thus turns levels and distinctions which, for him, had been only methodological, into the agitating devices of a pluralistic ontology and historical teleology. But the methods, and the distinctions within it, are Eleatic, as the title of Plato's dialogue would suggest, as well as the *Sophist*'s preoccupation with the results of an ontology grounded in non-identity and difference. The three Neoplatonic principles correspond to the distinction (used earlier in discussing Aquinas) between source (the One), archetype (Mind), and embodiment (Soul).

I have suggested that Parmenides' goddess collapses the later distinctions between existence and essence, together with elements in later ontology, into her methodology. Indeed, it would be a caricature to see Parmenides as Hegel does—the advocate of a distinctionless, negationless Being-in-Itself—given that her own speech is textured with negative predicates and modal metaphors (not including non-identity). It would also be an oversimplification to see her unnegated copulas as betokening pure existence, or a purely positive state of affairs without any negative propositions. The ontology of what a thing is, the source of later metaphysics from Socrates to Heidegger, together with a dialectical method in which negation is redeemed and included, radiate out from the nucleus of the Parmenidean Being.

Much of postmodern philosophy is concerned to restress a distinction between presentation and representation, as it is no longer taken for granted that speech—our way of representing reality—transparently gives us a grip on reality itself. Representations may bring Being closer to us, but they also partially obscure it, veil it, in the very act of bringing it closer, and Being itself, in transparent clarity, never appears unmasked on the tragic stage of philosophy and human life; there is no easy dialectical reconciliation between Being as it may be in itself and Being as it may be for us. I take that, even as early as Parmenides, what we have is not, *pace* Heidegger, a being free from domination by speech, but already a Being which gives itself to those who go in quest of it. The sources of representational thinking are to be found already in the Presocratics themselves, in a Being which makes itself one with those who would contemplate it.

# From Being to the World and Vice Versa

Jean Bollack

## Summary

The importance of the δόξα is accepted today by scholars; the problem is now the relation between the two parts of the poem. The most satisfactory solution is to consider the whole and to show that one part, the definition of Being, is made in reference to the other, as the projection of an organization of the world, and that both terms correspond perfectly to each other. This perspective allows us to reread the introduction as an initiation from a man who "already knows" better than anyone else, but lets himself be told everything by an honored authority: she discloses the truth of language and transmits, for the δόξα, the vision, in accord with Being, of a rigorous opposition.

## The starting point: getting rid of historical layers

Parmenides plays an important part, if not a capital part, at the horizon of the history of thought. In fact, it is largely thanks to the history of thought that Parmenides has reached us, mainly through Plato's ontological speculations. In the *Cratylus*, Plato lets representation overshadow language, and his Parmenides, as presented in the metaphysical dialogues, is reduced to a partisan of the One versus the multiple. When we apply this posterior interpretation back to Parmenides' "to be," which bears the origins of language, we lose track of the relationship between thought and speech. The text establishes such a relationship by implying a person who says "is," a speaker. The original text bears the marks of subsequent readings and borrowings.

I have chosen to locate Parmenides in his own time, at the moment of the elaboration of his poem, thus adopting a historical perspective, I had to take into account, as far as possible, the philosophical and, more broadly, intellectual context. In Parmenides' most audacious innovations, we sense his vision of his predecessors, as much in his extensive use of Homeric language—a debt that is currently underestimated—as in his treatment of Ionian unifying thought.

To grasp the relationship between the Truth and the Doxa, I have indicated in my book *Parmenides, from Being to the World,* published in 2006,[1] the passages that, in the elaboration of the 'Eόν, implicitly point toward the world, as later presented, and symmetrically the elements in the Doxa that point back to the previous part, which establishes their legitimacy.[2]

These correspondences are meaningful. The 'Eόν and the world depend on one another; the latter determines and structures the autonomy of the former, as much as it follows the pattern imposed by the preliminary definitions. The Ionian ἀρχή is proved both impossible and impracticable. It implies two orders—root and proliferation—that are mingled. Yet they do not mingle. The one can only be the principle of the other through a radical separation. This division becomes the method. It implies and corrects a link; it gives birth to two orders of knowledge, as exposed and coordinated by the voice of the goddess, master of speech. In this correlation, the world, built according to Being, is no less part of the final scheme; we cannot depreciate any of the parts. The second one could not be missing, if the first one were written for its purpose. In its difference, newly established, the purpose of Being is the world.

[1] Jean Bollack, *Parménide: De l'étant au Monde* (Paris: Verdier Poche, 2006).

[2] Cf. the list of quoted passages in the index, op. cit., p. 342, s.v. Doxa: "construite dans l'Étant," and, reciprocally, "l'Étant dans la Doxa."

## The unity of the poem: a tight correlation between the two parts

Non-being is excluded when we speak about being; there is no non-being in being. Yet this holds only when speaking about Being. Thus, in spite of incompatible levels of knowledge, we remain always on the same road, that which springs from the choice of "is," a choice that conditions everything, up to the patterns of the stars, and up to the human beings themselves. It is fundamental to understand the link between the two parts, a link responsible for the unity of the poem. But is it no less fundamental to understand how the link answers previous philosophical questioning. The radical distinction leads to a reconciliation of the two orders, reconciliation that takes the separation completely into account. It is impossible to contain error and ignorance, impossible to avoid arbitrary judgements or hypothetical guesses. Yet we have to live in the world, and cannot be satisfied with sole speculation. The bid will be won by the best possible approximation of truth. A crucial superlative. The strength of Parmenides' deductive argumentation remains unchanged from one order to the other, passing from Being to Doxa. There is no specific "doxic" language, as far as my analysis of the remaining fragments about the world proves. The continuity is obvious; it is sought after, from the metaphysical authority to its projection in the field of adaptation.

## The separation of the principle leads to the world

There is a χωρισμός—a very different one from Plato's, since Parmenides manages to integrate the world within the frame dictated by the Truth. At the same time, his Truth is much more autonomous, much more exterior to the world. But its principle is maintained in the transfer from definition to application: the separation that characterizes Being. This fundamental separation is transcended within the structure of a world in which men must live, because men cannot live with separation. Thus is the world elaborated as closely as possible to the cognitive operation that founded its principle. In turn, life will more surely lead to knowledge if it presents a structure strictly deduced from the principle.

## From ἐστι to ἐόν and τὸ ἐόν

The core "is" (ἐστι) is drawn from language and refers to it. In this state, the word represents the most universal element, both singular and open; it can be isolated, or it can represent a substitute for anything that has ever been said. It is presented as an irrevocable choice, without rival, qualified by its very choice. It is chosen as a basis on which is elaborated subsequent reasoning, a development that all the more reinforces the impact of the choice.

In a second phase, the word takes the shape of an object to be conceived and discussed, an object capable of existing, with matching qualifications and exclusions. The transformation of ἐστι into an object of representation corresponds to another grammatical formulation: ἐόν, a neutral participle. 'Eόν has a raw consistency given by its autonomy that allows it to occupy the former place of an ἀρχή. It is the unique formulation, throughout the elaboration of Being, up to the doorstep (fr. 8.32), where it finds its determination and completion, thus becoming τὸ ἐόν ("being," the participle). In German and in French, the infinitive form of the verb ("sein" and "être," respectively) is frequently used, but it is the participle ἐόν that denotes the process of constitution of the sphere. In this incarnated shape, it becomes the principle for the elaboration of the world. The attributes of Being are met by a material system.

## Abstraction takes a shape

In the course of the argumentation, the "signs" (σήματα) are enumerated first: they are the characteristics of Being, and analyzing them allows the establishment of a corporality true to the concept. It is as if abstraction itself could take shape from its separate field, opening up to totalization, a prefiguration of the world. The world springs from its very principle, logically deduced, contained within the logic and spherical in its conception, even before its birth. Becoming is banned, or rather redefined. The world has no birth. Eros acts on a very different basis, without fusion. Difference—that is, opposition—remains within a juxtaposition, and Parmenides' "mixture" is without mixing.

In fact, as much as Being remains an isolated model, shaped in abstraction, so does the world, deduced from it and born into the same abstraction. Division becomes a rule, strictly transmitted from Being to the world. It has a shape, sprung from logic and able to reproduce. Thus, the passage is easy, from truth to something like cheating, the ἀπάτη away from the road (the πάθος). The mode of dividing bodies, down to the infinitely small and without fusion, is part of the scheme, as much as difference is excluded from the initial speech. Being is shaped up; its destruction is no less planned, according to its essence. We could almost superimpose both types of knowledge, unable to meet one another yet desperately seeking to correspond. The structure of the world, proposed or imposed to the adepts, leads them to perceive that there is an arrangement that tells the true matrix. The part dedicated to the world is an interpretation, a very elaborate construction.

## Determinated Being and human language

When the Goddess determinates the ἐόν, using τό, she brings the demonstration to an end. She then goes back to the relationship between language and thought, a relationship that is based on the use of determination (fr. 8.34–36). The point is the identity between the act of thinking ("to think") and the object attributed by language "in the field of speech" (πεφατισμένον). In fact, the determination is initially present in the language: thought emerges when it recognizes the shape of a concept. The determinations echo one another in strict correspondence—or even collaboration—between language and thought. A subject projects itself onto language, which offers objects of confirmation and consolidation; Humboldt describes the process exactly in this way.[3] Parmenides also describes a phase in the history of the speaking man (*homo loquens*): that of the first determination, that gives birth to language, when words are distributed. When a man said he "was" or "was not," he was convinced he said the truth. These terms are almost the exact definition of the Doxa, which has no certitudes, and does not say the truth

[3] See his treaty, *On Comparative Study of Language.*

(fr. 1.30), not having the technical means, inherent to language, to establish the truth.

## The four levels of utilization of language

Four levels are determined by the essential differentiations. The first one is given by human language, as it was constituted at the origins. Being is not the speaker; the speaker is man, who voices his own "being." The second stage is the way history uses language, against its initial truth, particularly the first philosophers, who get the basic meanings mixed up. We reach the third phase, the true speech of Parmenides' Goddess: thought finds a rigor on the basis of the inherent distinctions of language.

Then we have Parmenides' Doxa, which does not deserve the same consideration, although it also relies on truth. It is not an untruthful attempt to confuse minds, like Heraclitus' doctrine—as presented by Parmenides—or Anaximenes. It is a truthfully negative definition in a field where all affirmations are random. None of these affirmations are founded on a sound knowledge of the material world. Such is the basis for the cosmological elaboration, that boasts being a device. The Doxa is the best projection onto the screen of uncertainty of a meaningful model, whose sole virtue is to be derived from truth. Truth, when transferred, offers the best guidance to interpret the phenomena occurring in an uncertain domain, when we need to.

## Ἀπάτη: the adaptation of a speech

The word "deceitful" has been considered an embarrassing one. How could rigor be called untrue? Karl Reinhardt[4] once decided to moved away from current presentations, and proposed to transfer the contempt to the object of the Doxa, the world of perceptions, a distinction really absent from Parmenides' doctrine. On the contrary, the material world receives a privileged treatment. It is the formulation that is "deceitful," because it rests on a biased truth, remodelled and distorted; it mixes truth and false exactly like Odysseus' speech. In the *Odyssey*, he freely

[4] Karl Reinhardt, *Parmenides und die Geschichte der griechischen Philosophie* (Frankfurt am Main: Klostermann, 1916).

speaks of himself in the third person, yet maintaining his faculty to adapt to circumstances. It seems to me that paronomasias must not be underestimated in the structure of the poem. We find ourselves walking either far from the road, on the outside of the road or altogether without a road (ἀπάτητος). The interpretation implies not only that truth gives the starting point but also that, conversely, it can be attained from the tale. Both aspects designate at once the purpose and the aim of the scheme.

## The fault inherent to dualistic wandering

Language is re-introduced in the presentation of the dualistic principles, at the beginning of the Doxa. We can be grateful to Simplicius for having included these verses in his quotation, in awareness of their importance regarding the interrelation of the two parts.

Men, these verses tell us, have proceeded to a repartition of the forms as they came into being; that is, they have opposed them to one another. The distinction enabled them to name two ideas (γνῶμαι): light and night, which shared the appearance of all things in the world. All perception was brought down to these opposite realms. The distinction through opposition is a system that stems from Truth, in a way that needs to be explained. Difference is radical because men find themselves in a world of wandering. But it is a positive definition: wandering is constitutive; it establishes an existential and cognitive frame. Men are not said to have erred in their choice, as if another choice could be made. For Parmenides, it is the best possible choice, therefore a necessary one.

## The noetic exteriority introduced into the world

In the open field of abstraction, Being has imposed its solitude, to the exclusion of non-Being. This operation cannot be repeated in the world of wandering, but the gain will be kept if absolute negation now intervenes at the place corresponding to Being. This place, alienated, is occupied by both principles, even if some sort of superiority is granted to light. Light and night are strictly equal, each being the strict negation of the other, its "non-being," in a reciprocal way. It is therefore clear that duality, along with exclusion, as established in fr. 2 for the constitution of Being, brings a double singularity. The second principle, the partner, called "one of the two," according to the point of view, is of no use (οὐ χρεών). It is the non-Being opposite the Being, and reciprocally. The solution, when outside the domain of Truth, to avoid ambiguity and confusion, companions to becoming and fusion, is to split the model in two distinct ones. Exclusion is double, each mutually rejecting the other, in a fierce assertion of its own individuality, as demonstrated by the enumerated table of opposites (fr. 8.55–59).

The rejection of mixture, the separation of Being and non-Being, becomes a leitmotiv throughout the construction of the world, down to sexual intercourse and the theory of knowledge. The fight is against mixing-fusion. The aim is to prove that everything can happen without it, including creation and reproduction.

Some interpreters have chosen a grammatically improbable translation of the difficult verse (fr. 8.54), convinced that Parmenides was criticizing the dualistic system for lacking the unity of the Truth.[5] Or that duality was criticized as such (one of the principles being always arbitrary).[6] But he was really establishing a divergence. The relative clause should not be analyzed as a denunciation of the erratic thesis, but as the determination of a distinct order of knowledge, characterized by wandering (the perfect tense designates a resulting state).[7] In reference to the demonstration made for Being, Parmenides then adds that one of the principles—any of the two, since they are equal—does not share the necessity of Truth. The whole statement is determined by obligation (χρεών).[8] Because a superior justification is lacking,

[5] See, for example, Denis O'Brien, *Études sur Parménide*, Vol. I (Paris: Vrin, 1987), p. 57 ad loc. ". . . Si l'on ne nommait qu'une seule forme corporelle, l'on se rapprocherait davantage de l'unicité de l'être." He nevertheless mentions two other possible interpretations.

[6] For example, Reinhardt, op. cit., p. 70.

[7] Because of ἐν ᾧ, it is not an interpolated clause, the relative clause is part of the statement. Panagiotis Thanassas, *Die Erste "Zweite" Fahrt* (München: Fink, 1997), p. 167, rightly analyzes the radical mutual exclusion, but strangely interprets the radical character to be the cause of the error.

[8] Μίαν means "one as such," for itself or separately, with an implicit reference (then made explicit) to Truth.

the artificial construction of the Doxa is legitimate. Difference, that is, relative inferiority, is only emphasized to stress the excellence of the proposed system.

## The road of strict negation

Some interpreters have considered that coexistence or "mixture" were being opposed to the absolute separation of principles. Such a position is in contradiction with the evidence we have of the Doxa. In fact, the Doxa precisely rests upon the strictest of separations, and non-Being is introduced by the way of pure negation: non-night is set against non-fire, without ever mixing. Thus does rigorous contradiction give the world of becoming a structure that matches that of Being. Each of the principles excludes the presence of the other, finding its constitution in its own autonomous self. Being has no share with non-Being, and mutual exclusion is absolute. The subject perceives the division that governs the sky because he bears opposing forces within himself. The construction of the world prepares him for this perception, from where he can reconstruct the unity of the separate entities.

The road of non-Being is presented in fragment 6: it is one of the choices to avoid, regarding Being. This road is clearly distinguished from another wrong way that is to be avoided at all cost. The two roads have a different status. The second one is descriptive. It belongs to mortals without knowledge, like Parmenides' philosophical predecessors. Short-sighted, they confuse Being and non-Being. The first one, on the contrary, is a rigorous road, the negative mirror of the affirmative path of "is." The hierarchy established in fr. 6, "first this path, then," announces the elaboration of the Doxa, a roundabout avoiding the dead end, disqualifying previous attempts. It is not mentioned for the sake of rhetoric: non-Being is central in Parmenides' dualistic system of opposition; its function is an accurate correction.[9]

---

[9] The relationship between the two roads of error is clearly exposed by Chiara Robbiano, *Becoming Being: On Parmenides' Transformative Philosophy* (Leiden University, 2005; Trade Edition, Sankt Augustin: Academia Verlag, 2006). The author is probably wrong to consider the "names" that establish the Doxa unrelated to Truth (p. 241).

## The cosmogonic model of duality: movement in stillness

The world is preceded by an anterior state of concentric spheres, alternating light and night in strict separation. The spheres get thinner and thinner toward the equatorial center of the global sphere, that is, equidistant from the center and the periphery.[10] At this place, infinitely fine layers alternate without ever mixing. This is where Eros appears, in prepared circumstances (the verse is often quoted, along with a reference to Hesiod, ever since Plato's *Symposium*). In what came down to us of Parmenides' text, Eros is the only truly divine name—as opposed to divinized entities. This is significant. Eros is the god that brings together what is divided, himself participating in his own game. We cannot but suspect the very name of Eros to be a declination of love's opposite, strife or "Eris." Indeed, Parmenides' Eros governs divided elements and takes care that strict division is preserved within the union.

## Combinations of unmixed bodies

According to Theophrastus, *De sensu* § 4, Parmenides uses the Greek word for mixture, κρᾶσις, in a way that distinguishes it from fusion, where frontiers are banned. His use of the word κρᾶσις redefines it as the coexistence of separate ingredients. The dosage of opposing elements determines the texture of bodies that are the battlefield of continuous reciprocal strife. This particular quotation refers to the modalities of knowledge: the subject is invited to respect the doses to avoid altering the nature of the dosage. He should master it and learn to make use of its power (the moral guideline is always present). Theophrastus discusses this quotation and calls into question the case of an equal dosage of the components (still, of course, distinct from one another); for him, the word μῖξις can designate a homogeneous mixture, whereas Parmenides employs it for disparity. In the fragment, though, difference is the source of

10 The analysis of Aëtius' testimony (II, 7, 1) has allowed me to distinguish an abstract pre-cosmogonic phase that opens the genesis of difference; see my article "La cosmologie parménidéenne de Parménide," in Brague Rémi and Courtine Jean-François, eds., *Herméneutique et Ontologie. Hommage à Pierre Aubenque* (Paris: Presses Universitaires de France, 1990), pp. 17–53. See "Le monde 2: Le diagramme" in my 2006 book.

knowledge: every man is able to fill a lack, following the principle of completion. Identification works in a circle, bouncing back on the subject itself (the determinations meet: τὸ αὖ τό), mirroring a process that takes place in the field of Being.

## The birth of mankind and the origins of language

Speech first emerged in circumstances that were inherited from the genesis of the world, as described by the goddess. Time works like in epic tales: it locates the events. In fragment 8, the episode of the emergence of names (8.38) is set before the study of the spherical shape, which leads necessarily to the determination of Being (8.46) and prefigures the structure of the world. Shape and language are themes that interact. Language speaks truth. At this stage of completion, men found words to designate birth and death (γίγνεσθαι and ὄλλυσθαι) and associated them to Being and non-Being (εἶναι and οὐχί), in the same terms used for the duality in the Doxa. Topography and language are morphologically connected. It seems that, within the very definition of Being, when the conditions of its constitution are put forward, the composition of the world, the Doxa, is already anticipated.

The Doxa did not seem to include any doctrine of the hereafter:[11] purpose remains internal, bound within the limits of the world's architecture. The knowledge of its structure is intimately linked with the moral guideline. Parmenides' ethics are implicit, and therefore have been widely underestimated. We believe that the disciple, to adapt his way of life, whether newly converted or coming from a Pythagorean community, needed to read the Doxa thoroughly, to decipher its logical link with Being. The transfer teaches that the real purpose was the elaboration of a cosmology. Parmenides' text was written for a selected circle. It is orchestrated in such a way. Following this hypothesis, the two parts of the poem are intrinsically linked, and the subject is synthetic. It is no wonder that commentators have hesitated when attributing some fragments to Being or to the Doxa. The criteria for the choice are missing if the correlation of the two

[11] See the discussion at the end of my book (2006), "La Migration des Âmes," p. 327f.

parts is not clearly established. Parmenides composed the world in the way of an exercise, to incite speculation and to bring back to Being. Being is what the Doxa leads to.

The workmanship of the text, despite its fragmentary state, gives indications that need to be integrated in the interpretation. The writing aims at intellectual—if not spiritual—exercise, and its difficulty has a purpose: meditation, as opposed to revelation. Parmenides guides contemplation with a system that leads thought beyond it. He does not propose a doctrine that offers peace to the soul with dreams of the hereafter. The aim is to seek out understanding. We must bear in mind the collective exercises, supported by books or contemplative, organized by the Pythagorean communities before Parmenides' times. The Eleatic used an existing longing, and directed it toward a speculative vision that we are able to restore.[12]

Translated by Aude Engel

[12] Parmenides substitutes the constructions that refer to perceptible phenomena, for a new interpretative or speculative model, so that the interpretation of our double-faced world becomes an obligation (p. 212f. of my book).

# Parmenides-Scholar of Nature[1]

Giovanni Casertano

## Summary

Aristotle's influence on what we could name the philosophical historiography of pre-Aristotelian times and the one still felt up to present times is huge. We can safely argue that the work of freeing pre-Aristotelian thinkers from Aristotelian interpretation has only been developing since last century, and it is an ongoing process. I personally believe that this is the historiographic direction to be followed and that much has still to be made clear and explained in this very direction. This kind of research does not just better "historically contextualize" the thought of any pre-Aristotelian, Parmenides in our case, by setting its roots in a real world of debates, quarrels, and stand-takings on different philosophical and scientific questions, but it also better underlines its originality and speculative strengths. My paper will thus be divided into two parts. Since I just aim to discuss the special stand of Parmenides' thought in the history of scientific thought, I will try and show first of all Parmenides' complete belonging in the very lively world of scientific debates and discussions of the fifth century. Then I will try to show how Parmenides, like the other great Sicilian Magna Graecia native, Empedocles, has foreshadowed concepts and doctrines of contemporary science and physics, even if just in the shape of ingenious intuitions.

1. Mankind has had its geniuses who marked the history of our culture for ages, exerting their influence on many different branches, following a pattern that goes from working as a trigger for research,

[1] Translations of ancient texts as well as of the texts by quoted scholars are my own.

(i.e., promoting the gathering of experiences and knowledge) to being a hindrance and a restraint to the progress of sciences. One of those geniuses is surely enough Aristotle: his influence has been practically felt for more than two thousand years in all branches of science, from logics to physics to astronomy, from biology to zoology, and, of course, philosophy. The ingenious nature of his "arrangement" of knowledge, in each and every field, in a consistently organized picture where experience and rationality would meld without evident conflicts, made his thought a set and binding reference point for philosophers and scientists, thus promoting the development and widening of human cognition. At some point though, his influence turned into a hindrance to the progress of scientific knowledge, and it became necessary to "dismantle" it, that is, to break free from the powerful methodological and theoretical structure of his system, in order to be able to make progress with cognition. This was a long and slow process, not free from conflicts of course: if we allow ourselves some concise schematizations—recognizing all the limits, but also the truths, schematizations do have—we could state that while Aristotelian physics and astronomy had to be left behind between the 16th and 17th century (say from Copernicus to Kepler to Galileo), it was only in the 18th but most of all in the 19th century (say from Mendel to Darwin to Bernard) that his biology and physiology had to give way to the new scientific thought.

So what about philosophy? As we all know, philosophy is not a science like all others. An ancient author can be as helpful as and sometimes more helpful than a contemporary one in thinking and considering as well as in theorizing ways to think and consider and means to analyze and understand the reality in which we live and think. It is not my intention here to discuss the influence that Aristotle's philosophic thought had, has and possibly will have on ours; I would just like to mention the influence he had, which we currently still have difficulty freeing ourselves from, on what we could call the philosophical historiography related to the pre-Aristotelian age. We are all aware that the success of Aristotle's scheme for interpreting philosophers and scientists who lived before him is basically due to two factors: the loss of their complete works—apart, of course, from Plato's dialogues—and the strong theoretical foundation on which Aristotle based the "quotations" of those authors. We can state that this work of freeing pre-Aristotelian thinkers from Aristotle's reading has only been starting to assert itself since the last century, and that it is still an ongoing process in which philosophy, philology, the history of culture and civilization and the history of scientific thought cooperate or should cooperate closely. Personally, I do believe this is the historiographic path to be followed, and that even on this path a lot still has to be explained and defined. Not only does this kind of research better "historify" the thought of any pre-Aristotelian thinker—in our case, Parmenides—rooting him in a defined world of discussions, polemics and stances on various philosophical and scientific questions, it also better highlights its originality and speculative strength. Before concluding this foreword, though, I would like to add one more comment: though it is right to try and read Parmenides without the influence of Aristotle's "spectacles," it is not possible, for the same reasons, to overlook Aristotle's testimony. It is true that Aristotle forces Parmenides' thought to fit into a scheme that is remote from it, but it is also true that that very reading offers lots of hints to correct it and even to get over it, given the cleverness and theoretical strength of the witness himself.

I intend to prove these statements through my paper, which will be divided into two sections. As I would like to discuss the particular position Parmenides garners in the history of scientific thought by simply mentioning his outlining of the methodological and philosophical question, I will try to show first of all the full participation of our author in a world of scientific discussions and polemics that was very lively in the fifth century. In no way was such participation devoid of signs showing a great originality. Secondly, I will try to prove how Parmenides, just like the other great Sicilian and Magna Graecia thinker Empedocles, foreshadowed—in the shape, of course, of ingenious intuitions—notions and principles of contemporary science, particularly physics.

2. The fact that Parmenides was a φυσιολόγος, that is, a scholar of nature, was well-known in ancient times. In the third

to fourth century AD, Iamblichus said that all those having anything to do with the science of physical things cannot avoid mentioning Parmenides.[2] And again in the sixth century AD, Simplicius, who was probably one of the last to read the whole poem by Parmenides and reported long passages from it, used to say that Parmenides was not only a philosopher but also a scholar of nature's things.[3] And even Aristotle himself, who, as mentioned, is mainly responsible for the distortion of some aspects of the Elean's philosophy, does not hesitate to place Parmenides inside what he saw as a trend shared by the whole line of research of the first Greek philosophers. Parmenides, philosopher of being, metaphysical thinker, "father of western metaphysics," is thus not an idea stemming from ancient times, but rather a modern (from Hegel on) and contemporary (from Heidegger on) reading. It is a legitimate reading, as all readings can be, but one that has little to do with Parmenides' texts and the cultural substrate of which they were a part.

In a well-known passage from the first book of the *Metaphysics*, Aristotle comments on the studies of the first Greek philosophers as follows: "Those who first philosophized thought that the only origins/principles (ἀρχάς) of all things were those of a material nature (ἐν ὕλης εἴδει), since the origin of the being of all things, from which they originally come and in which they eventually dissolve—though the substance (οὐσία) is kept but its qualities (τοῖς πάθεσι) change—this they say is the element (στοιχεῖον), this the origin/principle of things and so they think that nothing is generated and nothing destroyed (οὔτε γίγνεσθαι οὐδὲν οὔτ' ἀπόλλυσθαι), because such a nature is always preserved."[4] In this passage, and using, of course, a lexis of his own, the correspondence of which to the one used by ancient authors we are uncertain of, Aristotle is basically making three statements: 1)

[2] Iambl. *v. Pyth.* 166 = DK 28A4.

[3] Simplic. *De Cael.* 556, 25 = DK 28A14: he dealt "not only with hyper-physical things (περί τῶν ὑπὲρ φύσιν), but also with the things of nature (περί τῶν φυσικῶν)." But see also DL VIII 55 (from Theophr. *Phys. Opin.* fr. 3; *Dox.* 477) = 28A9; Menander (more specifically Genethlius) *Rhet.* I 2, 2 = 28A20: Parmenides, Empedocles and their disciples wrote physical hymns, I 5, 2; such hymns are hymns of nature's science; see also Suid. s.v. = DK 28A2.

[4] Aristot. *Met.* 983b6.

the very first Greek scholars were materialists;[5] 2) they clearly used to make distinctions between what always stays the same in its nature and what instead changes; 3) they thus thought that in reality nothing comes to be and nothing is destroyed. These three Aristotelian comments were not only confirmed by other influential scholars of old times (e.g., Alexander[6]), but are verified by the texts we have left from those first scholars. By clearly distinguishing between something that he calls τὸ ἐόν, which always stays the same, which is eternal (that is, it does not come to be and is not destroyed), which is one, compact and still; and something that he calls τὰ ἐόντα, which changes, which comes to be and is destroyed, which always looks different, Parmenides is neither operating from a purely linguistic or grammatical point of view nor drawing a contrast between reason and senses or, even worse, between metaphysics and physics. Instead, he is stating and proving through a new and accurate methodology what was a common notion not only among the philosophers who lived before him but also among those coming after.

Ever since the Greeks started thinking about the world, say, from Thales onward, they were distinguishing a world without birth or death from the world of births and deaths; that is to say, they were thinking about one reality, unchangeable, within which the occurrence of changing and developing things took place. These were not two separate realities, but one reality that, in order to be understood, must be examined and thought of from two points of view: the point of view of uniqueness and totality and the one of particularity and multiplicity. Parmenides systemizes this concept in the last lines of fragment 1 and in fragments 8 and 9, but he also supports it with a completely original comment on the different methodology that needs to be used in our discourses on the two aspects of that reality (fragments 2–7). The concept was, in fact, a deeply rooted notion in Ionian philosophy and science. Thales already used to say ἕνα τὸν κόσμον,[7] and Anaximenes used to talk about an

[5] Strictly speaking, even the term "materialist" is a modern one, not an old one, but I believe it does convey what Aristotle meant.

[6] Alex. *Metaph.* 31, 7 = DK 28A7.

[7] Aët. II 1, 2 = DK 11A13b.

"eternal one" whose movement produces change[8] and one world that ever lasts but always changes.[9] Anaximander stated even more clearly that this sole reality is still and unchangeable if it is thought of as the whole, and mobile and changeable if thought of as the parts making that whole up: τὰ μὲν μέρη μεταβάλλειν, τὸ δὲ πᾶν ἀμετάβλητον εἶναι.[10] Only one reality, and one that is eternal in its constituents, inside which all processes of change take place from births to deaths, is an active notion even after Parmenides, as we all know: it is indeed stated, and sometimes literally using Parmenides' wording, by Empedocles,[11] Anaxagoras,[12] Hippocrates,[13] Melissus,[14] Democritus,[15] and even by Aristotle, who also confirms it in passages other than the abovementioned one.[16]

So we are facing a dialectics eternal/time, which is also built like a whole/parts relationship. In Parmenides, this conclusion comes not just from the leftover fragments that endure but is also a feature noted by the old scholars interpreting him. I will quote two examples apart from Aristotle. Between the second and third century AD, Alexander wrote, quoting Theophrastus: Parmenides "states the whole to be eternal, and also he wants to assign an origin to beings. Not from the same point of view (οὐχ' ὁμοίως), though: κατ' ἀλήθειαν he thought the whole is one and ungenerated and spherical, κατὰ δόξαν, in order to explain the

8 DK 13A5.

9 DK 13A11.

10 DK 12A1; cf. 12B2, B3, B1.

11 DK 31B8 (ὀνομάζειν); B9, B11 (γίγνεσθαι, οὐκ ἐόν, ἐξόλλυσθαι); B12 (ἄπυστον); B13, B14, B17.30–35, B17.36: Empedoclean terms more explicitly recalling Parmenides' lexis are put in parentheses.

12 DK 59B17: "Greeks do not consider coming to be and perishing correctly, though: no thing indeed comes to be and perishes, but starting from those things that are, a process of composition and separation develops; therefore they should correctly name coming to be composing, perishing separating."

13 *De Victu* I 4: "Of all things, thus, none perishes, none comes to be that was not already before: and they alter through composing and separating."

14 MXG 1–2 = DK30A5; 30B1, B2.

15 DK 68A1, A37, A38, A39, A41, A58, etc.

16 See *Phys.* 187a: "all that originates . . . it is impossible that it originates from the not-being: on this notion all naturalists agree"; see also *Metaph.* 1062b24–25; *Metaph.* 984a27 (added by Albertelli to DK 28A24): "the one, and all nature, is still . . . as far as coming to be and perishing are concerned: this is in fact an ancient notion shared by all primitives."

origin of phaenomena, he posited two principles, fire and earth, the first as matter (ὡς ὕλην), the latter as cause and active principle (ὡς αἴτιον καὶ ποιοῦν)."[17] And in the same period, Hippolytus stated that "Parmenides says the whole (τὸ πᾶν) is one, eternal, ungenerated and spherical, not being himself able to free himself from the opinion of the many, since he says the principles/origins of the whole are fire and earth, earth as matter (ὡς ὕλην), fire as cause and shaping principle (ὡς αἴτιον καὶ ποιοῦν). He said that the cosmos is subject to destruction but did not explain how. At the same time he maintained the whole is eternal, not generated, spherical, homogeneous and, having no space (τόπον) in itself, also still and limited."[18] We will come back to the distinction between truth and opinion, and also to the two principles explaining the origin of phenomena. But it seems evident to me that both authors clearly point to that dialectics eternal/time, whole/parts, that from Anaximander to Xenophanes to Parmenides is deeply rooted in the scientific and philosophical culture of the sixth to fifth centuries BCE, and Hippolytus, in his "Rebuttal of All Heretics," underlines exactly that the notion of the eternity of matter or, if you like, of reality, is deeply rooted in those ancient authors who did not know the Christian doctrine.[19]

It means a necessary distinction has to be made between two ways of looking at one and only reality and not an opposition between a reality and a non-reality, which can be read, in my opinion, in the second part of fragment 8 and in fragment 9. It also perfectly fits, as a famous scholar of Aristotle stated during the 1960's, in the picture made up of those "Presocratic interpretations of the process of nature resulting in the statement that it is possible to reconcile generation, changing and corruption with the idea of the unchangeable nature of the universe as a

---

17 Alex. *Metaph.* 31, 7 (from Theophr. *Phys. Opin.* fr. 6; *Dox.* 482) = 28A7. On eternity, see also the testimonies gathered in A24, A25, A22: a set of testimonies that can be a satisfactory comment on B8.53–59, B9, and confirming that the second part of Parmenides' poem is not a list of men's mistakes but rather a well-organized ordering of his own doctrines.

18 Hippol. *Ref.* I 11 = 28A23.

19 What is also interesting is Hippolytus' conceptual distinction between the whole and the cosmos, the former being eternal and indestructible, the latter (clearly the ordering of ἐόντα) subject to destruction.

wholeness."[20] In the abovementioned fragments, Parmenides does indeed make a distinction between the way one looks at reality meant as a whole and a unity (that he calls τὸ ἐόν) and the way one looks at reality meant as parts coming to be and dying (that he calls τὰ ἐόντα). Here arise those two μορφαί, principles or elements that can explain the world of changing and that Parmenides calls fire (πῦρ) and night (νύξ), in B8.56 and 59, or light (φάος) and night (νύξ) in B9.1. But this is also where Aristotle comes in heavily. First, though, one has to point out that Aristotle's interpretation, though absolutely not denying the picture we have just drawn—one which he himself indeed helped to draw—*historically* leads the way to a more and more philosophical and less and less scientific interpretation of Parmenides' conceptions, bent in a metaphysical direction that did not belong to the Elean.

Let us consider it now. Parmenides talks about the two principles fire and night as making up the reality of phenomena; they are always there in all phenomena (B9.3) that always result from a relationship implying both principles (B9.4); they can thus be recognized and named by observing all things (B9.1). Seeing or naming only one of them (B8.54: μίαν), or even worse, opposing one to the other (B8.55: τἀντία; B8.56: χωρὶς ἀπ' ἀλλήλων), is one of men's mistakes (B8.54).[21] This remark by Parmenides is on one hand a statement of principle, in the sense that it expresses his own cosmogony and cosmology theory, and on the other hand a polemic statement addressing that Pythagorean culture that, in Parmenides' time and even after him, was widely spread in the Magna Graecia milieu in which he lived.[22] The "theory of the opposites" was surely a common doctrine to Presocratics (as again Aristotle testifies in his first book of *Physics*: "everyone sets opposites as principles"[23]), but surely the Pythagoreans were among the first to theorize it. Again,

[20] Düring, *Aristotele*, p. 238.

[21] For the justification of μίαν as "only one," see Casertano, *Parmenide*, pp. 217–221.

[22] On the relationships between Pythagoreanism and Eleatism, I refer to my article "Pitagorici ed Eleati."

[23] Aristot. *Phys*. 188a19.

Aristotle testifies to a tendency of the first Pythagoreans and Alcmaeon to "classify" the opposites and reports on the so-called "chart of the opposites."[24] It is a chart drafted κατὰ συστοιχίαν,[25] and it includes ten matches of opposites expressing a fundamental polarity of reality and of the life of all beings, humans included, and including various branches from mathematics to geometry, from physics to cosmology, from physiology to ethics. A characteristic of Pythagorean thought was to consider the two series of opposites according to the scheme positive/negative or good/bad.[26] Now, if our understanding of Parmenides' fragments holds true, it is clear that Parmenides' polemics at the end of B8 and B9 were directed against this aspect of the Pythagorean doctrine, to which he himself had been initiated: according to the Elean, it is not possible to think of opposites in terms of positive and negative, since both terms of the opposition do necessarily come in the makeup of all things, and each thing is the result of their makeup. On this aspect, Empedocles, as we know, perfectly agrees with Parmenides.

But it is at exactly this point, we said, that Aristotle "comes in" Parmenides' text, interpreting it—that is, "bending" it—to the principles founding his own philosophy. Overall, the Aristotelian picture of Parmenides is the one that has been more or less handed down to our time; the picture of Parmenides devaluating experience and favoring an abstract λόγος operating absolutes, thus supporting an opposition of truth and opinion. This occurred in spite of Aristotle himself conveying that other picture of Parmenides perfectly in tune with the naturalistic tradition before him. But it also has to be underlined that, as has been noticed by scholars, maybe never as in this series of testimonies does Aristotle keep on highlighting the Elean's lack of experience on one side and how wrong his theses are on the other.

---

24 Aristot. *Metaph.* 986a15 (= DK 58B5). More specifically, Aristotle makes a distinction between those classifying opposites and Alcmaeon, who just listed them randomly.

25 Συστοιχία is a series of items arranged in a given order, and since the following sentences in the passage make it clear it is "oppositions" (ἐναντιότητας), thus "opposites" (τἀναντία), we can say "according to pairs of opposites."

26 See again Aristotle, *EN* 1096b5 (= DK 58B6), 1106b29 (= DK 58B7).

Let us take a concrete look. In *Physics*, it is held that "the first ones who started to philosophize searching for the truth and the nature of beings deviated, so to say, to a different direction, driven by inexperience (ὑπὸ ἀπειρίας). They said nothing in the being originates or perishes, for they thought it necessary for what originates to originate either from the being or from the not-being, while neither is possible. In fact, it is not the being that originates (because it already is) and from the not-being nothing can originate. Having thus laid out the question, and worsening the consequences (τὸ ἐφεξῆς συμβαῖνον αὔξοντες) they said not even the manifold exists, but only the being in itself."[27] In this passage, where not just the "naturalistic" concept of "nothing comes to be and nothing perishes" is clear, but also the Gorgian logics, it is equally clear that it is not the ancient scholars who "worsen the consequences," but rather Aristotle himself: the move to the nonexistence of the manifold is actually a completely arbitrary one. In *Metaphysics*, though recognizing the thesis of the motionless one as an old and "normal" one, he piles it on, even stating that those ancient scholars, including Parmenides, not only examined these questions only superficially, but were not even capable of the task.[28] The wrongness and falsity of Parmenides' thesis, placing him even in the league of the Eristics,[29] is after all given by the fact that it postulates the being

[27] *Phys.* 191a24. Many of the testimonies referred to are not in DK, but are translated by Albertelli.

[28] *Metaph.* 984a27: "the very first ones beginning this study and saying the substrate to be one, *did not worry about the problem in the least* (οὐθὲν ἐδυσχέραναν ἑαυτοῖς); some supporters of unity though, *overcome, so to speak, by this search* (ὥσπερ ἡττηθέντες ὑπὸ ταύτης τῆς ζητήσεως), say the one and all nature are still, not just as far as their coming to be and perishing are concerned (this is actually an old notion shared by all primitives), but also as far as any other transformation is concerned, and this is their peculiarity . . . among them there is Parmenides."

[29] Cf. *Phys.* 186a6: Melissus and Parmenides "argue in an eristic way. They assume the wrong premises and their reasonings are not rationally consistent with them." *Phys.* 186a22: "this premise is false, because he assumes that 'what is' is said in an absolute sense (ἁπλῶς λαμβάνειν τὸ ὂν λέγεσθαι), while it is said in many ways (πολλαχῶς). Even his conclusion is wrongly inferred (ἀσυμπέραντος) . . . But this Parmenides had not noticed yet." See also *Phys.* 187a3, 191a24.

as unequivocal, whereas it can be said in many ways.[30] From the nonexistence of the many, one too easily and consequently gets to the devaluation of experience and of the world of phenomena, so in Aristotle's *On the Heavens,* Parmenides denies (ὅλως) birth and death[31] completely, and in *On Generation and Corruption*, devaluating experience, Parmenides is even madness-stricken (μανία).[32]

Where Aristotle's forcing is particularly evident is in his reduction of the two opposite principles of fire and night to fire and earth and warm and cold. "Forced then to follow phenomena and believing the one is in accordance with the logos (κατὰ τὸν λόγον) but is manifold according to opinion, he then supposes two causes and two principles, warm and cold, that is to say (οἷον . . . λέγων) fire and earth. He supposes the former, warm, at the side of the being (κατὰ τὸ ὄν), the latter at the side of the

[30] See *Phys.* 185a9–10: "both Melissus and Parmenides assume the wrong premises and develop their reasoning incorrectly." 185a21: "the most appropriate starting point is that 'what is' is said in many ways (πολλαχῶς λέγεται τὸ ὄν)" . . . 185b24: "their reasoning will not be that 'all things are one,' but rather that 'all things are nothing' (οὐ περὶ τοῦ ἓν εἶναι τὰ ὄντα ὁ λόγος ἔσται περὶ τοῦ μηδέν)." As we all know, the same mistake in thinking is univocally attributed by Aristotle even to Plato.

[31] *On the Heavens* 289b14: "Some of them completely (ὅλως) denied coming to be and perishing. They say in fact that nothing among the beings is, neither comes to be nor perishes, but it only looks like they do, to us. They are Melissus and Parmenides and their disciples who, even supposing they can provide good arguing for the rest, can't be supposed to be arguing like physicists." The attribute of "a-physicists" assigned to Parmenides and the Eleans by Aristotle is also reported by Sextus Empiricus, *Adv. Math.* X 46: "Aristotle called them [Περί φιλ. fr. 9 Walzer = fr. 9 Ross] blockers of nature and also aphysicists (στασιώτας τῆς φύσεως καὶ ἀφυσίκους) blockers from stasis, aphysicists because the principle of movement is the nature, that nature they deny when they say nothing moves." This Aristotelian phrase, with the relevant replacment of the word τὸ ὅλον with φύσις, recalls a definition by Plato (*Theaet.* 181a: "blockers of the whole: τοῦ ὅλου στασιῶται)" that was more exact, since it assigned stillness only to the whole thought as one and did not imply that *nothing* moves.

[32] *On Generation and Corruption* 325a13: "Going by these arguments and making sensation not relevant and devaluating it (παριδόντες), since they believe one has to proceed according to reasoning (λόγῳ δέον ἀκολοθεῖν), they say the whole is one and still, and some of them say it is infinite . . . Then, according to reasoning, it seems these should be the consequences (ταῦτα συμβαίνειν), while according to things (πραγμάτων) thinking like that is almost insane (μανίαν παραπλήσιον εἶναι)."

not-being (κατὰ τὸ μὴ ὄν)."[33] This passage can be considered as the key to Aristotle's interpretation of Parmenides, with its threefold assimilation of the two μορφαί of fragments 8 and 9 to warm and cold, fire and earth, being and not-being. We are obviously facing an *interpretation* of Parmenides' doctrine and not a real testimony, one which is indeed functional to "Aristotle's tendency to get the implications of his own doctrine from others' doctrines,"[34] which, like many of his other interpretations, got to mark the authentic thought of the Elean[35] in old and contemporary historiography. I believe that one of the brightest discussions of this question is still the one by Cherniss: in these passages "'fire' and 'earth' are given as the two elements, though Parmenides calls them 'fire' and 'night' [. . .]. Aristotle himself prefers to call them 'the hot and cold' and implies that this is really what Parmenides meant. Having identified the 'fire' of the poem with his own primary quality 'hot,' in order to assert that Parmenides, too, posited contraries, he had to suppose that the other element was what in his own terminology was called 'cold.' But 'night' could not be equated with 'cold,' nor could it be considered the contrary of 'fire,' so that Aristotle, to maintain the argument, had to change it to earth, which was the easiest to do, since of his own primary sensible bodies fire and earth are the two limiting terms."[36]

The question of old Aristotelians, from Theophrastus through Alexander to Simplicius, is a more complex one. In the already mentioned passage by Theophrastus, though he overall accepts Aristotle's interpretation positing the two Parmenidean principles one on the side of the material substrate (ὕλη) of all continuous changes and the other on the side of the efficient cause (δημιουργός) of those changes based on the match acting/

[33] *Metaph.* 986b27. See also *On Generation and Corruption* 330b13; *Phys.* 188A19.

[34] Reale, "Eleati," p. 254. Talking about ἀναγκαζόμενος, Untersteiner (*Parmenide,* note to A24 and ch. I) notes that "Aristotle presents, as if it was by the Elean, the objection he himself was raising to him."

[35] Among ancient scholars Cicero (*Ac. Pr.* II 37,118 = DK 28A35), Diogenes Laertius (DL IX 21–23 = DK 28A1), Hippolytus (*Ref.* I 11 = DK 28A23), Clement of Alexandria (*Protr.* 5, 64 = DK 28A33); among modern ones, at least starting from Zeller and Ross (*Aristotle's Metaphysics,* p. 133), many.

[36] Cherniss, *Criticism,* p. 48 n192. Also Untersteiner, *Parmenide, ad* A24.

suffering, he clearly indicates the different points of view taken by the Elean while talking about the one and the many. Let us read it once more: "[Parmenides] states the whole is eternal, and also he wants to assign an origin to beings. Not from the same point of view (οὐχ ὁμοίως), though: κατ' ἀλήθειαν he thought the whole is one and ungenerated and spherical, κατὰ δόξαν, in order to explain the cause of phaenomena, he posited two principles, fire and earth, the first as matter (ὡς ὕλην), the latter as cause and active principle (ὡς αἴτιον καὶ ποιοῦν)."[37] The phrase οὐχ ὁμοίως, used by Theophrastus here, is very relevant, signaling the difference in the approach to the study of reality with respect to Aristotle's ὅλως, which signified a philosophical inexperience.[38] Even Simplicius, though sharing Aristotle's reading,[39] significantly corrects both Aristotle and Alexander: "Parmenides—Alexander says—drawing physics in accordance with the opinion of the many and according to phaenomena, and stating no longer that the being is one nor that it is ungenerated, posited as principles of becoming fire and earth, making the earth work as matter and fire as efficient cause; and he calls (καλεῖ)—says Alexander—light the fire, darkness the earth. If Alexander means the phrase 'according to the opinion of the many and according to phaenomena' in the sense Parmenides means when he calls the sensible δοξαστόν, then he is right. But if he believes those discourses completely untrue and thinks light or fire are said the efficient cause, then he is wrong."[40] Simplicius, who knew Parmenides' poem well, is thus perfectly aware of both the "translation" in Aristotle's language and then Alexander's translation of Parmenides' terminology, and of the forced understanding of opposites in terms of efficient cause and material cause. And again, in a different passage, Simplicius corrects Aristotle's translation: "Among those stating the principles are limited, some posit two, like Parmenides who, in the part of his work related to opinion, posits fire and earth (πῦρ καὶ

---

[37] Theophr. *Phys.* I (Theophr. *Phys. Opin.* fr. 6; *Dox.* 482, in Alex. *Metaph.* 31, 7 = 28A7).

[38] See the passage from *De Caelo* quoted above, n31.

[39] See Simplic. *Phys.* 115, 11 = DK 28A28.

[40] Simplic. *Phys.* 38, 20 (not in DK).

γῆν) as such, *or rather* light and darkness (ἢ μᾶλλον φῶς καὶ σκότος)."[41] What should be noted in this very short "history" of Parmenidean principles is, first of all, that even those following Aristotle's interpretation do point out his forcing, reasserting the equivalence of the two opposites in the poem and the fact that they cannot be separated: this was, after all, Parmenides' originality in his polemics, both against the Pythagoreans and against the traditional view, say, Hesiodean,[42] on one side, and on the other side his sharing of certain traits of the Presocratic scientific, say, Empedoclean thought.[43] Second, it should be noted that in none of these interpreters, but actually not even in Aristotle, is the second part of the poem seen as a list of humans' false opinions or as a non-Parmenidean doctrine: they are indeed opinions and thus different from the reality that can be built on τὸ ἐόν, but they are the likely opinions that the λόγος builds on

[41] Simplic. *Phys.* 25, 15. "Exact exegesis" is Untersteiner's comment (*Parmenide,* p. clxix n9. Even Hans Schwabl, keeping this correction in mind, points out that Aristotle's assimilation of one of the two principles to the being and the other to the not-being "lässt sich nach dem parmenideischen Sprachgebrauch nicht mehr rechtfertigen" (p. 406). The same opinion (i.e., Cherniss's opinion, see *Criticism,* pp. 220–221, and "History of Ideas," p. 108) is also shared by Tarán (*Parmenides,* pp. 269–291) and Mourelatos (*Route,* p. 130). See also Düring, *Aristotele,* p. 263: "The criticism of the Eleans [by Aristotle] is surely interesting in the history of philosophy—philosophically, though, unlike the discussion in Plato's *Parmenides,* it is irrelevant: Aristotle never tries to confront Parmenides on his very ground"; p. 268, n330: "It is interesting to compare Plato's reverent approach to his spiritual father Parmenides, even when he criticizes his opinions, to the arrogant tone of young Aristotle." He also quotes *Phys.* 191a25–35, noting that "in this book Aristotle repeats ἡμεῖς λέγομεν six times." See also Long, "Principles," p. 95: the "not necessary step" taken by Aristotle was the identification of μορφαί with the two opposites being-not being; once this had been done, the "parallel between not-being and the earth (night) perfectly fits into his doctrine of deprivation and potentiality."

[42] To Hesiod, *Theog.* 748–766, light and darkness are two Gods, the former positive and beneficial, the latter negative and malignant; see Cerri, *Parmenide di Elea,* p. 89; "Parmenides . . . enlists precisely Hesiod as his privileged addressee, together a model to imitate and the target of his polemics."

[43] According to Empedocles, for instance, fr. 17.27, the elements and the two principles are "all equal and contemporary"; see also the Pythagorean dissenter Alcmaeon (fr. 4) who believes that health is the ἰσονομία of the elements and their harmonious mixing, while sickness is the μοναρχία of one of them. See Pasquinelli, *I Presocratica,* pp. 407–408 n56: "The goddess has by now entered the field of δόξα and gives the two forms an equal measure of reality."

the multiplicity of phenomena, making it up in a διάκοσμος,[44] and they are Parmenidean doctrines.

3. We cannot actually say much about Parmenides' scientific doctrines, though we can draw an almost complete picture of its general outline, as they seem deeply rooted in the structure of his poem. After the epic-style introduction telling the story of his journey to meet a goddess, the same goddess shows him a program that includes all branches of knowledge: "you must learn every thing (B1.28) both (B1.29: ἠμέν) truth with no

[44] On the significance of this word, see Diller, *Der Vorphilosophische Gebrauch,* p. 51 n1; quoted by Untersteiner, *Parmenide,* p. clxxvii n41: "Notice the coming back of κόσμος in διάκοσμος: the artistic order of words will express the real order of things, an arrangement which is precisely διάκοσμος and not simply κόσμος 'since it has to be consistent (ἐοικότα) in its very last peculiarities.'" Even Cerri (*Parmenide di Elea,* pp. 215, 253) rightly points out: "The goddess (Parmenides) will make a systematic (διάκοσμος) rational review of human ideas/opinions, so that they are no longer elements of mistake but rather objects of conscious thinking." Even believing Parmenides a scientist and not a metaphysician (cf. p. 65), Cerri, though, misunderstands the being/existing of ἐόντα in the second part of the poem when he states that they are "beings that in fact do not exist" (p. 74); see also p. 185, where he talks about beings "that, seen in the light of scientific reason, cannot be wholly real," to which one could raise the following objection, as Cornford ("Parmenides' Two Ways," p. 101) does: "How can a thing exist and yet not be wholly real?" In fact, B8.51–52 have long been discussed: "from now on learn about human experiences listening to the order, which can draw into deception, of my words: δόξας δ' ἀπὸ τοῦδε βροτείας μάνθανε, κόσμον ἐμῶν ἐπέων ἀπατηλὸν ἀκούων)." The fact that he is talking about the second part, from now on, of the general program of knowledge expressed by the goddess in B1.31–32, and that Parmenides has to learn, seems to me confirmed from the imperative form of the verb used here, which is the same one found in B1.31. Even though my translation of ἀπατηλόν (= deceptive), "which can draw into deception," is a non-literal one intended to express the *meaning* of what the goddess is stating here: now human experiences will be considered, and they can be deceptive if they are not placed in a rational order, that is, in a well-coordinated, rational system that will account for them, making them likely, precisely, if not truths (see B1.32: δοκίμως, on whose meaning see Casertano, *Parmenide,* n33, pp. 59–63; and B8.60: ἐοικότα, on which see Casertano, *Parmenide,* pp. 226–229). This is actually the point around which the whole general interpretation of Parmenidean *doxa* by the different scholars, from Aristotle on, revolves. Close to the interpretation that is given here, we find, for instance, De Santillana, Cornford, Verdenius, Schwabl, Heitsch, Popper, Ruggiu, Untersteiner, Matson, and Cerri, with different nuances. What Heitsch says is relevant (*Parmenides,* p. 73): "the goddess calls the 'order of my words,' i.e., her presentation ἀπατηλόν, 'deceptive, misleading.' She is of course not saying she wants to deceive her audience . . . 'deceptive' is the exact correspondent of 'likely,' for there, where basically only likelihood lies, the possibility of a mistake is always to be found."

contradictions, and (B1.30: ἠδέ)[45] experiences, or opinions, of men, where no true certainty lies."[46] Then, and herein lies the Elean's originality, the method is explained (it is the main theme of the "ways") that is needed in order to talk both about the nature meant as a whole and the nature meant as the manifold of phenomena making that whole up, and here is where the dialectic relationship between truth (B1.29) and likelihood (B8.60: ἐοικότα)[47] is set. Finally, there is the description of the world of phenomena through the parameters of physics, cosmology, anthropology, biology and embryology. And though there are no genuine fragments here, we do have many testimonies helping us draw the picture of Parmenidean doctrines.

At the center of the eternal whole, ungenerated and spherical,[48] lies the spherical earth;[49] Parmenides was the first

---

45 'Ημέν and ἠδέ, epic conjunctions, denote a correlation and not an opposition.

46 The need to learn all is stated again in line 31: "but at all costs you will learn also this (ἀλλ' ἔμπης καὶ ταῦτα μαθήσεαι)." For the justification of this translation, I refer to my *Parmenide,* pp. 54–64.

47 The term ἐοικότα, likely, does not have to be understood in a negative sense, exactly like in Plat. *Tim.* 29b–d. Cornford (*Plato and Parmenides,* p. 46 n2) even believes this passage to be "a paraphrase of line 61." Popper (*Ulteriori,* p. 690) on παρελάσσῃ: "the word 'winning' (or similar terms pointing out that the goddess's aim is for Parmenides to be the winner in any dispute or verbal conflict against other mortals) would turn out to be . . . fatal to the seriousness of the goddess's message, since her first aim is to disclose the truth, while her second aim is to provide Parmenides with the intellectual equipment he needs to avoid the mistakes derived from traditional belief, and not to be misled by it."

48 Actually, in B8.43, referring to the whole, Parmenides says "εὐκύκλου σφαίρης ἐναλίγκιον ὄγκῳ: similar to the mass of a well-rounded sphere"; the word ἐναλίγκιον can mean both "similar, alike" and "equal." There is, though, a whole cultural tradition before and after Parmenides understanding physical reality in terms of spheres. See the discussion of bibliography in Casertano, *Parmenide,* pp. 187ff. and footnotes.

49 DL IX 21–23 = DK 28A1. Here Diogenes uses the word σφαιροειδῆ, whereas in a different passage (DL VIII 48 = DK 28A44), referring to Pythagoras and Parmenides, he uses the word στρογγύλη, which properly means convex or round. But Cherniss (*Criticism,* p. 396) points out that στρογγύλη is not as accurate as σφαιροειδῆ: it is to this term as "round" is to "spherical," so that only the universe would be spherical. Mondolfo, though, points out, drawing on Plat. *Phaed.* 97e1, where a flat shape of the earth is opposed to a spherical one, using precisely the term στρογγύλη, that it must mean spherical. Untersteiner, ad loc., points out in this regard Parmenides' closeness to the Pythagoreans: "whether this idea of a spherical earth is derived by Parmenides from the Pythagoreans or is his own intuition, it is difficult to tell."

to determine the climatic zones and the inhabited areas.[50] As for the roundness of earth and universe, Parmenides is following a tradition belonging to the previous philosophical thought, from Ionians to Pythagoreans. It is indeed true that in Anaximander, the earth has a bent shape, "like a stone column,"[51] but references to the sun or the celestial bodies as *spherical* bodies are not missing in his texts: around the earth and the air surrounding it there is actually a "fire sphere (φλογὸς σφαῖρα)" wrapping it all and from which all stars originate.[52] It seems Anaximander had written a book titled σφαῖρα.[53] Even among the Pythagoreans we have many testimonies talking about the roundness not just of the earth, but also of the cosmos and the bodies in it.[54] And, of course, the roundness of the whole and of the earth is a quality that gets repeated even after Parmenides, by his great disciple Empedocles,[55] and then by Ecphantus,[56] Leucippus and Democritus.[57] Parmenides' originality, and here he was also following the scientific spirit of Ionians,[58] was in trying a climatic and anthropologic partitioning of the earth.

What proves to be harder is to exactly define the διάκοσμος, Parmenides' cosmic system. Going by fragments 10–12 and some

[50] Strab. I 94 = 28A44a says Posidonius (who, through Eudoxus, uses Theophrastus) stated that the first adoption of the division of the earth in five zones (ζώνας) was by Parmenides. Aëtius (III 11, 4) instead tells us Parmenides was the first to determine the inhabited areas of the earth (τοὺς οἰκουμένους).

[51] See DK 12A10, A11, B5.

[52] See DK 12A10. According to Anaximander, stars are fire spheres that come off the cosmos's fire (12A11); the sun's sphere is 27 times that of the earth (12A11, A21, A22).

[53] See DK 12A2.

[54] See DK 58B1a, DK 44A15, B12; DK 31B129. For some Pythagoreans, sphericity seemed to also determine time, understood as σφαῖρα τοῦ περιέχοντος (DK 58B33).

[55] See DK 31B26, 27, 27a, 28, 29. Even in Xenophanes, sphericity is referred to the one-whole and to god: DK 21A1, A28, A31, A33, A34, A35, A36.

[56] DK 51.1.

[57] DK 67A22. Probably the idea dated further back, if Hecataeus' news is true (*On the Philosophy of Egyptians*: cf. DL I 11 = DK 73B6), ascribing it to the ancient Egyptian wise men.

[58] Anaximander was probably the first to draw a geographic map, with the borders of the earth and sea: see DL II 2 = DK 12A1, Agathemerus I 1 = DK 12A6; Strab. I 7 = DK 12A6 tells us that his map was improved upon by Hecataeus, "tireless voyager."

testimonies (basically Aëtius, Clement, Plutarch and Simplicius), Giovanni Cerri classifies the astronomic space drafted by Parmenides in a series of "coronas": "The most external corona, that worked as a borderline for the visible universe, was made of a layer of stiff ether, after which, and moving towards the centre one more corona would be found, made of rarefied and fire ether, called οὐρανός, the ὄλυμπος ἔσχατος, 'the last Olympus' we found quoted in fragment 11."[59] This scholar, going by B12.1–2, rightly wonders: "Why do the lower coronas contain pure fire, while the upper ones hold a mix of night and fire? It is hard to understand the *ratio* in this theory. It might be that Parmenides, who thought that the sun and the moon were to be found in the innermost coronas, wanted to explain why these stars could light the earth up and even generate a significant series of events (ἔργα, fragment 10), while every other star would just be shining points, unable to diffuse light, let alone warmth: he might have thought that the most economical solution was assuming that the sun's fire is pure, while that of stars is not."[60] Parmenides must have undoubtedly known the Pythagorean cosmology of his times, the pre-Philolaus one. Traditional positioning saw the earth in the center and, in order, the moon, the sun, the five planets (Venus, Mercury, Mars, Jupiter, Saturn), and the fixed stars. This is the prevailing positioning that comes down to Democritus,[61] Plato,[62] and Aristotle.[63] Philolaus changed this order[64] and put one fire at the center of the cosmos, another one at the top, under which the ten celestial bodies (fixed stars) revolve, under these the five planets, then the sun, then the earth, and the anti-earth, all of them revolving around the "fire of the hearth that has its place in the centre." And he calls "Olympus" the remotest part, where the elements in their purity are, "cosmos," the part underneath Olympus, where the five planets with the sun and the moon are; "heaven," the part underneath the moon and around the

59 Cerri, *Parmenide di Elea*, p. 266.
60 Cerri, *Parmenide di Elea*, p. 270.
61 Aët. II 15, 3 = DK 68A86.
62 *Tim.* 38c–e.
63 *On the Heavens* 291a29–b10.
64 Aët. II 7, 7 = DK 44A16.

earth. Anaximander represented a different tradition: the sun, moon, fixed stars, five planets, motionless earth at the center of the sphere,[65] between the two traditions, Parmenides looks much closer to the Ionian one, thus confirming once again his anti-Pythagorean polemics.[66]

A reconstruction of Parmenides' cosmology is, in fact, if we wanted to carry it out in its details, quite difficult. What is certain is that he states that there is an outmost part of the cosmos, an extreme Olympus or a heaven surrounding everything, inside which the stars, the sun, the moon and the earth move. One could maintain, and it has been maintained, that ether, heaven and the Olympus are synonyms and define one and the same reality, making heaven and the Olympus the same thing and distinguishing them from ether,[67] but I am not sure it would be right. On the other hand, it is not easy to explain B12 on the basis of Aëtius: in the first part of his testimony, it is said that what surrounds all coronas (τὸ περιέχον πάσας) is a kind of wall (τεῖχος), while later on, the ether is said to "be all around in the outmost circle." Aëtius would thus provide us with two schemes of Parmenides' cosmology: 1) given that the "rarefied" (ἀραιόν) and the "dense"

---

[65] Hippol. *Ref.* I 6, 1–7 = 12A11. Remember Anaximander built the first armillary sphere representing the celestial sphere with the orbits of the stars (DK 12A6, 12A1, 2; 12A2).

[66] Even in this, Parmenides is followed by Empedocles: see Aët. II 1, 4 = DK 31A50. But for Empedocles, there is also a testimony of a theory with two suns: one is the archetype, and it is in the other hemisphere of the cosmos filling it all up—external fire?—and the other one is the one which appears, the reflected image in the other hemisphere: Aët. II 20, 13 = 31A56. There were, though, even "heterodox" theories, so to speak, like the one by Hicetas from Syracuse (a Pythagorean of the fourth century, master of Ecphantus), according to whom all stars are still, and only earth revolves at high speed around its own axis, thus making the stars seem to move (Cic. *ac. pr.* II 39, 123 = DK 50A1); and Ecphantus from Syracuse (Hicetas' pupil or, according to other scholars, Heraclides Ponticus'). Hicetas and Ecphantus could stand for two instances of that process developing from Philolaus to Aristarchus, through which celestial mechanics gets more and more certain. Ecphantus was the first to say that Pythagorean monads are bodily (Aët. I 3, 19 = 51A2); according to him the earth is the center of the cosmos, and it revolves around its axis from west to east (Hippol. *Ref.* I 15, p. 18 = 51A1). Remember that even Plato mentions a movement of the earth, in *Timaeus* 40b, against which Aristot. *On the Heavens* 293b30–32.

[67] Gilardoni, pp. 91–93.

(πυκνόν) quoted by Aëtius are light and night, though this is no obvious assumption, we will have a rarefied sphere (of fire) at the extreme boundary, a dense sphere (of night) in the innermost part, and mixed spheres with both elements in the middle; 2) an outmost sphere and an inmost one formed by a solid and heavy element (hard as a τεῖχος), immediately underneath the first and above the second a sphere of fire, between these two spheres of fire the mixed spheres of light and night. Indeed, even the air, considered a secretion of earth and fire, and the Milky Way, as an exhalation from fire, would make the earth and fire opposite (since primal) elements, on the basis of the Aristotelian assimilation of earth and night, while B10 and B11 put the earth, sun, galaxy and moon on the same level as σήματα ἐν αἰθέρι.[68] It is significant, however, that, in his cosmological picture, on the one hand, Parmenides states again that the light of the moon is a reflection of the light of the sun, a theory also ascribed to Thales and Pythagoras,[69] and on the other, he reasserts the findings according to which Hesperus, the evening star, is the same star as Phosphorus, the morning star, bearer of light.[70] I use the term "reasserts" on purpose, since these facts were already determined by the scientific culture of ancient times, perhaps even by Babylonian culture,[71] and definitely by Greek astronomers of the sixth century; even so, the fact remains, as Cerri[72] rightly points out, that Parmenides was the first to write them down.

Parmenides' anthropology is strongly linked to his cosmology. Diogenes Laertius[73] states that, according to Parmenides,

---

[68] It is relevant to note that the term σήματα, referring in B8.2 to the qualities of "what is," in B10.2 refers to stars.

[69] Aët. II 26, 2 = DK 28A42; see DK 28B14–15. Parmenides (B14.1: "light shining at night of a light not its own, wandering around the earth [νυκτιφαὲς περὶ γαῖαν ἀλώμενον ἀλλότριον φῶς]") uses the term νυκτιφαές, found just here and in the Orphic hymns (*Hymn.* 54, 10). Untersteiner also admits a different wording by Parmenides, that one also a *hapax legomenon*, and quotes it like DK 28A13a: νυκτικρυφές "hidden at night," referring it to the sun. In Empedocles B45, the phrase ἀλλότριον φῶς reappears.

[70] See DL in DK 28A1 and VIII 14, where Pythagoras is said to be the first to maintain this theory.

[71] See Untersteiner *ad* DK 28A1.

[72] Cerri, *Parmenide di Elea*, p. 55.

[73] DL IX 21–23 = DK 28A1.

there are two principles: "fire and earth, and the one is the demiurge, the other the matter (ὕλη).[74] . . . Men get their first origin from mud,[75] and both warm and cold, that make up everything, are in them." Indeed, the origin of living species from the earth, and in particular, the origin of human species from other animal ones—what we would call a first draft of evolutionary theory—is testified to at least in Anaximander, Xenophanes, Parmenides and Empedocles. According to Anaximander, man was first generated by animals of a different species;[76] the first living creatures were generated in the damp . . . and as time went by they landed on dry ground;[77] from warmed-up water and earth, fishes or creatures very similar to fishes were born, and in the latter and together with them, men grew.[78] Even Xenophanes thinks the human species is born from earth and water,[79] as anything that is born and grows,[80] and it proceeds subject to the endless transformation (μεταβολή) to which all worlds are subject together with the living creatures in them.[81]

---

[74] As has already been pointed out, the replacement of φάος and νύξ by πῦρ and γῆ started with Aristotle and Theophrastus, and has then been ascribed to Parmenides.

[75] We have here a double lesson: ἐξ ἡλίου or ἐξ ἰλύος, as in Albertelli, based on Aldobr. code: *limo*.

[76] [Plutarch.] *Strom.* 2 (from Theophrastus) = DK 12a10.

[77] Aët. V 19, 4 = DK 12A30.

[78] Censorin. *De D. Nat.* 4, 7 = DK 12A30. Even Plutarch (*quaest. conv.* VIII 8, 4 p. 730 E = DK 12A30) testifies to this doctrine much older than Anaximander's; as a matter of fact, he sets it against the latter: "the descendants of the old Hellen sacrifice to first-born Poseidon because they believe, like Syrians, that man is born from a damp substance: that's why they venerate fish since it is of our own descent and fed together with us. And so they reason better than Anaximander. He does in fact not admit that men were first born in fishes and were fed like sharks: once they were able to take care of themselves, they got out and came ashore." Sharks are mentioned because of the doctrine according to which these fishes fed their offspring by keeping them in their mouth; see Longo, *passim*.

[79] Sext. Emp. *adv. math.* X 314 = DK 21B33.

[80] Simplic. *phys.* 188, 32 = DK 21B29.

[81] Hippol. *Ref.* I 14 p. 17, 12 = DK 21A33. To confirm what was stated above about the dialectics whole/parts, which is certain and validated even in Xenophanes, see what bishop Theodoret, a witness in the fourth to fifth centuries and a passionate defender of Christian orthodoxy, said about the Colophonian: "he said everything is one and spherical and limited, not generated but eternal and completely still. But then, *forgetting his statements*, he said everything originates from earth" (Theodoret. IV 5 = DK 21A36).

And it is so even for Parmenides, who, also for this side of his doctrine, has been linked to Empedocles since ancient times: "Empedocles . . . asserts [31A72] a similar thesis, that is, he maintains that at first the single limbs came randomly out of the earth, that was pregnant with them; then they got together and formed the matter of the complete man (*solidi hominis materiam*), that is a mixture of fire and water. . . . This same opinion shared Parmenides from Velia: apart from a few non relevant points, he does not dissent from Empedocles."[82] Thus, the earth originated from a primal matter, like all stars did: it shares the nature of the cosmos, that is, it is made up of fire and night. But it is not populated by living creatures. Life only comes in later on, as a particular form of existence of the matter, a new product in the evolutionary process of the world. What is clearly found here is the intuition of the sequence of phases, of development stages of matter, where more and more complex forms of existence get defined, equipped with new qualities. The fantastic and poetic language used by Parmenides and Empedocles forecasts modern scientific beliefs. The single limbs coming out of the earth hint at a notion of seeing in the endless development of matter a series of "tries," through which more and more complex forms of life get defined: organic matter, living substance, living creatures. Even men, like all living creatures, are actually made up of the same elements that make up the cosmos.

Spontaneous birth of all living creatures from earth and water is just a first step in the history of life, though. At a given point of its evolution, the birth of men and other animals gets sexed. Generation is caused by Eros, the first among gods born[83] from the firstborn goddess who rules on everything,[84] a relentless force pushing the male and the female to couple.[85] Thus, from the painful delivery following the coupling, more men are born. Clear signs of a Parmenidean embryology can be found in fragments 17–18 and in some testimonies. The *Virtutes* (i.e., δυνάμεις) of both male and female contribute to the developing of the fetus: when they

[82] Censorin. *de d. nat.* 4, 7–8 = DK 28A51.

[83] DK 28B13.

[84] DK 28B12.3.

[85] DK 28B12.4–6.

mix up in a balanced ratio, well-shaped organisms are born; when, instead, they confront each other and are not able to join up in the organism resulting from melting, creatures with a troubled sex are born (i.e., effeminate men or mannish women). Usually (B17), when the right part of the uterus is inseminated, males are born; when the left part is, then females are born. Ancient interpreters confirm this idea,[86] testifying moreover to the existence of two "schools of thought" on the subject, one stating that the female seed was of no use to generation, the other that both the father's and the mother's seeds contributed to the conception of children: Parmenides is thus in these latter ranks.[87] The theories on the generation and differentiation of sexes were in any case very old, and they assigned a particular relevance to the right and left side of the body. These ideas were present in the medical schools in Knidos and Kos—that is to say, in an environment with Carian background, and thus a pre-Indo-European one—and that is why they can also be found in Indian medicine and are shared by the whole Indo-Mediterranean region.[88] We are facing here a theory of generation that lasted millennia, linking the origin of the male sex to the right part of the body and that of the female sex to the left part. This theory, born in India, was brought into the scientific conceptual domain by Greeks. Pythagoreans brought it up, for they thought that in the table of opposites on the origin of things,

[86] According to Aëtius, V 11, 2 = DK 28A54, when the seed comes from the right side of the uterus, children look like their father; when it is placed on the left, they look like their mother (same in Censorin. *De D. Nat.* 6, 8); according to Lactantius, *De Opif. D.* 12, 12, when the male seed falls in the left side of the uterus, womanly males are born, while when a female seed gets in the right side, mannish females are born. Galen, *in Epid.* VI 48 = DK 28B17, believes the male fetus is produced from the fertilization of the right side of the uterus. See also Aët. V 7, 2; V 7, 4; Aristot. *De Gen. Anim.* 763b30; Censorin. *De D. Nat.* 5, 2.

[87] See Censorin. *de d. nat.* 5, 3: "Even on this there's no agreement between the authors' opinions, whether a child is just born from the father's seed, like Diogenes of Apollonia [DK 64A27], Hippon [DK 38A13], Aristotle and the Stoics wrote, or also from the mother's seed, like Anaxagoras [DK 59A107] and Alcmaeon [DK 24A14] thought, and also Parmenides, Empedocles [DK 31A81], Epicurus." In fact, even Democritus is to be placed in this second list (see 68A142–143: Christian Nemesius' testimony in the fourth to fifth centuries, *De Nat. Hom*, c. 25 p. 247, stating the opposite, comes from an oversimplified assimilation of Democritus to Aristotle).

[88] See Lesky, pp. 39–40.

the opposition male/female was to be found right after the right/ left one; thus, a people's belief enters into a scientific system for the first time. Parmenides, then, was the first to make the theory about "right and left" part of an explanation of the biological mechanics that, indeed, he also used to explain such phenomena as sleep and death, deriving the former from a moderate cooling of blood's warmth, and the latter from its absolute cooling.[89]

Then, to confirm Parmenides' "materialism," there is of course fragment 16, a fragment expressing the genuine Parmenidean doctrine, the evidence being that it is only found handed down in Aristotelian[90] texts or texts from Aristotelian school,[91] and in such contexts where the quoting was used polemically, namely, to prove the "mistake" that Parmenides, just like other pre-Platonic philosophers, had made. According to this fragment, man is an unsplittable oneness of body and thought, and this is one more piece of evidence of how impossible it is in Parmenides to separate and oppose sensibility and reason. This is also indirectly proven by the efforts of those scholars, efforts who wanted to find that separation and opposition in him and thus had to justify their theory with complex explanations that would highlight the claimed clash between this fragment and the previous ones.[92] The fragment actually tells us that there is a very strong tie (ὡς . . . τώς) among the μέλεα making up every man and his mind (16.1–2); the sense of this link is that it is always φύσις μελέων, that is, the special form that is taken in each man by the combination[93] of

[89] Tertull. *de an.* 45 = DK 28A46b; even here, Parmenides is close to Empedocles: see Aët. V 24, 2 = DK 31A85.

[90] Aristot. *Metaph.* 1009b21.

[91] Theophr. *De Sens.* 3; Alexandr. *Metaph.* 306, 29 (he quotes only the first two lines and gives a paraphrase of the rest).

[92] For instance, see Somigliana ("Interpretare," p. 85): "The verbs to see, to hear, to know were much used in the old metaphysics with this allegorical meaning, and they defined the direct perception in the order of transcendent knowledge. . . . A similar value has to be attached to the verb αἰσθάνομαι in Parmenides' discourse, . . . αἴσθησις instead stands for the understanding of the Divine."

[93] It is important that at line 1 the word κρᾶσιν is used instead of μῖξις in DK B12.4: here, that term was used to mean the union, the coupling of male and female—particular forms of that duality expressing itself in the whole universe—suggesting it is a particular case of that general law, according to which the opposites search for each other and unite even while staying distinct from one another. Here κρᾶσις is meant instead as a more intimate and complete union:

his constituents, which determines his thought: it is in fact (τὸ γὰρ αὐτό) the very part of men that thinks (φρονέει), and indeed the νόημα actually expresses man's wholeness (τὸ πλέον): it is the meaningful sense of his fullest *being*. So the fragment tells us about a tight unity between sensibility and reason that makes thought not alien at all to bodily nature, in the sense that being physical does somehow affect the way one thinks. This does not mean that thinking *is* immediately feeling; though it is linked to it, since its features are what they are because they are related to the bodily nature of man, it is nevertheless something different from it, given its ways of being and working and its abilities to think about sensibility and itself.

The subjugating of thinking to feeling, or their identification, is one more feature assigned not just to Parmenides but also to most of the pre-Platonics by Aristotle, in order to underline their being old, primitive, and rough—to underline, as a matter of fact, that their doctrines were wrong. In the fifth chapter of the fourth book of his *Metaphysics,* Aristotle is arguing against Protagoras' cognitive relativism; more specifically, against those who tightly linked intellectual knowledge to the sensible one; and in more general terms, against those denying the principle of noncontradiction. This tight link, as mentioned, does of course exist; the *identification* is a consequence unduly drawn by Aristotle: "By observing sensible things, some philosophers were induced to maintain that *everything that appears, is true.*"[94] In general terms, these philosophers

the parts making up a man are not just "set one next to the other," put together; rather, they compose a unity in which each constituent does not stay itself but changes the others and is changed with the others, producing something new that could not be produced by the simple separate existence of each single part: the mind, to be precise. Parmenides' doctrine is original at this point, and it will be referred to by Empedocles DK 31B8, 9, 21, 23, 26, 31, 35, 62, 71, 96, 98; also B110.10: "you should know in fact that all things have knowledge (φρόνησιν) and the devoted part of thought (νώματος αἶσαν)." Martano appropriately comments (*Empedocle d'Agrigento,* p. 63): "Μῖξις, μίγνυμι, have a general meaning, a broad sense; κρᾶσις, κεράννυμι have a more specific meaning. The semantic difference between the two terms and their related *abgeleitete Wörter* looks clear: the first family randomly gives the sense of mixture, blend, the other a sense of melting, special tie between two substances . . . that does not provide the qualities of a mixture but those of a new substance with its characteristic qualities."

[94] *Metaph.* 1009b1–2.

state that everything that appears to our senses is necessarily true, because they think that thought (φρόνησιν) is sensation (αἴσθησις) and that the latter is an alteration (ἀλλοιώσει).[95] The philosophers Aristotle is referring to are Democritus[96] and Empedocles,[97] and he then adds, "Parmenides also says the same thing" and quotes fragment B16.[98] After Parmenides, Aristotle quotes Anaxagoras[99] and Homer.[100] The question Aristotle asks himself at this point is a bewildering but extremely symptomatic one: "If those who more than anyone searched for the truth we are able to grasp (and they are those who search it and love it the most), if precisely these hold such opinions and maintain such doctrines on truth, how will those beginning philosophizing be able not to get disheartened, and rightfully so?"[101] And his explanation is, confirming what we are saying: "they were, indeed, searching for truth about beings, *but they thought that only sensible things were beings.*"[102]

Of course, we modern scholars do have to keep the two levels distinct. On one hand, there is the testimony—there is undoubtedly, according to Democritus, Empedocles, Parmenides and Anaxagoras, a very strong link between the activities of νόησις (or of φρόνησις) and those of αἴσθησις. Thought is linked to the physical and biological constitution of man. From this point of view, Aristotle's testimony perfectly captures the conceptual and doctrinal substance of a thesis and cultural attitude that are shared by the philosophers he is

---

95 1009b13–14.

96 Democritus' fr. 117 is quoted: "nothing we know in truth, for the truth is in deep." Actually, if this means that Democritus, according to Aristotle, believes the truth is unknowable because it lies beyond sensations, Aristotle "forgets" that Democritus thought that atoms and the vacuum are the most certain knowledge, and they are certainly not perceptible through sensations.

97 Empedocles' fr. 106 is quoted: "connected with things present to senses, the mind (μῆτις) grows in men," along with B108: "to the extent in which men change, thoughts occur to them always different (τὸ φρονεῖν)."

98 See also *On the Soul* 427a, where it is confirmed that according to some, νοεῖν and φρονεῖν are the same as αἰσθάνεσθαι, quoting *Od.* 18, 136.

99 A statement of his is reported, a "statement made to some of his disciples, saying that beings were to them what they thought they were" (= DK 59A28).

100 *Il.* 23, 698: the hero, delirious because of a wound, "was lying with changed thoughts in his mind."

101 *Metaph.* 1009b33–37.

102 *Metaph.* 1010a1–3.

referring to. On the other hand, there is the use Aristotle makes of those doctrines for his own aims, and thus his judgment on them. The overall presentation of those philosophers is intended to make them all look like relativists or, even worse, subjectivists, while it is right to maintain that they thought science, knowledge and even truth had a value of objective force. Later on, Aristotle states: "those maintaining that the being and the not-being exist together, should state that everything is still, not that everything moves/changes: according to this doctrine, in fact, there cannot be something into which the object turns because everything already exists in everything."[103] This statement is explained through the intention to criticize all those who, precisely like the quoted philosophers, do admit a changing and developing, but assign no aim to them, as he instead thought necessary.[104] And eventually, closing the chapter, and to reassert the perspective Aristotle thought inescapable, the following statement is made: "And, generally speaking, if only what can be perceived by senses exists, if no lively beings existed nothing could be: for, in this case, neither sensibles nor sensations would exist (sensations are, in fact, affections of the one who feels); but the objects causing sensations cannot possibly exist also independently from the sensation. For sensation is not self-sensation, but there is something other than sensation and beyond sensation that exists, necessarily, before sensation itself. What causes movement is in fact, for its very nature, prior to what is moved: and this is not less true if we state that sensation and sensible are correlative."[105] Aristotle offers this perspective as an argument against those philosophers who tightly linked sensible knowledge to the knowledge derived by cognition, reasserting the priority of the object causing the sensation on the sensing subject, that is, its existence independently of the sensation itself; an assertion, in any case, that would have been easily accepted by each and every philosopher he named, albeit in their own perspective:

[103] *Metaph.* 1010a34–37.
[104] See Reale, *Aristot.* = Aristotele, p. 348 n32.
[105] 1010b30.

no pre-Platonic philosopher would agree on the idea that the world outside man could be a projection of the thinking Self. The same perspective would then be reasserted by the great Aristotelian pupil Theophrastus, who, moreover, testifies to a Parmenidean theory that unfortunately cannot be confirmed through any of the fragments we have left, but can easily be found in Empedocles—that, if the way one thinks is linked to the way one feels, then all living beings must have some cognitive ability (ὅλως δὲ πᾶν τὸ ὂν ἔχειν τινὰ γνῶσιν),[106] which of course differs from species to species.

Aristotle found himself facing a philosophical and scientific tradition of thought, which was by that time deeply rooted in Greek culture, that expressed a clear break with a kind of mythical argumentation: even man and the particular world of his thought are a subject matter of scientific analysis, and not just the subject of religious or ethical thinking. The fact that man's νόος and its θυμός were "variable functions" had already been asserted by Greek culture long before. Homer had already stated that man's νόος is what day by day the father of gods and men causes it to be,[107] and Archilocus had said that "men's nature is coated in the days that Zeus brings us day after day, and they adjust the idea to the action taking them up."[108] Thus, there was a strong relationship linking thought to real life, their way of feeling and their behavior to their actions, their being concretely "in situation." But if the poets still have the sense of men's dependence on God, the first Greek "philosophers" clearly exhibit a shift in mentality. Alcmaeon[109] and Zeno[110] can be found at Parmenides' level. But

[106] Theophr. *de sens.* 1–3 = DK 28A46.

[107] *Od.* 18, 136–137. See Snell, *Cultura*, pp. 92–93: according to Homer νόος and θυμός are "organs" or "functions" that can be distinguished but not separated: "the soul's organs are not substantially distinguished by those of the body."

[108] Archilochus fr. 68 Diehl.

[109] To whom health is a harmonious blend of opposite qualities (DK 24B4); the brain has the task of coordinating and reconciling the manifold of sensations deriving from the different organs of sense: the changing of the brain, and thus of knowledge, is thus connected to the changing of this reconciliation (DK 24A5).

[110] "Men originate from the earth and the soul is a mixture of elements where none of them prevails": DK 29A1.

the closest to the Elean are, as noted repeatedly, Empedocles[111] and Democritus.[112] And finally, to confirm this so deeply rooted mentality in the Greek ancient culture, here is one more passage by Theophrastus: thought depends on "physical changes, and this is a very old opinion, since all, both ancient poets and philosophers, explain thought as dependent on our disposition."[113] Thus, agreeing with Cerri, "a completely materialist notion: psyche is nothing else than a function of the body, the properties of the former depend on those of the latter."[114]

---

[111] His belief that thought depends upon the particular way of being of man is widely testified to. See DK 31B2: the evils occurring to men cloud their thoughts; DK 31B3.9–13: all senses and limbs need to be trusted, they hold "ways to know (πόρος ἐστὶ νοῆσαι)"; the connection of thinking to being, with phrases literally similar to Parmenides' phrases, is the explicit topic of fragments 105–110. B105: thought is the blood of man; B106, B109: thought is the sensations man feels; B107: thought is the crasis of all elements it is made of; B108: thought is the particular condition he is in and its changing in connection with outside situations; B109: thought is his individual character (ἦθος), B110: all his φύσις. See Kahn, *Religion*, p. 439 n34; explicitly linking these fragments to Parmenides' B16: "Both philosophers represent, in a more rigorous way, the general 5th century tendency to consider ψυχή the 'mental correlate of σώμα'. But both philosophers avoid the ambiguous term ψυχή and speak more concretely of νόος, νοεῖν, or φρήν, φρονεῖν." We do not actually find the term "soul" (ψυχή) in Parmenides: we have a testimony by Macrobius (*s. Scip.* I 14, 20 = DK 28A45) saying that the soul is made up of earth and fire; one by Diogenes Laertius (IX 22 = 28A1, probably derived from Theophr. *phys. opin.* fr. 6) saying that soul and mind are the same thing. There are two more by Aëtius: in the first one (IV 3, 4 = DK 28A45), Parmenides and Hippasus are said to have maintained the soul is igneous, and in the second (Aët. IV 5 12 = DK 28A45), Parmenides, Empedocles, and Democritus identify mind and soul, so to them no animal is completely irrational. And eventually, soon after having quoted B12.3, Simplicius tells us (*phys.* 39, 18) that the "goddess ruling on all" sometimes sends the souls from the visible to the invisible and sometimes the other way round, but we do not have any clue to judge on this point.

[112] See DK 68A135: thought derives from "the blending (κρᾶσις) [of the elements] of the body" and "is produced when there is balance in the eternal blend of the soul"; 68B9: "We actually do not know anything which is invariable, but rather just changing aspects according to the attitude of our body and to what slips into it or resists to it."

[113] *De sens.* 72 = DK 68A135.

[114] Cerri, *Parmenide di Elea*, p. 281. But see also Mansfeld, *Offenbarung*, p. 193: "Spirit is the quality aspect of the physical quantities with which it identifies"; and Kafka, *Die Vorsokratiker*, p. 70: ". . . it is surely not by chance that the formula of the identity of thought and being, that otherwise served, as it could materially be expressed, for representing the Being (ideal) as a function of the Thought (rational), is here somewhat reversed in the inverted formula where the Thought (derived from the senses) turns up to be a function of the Being (material)." On the

4. I will close my contribution with some quotes in order to show how some Parmenidean doctrines, which could seem paradoxical (i.e., against common opinions), are in fact very close to relativistic physics, developed last century. First of all is the question of the structure of the spherical universe, finite but unlimited. In an article called *Cosmological Considerations on the General Theory of Relativity*, published in the Prussian Academy proceedings in 1917, Einstein pointed to the earth's surface as a good example of such a universe.[115] The most suitable model to represent the universe is precisely the bidimensional spherical surface: a spherical surface has neither a center nor privileged points—a concept that could be a comment to 28A5. If a voyager moved in a straight line on this hypothetical surface, leaving from a point P, he would start by going away from it but then, after reaching the point diametrically opposite the starting point, would start getting close again and eventually he would reach P again. The length of the semicircle from P to the diametrically opposed point is the "radius" of this bidimensional universe.[116] Likewise, according to the original model by Einstein, our universe would have similar qualities to that of the bidimensional spherical surface. This means that a hypothetical voyager moving across the universe following a geodetic line (the line traced by a ray of light in space), getting away from the earth, would end up coming back to earth. This universe, like Parmenides', is finite, since it is confined to the total area of the surface or to the wholeness of the tridimensional spherical space, and unlimited at the same time, since the voyager does not get stopped in his journey from any geometrical obstacle.[117] With regard to B8.44–45,[118] we

---

Aristotelian distortion of the first Greek science and the victory of his scientific outline, see Longo, *Scienza*, in particular where he talks about biology, with the defeat of the evolutionary theory and of the genesis of the living world.

[115] See Infeld, *Albert Einstein*, p. 87.

[116] See Coleman, *Origine*, ch. I.

[117] Einstein and Infeld, *L'evoluzione*, part III.

[118] Which has been understood by some scholars as defining a figure "eternally growing with respect to its centre" (see Calogero, *Studi sull'eleatismo*, p. 27; Mondolfo, *Problemi del pensiero antico*, pp. 159–160; Mondolfo, *L'infinito*, pp. 364–366; De Santillana's *Le origini*, p. 107 and "Prologo a Parmenide," p. 31; Martano, *Contrarietà*, pp. 105–106).

can read the following passage by Infeld: "Such expanding sphere, and not a sphere with unchanging radius, is the bi-dimensional model of our universe! We see this principle satisfies both the uniformity principle and the rule of moving towards red. In fact, our nebulae (the golden points on the expanding sphere) will stay uniform, because they were designed in a uniform way and because in the expansion the spherical form is kept and only the radius changes. The distances between the nebulosae measured on the sphere will increase. An observer from any one of these nebulosae will see the others moving away."[119]

More specifically, it is the features of Parmenides' cosmos themselves that can be compared to those of Einstein's universe. First of all, the feature of *continuity*, stated by Parmenides in B4.2–4, B8.22–25, B8.5–6, is precisely proper of geometric, mathematic-physical space—in modern terms, we would say precisely that space is a continuous unity. Then the feature of *homogeneity*, stated by Parmenides in B8.2–4, B8.22–25, B8.29–30, B8.32–33, B8.45–48: the whole set of stars, galaxies and all that makes the universe up is evenly distributed in a continuous mass, with no remarkable irregularities. As such, "Einstein considered it from a mathematic point of view as if the whole matter making the universe up was almost evenly distributed in a regular mass filling the whole space up."[120] Finally, the feature of *isotropy*, stated by Parmenides in B8.42–45, 49: no part of the universe has remarkable differences compared to the others; there is no place differing in some way or another from the rest of the universe. "If with our telescopes we look in different directions, we see that—statistically—there are no privileged directions. We also see that the number of nebulosae per volume unity stays the same, no matter how far our telescopes can reach. In our universe matter seems to be distributed somehow evenly. There are of course some irregularities, but they are so small that we can assume, with some certainty, that there is no

[119] Infeld, *Albert Einstein*, p. 97.
[120] Coleman, *Origine*, p. 31.

privileged direction and that there is no difference among the many points in space."[121]

Some fundamental intuitions of modern sciences are thus remotely but clearly rooted in the bright intuitions of "ancient primitives." The same holds for the *vacuum*. According to Parmenides, a vacuum does not exist, and this idea will be reasserted by physics from the relativistic revolution onward. At the beginning of the nineteenth century, the whole conception of physics seemed based only on the notion of matter. During that century, thanks especially to studies of electromagnetic phenomena, the need for one more concept was felt: the concept of *field*. Later on, the relativity theory laid the foundations for overcoming the binomial field-matter in a higher unitary perspective. Relativity theory has actually assimilated the notions of mass and energy, proving that matter represents big energy reserves and that energy represents matter. If the distinction between mass and energy, though, is just a quantitative one, even the one between matter and field cannot be qualitative anymore: matter is in fact given where there is a strong concentration of energy, field where the concentration is weak. In other words, if matter is a strong concentration of energy in a relatively limited space, it can be assimilated to a space area where the field is extremely strong.[122] So a vacuum does not exist: a vacuum should be a complete absence of energy, but there will always be a field (an electric, magnetic, gravity, or thermal field) in what we call a vacuum. According to Schrödinger:[123] "A physicist cannot reasonably distinguish, inside his research area, between the matter and 'something else.' We can't oppose forces or force fields and matter like they were something different, we now know that the two notions have to be melted in one. It is true that we say an area in space is empty from matter if it is just filled by a gravity field. But that is not correct, since even in sidereal space, so far away from us, there's the light of stars, and this 'is' matter."

Even when we consider the well-known correspondence between being and thought, explicitly stated by Parmenides in

121 Infeld, *Albert Einstein*, p. 94.
122 Einstein and Infeld, *L'evoluzione*, pp. 251–253.
123 Schrödinger, *L'immagine*, p. 35.

B3, B8.8–9, B8.34–36, B2.7–8, which from Plotinus to Hegel and onward has been read in an "idealistic" perspective, we can state that this is the essential requirement of any scientific research. Some quotes: Einstein and Infeld: "Without the belief that reality can be reached through our theoric constructs, without the belief in an inner harmony of our world, no science could ever be."[124] Planck: "What a philologist supposes and must suppose, if he wants to work successfully, is for his document to have some reasonable meaning. Thus even the physicist has to suppose that real world obeys to some rules we can understand."[125] De Broglie: "This . . . is not a posit of no importance: it leads to admit the rational character of the physical world, to recognize that there's something in common between the material structure of the universe and the rules operating in our thought."[126] We can also read the enthusiasm upon the discovery of this principle in a beautiful passage by Plank, from his "posthumous essay," *Scientific Autobiography*: "My decision to devote myself to science was a direct consequence of a finding, that never ceased filling me with enthusiasm since I was very young: *the rules of human thought coincide with the rules regulating the series of sensations we get from the world around us, so that logics can make us see through its mechanism.*"[127]

And eventually, even on the relationship between experience and science, between the world of the senses and the rationally built image of the world, a relationship defined by Parmenides starting from B8.50–53, and one on which the opinions of philologists and philosophy scholars have already been quoted, we can now quote scientists' "testimonies." For instance, Einstein: "Thought and ideas and not formulas are the origin of any theory in physics. Only afterwards do ideas have to wear the mathematical clothes of a quantitative theory, for the purposes of experimental control."[128] Also: "Science is not . . . a catalogue of unrelated facts. . . . The theories of physics try and design a representation of reality and define the links with the wide

[124] Einstein-Infeld, *L'evoluzione,* p. 203.
[125] Planck, *Conoscenza,* p. 245.
[126] De Broglie, *Sentieri,* p. 300.
[127] Planck, *Conoscenza,* p. 11: my italics.
[128] Einstein and Infeld, *L'evoluzione,* p. 285.

world of sensations."[129] There is also De Broglie: "Data coming from our senses can help us in the construction of science only after we have interpreted them properly and in doing so some notions held in our spirit, that is theorical ideas, necessarily operate. It is enough to prove that one cannot distinctively separate experimenting and theory, and think of the experimental fact as something independent from any interpretation. The existing relationship between experimental facts and theory is deeper and more complex: *experimental observations acquire their scientific value only after having been processed*"[130] [my italics]. Scientific research brings order and regularity in the heterogeneity of sensible experiences; "it reduces the manifest complexity of natural phenomena to a few and simple fundamental ideas and relationships,"[131] so there is no opposition between common sense and scientific research, which presuppose and deny each other in a dialectical relationship. And finally, I present one more beautiful passage by Planck: "Sensation is always a fact, thus indisputable. The conclusions each one attaches to it, that's something else. . . . To the content of sensory impressions is the most suitable foundation, and the only irreproachable one, on which to base the building of exact science. If we define the set of sensory impressions with the term *world of senses*, we can briefly assert that exact science is born from the world of senses that we experience. . . . So what is the meaning of this work of science? Briefly, it lies in the task of bringing order and regularity in the richness of the heterogeneous experiences coming from the different fields of the world of senses. . . . From this common way of thinking scientific thinking does not differ in its substance, but rather just in its level of subtlety and precision, more or less like the performance of a microscope differs from that of the naked eye."[132]

Translated by Silvia Casertano

[129] Einstein and Infeld, *L'evoluzione*, p. 301.
[130] De Broglie, *Sentieri*, p. 156: my italics.
[131] Einstein and Infeld, *L'evoluzione*, pp. 64–65.
[132] Planck, *Conoscenza*, pp. 357ff.

# Bibliography

Aubenque, Pierre, ed. *Études sur Parménide*, Tome I et II. Paris: Vrin, 1987.

Calogero, Guido. *Studi sull'eleatismo. Roma: Tipografia del Senato,* 1932. Reprinted, Firenze: La Nuova Italia, 1977.

Casertano, Giovanni. "Astrazione ed esperienza: Parmenide (e Protagora)." In Paolo Impara (a cura di), *Il Problema del Linguaggio nella Filosofia Greca* (pp. 41–59). Roma: Casa Editrice "La Sapienza," 1988.

_____. "Una nuova lettura di Parmenide." In *Atti dell'Accademia di Scienze Morali e Politiche della Società Nazionale di Scienze, Lettere ed Arti in Napoli* (pp. 379–421). Napoli: Giannini Editore, 1974.

_____. *Parmenide il Metodo la Scienza l'esperienza.* Napoli: Loffredo Editore, 1989.

_____. "Pitagorici ed Eleati." In Maurizio Bugno, ed., *Senofane ed Elea tra Ionia e Magna Grecia* (pp. 213–240). Napoli: Luciano Editore, 2005.

Cassin, Barbara. *Parménide, sur la Nature ou sur l'étant.* Paris: Éditions du Seuil, 1998.

Cerri, Giovanni. *Parmenide di Elea. Poema sulla Natura.* Milano: Biblioteca Universale Rizzoli, 1999.

Cherniss, Harold. *Aristotle's Criticism of Presocratic Philosophy.* New York: Octagon Books, 1976.

_____. "The Characteristics and Effects of Presocratic Philosophy." *Journal of the History of Ideas* 12 (1951): 319–345. Reprinted in David J. Furley and R. E. Allen, eds., *Studies in Presocratic Philosophy*, Vol. 1 (pp. 1–28). London: Routledge & Kegan Paul, 1970.

_____. "The History of Ideas and Ancient Greek Philosophy." In *Estudios de Historia de la Filosofia en Homenaje al Profesor R. Mondolfo*, Fasc. 1 (pp. 93–114). Tucumán: Univ. Nac. De Tucumán, 1957.

Coleman, James A. *Origine e Divenire del Cosmo.* Milano: Feltrinelli, 1961.

Cordero, Néstor-Luis. *Les Deux Chemins de Parménide.* Paris-Bruxelles: Vrin-Éditions Ousia, 1997[2].

Cornford, Francis Macdonald. "Parmenides' Two Ways." *Classical Quarterly* 27 (1933): 97–111.

_____. *Plato and Parmenides: Parmenides' Way of Truth and Plato's* Parmenides, *translated with an introduction and a running commentary.* London: Routledge & Kegan Paul, 1939.

Couloubaritsis, Lambros. *Mythe et Philosophie chez Parménide.* Bruxelles: Éditions Ousia, 1986.

De Broglie, Louis. *Sui Sentieri della Scienza.* Torino: Bollati Boringhieri, 1962.

De Santillana, Giorgio. *Le Origini del Pensiero Scientifico*. Firenze: Biblioteca Sansoni, 1966.

_____. "Prologo a Parmenide." *De Homine* 22–23 (1967): 3–50.

Diels, Hermann. *Parmenides Lehrgedicht*. Berlin: Reimer, 1897; Sankt Augustin: Academia Verlag, 2003.

Diller, Hans. "Der Vorphilosophische Gebrauch von KOSMOS und KOSMEIN." In *Festschrift Bruno Snell* (pp. 47–60). München: Beck, 1956; reprinted in H.-J. Newiger and H. Seyffert, eds., *Kleine Schriften zur antiken Literatur* (pp. 73–87). München: Beck, 1971.

Düring, Ingemar. (1966) *Aristotele*. Milano: Mursia, 1976.

Einstein, Albert, and Leopold Infeld. *L'evoluzione della Fisica*. Torino: Bollati Boringhieri, 1960.

Fränkel, Hermann. "Parmenidesstudien, VI: Parmenides und Anaximander." In *Nachrichten von der Gesellschaft der Wissenschaften zu Göttingen. Philologisch-historische Klasse. Sonderabdruck Fachgruppe I (Altertumswissenschaft)* (pp. 153–192). Berlin: Weidmann, 1930. English Translation by David J. Furley and R. E. Allen, eds., in *Studies in Presocratic Philosophy*, Vol. II (pp. 1–47). London: Routledge & Kegan Paul, 1975.

Gilardoni, Giovanni. *Parmenide. I frammenti*. Firenze: Le Monnier, 1969.

Heitsch, Ernst. *Parmenides. Die Anfänge der Ontologie, Logik und Naturwissenschaft*. München: Heimeran, 1974.

Infeld, Leopold. *Albert Einstein*. Torino: Einaudi, 1962.

Kafka, Gustav. *Die Vorsokratiker*. München: Ernst Reinhardt, 1921.

Kahn, Charles H. "Religion and Natural Philosophy in Empedocles' Doctrine of the Soul." *Archiv für Geschichte der Philosophie* 42 (1960): 3–35. Reprinted in Alexander P. D. Mourelatos, ed., *The Pre-Socratics* (pp. 426–456). Garden City, NY: Doubleday-Anchor Press, 1974.

Lesky, Erna. *Die Zeugungs- und Vererbungslehren der Antike und ihr Nachwirken*. Wiesbaden: Steiner, 1951.

Lloyd, Geoffrey E. R. *La Scienza dei Greci*. (1970–1973). Roma-Bari: Laterza, 1978.

Long, Anthony A. "The Principles of Parmenides' Cosmogony." *Phronesis* 8 (1963): 90–107. Reprinted in David J. Furley and R. E. Allen, eds., *Studies in Presocratic Philosophy*, Vol II (pp. 82–101). London: Routledge & Kegan Paul, 1975.

Longo, Oddone. *Scienza Mito Natura. La Nascita della Biologia in Grecia*. Milano: Bompiani, 2006.

Mansfeld, Jaap. *Die Offenbarung des Parmenides und die Menschliche Welt.* Assen: Van Gorcum, 1964.

Martano, Giuseppe. "Bagliori della Chimica Moderna in Empedocle d'Agrigento" (1963). In *Studi di Storia del Pensiero Antico* (pp. 53–81). Napoli-Firenze: Il Tripode, 1968.

_____. *Contrarietà e dialettica nel pensiero antico*, I. Napoli: Il Tripode, 1972.

Matson, Wallace. "Parmenides Unbound." *Philosophical Inquiry* 2 (1980): 345–360.

McDiarmid, John B. "Theophrastus on the Presocratic Causes." *Harvard Studies in Classical Philology* 61 (1953): 85–156. Reprinted in David J. Furley and R. E. Allen, eds., *Studies in Presocratic Philosophy*, Vol. 1 (pp. 178–238). London: Routledge & Kegan Paul, 1970.

Mondolfo, Rodolfo. *L'infinito nel Pensiero dell'antichità Classica.* Firenze: La Nuova Italia, 1967.

_____. *Problemi del Pensiero Antico.* Bologna: Cappelli, 1936.

Mourelatos, Alexander P. D. *The Route of Parmenides.* New Haven and London: Yale University Press, 1970. Revised and Expanded Edition, Las Vegas: Parmenides Publishing, 2008.

Pasquinelli, Angelo. *I Presocratici. Frammenti e Testimonianze.* Torino: Einaudi, 1958.

Pfeiffer, Horand. *Die Stellung des Parmenideischen Lehrgedichtes in der Epischen Tradition.* Bonn: R. Habelt, 1975.

Planck, Max. *La Conoscenza del Mondo Fisico.* Torino: Bollati Boringhieri, 1964.

Popper, Karl R. "Ulteriori Osservazioni sui Presocratici e in Particolare su Parmenide." In *Addenda* n. 8 a *Congetture e Confutazioni* (1958–1959), Vol. 2. Bologna: Il Mulino, 1972.

Reale, Giovanni G, ed. *Aristotele, La Metafisica. Translation, Introduction and Commentary.* Vol. 2. Napoli: Loffredo, 1968. Reprinted 1978.

_____. "Eleati." In E. Zeller and Rodolfo Mondolfo, *La Filosofia dei Greci nel suo Sviluppo Storico*, Part I, Vol. III. Firenze: La Nuova Italia, 1967.

Robbiano, Chiara. *Becoming Being: On Parmenides' Transformative Philosophy.* Sankt Augustin: Academia Verlag, 2006.

Ross, William D. *Aristotle's Metaphysics.* Oxford: Clarendon Press, 1924.

Ruggiu, Luigi. *Parmenide.* Venezia-Padova: Marsilio, 1975.

Ruggiu, Liugi, and Giovanni Reale. *Parmenide. Poema sulla Natura.* Milano: Rusconi, 1991.

Santoro, Fernando. *Parmênides. Da Natureza*. Rio de Janeiro: Laboratório Ousia, 2006.

Santos, José Trindade. *Parménides. Da natureza*. Queluz: Alda Editores, 1997.

Schrödinger, Erwin. "L'immagine Attuale della Materia." In Werner Heisenberg, Erwin Schrödinger, Max Born, and Pierre Auger, *Discussione sulla Fisica Moderna*. Torino: Bollati Boringhieri, 1960; 2nd editon, 1980.

Schwabl, Hans. "Sein und Doxa bei Parmenides." *Wiener Studien* 66 (1953): 50–75. Reprinted in Hans-George Gadamer, ed., *Um die Begriffswelt der Vorsokratiker* (pp. 391–422). Darmstadt: Wissenschaftliche Buchgesellschaft, 1968.

Sichirollo, Livio. "Aristotelica." *Studi Urbinati* 27 (1953): 220–264 and 28 (1954): 387–405.

Somigliana, Ada. "Come Interpretare in Parmenide l'equivalenza di 'Sentire' e 'Pensare.'" *Sophia* 1–2 (1969): 83–86.

Somville, Pierre. *Parménide d'Élée. Son tempe et le nôtre*. Paris: Vrin, 1976.

Snell, Bruno. *La Cultura Greca e le Origini del Pensiero Europeo*. (1955$^3$). Torino: Einaudi, 1963$^2$.

Tarán, Leonardo. *Parmenides: A Text with Translation, Commentary and Critical Essays*. Princeton: Princeton University Press, 1965.

Untersteiner, Mario. *Parmenide. Testimonianze e Frammenti*. Firenze: La Nuova Italia, 1967.

Verdenius, Willem J. *Parmenides: Some Comments on His Poem*. Groningen: J. B. Wolters' Uitgevers-Maatschappij, 1942; Amsterdam: A. M. Hakkert, 1964.

Zeller, Eduard, and Rodolfo Mondolfo. *La Filosofia dei Greci nel suo Sviluppo Storico*, Part I, Vol. III. Firenze: La Nuova Italia, 1967.

# Parmenides Lost in Translation

Barbara Cassin

## Summary

I would like to show in this text the successive difficulties to be overcome when one tries to translate Parmenides. Translation is the extreme degree of interpretation. For that purpose, one needs to triumph over the impossibility of confronting the original "venerable and awesome" as well as of confronting "historial" language such as Greek. Then, one must sort out the alternatives that make it possible to select and fix a fragmentary text. Finally it is necessary to explore all the connections permitted by semantics and syntax. My study is focused on the play of "θυμὸς ὁδοῖο / μῦθος ὁδοῖο," and on possible interpretations of the text traditionally retained since the 5th edition of Diels, between the heroism of being, described as Odysseus, and the storytelling of language.

Permit me to write this text in the form of a number of theses, imperatives and questions, supported by quotations describing the translation of the venerable and formidable Parmenides, "the first to," as Plato tells us still, in the long duration of the history of the transmission and reception, as well as in the history of philosophy and the history of translation.

## 1. Making hermeneutics less of a drama

"It is easier to raise a shrine
than bring the deity down to haunt it."
S. Beckett, *The Unnameable*
(Exergue to T. W. Adorno, *The Jargon of Authenticity*[1])

[1] The quotation is placed as an exergue to the French translation of Adorno's text [trans.].

To begin our work, we must recover from being left dumbstruck by three shocks. Their expression by Heidegger might give us the shivers, in several ways, and with good reason.

—Regarding text-origin:

"These few words stand there like the Greek statues of the early period. What we still possess of Parmenides' didactic poem fits into a thin brochure, but this little brochure is one which might perfectly well replace whole libraries of supposedly indispensable philosophical literature. Anyone living today who knows the measure of such thinking discourse must lose all desire to write books."[2]

—Regarding historical language:

"The *Greek language is philosophical,* i.e. not that Greek is loaded with philosophical terminology, but that it philosophizes in its basic structure and formation [*Sprachgestaltung*]. The same applies to every genuine language, in different degrees to be sure. The extent to which this is so depends on the depth and power of the people who speak the language and exist within it [*Der Grad bemisst sich nach der Tiefe und Gewalt der Existenz des Volkes und Stammes, der die Sprache spricht und in ihr existiert*]. Only our German language has a deep and a creative philosophical character to compare with the Greek (cf. Meister Eckhart and Hegel)."[3]

—Regarding the essence of translating:

". . . All translating is of necessity an interpreting. But the inverse is equally true: every interpretation and everything which results from it is a translation. This incidental remark on the essence of translating seeks to remind us that the difficulty of a translation is never simply technical, but concerns the relationship of man to the essence of speech and the dignity of language [*zum Wesen des Wortes und zur*

[2] Martin Heidegger, *An Introduction to Metaphysics,* trans. Ralph Mannheim (New Haven: Yale University Press, 1959), p. 96.

[3] Martin Heidegger, *The Essence of Human Freedom: An Introduction to Philosophy*, trans. Ted Sadler (London: Continuum, 2002), p. 36.

*Würde der Sprache*]. Tell me what you make of translation and I will tell you who you are."[4]

"We do not ask whether ὄν is correctly translated as 'being' and εἶναι as 'to be'; we ask only whether in the correct translation we think correctly. We ask only whether in this most common of all translations anything at all is thought."[5]

## 2. Translating philosophy?

> "Whoever finds language interesting in itself is different from whoever only recognizes in it the means for interesting thoughts."
> F. Nietzsche, "Fragments sur le langage"

To translate philosophy, one has to deal with two types of contradiction, which the *Dictionnaire des Intraduisibles*[6] enabled me to point out more clearly:

—The contradiction between logical universality and linguistic expression:

"When disagreements arise, there will be no more need for discussion between two philosophers than there is between two calculators. In truth it will be enough for them to take their pens, to sit down at a table and to say to each other (after having called a friend, if they wish): *calculemus*, let us calculate" (G. W. Leibniz, Vol. 7, Gerhardt edition, p. 1980).

"Here [in authentic philosophy], more so than in any other domain—and despite the range of contemporary or successive opinions—language contains *a* system of concepts. Precisely because they touch each other, are united and made complete in the same language, these concepts form *a* whole. With the exception, if any, of God and of Being, the first substantive and the first verb, the different parts of such a system do not correspond with those of any of the systems

4 Martin Heidegger, *GA53*, p. 75.

5 Martin Heidegger, "The Anaximander Fragment," in *Early Greek Thinking*, trans. David Farrell Krell (New York: Harper Row, 1984), p. 23.

6 Barbara Cassin, *Vocabulaire Européen des Philosophies: Dictionnaire des Intraduisibles* (Paris: Seuil, 2004).

of any other language, because even the absolutely universal, although located outside of the domain of particularity, is illuminated and coloured by language" (F. Schleiermacher, *On the Different Methods of Translating* [1813][7]).

—The contradiction between ontological nationalism and deterritorialization:

"What begins with Fichte, parallel to a cultural movement in which poetry and politics play a major role, is a deliberate reappropriation by German thought of what is most specific, original and irreducible about its mode of expression. At the limit, untranslatability becomes the criterion of truth, and this ontological nationalism, comforted by the gawping admiration it occasions on the other side of the Rhine more than anywhere else, will culminate with Heidegger, who nonetheless remains one of the greatest philosophers of his century" (Jean-Pierre Lefebvre, "Philosophy and Philology: The Translations of German Philosophers," in *Encyclopedia Universalis,* Symposium, Les Enjeux 1 [1990], p. 1970).

"The plurality of languages is far from reducible to a plurality of designations of a thing; they are different perspectives on the same thing, and when the thing is not the object of the five senses, one is often dealing with as many different things, fashioned differently by each language [. . .] The diversity of languages is the immediate condition for us of a growth in the richness of the world and the diversity of what we know about it. At the same time, this is how the region of human existence expands, and new ways of thinking and feeling are offered to us with determinate and real characteristics" (W. von Humboldt, "Fragment of a Monograph on the Basques" [1822]).

"What does it mean, metalanguage, if not translation? One can only speak of one language in another" (Jacques Lacan, "Towards a New Signifier," Séminaire 1977–1978 [Paris: Association Lacanienne Internationale, 2004]).

[7] Translated from the French translation: Friedrich Schleiermacher, *Des Différentes Methodes de Traduire,* trans. A. Berman (Paris: Seuil, 1999).

## 3. Translating a Presocratic?

> "Erudition is the modern form of the fantastic."
> J. L. Borges

To translate a Presocratic, one must first understand how a fragment is fabricated. It is a matter of a series of operations that arise from the trafficking of the letter. A fragment is the result of a cascade of arborescences all aiming to produce the One. The "authentic text" is fabricated by tradition from a multiplicity of sources, which in turn may themselves cite the fragment a multiplicity of times, from a multiplicity of manuscripts each time, each susceptible in turn to a multiplicity of readings and corrections. Translators, editors, citers, and scribes all contribute to reproducing the text that was originally lost, according to the following schema:

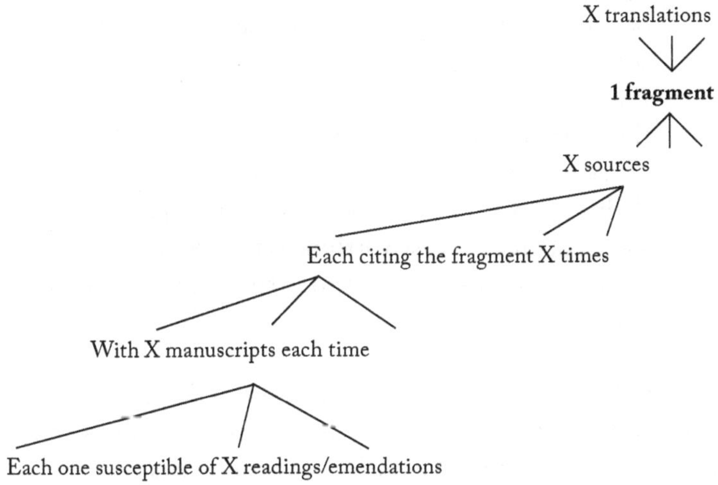


In fact, this is how the great German philology of the 19th century operated. The *Presocratic Fragments* gave both itself and us the possibility of a return upstream to the source, seeking to identify what Diels calls in the preface to his *Doxographi Graeci* the "first lips." The ensemble constitutes an imposing construction of knowledge and competence, which I like to call—with a plurilingual play on etymologies heavy with meaning—the *building* of the *Bildung*. As we "professionals" know, it is articulated around the labor of one man, Hermann Diels, who intervened at every link in the chain. In particular, he was the author of the following works:

- *Doxographi Graeci* (1879), which identifies the transmitters of the opinions in Antiquity and the modalities of that transmission (doxography: "writing of opinions");
- *Simplicii in Aristotelis Physicorum Libros quattuor priores Commentaria* (1882), which edits the commentary of Simplicius on Aristotle's *Physics*, a commentary which constitutes one of the goldmines for quotations of the Presocratics and, in particular, of Parmenides;
- *Parmenides Lehrgedicht* (1897), which proposes an edition of Parmenides on these bases;
- *Poetarum Philosophorum Fragmenta* (1901), which gives a first edition of the "poet-philosophers," that is, those he will subsequently call "Presocratics"; this edition serves as the matrix for . . .
- *Fragmente der Vorsokratiker* (1st edition 1903, 1934 for the edition revised by W. Kranz), which edits these "Presocratics" by distinguishing their texts from their contexts and the apocryphal fragments, with such a degree of trustworthiness that contemporary editions make use of it as *editio princeps* and only ever amend and augment it.

The basic principle of such an undertaking is frighteningly simple: one must endeavor to "de-deform" so as to find the authentic (the true, the one) version. The basic idea of this method is that the more recent the manuscript, the less chance it has of being reliable, as it has passed through a series of transmitters, who, intentionally or not, are likely to have introduced errors and deformations—in short an opacity—into the understanding of the fragment.

## 4. Translating Parmenides?

"One language, among others, is nothing more than the integral of equivocations that its history has allowed to persist in it."
J. Lacan, "L'Étourdit"

To translate Parmenides, let us—we philologists, philosophers stumbling one foot over the other like Nietzsche's centaur—get back to interpretation. And let us examine a textbook case, a bit of a phrase from Parmenides, transmitted twice in very different ways.[8] This phrase is the product of a series of interpretative operations of which translation is the final point and the final point only. The most adequate name for this series of operations is *fixion*, with a Lacanian *x* to emphasize that the fact is a fabrication, the *factum* a *fictum* that it has been decided to fix.

## 4.1 Fr. 1 / Fr. VII–VIII θυμὸς ὁδοῖο / μῦθος ὁδοῖο: the fixion of the fragment, or the sense of a spoonerism

### A. Sextus Empiricus: θυμὸς ὁδοῖο, one more effort to be a skeptic

Sextus (*Adversus Mathematicos*, VII, 111) is the sole transmitter of one of the two longest fragments, the one generally considered to be the "proem"—a little over thirty opening verses, edited as fragment 1 by Diels. In Sextus, the proem closes with a version of our phrase: μόνος δ' ἔτι θυμὸς ὁδοῖο λείπεται, which can be rendered, provisionally and approximately, by something like "for the heart by itself still misses the route." In the commentary by Sextus, then, Parmenides is explicitly a step on the route leading to skepticism. Parmenides would in fact think—as would Plato—that neither sensibility nor the heart (the first two "faculties" of the soul) are sufficient for knowledge. By this account, Parmenides would be saying that one more effort (the mind, νοῦς) is required in order to be a rationalist. To this, Sextus would add that a further effort is required in order to place not only sensibility and the heart in doubt, but reason itself, to become a skeptic.

It is in this form that the phrase and the fragment figure in the first four editions of the *Presocratic Fragments* of Diels (up to 1922). Here is the verse and its immediate context, in this first version:

[8] Here I am only taking up, in a different way, the analyses found in my book *Parménide, Sur la Nature ou sur l'étant: La Langue de l'être?* (Paris: Seuil, 1998).

**Fr. 1**

[. . .] χρεὼ δέ σε πάντα πυθέσθαι
ἠμὲν ἀληθείης **εὐπειθέος** ἀτρεμὲς ἦτορ
ἠδὲ βροτῶν δόξας, ταῖς οὐκ ἔνι πίστις ἀληθής.
ἀλλὰ σὺ τῆσδ' ἀφ' ὁδοῦ διζήσιος εἶργε νόημα
μηδέ σ' ἔθος πολύπειρον ὁδὸν κατὰ τήνδε βιάσθω,
νωμᾶν ἄσκοπον ὄμμα καὶ ἠχήεσσαν ἀκουὴν
καὶ γλῶσσαν, κρῖναι δὲ λόγῳ πολύπειρον ἔλεγχον
ἐξ ἐμέθεν ῥηθέντα. μόνος δ' ἔτι **θυμὸς** ὁδοῖο
λείπεται.

You must learn all things,
both the unwavering heart of persuasive truth
and the opinions of mortals in which there is no true trust
Restrain your thought from this road of inquiry
and do not let custom, based on much experience, force you along this road,
directing unobservant eye and echoing ear
and tongue; but judge by reason the battle-hardened proof
which I have spoken. **The heart by itself still misses the route.**[9]

## B. Simplicius: *muthos hodoio,* the affirmation of being

Four centuries later, Simplicius, not a doctor-skeptic from the second century CE but a Neoplatonic of the sixth century CE (the same lapse of time as that between Ronsard and Mallarmé), cites, then, the same—or nearly the same—verses when he comments on Aristotle's *On the Heavens* (*in Aristotelis de Caelo Commentaria,* I. L. Heiberg, ed., *Commentaria Aristotelem Graeca,* Vol. 7, Berlin: Georg Reimer, 1894, pp. 557, 255–558, 2).

1. With regard to fragment 1, Simplicius cites the final verses only; like Sextus, he cites 28b–30, but he proposes another ending of which there is no trace in Sextus nor others who cite the prologue and stop at 30. Nowadays, editors generally stick

9 Translation note: Up to the final phrase, the translation is adapted from Barnes's version of the poem. Idem for the fragment from Simplicius. See Jonathan Barnes, *Early Greek Philosophy* (London: Penguin, 1987).

to Simplicius' first version, but with the adjective *eupeitheos*, "highly persuasive," transmitted by Sextus, in verse 29.[10] Thus, the end of fragment 1 goes:

> [. . .] χρεὼ δέ σε πάντα πυθέσθαι
> ἠμὲν ἀληθείης **εὐκυκλέος** ἀτρεμὲς ἦτορ
> ἠδὲ βροτῶν δόξας, ταῖς οὐκ ἔνι πίστις ἀληθής.
> ἀλλ' ἔμπης καὶ ταῦτα μαθήσαι, ὡς τὰ δοκοῦντα
> χρῆν δοκίμως εἶναι διὰ παντὸς πάντα περῶντα.
>
> [. . .] You must learn all things,
> both the unwavering heart of well-rounded truth
> and the opinions of mortals in which there is no true trust.
> But nevertheless you will learn this too—how what appears
> had apparently to be, forever traversing everything

2. Elsewhere he cites the final phrase from Sextus three times, but with μῦθος instead of θυμός, followed by another sequence, constituting the beginning of fragment 8 for modern editors (fragments 7–8 are thus essentially a mixture of Plato, *Sophist*, 238a8–9, 258d2–3 [for VII 1–2]; of Sextus [for VII, 2–6 and VIII, 1–2] and of Simplicius [for VII, 1–2, and for VIII]). So he places our phrase, or one that is nearly the same, at the heart of the poem, immediately following the fragment subsequently identified as fragment VII. This timc thc phrasc significs thc affirmation of being. But it is not quite the same phrase. There is the matter of an inversion of consonants, like a spoonerism: μῦθος instead of θυμός, "discourse, story" instead of "heart, drive, will, desire," and also a clause is added, made of two words: it is a story ὡς ἔστιν, "that is." Parmenides becomes different, he is not caught up in the direction of a sequence of the history of philosophy any longer, where he was already Platonic but not yet skeptical, but he is, as

---

10 On the choice in favor of the "beginning" with Simplicius, see, for example, Denis O'Brien, *Études sur Parménide* I (Paris: Vrin, 1987), pp. 239–245. On the choice of *eupeitheos*, see p. 11.

Plato put it, the father at the origin of ontology. Here is the verse and its new context, in the second version:

**Fr. VII**

οὐ γὰρ μήποτε τοῦτο δαμῇ εἶναι μὴ ἐόντα·
ἀλλὰ σὺ τῆσδ' ἀφ' ὁδοῦ διζήσιος εἶργε νόημα
μηδέ σ' ἔθος πολύπειρον ὁδὸν κατὰ τήνδε βιάσθω,
νωμᾶν ἄσκοπον ὄμμα καὶ ἠχήεσσαν ἀκουὴν
καὶ γλῶσσαν, κρῖναι δὲ λόγῳ πολύδηριν ἔλεγχον
ἐξ ἐμέθεν ῥηθέντα.

VIII μόνος δ' ἔτι **μῦθος** ὁδοῖο
λείπεται **ὡς ἔστιν·** ταύτῃ δ' ἐπὶ σήματ' ἔασι
πολλὰ μάλ', ὡς ἀγένητον ἐὸν καὶ ἀνώλεθρόν ἐστιν,
οὖλον, μουνογενές τε καὶ ἀτρεμὲς οὐδ' ἀτέλεστον·

VII Because this will never be overcome: to be non-beings.
You, separate then your thought from this route of research,
and that the custom of numerous experiences not force you the length of this route
to turn a gaze without aim, a hearing echoing with noise
and a tongue, but judge by the saying of this test of many struggles
such as I have spoken it.

VIII **Sole remains then the story of the route "is."** On it, the marks are
very numerous: in being without birth and without death it is,
complete, alone of its kind, without trembling and not without end.[11]

[11] Translation note: Where the author is making specific points about the French rendering of the Greek, I have elected to provide a more literal rendering of the French. It is less elegant, but aims to make the syntactic and semantic distinctions more evident.

Such, then, is the sequence and the lesson that all the editors and interpreters draw from it today, in this way doing nothing but conforming to the 5th edition of Diels (dated 1934), which is followed *ne varietur* in all subsequent versions and remakes.[12]

## 4.2 Fr. VIII, 1–2, on translation as multiple: the blooming of possibilities

Translation is the culminating point of fixion. When I attempted an edition-translation of Parmenides' poem, I would have liked to have been able to set out a table of the semantic and syntactic alternatives of each sequence, nested inside each other. But, lacking any way of laying this out on the printed page (among other reasons), I was unable to. We should be able to render this opening up of possibilities materially, like a calculus. This would display its compossibilities, in the Leibnizian sense, and the paths that close down as soon as certain interpretations, possible at the preceding step of the temporally enunciated discursive sequence (that is what "discursivity" signifies), are rendered impossible by the subsequent word. In this way, a translation would have more of an arborescent order than a linear one.

Here are some of the principle semantic and syntactic bifurcations that can be envisaged for the sequence as it is always edited nowadays. They are followed by some examples of the translations of the sequences and descriptions in relation to the bifurcations chosen.

μόνος δ' ἔτι μῦθος ὁδοῖο
λείπεται ὡς ἔστιν·

—Syntactic and semantic bifurcations:

1. The meaning of *muthos*: a) word / b) story?
2. ὡς ἔστιν completing: a) μῦθος / b') ὁδοῖο the route?

[12] The reasons concerning both the form and the deeper sense of the text transmitted by Simplicius are summarized well in Denis O'Brien and Jean Frère, *Le Poème de Parménide: Texte, Traduction, Essai Critique* (Paris: Vrin, 1987), pp. 239–242.

3. The meaning of ἔστιν: a) existence / b) copula / c) verificational / d) possibility?
   The construction of ἔστιν: a′) without an elided subject / b′) with an elided subject?
4. The meaning of ὡς: a) that (attenuated = "…" ) / b) how?

—Example translation-bifurcations:

**Tarán**: "There is a solitary word (1a) still left to say of a way: exists (2a + 3a a′ + 4a)."
**Mourelatos**: "Sole the account (1b) still remains of the route, that is (2b + 3 a a′ + 4a)."
**Collobert**: "Une seule parole (1a) demeure: celle du chemin est (2b + 3 a a′ + 4a)."
**Heitsch**: "Allein also noch übrig bleibt die Beschreibung (1b) des Weges 'es ist' (2b + 3a b′ + 4a)."
**Barnes**: "A single story (1b) of a road is left—that it is (2a + 3a b′ + 4a)."

I will drop the idea of the syntactico-propositional calculus. The sometimes grandiose, sometimes minimal "stylistic" invention refers also to the difference between languages:

**Diels-Kranz**: "Aber nur noch eine Weg-Kunde bleibt dann, dass IST ist."
**Heidegger**: "Die Sage des Weges [. . .] (auf dem sich eröffnet), wie es um sein steht" [*Introduction to Metaphysics*, pp. 73–96: "But only the legend remains of the way (along which it is disclosed) how it stands with being"].
**Beaufret-Rinieri**: "Il ne reste plus qu'une seule voie dont on puisse parler, à savoir qu'il est."
**O'Brien**: "Il ne reste plus qu'une seule parole, celle de la voie énonçant: 'est'" / "The only tale still left is <that> of the way <which> tells us that is."
**Cordero**: "Il ne reste qu'une proposition du chemin: (il) est."
**Conche**: "De voie pour la parole ne reste que: 'il y a.'"
**Bollack**: "Seul reste encore en lice le récit du chemin que 'est.'"

**Santoro**: "Ainda uma so palavra resta do caminho: que é."[13]

## 4.3 The motives for a choice

It is on the basis of this plurality of more or less philologically and linguistically masterable resources that I have personally chosen to privilege two translations, in both an arbitrary and a motivated manner (as Gerard Genette said "who reads last, reads best"). Just the fact of keeping two translations is itself unusual.

Here are the two translations that I consider simultaneously.

First Translation: "Reste à faire le récit de la route du est"[14] / "There remains to tell the story of the route that 'is'" [μῦθος = story, ὡς ἔστιν completes ὁδοῖο; ἔστιν "total'" without subject; ὡς that. Or: 1b + 2b + 3abcd a′ + 4a].

Second Translation: "Seul demeure le mot du chemin: 'Est'", "Sole remains the word of the path: 'Is'" [μῦθος = word; ὡς ἔστιν completes μῦθος; ἔστιν "total" without subject; ὡς that. Or: 1a + 2a + 3abcd a′ + 4a].

With an almost (but not quite) identical analysis, we can see once again the force of a "style" that, taking into account connotations and the play on case, for example, allows for profound transformations, as violent as changes of the horizon. Let us explore the world opened up by each translation.

[13] For the references to the works from which these translations are taken, see the bibliography of Cassin 1998, op. cit., adding to it Jean Bollack, Parménide: *De l'étant au Monde* (Paris: Verdier, 2007) and Fernando Santoro, *O Poema de Parmênides: Da Natureza* (Rio de Janeiro: Azougue, 2008), but I rely on the manuscript F. S. had the kindness to provide me before the symposium.

[14] In French, "la route du 'est'" could be heard as a proper name like "la route Napoléon," from Golfe Juan to Grenoble through the Alps.

## A. "The story of the route that is," or the heroism of the being and the Homeric palimpsest

> "Quotation is something which conceals itself [. . .]
> The hand that belongs to the finger must be somewhere.
> Often a single particle is a hidden formula for a quotation.
> But one must admittedly have placed oneself
> in the same sphere as the utterer."
> F. W. Schleiermacher, "General Hermeneutics"[15]

With the "story of the route that is" we are in Kerouac or *Easy Rider.* More precisely, we are in Homer's *Odyssey* with Odysseus. Palimpsest is the modality par excellence of Ancient Greek writing; it is even what they call *paideia*—"culture" or "training." Parmenides' *On Nature*, written in the dactyl hexameter of the epic, describes the voyage of a man under divine guidance who risks going astray, risks error and the loss of self. Parmenides takes hold of all the major earlier stories and their supreme matrix, which is Homer's epic, and rearticulates them to create philosophy. The key moment that signals all the others is the appearance in the middle of *On Nature* of τὸ ἐόν, "the being," described in the same words as those used in *The Odyssey* to describe Odysseus. Surrounded by his oarsmen, their ears blocked with wax, and tied to the mast so as not to succumb to the charms of the Sirens' singing and dive into the sea to perish like all other sailors, Odysseus sails past the island of the Sirens, who are singing to "the much praised Odysseus, honor of the Achaia." The reference is inescapable:

### Fr. VIII: Being as Odysseus, "tel qu'en lui-même"

> αὐτὰρ ἀκίνητον **μεγάλων ἐν <u>πείρασι</u> δεσμῶν**
> ἔστιν ἄναρχον ἄπαυστον, ἐπεὶ γένεσις καὶ ὄλεθρος
> τῆλε μάλ' **<u>ἐπλάχθησαν</u>**, ἀπῶσε δὲ πίστις ἀληθής.

[15] Friedrich Schleiermacher, "General Hermeneutics," in *Hermeneutics and Criticism and Other Writings,* trans. Andrew Bowie (Cambridge: Cambridge University Press, 1998), p. 253.

Ταὐτόν τ' ἐν ταὐτῷ τε μένον καθ' ἑαυτό τε κεῖται
**χοὔτως ἔμπεδον αὖθι μένει·** κρατερὴ γὰρ Ἀνάγκη
πείρατος **ἐν δεσμοῖσιν** ἔχει, τό μιν ἀμφὶς ἐέργει,
οὕνεκεν οὐκ ἀτελεύτητον **τὸ ἐὸν** θέμις εἶναι·

So, immobile **within the bounds of great limits**
It is without beginning, without end, since birth and loss
Are very much **errant** in the distance, true belief has pushed them away.
The same and remaining in the same, it holds itself in itself
**and in this way remains there rooted to the ground**, because powerful necessity
holds it **in bonds** of the limit which encloses it all around;
that is why it is right that **the being** is not devoid of end

## Homer, *Odyssey*, XII, 158–164: Odysseus' identity

Σειρήνων μὲν πρῶτον ἀνώγει θεσπεσιάων
φθόγγον ἀλεύασθαι καὶ λειμῶν' ἀνθεμόεντα.
οἶον ἔμ' ἠνώγει ὄπ' ἀκουέμεν· ἀλλά με **δεσμῷ**
δήσατ' **ἐν ἀργαλέῳ, ὄφρ' ἔμπεδον αὐτόθι μίμνω,**
ὀρθὸν ἐν ἱστοπέδῃ, ἐκ δ' αὐτοῦ **πείρατ'** ἀνήφθω.
εἰ δέ κε λίσσωμαι ὑμέας λῦσαι τε κελεύω,
ὑμεῖς δὲ πλεόνεσσι τότ' **ἐν δεσμοῖσιν** πιέζειν.

[Circe] warned first to flee from the voices of the Sirens
with their divine song and their meadow in flower,
while she commands that I hear their voices;
but **tie me, with a painful binding so that I remain there rooted to the ground,**
straight on the mast, and that I be held within the limits of the bonds around it.
But if I beg and command you to release me,
then you will bind me tighter **in bonds** that are more numerous.

In this tradition, our tradition, the being, or Being, becomes forever the hero of philosophy, just as Odysseus will forever be the hero of the epic. It is in order to open up this world that I hold to the translation "the story of the route that 'is'" and to the perception of the poem—and of philosophy—that it induces.

### B. "The word of the path: 'Is'", or the ontology of Grammar

> "[. . .] the relationship of the utterer to the language:
> he is its organ and it is his."
> F. W. Schleiermacher, "General Hermeneutics"[16]

This second translation relates to the manner in which the Greek language is deployed throughout the poem, that is to say, to the modality of Parmenides' writing itself. What is at stake here is the distance from ordinary language which makes the poem a singular work. The Greek language both exists in and pre-exists the poem, even if it has a history and undergoes an evolution (thus the definite article, which is in the first place a deictic or is demonstrative, and on which the poem plays and has an impact). However, the poem points out and underlines how language is made, how it fabricates itself and how syntax and semantics intervene together. In this way, in the course of the poem, the subject is secreted by the verb via a series of clearly legible steps: "is" (*estin*, fr. II, 3, the third person singular of the present indicative which, right at the start, names the path of research to follow, and of which our little bit of phrase evidently makes itself the internal echo), "to be" (*einai*, infinitive, VI, I), "being" (*eon*, participle, VI, 1), finally "the being" (*to eon*, substantivized participle, VIII, 32) thus named just after the Homeric palimpsest. "Being," identifiable at last, enters into eternity, as does "Odysseus" when named by the Sirens.

[16] Schleiermacher, op. cit., p. 229.

Here are the principal traces, or proofs:

**Fr. II**

Εἰ δ᾽ ἄγ᾽ ἐγὼν ἐρέω, κόμισαι δὲ σὺ μῦθον ἀκούσας,
αἵπερ ὁδοὶ μοῦναι διζήσιός εἰσι νοῆσαι·
ἡ μὲν ὅπως **ἔστιν** τε καὶ ὡς οὐκ ἔστι μὴ εἶναι,
πειθοῦς ἐστι κέλευθος, ἀληθείῃ γὰρ ὀπηδεῖ,
ἡ δ᾽ ὡς οὐκ ἔστιν τε καὶ ὡς χρεών ἐστι μὴ εἶναι,
τὴν δή τοι φράζω παναπευθέα ἔμμεν ἀταρπόν·
οὔτε γὰρ ἂν γνοίης τό γε μὴ ἐόν, οὐ γὰρ ἀνυστόν,
οὔτε φράσαις.

Come, so I may tell you—but you, take care of the story you will have heard—
which paths of research alone are to be thought:
the one that **is** and that is not not to be;
it is the path of persuasion, because it follows the truth;
the other that is not and that is needed not to be,
that one, I indicate to you that it is a path of which nothing can be known
because you cannot know that which, in any case, is not
(because one cannot exhaust it) nor express it.

**Fr. VI**

χρὴ τὸ λέγειν τὸ νοεῖν τ᾽ **ἐὸν ἔμμέναι· ἔστι γὰρ εἶναι**
μηδὲν δ᾽ οὐκ ἔστιν· τά σ᾽ ἐγὼ φράζεσθαι ἄνωγα.
πρώτης γὰρ σ᾽ ἀφ᾽ ὁδοῦ ταύτης διζήσιος <εἴργω>

Here is what it is necessary to say and to think: **is as being because to be is.**[17]
But nothing is not: it is in this way that I push you to express yourself,
because it is primarily from this path of research that I am separating you.

[17] "Est en étant, car est être."

**Fr. VIII**

τῷ ξυνεχὲς πᾶν ἐστιν· **ἐὸν γὰρ ἐόντι** πελάζει.
αὐτὰρ ἀκίνητον μεγάλων ἐν πείρασι δεσμῶν
ἔστιν ἄναρχον ἄπαυστον, ἐπεὶ γένεσις καὶ ὄλεθρος
τῆλε μάλ' ἐπλάχθησαν, ἀπῶσε δὲ πίστις ἀληθής.
ταὐτόν τ' ἐν ταὐτῷ τε μένον καθ' ἑαυτό τε κεῖται
χοὔτως ἔμπεδον αὖθι μένει· κρατερὴ γὰρ Ἀνάγκη
πείρατος ἐν δεσμοῖσιν ἔχει, τό μιν ἀμφὶς ἐέργει,
οὕνεκεν οὐκ ἀτελεύτητον **τὸ ἐὸν** θέμις εἶναι·
ἔστι γὰρ οὐκ ἐπιδεές, μὴ ἐὸν δ' ἂν παντὸς ἐδεῖτο.
ταὐτόν δ' ἐστὶ νοεῖν τε καὶ οὕνεκεν ἔστι νόημα
οὐ γὰρ **ἄνευ τοῦ ἐόντος**, ἐν ᾧ πεφατισμένον **ἔστιν**,
εὑρήσεις τὸ νοεῖν· οὐδὲν γὰρ <ἢ> ἔστιν ἢ ἔσται
ἄλλο πάρεξ **τοῦ ἐόντος**, ἐπεὶ **τό γε** Μοῖρ' ἐπέδησεν
οὖλον ἀκίνητόν τ' ἔμεναι·

so it is entirely continuous, because **being touches being.**
Then, immobile within the bounds of great limits,
it is without beginning, without end, since birth and loss are very much errant in the distance, true belief has pushed them away.
The same and remaining in the same, it holds itself in itself
and in this way that it remains there rooted to the ground, because powerful necessity
holds it in bounds of the limit which encloses it all around;
that is why it is right that **the being** is not devoid of end
because it is not lacking, whereas not being it would lack everything.
It is the same thing, to think and the thought that "is"
because, **without the being** in which **"is"** finds itself formulated,
you will not find thinking. Nothing else in fact is nor will be
apart from **the being**, because it is **this** that destiny has attached
so that complete and motionless it be.

I do not wish, nor am I able, to choose between these two translations. But why stop with just these two? The only answer is because they interest me, because in my eyes they present more meaning than the others, meaning to which it is essential to be rendered sensible. This choice, which is explicitly presented as a choice, is much more savage than a description adjusted in terms of the hermeneutic circle of expectation and interpretation. It underlines the type of consistency of the normal interpretative operations: cultural construction, fixion of the text, trafficking of the letter, translation as culminating point of interpretation. They are correctly described only in the plural and are measured by the interest that they present. Gilles Deleuze opens the door to well-thought-out relativism by putting truth in its place: "the notions of importance, of necessity, of interest, are a thousand times more determining than the notion of truth. Not at all because they replace it, but because they measure the truth of what I am saying."[18]

## 5. Conclusion / Appendix

Every language introduces its own form and manner of equivocating and/or of disambiguating, on both the syntactic and the semantic planes.

To the extent that Parmenides' poem plays on multiple senses of *esti* in order to function, the disambiguation necessary for translation risks being one interpretative step too many, interfering with the very functioning of the poem. I call this the scheming of language. Doing the same thing as Gorgias had already done with Parmenides, it projects a categorical perspective of an Aristotelian type onto another state of language, a historically and deliberately different or ambiguous state.

When Néstor Cordero says that one should not project Platonism or Sophistry onto Parmenides, we can easily agree on the principle of the matter (even without necessarily agreeing on the definition of what derives from Sophistry and what from Platonism). But a maximal mental restriction is needed, analogous to that of the anthropologist who knows that he cannot *not* have a "point of view," or the Hegelian philosopher who

[18] Gilles Deleuze, *Negotiations,* trans. M. Joughin (New York: Columbia University Press, 1995), p. 67 (translation modified).

knows that he cannot "leap beyond his own time." When one translates, one projects one's own language onto the other and the state of one's own language onto the state of the other's language, even if—as Schleiermacher says—there are two, and only two, ways to translate: "either the translator leaves the writer alone as much as possible and makes the reader go to meet him, or he leaves the reader alone as much as possible and makes the writer go to meet him."[19] Even if the only good way is adopted—leave the original language alone as much as possible and trouble the destination language, deterritorialize one language by another and thus realize that it is one language, among many, that one speaks. There is no reason to make a big Heideggerian drama out of this, linking it to the loss of an originary unconcealment. The disorienting effect that one language has on another can be given a positive spin: it is the "shelter of the distance," "l'auberge du lointain," as Berman put it.

My French ear is particularly sensitive to this issue with Spanish and Portuguese, which constrain us to make a further disambiguation of *esti.* Is it "ser," with the sense of "essence"? Or "estar" with the sense of "accident"? And this is to say nothing of *ficar, haver* and *ha,* words with whose strangeness the French have been familiarized by Alfonso Correa-Motta and Fernando Santoro, in their collaboration in the *Dictionnaire des Intraduisibles.*

At the end of his *Parmenides,* Fernando Santoro chooses to set out a "Table of the Functional Values of the Verb *Eimi.*" Evidently, this is an undertaking that cuts both ways. The table makes the disambiguations chosen by the interpreter manifest, disambiguations which are generally chosen with reason, but often less consciously and with less subtlety. Immediately, one notices the supplementary strength/weakness of Portuguese. Besides *ficam,* which introduces its own tonality, as does *es gibt, there is* or *il y a* (I, 11, "locative," but all VIII, 27, "predicative"), one finds *ha* three times (VI, 1 and 2, VIII, 47: "existential"; see also XX, 1). Above all, we find *esta* four times:

[19] Schleiermacher, *Traduire,* p. 49.

- VIII, 15, "existential" for ἡ δὲ κρίσις περὶ τούτων ἐν τῷδ' ἔστιν, "a decisao sobre tais esta histo," which is certainly not existential in the same sense as ἔστιν ἢ οὐκ ἔστιν, "ê ou nao ê"!;
- VIII, 35, "predicative," οὐ γὰρ ἄνευ τοῦ ἐόντος ἐν ᾧ πεφατισμένον ἐστὶν, "pois sem o ente, no qual esta apalavrado," a heavy and contentious interpretative decision;
- VIII, 54, "predicative," ἐν ὧι πεπλανημένοι εἰσίν, "ne que estao desgarrados";
- IX, 3, "predicative," πᾶν πλέον ἐστίν, "tudo esta cheio."

"Tudo esta cheio": every translation and interpretation is certainly full, too full.

Translated by Andrew Goffey
Middlesex University

# The Astronomical Section in Parmenides' Poem

Giovanni Cerri

**Summary**

I have collected all the data (*testimonia and fragmenta*), which demonstrate that in Parmenides' poem *On Nature* there was a long section concerning astronomy, where he described the heavens and also illustrated recent, astonishing discoveries accomplished by astronomical research of his time. Such a section, which is very important in the history of ancient science, could not be a mere digression, not related to his general theory of nature. Therefore, every modern interpretation of his philosophical thought based on the removal of this aspect should certainly be considered inadequate to explain the whole doctrine in its very essence.

In the first half of the third century BCE, Colotes of Lampsacus, himself a pupil of Epicurus, wrote a polemical book with the purpose of demonstrating that all philosophical teachings other than those of Epicurus denied legitimacy to real life, this on account of the fact that all of them, though in different ways, did not rely upon the testimony of the senses. This work was lost in late antiquity, but we know its contents well, thanks to Plutarch's scrutiny in his opuscule *Against Colotes.* Among philosophers criticized by Colotes there was also Parmenides. This is Plutarch's summary of the critiques leveled against him by the Epicurean: Parmenides, "by saying that 'the universe is one,' has—I do not know why—prevented us from living" (Plutarch, *Moralia* 1114a, translated by B. Einerson and P. H. De Lacy, slightly adapted).

The addition "I do not know why" is just an anticipation of the objection he will expound shortly after:

> But Parmenides for one has abolished neither 'fire' nor 'water,' neither 'a precipice' nor 'cities lying in Europe and Asia' in Colotes' words. (Plutarch, *Moralia* 1114b, translated by B. Einerson and P. H. De Lacy)

The sentence is clearly a negative paraphrase of the mocking phrases employed by Colotes himself, when he argued that Parmenides, with his theory of the All-One, denied the evidence of things we come across in our real life. Yet—insinuates Plutarch—Colotes evidently ignores Parmenides' work; rather, he confines himself to reaching inferences, both facile and rash ones, from fragmentary and second-hand information, since a reader of the poem undoubtedly knows that its content is quite different:

> He [sc. Parmenides] has actually made a cosmic order (διάκοσμον πεποίηται), and by blending as elements (στοιχεῖα) the light and the dark produces out of them and by their operation the whole world of sense (τὰ φαινόμενα πάντα . . . ἀποτελεῖ). Thus he has much to say about earth, heaven, sun, moon, and stars, and he has recounted the genesis of man; and for an ancient natural philosopher—who has put together a book of his own, and is not pulling apart the book of another—he has left nothing of real importance unsaid . . . (Plutarch, *Moralia* 1114b, translated by B. Einerson and P. H. De Lacy)

The opening expression διάκοσμον πεποίηται is very significant: πεποίηται = "has composed," *perfectum praesens*, can only refer to the text of the poem composed by Parmenides. Therefore, at this time, it has been both composed and concluded and, furthermore, is open to be consulted by the one who is speaking. This text is evoked again at the end of the sentence with the reference to the composition of an original work. Besides, the whole opuscule *Against Colotes* parades the opposition between the ancient Epicurean opposing older and contemporary philosophers without reading their works, and Plutarch himself, with his circle of friends and disciples with a rich library at their disposal and therefore able to realize how much his rash statements outrage the letter and the spirit of the writings in question.

A clue of Plutarch's direct personal consultation is the term διάκοσμον, which precisely takes up the term employed by Parmenides in the protasis to the second part of the poem, namely in its last two lines, which must have immediately preceded the beginning of the treatment subsequent to that of the Being per se (fr. 8.60–61 DK):

> I tell you all the likely arrangement (διάκοσμον) in order that no opinion of mortals may never outstrip you. (translation by L. Tarán, slightly adapted)

Thus Plutarch's summary of the second part of the poem is trustworthy: for the arguments he explicitly invokes he has to have found there a more or less extensive treatment. And there is no doubt that the summary implies the presence of an astronomical section in the poem. Let us read once more the arguments concerned: "he has much to say about earth, heaven, sun, moon, and stars." From this overall testimony, as it were, let us move to the discussion of proper fragments as well as more specific *testimonia* about single items of the treatment.

> You will know the nature of the ether and all the signs in the ether and the destructive works of the pure torch of the resplendent sun, and whence they came into being. You will know, too, the wandering works and the nature of the round-faced moon. You will know also the sky which embraces all, whence it was born and also how Necessity guiding it fettered it to hold the limits of the stars. (fr. 10 DK, translation by L. Tarán)

The lines evidently derive from the protasis of the astronomical section of the poem or from one of its subsections. The list of arguments almost completely overlaps with that envisaged by Plutarch, except for the addition of the ether (αἰθήρ). It is not clear to what degree, or whether, this is meant to be distinct from the sky (οὐρανός). Furthermore it is clearly stated that the latter includes in itself the whole astronomical system; actually it represents its outermost limit, having the geometrical shape of a spherical crown, as can be gathered from other fragments and *testimonia*.

A distinctive feature of Parmenides' treatment, as it emerges from this protasis, is that it had to have a double outlay, synchronic on one hand, that is, a depiction of the structure of the starlit sky as it is or appears, diachronic on the other hand, that is, a tentative reconstruction of the probable origin of the stars and of their orbits. Apart from the reiterated use of the term "nature" (φύσις), which may refer either to the current structure or to the causal origin of the thing <in question>, phrases such as "whence they came into being" (1.3) and "whence it was born" (1.6), unmistakeably allude to the cosmogonic history. Did Parmenides narrate a beginning explosion, a sort of *Big Bang*? Yet of what? And why? We have no evidence from which to sketch an answer.

> How the earth and the sun and the moon and the common ether and the heavenly milky way and the outermost Olympos and the fiery stars strove eagerly to come into being. (fr. 11 DK, translation by L. Tarán)

In some respects, fr. 11 seems to be a doublet of fr. 10, another proposition, with different words and more concisely phrased, of the astronomical themes to tackle. It is not easy to figure out how the two passages were actually placed in the text, so that they did not seem a pointless repetition of each other. We may guess they both belonged to the general protasis of the whole astronomical section, perhaps one to its beginning, the other to its conclusion, with intentional repetition, according to the technique of ring composition. After all, the lengthy proem of the Hesiodic *Theogony* also exhibits something similar: the clusters of lines 11–21, 36–52, 105–115 all assert the contents of the Muses' song, which will be later the contents of the poem itself, by means of similar lists, pleonastically repetitive, made up by more or less the same items. Yet we may also think that the astronomical section was composed of several subdivisions, and that consequently, along with the opening protasis, it included other subordinate protases; that therefore fr. 10 and fr. 11 derive from distinct protases.

Be that as it may, the comparison with fr. 10 makes it clear that fr. 11 stands out for two reasons: the earth (γαῖα), in this case to be understood as a heavenly body among others, and the "heavenly milk" (γάλα οὐράνιον), that is the Milky Way. The "farthest Olympus" ("Ολυμπος ἔσχατος) clearly is identified with the sky (οὐρανός), on which fr. 10 states that it "embraces all" and that "Necessity guiding it fettered it to hold the limits of the stars." It is therefore "outermost," "farthest" in comparison with the whole, for it represents the outer wrapping of this whole.

In Homer and in Hesiod the Olympus, the very high mountain whose top was the abode of the gods, and the sky, οὐρανός, are usually thought of as two quite distinct things; in a few places, however, one may find a sort of assimilation between the two. For instance, in *Odyssey* 20, 103 we are told that Zeus hurls a thunder from Olympus, but straight after it is stated that he has thundered "from starlit sky"; in Hesiod, *Theogony* 689–691, Zeus hurls lightnings and thunders "from the sky and from Olympus." Apparently in *Iliad* 5, 749–751 there is straightforward identification, for the gate of the sky and of the Olympus are one. The reason for such an assimilation-identification is clear enough: the Olympus is so high that its top reaches the sky, therefore it is in the sky; most of all, two notions of the divine dwelling interfere with each other—both are mythic, but one is in more actual terms topographic (the Olympus), the other one leaning toward a deanthropomorphizing sublimation (the high heavens). Parmenides stresses the identification according to a precise programme of reinterpreting the traditional pantheon in terms of his own philosophy.

In the end, fr. 11, consisting of a single indirect interrogative sentence with several subjects and only one verbal predicate, is brought by the latter to that very ground of cosmogonic history already detected with respect to fr. 10: "how (v. 1) . . . they came into being" (vv. 3–4).

Can one doubt that in these two fragments Parmenides is doing anything other than promising exactly an extensive and detailed astronomical treatment? Or that the facts followed the promise, that is, that the rest of the poem tallied with the protasis? If one cannot reasonably doubt either possibility, we are prompted to admit that, at least in large part, Parmenides' poem had to belong to the same genre and to be quite similar to the later *Phaenomena*, Aratus' didactic-astronomical poem; and further that, thanks to this section, Parmenides' was the oldest astronomical poem of Greek literature, since it seems that in Xenophanes' poem *On nature* there was not anything so full-fledged, rather just dispersed cues of astronomical teaching. Anaximander's work, even older, was only a very short handbook (Diogenes Laertius 2, 2, who derives from Apollodorus of Athens = Anaximander test. 1, 2 DK), and further this was not a poem, but a prose pamphlet.

> For the narrower [rings] were filled with pure Fire and those which come after them with Night, but a portion of flame is discharged also there. In the middle of these is the goddess who governs all things. For everywhere she is the beginner of union and of painful birth, sending the female to unite with the male and again to the contrary the male with the female. (fr. 12 DK, translation by L. Tarán, slightly adapted)

"The narrower" (αἱ στεινότεραι), "those which come after them" (αἱ ἐπὶ ταῖς): which feminine noun do these two pronominal phrases refer to? Paradoxically, in the two passages from Simplicius representing our sources for this fragment there is no explicit reference to the entities mentioned as subject of the sentence. Yet we are lucky enough to be helped by the doxographer Aëtius (2, 7, 1 = test. 37 DK): he summarizes a teaching included in the poem that clearly represented the context from which our fragment derives and therefore allows us to solve the unknown factor: Parmenides divided the astronomical space in a series of "rings" (στεφάναι), that is, concentric globe-shaped crowns, in each of which was placed a star. Therefore the two pronouns in ll.1f., αἳ . . . ταῖς, evidently referred to the noun "crowns" (στεφάναι). And at last the opposition between the "narrower," that is the lower ones, closer to the center of the whole sphere and then with shorter diameter, and "those after them," that is the higher crowns, farther from the center, closer to the outer round surface and then with longer diameter, becomes clear.

In fact, the integration of data granted by both fragment and source inevitably leads us to the conclusion that Parmenides' depiction of the starlit sky resulted in a tentative heavenly map composed of concentric spheres keeping up and developing the notion that had already been outlined by Anaximander. Anaximander did not confine himself to the spoken and written word, but even built the first armillary sphere, thus describing the heavenly sphere with the stars' orbits sloping down toward the center (testt. 6; 1, 2; 2 DK). Both in Anaximander's and in Parmenides' system this center was taken up by the earth. This is how the foundations of that geocentric system were laid down, that for two millennia would give a most effective key with which to interpret astronomical phenomena until it was replaced, after the Copernican revolution of the 15th and 16th centuries, by the heliocentric system, more refined and exhaustive.

The tenor of the fragment is markedly narrative: "the narrower were filled with pure Fire," etc. Thus it seems that Parmenides is keeping his proemial promise to tell how the astronomical universe took shape: at some point the "narrower" heavenly spheres, that is those more inner and closer to the earth, were overrun by flows of pure fire, whereas those more outer and farther from the earth were invaded by a magmatic blending of fire and night. If we ask ourselves how, in Parmenides' reconstruction, these incandescent spherical layers then clotted into distinct celestial bodies, one might suggest that this subsequent process of amalgamation was prompted by the whirling motion of the spheres themselves, revolving around the center of the system. However in his cosmogony such a process did take place, for in his account stars were clots of fire (cf. Aëtius 2, 13, 8 = test. 39 DK: "Parmenides and Heraclitus thought of stars as πιλήματα πυρός").

Coming back to the synchronic dimension of Parmenides' teaching, we are not able to reconstruct the arrangement of stars and related spherical crowns in their sequence from the center, that is, from the earth up to the outermost limit represented by the "sky which embraces all" (fr. 10.5) with confidence and completeness: fr. 10–12 tell too little on this aspect, and Aëtius' testimony, very valuable for reconstructing the type of overall architecture, is however too confused and inconsistent when it comes to details of the system. Only one detail of such an arrangement is defined by fr. 12: halfway (ἐν μέσῳ) between the surface of the earth and the highest sky is the "goddess who governs all things," whose power, as specified in the following lines, is to inspire with erotic attraction, to induce intercourse between males and females and, consequently, birth.

Yet this is a problematic detail, one which at first reading has raised many doubts. Let us begin with this: did Parmenides mean, by attributing a divine status (as implied in the noun δαίμων) to this principle, to equate it with any divinity of positive Greek religion or not? The answer lies in a careful scrutiny of the sources handing down another fragment:

> She devised Eros as the very first of all gods . . . (fr. 13 DK, translation by L. Tarán)

While quoting this isolated line, Simplicius attests that the subject of the verb, namely the mother of the god Eros, was in the text of the poem the same δαίμων of fr. 12, whereas according to Plutarch it was Aphrodite. Both sources are trustworthy, for both Plutarch and Simplicius had first-hand knowledge of the poem: on account of their common knowledge, one can safely infer that the δαίμων and Aphrodite were in Parmenides the same goddess, the mother of Eros.

Another problem: the goddess of fr. 12 and fr. 13 is in the middle (ἐν μέσῳ) of the heavenly space; but does this amount to saying that she finds her place at the boundary between two crowns, each of them central with as much right as the other, or rather that she is in a crown occupying all alone the central place in comparison with the others? The question is far from irrelevant: in the first case we would be dealing with an incorporeal physical-divine entity; in the second case, as holder of her own crown, she could not help being identified with a star, thus a star named Aphrodite. The continuation of this study will prompt us to prefer the second assumption.

According to the ancient tradition, Parmenides would have been the maker of three astronomical discoveries still effective today: the earth's roundness; the identity of moon and sun light, a fact explaining the phases of the moon; the identity of the evening and morning star. Some sources attribute these discoveries to Pythagoras rather than to Parmenides, which in itself does not alter the picture, for Parmenides, even if not "the first discoverer" (πρῶτος εὑρέτης), would nevertheless have been the direct continuer of the discoverer himself, and thus a scientist of the first rank all the same. On the other hand, we are well aware of his Pythagoricism. But here, with respect to the study we are carrying out, we are not at all interested in determining who may legitimately lay claim to each of these discoveries, but rather in ascertaining whether they were dealt with in his Περὶ φύσεως, whose astronomical section we are trying to reconstruct. That Parmenides might have expounded and demonstrated them in his poem seems more than probable, basically for two reasons:

1) From where could the ancients know that he had defended those assumptions, if not from the reading of his own poem? This is easier to assume than to suppose an oral tradition beginning in the sixth and fifth century BCE, and only later flowing into the writings of scholars.

2) As we have just seen, Parmenides himself stated in the proemial passages his intention of holding a thoroughly astronomical discussion and his first-hand readers testify that he actually did so: why should he have skipped exactly the propositions which earned him renown in his own time and in times to come?

But, apart from this abstract possibility, at least for his theses on the moon and the evening/morning star we are on safe grounds of documentary certainty.

> Wandering around the earth shining in the night with a borrowed light. (fr. 14 DK, translation by L. Tarán)

The source makes us sure that these words were used to refer to the moon. The phrase is technically precise to the point of meticulousness, absolutely unmistakable: the moon revolves round the earth (περὶ γαῖαν ἀλώμενον), by night reflects the light of the sun, invisible to men because below the horizon, giving the false impression of shining with its own light (νυκτιφαές), like the sun and the other stars, whereas on the contrary its light is actually other's (ἀλλότριον φῶς).

> Always looking towards the shining glance of the sun (fr. 15 DK).

The moon is assimilated to a woman in love who, anxiously looking around, always succeeds in meeting the eyes of the man she worships. The loveliness of this poetic image has caused critics to lose the literal and scientific meaning of the line: the moon, whose body is in itself as bereft of light as the earth's, always manages to sight the sun from one side or the other, as much lighted up by the sun as allowed each time by the position it assumes with respect to the sun itself and to the earth, our look-out point: at best full moon, otherwise crescent or decrescent, with its bump now eastwards, now westwards.

As to the identification of evening and morning star, we actually do not have fragments but a very important testimony that the proposition was included in the poem *On Nature*. Diogenes Laertius (9, 23 = test. 1 DK) writes:

> He [sc. Parmenides] is believed to have been the first to detect the identity of Hesperus, the evening-star, and Phosphorus, the morning-star; so Favorinus in the fifth book of his *Memorabilia*; but others attribute this to Pythagoras, whereas Callimachus (*Pìnakes*, fr. 442 Pfeiffer) holds that the poem in question was not his. (translation by R. D. Hicks, slightly adapted)

In some respects the testimony is anything but plain. In the first instance it is left unclear whether Diogenes attributes to Favorinus the whole passage; alternatively, after reporting Favorinus' point of view, Diogenes himself might add the opinion held by others, gathering it from different sources assembled by himself. In the second instance, it is doubtful whether the concluding sentence—"Callimachus holds that the poem in question was not his"—is meant to refer Callimachus' judgment of inauthenticity to Parmenides' poem or to one of the poems that in antiquity went around by the name of Pythagoras and that included lines about the identity of morning and evening star. I do not mean to develop a hermeneutical analysis here, both because it would deserve further depth, and because it would have no bearing on the approach I am suggesting; also, because it already is the object of study of other scholars. (A. Gostoli, in AA.VV., *Samo: storia, letteratura, scienza*, "AION (filol)" Quad. 8, Pisa-Roma 2004, 159–165). I shall confine myself to suggest what follows: the overall line of reasoning of Diogenes' passage—regardless of the doubt whether it belongs to Diogenes himself or Favorinus, his source—concerns the authorship of an astronomical discovery; the author of the reasoning found the identification of morning and evening star both in Parmenides' poem and in a poem attributed to Pythagoras; considering the regrettable ambiguity of the last sentence, we are unable to understand the conclusion of the reasoning, in any event based on the reading of two books. As far as our point of view is concerned, what is relevant is that in Parmenides' poem there was such identification; consequently, there was also this astronomical proposition.

By now we are in the position to convincingly put forward some further inductions, so far curiously neglected by critics. After their identification by either Pythagoras or Parmenides between the sixth and fifth centuries BCE, evening and morning star ceased, on a scientific level, to be two stars, and became one. What was the name given this star by the ancient astronomers? We have evidence for periods later than the two archaic philosophers-scientists: the Greeks called it Aphrodite, the Romans Venus, the goddess corresponding, in their pantheon, to the Greek Aphrodite, openly identified with her. But when did this name come into use? Already in Pythagorars' and/or Parmenides' times or only after it?

Generally speaking, we know that in antiquity, when an astronomer "discovered" or in any event wished to single out a new star, he definitely proceeded to give it the name of a god or a hero, which among other things expressed a sort of identification between the star and the god or hero, and that usually this name was unchanged from then on in the astronomical onomastics. Why should not one suppose that the discoverer of the identity of morning/evening star, may he be Pythagoras or Parmenides, may have himself given the new star, born from the *reductio ad unum* of the two preceding ones, the name of Aphrodite? The more so, if we consider that the evening star was always conceived, in common perception as well as in the wedding songs, as erotic star, propitiator of the first sexual intercourse of the newlyweds.

We wondered above whether the goddess-Aphrodite in fr. 12–13, put by Parmenides in the middle of heavenly space, was an incorporeal divine entity, placed between the two central crowns, or rather an actual star, revolving in the central crown. By now, after what we have noted on the identification of evening and morning star, our reasoning reaches its conclusion: the new star was named Aphrodite by its discoverer, Pythagoras or Parmenides; this is in any case the name it had in the poem of Parmenides, who placed it halfway between the surface of the earth and the highest sky and assigned a cosmic generative influence to it, apt to give it a leading status in comparison with the whole phenomenal universe. Yes, for the rising astronomical science was inheriting from the cultural tradition, already attested in Homer and Hesiod, the notion that each single star exerts a specific influence on the sublunary world, on vegetation, animals and men; nor would it have ever laid aside such a heritage, not even in its most sophisticated developments in Hellenistic and imperial ages. The distinction between astronomy and astrology is a modern one, and in antiquity the study of starlit sky was always indifferently *astrology* or *astronomy*; and it was concerned with mathematical reckonings as well as astral influences.

As a matter of fact, both astronomical discoveries whose presence in Parmenides' poem we have argued for, namely both the doctrine of lunar phases and of lunar light as reflected light of the sun, on the one hand, and the doctrine of the identity of evening and morning star, on the other hand, amount to notably sophisticated scientific truths-hypotheses, implying meticulous and deliberately planned surveys, quite complex reckonings, geometrical-temporal projections far from elementary. Thus science, and science on the cutting edge, for those generations that lived between the second half of the sixth and the first half of the fifth century BCE. One was then in the position of unveiling—with the ready support granted by mathematics—the fallaciousness of a traditional and rooted belief as was the case for the supposed diversity of evening and morning star, but at the same time of acknowledging, for the new star, the same erotic influences up to then attributed to the old evening star, of even identifying it with the supreme goddess of love, and of naming it Aphrodite.

## Conclusions

On account of the evidence collected so far, in my opinion, objective and indubitable, it is curious that, for the most part, modern scholars of Parmenides keep on discussing his philosophical thought and his poem as if it were bereft of a scientific-astronomical dimension, as if—literally—it had not had a dense section set out as a sort of map of the heavens. Hundreds, perhaps thousands of lines, as has already been shown, are similar in content to Aratus' *Phaenomena* or Manilius' *Astronomica* (just to mention poems which have reached us by means of direct tradition), and are much closer to these two poems than to the first part of Parmenides' poem itself, usually known by the name of ἡ Ἀλήθεια.

The admission of natural science to the bulk of the poem in no way can be considered irrelevant, as if it were a heterogeneous appendix, not concerned with the content of the other sections. Yet in any event one still has the interpretive task of reconciling the monism of the first section of the poem with the simultaneous presence of teachings which manifestly consider the plurality of things as object of rational systematization and positive knowledge; a further reflection seems to me necessary in order to reconcile the science of the Being per se with physical, physical-mathematical and physical-empirical sciences; to reconcile, in the last analysis, Parmenides as thinking of the world as an absolute, not generated, imperishable, unchangeable, timeless, and Parmenides as geometrically studying the plurality and the course of the stars. Every interpretation of his thought effacing or marginalizing such a scientific dimension is manifestly inadequate to answer for the whole of the evidence we possess.

Translated by Dr. Massimo Giuseppetti
Università degli Studi Roma Tre

# Parmenidean "Physics" is not Part of what Parmenides calls "δόξα"

Néstor-Luis Cordero


## Summary

Parmenides, as were all the philosophers of his time, was certainly interested in "physical" questions, even if the response to these questions was necessarily conditioned by his big "discovery": that there is being. But the only way to respect the value of his "physical" theories is by keeping them out of the so-called "δόξα" because, *for Parmenides,* opinions are deceitful and not true. The hazardous reconstruction of Parmenides' text invites the researcher to find the "δόξαι" between the end of fr. 8 and fr. 18. This prejudice, together with the anachronistic idea according to which Parmenides spoke of "appearances" (and the δόξαι would be their description), leads to the exaggerated place the δόξαι occupy in the present reconstruction of the Poem. Parmenides exposes—and criticizes—the δόξαι of "others." There are no Parmenidean δόξαι.


The hypothesis I would like to offer here is that if there is a "Parmenidean physics"—and everything seems to indicate that this is the case—it cannot be a part of the δόξα, simply because it would be contradictory to what Parmenides asserts explicitly about what he understands by δόξα: a deceitful discourse, something not true. In order to justify my hypothesis, we need to put under critical analysis two essential points of the existing interpretation of Parmenides' philosophy.

First, I propose to question the order of the quotations (usually—and wrongly—called "fragments") that has led to the present reading of the Poem. Second, I intend to question the tendency to assume that all affirmations about physical entities (such as the stars, the day, the night, the human being, etc.) belong to the realm of "appearances." In fact, the interpreters, and not Parmenides, are responsible for these two. Once both points have been discussed, I will make arguments to support my hypothesis.

The conjunction of both prejudices has caused the so-called "δόξα of Parmenides" to become the most discussed part of the Poem. About the "δόξα," one thing and the contrary has been said and continues to be said today, for example, that it is only a fiction proposed by the erratic mortals' intellect, or that it contains a genuine Parmenidean theory about the sensible reality, which changes continually. I hope that a critical analysis of these two prejudices will help us understand which *for Parmenides* is the meaning of the "δόξαι" and, at the same time, justify a "physics" in Parmenides.

In order to begin at the beginning, we must admit that, without doubt, the δόξαι are part of the program the Goddess presents to the young man who decides to undertake an arduous trip in order to find her. The Goddess affirms without ambiguity that he must be informed (πυθέσθαι) of the heart of the truth *as much as* of the δόξαι βροτῶν (fr. 1.28–30). In fragment 8, she affirms that it is necessary to learn (μάνθανε, 8.52) the δόξαι that she is going to expose, and in fragment 19, she concludes that "thus, these things arose according to the δόξα." One question immediately arises: are these three occurrences of the term δόξα enough to justify the great number of works devoted to the subject? It does not look like it. On the contrary, I believe that if so much has been written, is currently written and probably will be written about Parmenidean δόξα, it is because what is placed in the *dossier* "δόξα" is actually more than what Parmenides himself put in it. This will be the central thesis of this paper.

In my opinion, prejudices have darkened the understanding of a "dark," or at least difficult to understand, philosophy. According to the *present* arrangement of the fragments,[1] the section called

[1] Since the edition of H. Diels. *Parmenides Lehrgedicht* (Berlin: G. Reimer, 1897), the "fragments" are cited by a number: "fr. 1," etc. The present arrangement is due to H. Diels and W. Kranz, *Die Fragmente der Vorsokratiker*, 5th ed. (Berlin: Weidmann, 1934–1937).

"δόξα" begins with line 52 of fragment 8 and finishes with fragment 19. But this set of lines has always been analyzed according to anachronistic schemes that were valid a century later, especially schemes from Plato's times. For Plato, reality is divided into "being" (the Forms) and "appearances" (the sensible universe). In line with this perspective, "physical" realities are only "appearances" and therefore, the "physical world" can only be explained by "opinions." This scheme was consequently applied to Parmenides.

## The reconstruction of Parmenides' text

Let us begin, then, by a critical analysis of the first of the *items* mentioned above: the reconstruction of the text of Parmenides. In the current arrangement of the Poem, fr. 19, placed at the end, seems to close not only the Poem but also a "section": the δόξα. As we will see, this detail provokes a misunderstanding that did not exist in the first attempts to restore the Poem, when fragment 19 was yet unknown. Henri Estienne, who succeeded in finding the sum of sixty-seven authentic lines, made the first assay at reconstruction. The quotations of Parmenides were not identified by a number, as they are now (e.g., "fragment 1," etc.), but according to the name of the author who made the quotation, that is, the source. Estienne's reconstruction[2] began with the extensive quotation from Sextus Empiricus, considered today as a Proemium (which is apropos, because Sextus himself said that Parmenides' text began with these words). After that, Estienne added further quotations, preceded by the words "ex Simplicio," "ex Clemente," "ex eodem." And following the present fragment 8, he placed a series of texts about "physical" questions.

Enormous progress was achieved a few years later, by the end of the sixteenth century, when Joseph Scaliger, who had already added an appendix to the work of Estienne, was able to find 148 lines of Parmenides (that is, *eighty-one* more lines than Estienne). Most unfortunately, this important reconstruction remained unpublished and was considered lost for several centuries. Eminent Parmenidean researchers in the eighteenth and nineteenth centuries, such as Fülleborn and Brandis, complained

[2] H. Estienne, *Poesis Philosophica* (Geneva: Excudebat Henr. Stephanus, 1573).

of not being able to consult it. Four centuries had elapsed when I was lucky enough to rediscover Scaliger's work myself in the archives of the University of Leyden Library and publish this finding in *Hermes* (1982).[3]

Parmenides' Poem acquired a new look in 1810, when Amédée Peyron edited the manuscript found in Turin of the Commentary of Simplicius of the *De Caelo* of Aristotle, in which he found new quotations of Parmenides' Poem.[4] One of them, the present fr. 19, seemed to be a summary of cosmogony and physical subjects, which is today grouped after fragment 8. (Neither Estienne nor Scaliger knew the Parmenidean quotations contained in the *De Caelo* of Simplicius, and, for that reason, the texts following fragment 8 were presented without a conclusion.) In 1813, C. A. Brandis located the current fragment 19 at the end of the Poem.[5] Since then, the reconstruction of the Poem has seen little modification.

We must recognize that from a formal point of view, the reconstitution seems impeccable: it begins with the text that Sextus quoted as the opening of the Poem and continues with the treatment of the way of truth until line 51 of fragment 8, where the Goddess says that she is now going to expose the opinions (δόξαι) of the mortals. Subsequently follow ten fragments that seem to honor this pledge, as they concern cosmological, "physical" questions in a very large sense, that is, the stars, the Milky Way, human beings, etc. And finally, in the text known today as fragment 19, we read "thus, these things were born, according to δόξα, and hence they exist now." It is true that, in the presentation of the δόξαι, there is a point of departure (line 52 of fragment 8) and a final point (fragment 19). This set of texts constitutes the so-called "δόξα" of Parmenides.

[3] N.-L. Cordero, "La Version de Joseph Scaliger du *Poème* de Parménide," *Hermes* 110 (1982), 391–398.

[4] A. Peyron, *Empedoclis et Parmenidis Fragmenta: Ex Codice Taurinensis Bibliothecae Restituta et Illustrata* (Lipsiae: I. A. G. Weigel, 1810), pp. 55–61.

[5] C. A. Brandis, *Commentationum Eleaticarum.* Par Prima: Xenophanis, Parmenidis et Melisii Doctrina Propriis Philosophorum Reliquiis Exposita (Altonae: J. F. Hammerick, 1813).

## Parmenides' judgment about the δόξαι

In fact, between fragment 8, line 51 (where Parmenides uses the word "δόξαι"), and fragment 19 (where he repeats the same word), there are nine texts where the notion of δόξα is absent. These texts, however, relate to questions today identified as "physical." Using a modern formula, we could say that the insertion of these texts between 8.51 and 19 constitutes a genuine process of *disinformation*, because nothing proves that they were originally placed in that section of the Poem.

I dare speak of *disinformation* because a naïve reading of Parmenides' "fragments," taking each quotation as an independent text, would not justify a possible "Parmenidean δόξα." It is only through an arbitrary, un-Parmenidean arrangement of the texts that interpreters (a) feel obliged to justify why Parmenides dedicates so much effort to the question of "opinions" (remember that if we accept the hypothesis put forth by Diels, only one-ninth of the original of this section has been preserved); and (b) are compelled to try to explain the possible "theory" exposed in this hypothetical section.

Let us begin with the first question. Although Parmenides includes the notion of δόξα in his Poem, its value is denied twice, not just on one occasion, as is usually claimed: in fr. 1.30, he says that "there is no true conviction" in the opinions (that is to say that the δόξαι are not "truthful"); and in fr. 8, he states that the δόξαι are a "deceitful (ἀπατηλόν) order of words" (8.52). With regard to this, interpreters have adopted, *grosso modo,* three attitudes. Some researchers (among whom I include myself) have respected Parmenides' criticism to the letter and have maintained the deceitful and false character of what Parmenides calls δόξαι, as presented in the final lines of fragment 8, in order to warn the listener against other mortals' points of view. Other authors, the majority, have diluted the strongly negative and false character of the δόξα. And finally, one author—I do not believe that there are others—has maintained that Parmenides never said that the δόξαι were false or deceptive. Let us quickly examine the three possibilities, beginning with the last one.

According to Karl Popper, Parmenides did not want to say that the δόξα is something ἀπατηλόν, but rather intended to explain that the δόξα was something ἀπατητόν, "unusual." Alas, Parmenides himself, or a copyist, mistook a letter. Therefore, Popper simply proposes to replace ἀπατηλόν "with a word that differs only by one letter, ἀπάτητον, that was in the mind of Parmenides."[6] For us humble researchers, it is impossible to know what word Parmenides had in mind, but I am convinced that the great Popper was not worthy of his reputation when he wrote this. If each time we find a word difficult to interpret we decide to change it, the history of philosophy would be but a long list of the unconscious desires of philosophy historians.

Some other scholars, more reliable than Popper here, weaken the Parmenidean criticism of the δόξα by arguing that if a great part of the Poem refers to the δόξαι, there must be a reason, and they propose a sort of axiom: the δόξαι are a description of appearances, and appearances are deceptive (actually, who can deny that appearances deceive?); thus, the opinions explaining the appearances are also deceiving. This type of apparently logical interpretation leads to a severe illness that I call "terminal Platonitis," as we will further see.

I have left aside the third possibility, the position of the authors who take not only the term ἀπατηλόν literally but also the passage where Parmenides denies all positive value to "opinions" (fr. 1.30). This group of scholars (myself included) accept the strong negative sense of ἀπατηλόν. The Poem of Parmenides is eminently didactic, and if a speech is called ἀπατηλός it is to emphasize its danger, because deceit (ἀπάτη) is the opposite notion to persuasion, and persuasion is what characterizes the true way (which, in fact, "accompanies" truth, and is, then, the "way of persuasion," πειθώ). Furthermore, the notion of ἀπάτη is particularly dangerous because it signifies that something can be imposed by deceitful ways. In a clear reference to Parmenides, Gorgias maintains the contrary: for the great sophist, because the *logos* does not "reveal" reality, it can deceive and persuade *at the same time,* as in the case of Helen: the λόγος πείσας καὶ

[6] K. Popper, *The World of Parmenides* (London: Routledge, 1998), pp. 131–133.

ἀπατήσας her ψυχή (Gorgias, fr. 11 § 8). In Parmenides, it is impossible to weaken the strong negative sense of ἀπατηλόν.

However, I have already stated that there is another passage that completes the presentation of the negative character of the δόξαι: in line 30 of the Proemium, the Goddess affirms that in the δόξαι "there is no true conviction" (οὐκ ἔνι πίστις ἀληθής). The δόξαι are not reliable, and the adjective "ἀληθής," denied, places the δόξαι in an opposite position with respect to the way of persuasion, which is accompanied by truth. Πίστις is, in Parmenides, synonymous with πειθώ, "persuasion." Only what has "credit" (sense of πίστις, also in Modern Greek) persuades. All credit needs to be guaranteed, and opinions, which are only empty words, lack real guarantee. Moreover, for that reason, they are the contrary of true speech, which is a πιστὸν λόγον (line 8.50). Opinions are παναπευθεῖς (cf. fr. 2.6), an adjective related in Parmenides to the erroneous way.

There is no doubt that, for Parmenides, the δόξαι are not true (in the preserved texts of the Poem, the word "false" does not appear, but, in a dualistic logic, something that is not true can only be false). The δόξαι are not credible, and worse, they are deceptive. Consequently, many authors have wondered why Parmenides presents a deceptive speech. They seem to ignore that Parmenides himself explains why: to be able to recognize it and avoid it, because it leads to nowhere.

## Some anomalies in the set of texts that constitutes the δόξα

Let us return to the set of texts that constitutes the so-called Parmenidean δόξα, from line 52 of fr. 8 through fr. 19. We see that Parmenides says in a clear and distinct manner that opinions are deceptive and that they are not true. However, even a superficial reading of the set of texts that are supposed to constitute the δόξα shows that the critical judgment of Parmenides is justified *only* on certain occasions (e.g., in the case of fr. 9, which affirms that there is *nothing* outside of light and night, an idea that is evidently absurd). But in other passages, a negative judgment is not relevant: why would it be deceptive to affirm that the Moon lacks a proper light, or that it turns around the Earth, or that Eros was one of first (or the very first) of the gods (Hesiod *dixit*), or that opposite sexes mixed "the seeds of love"? In addition, in a text placed usually in the δόξαι (fr. 10), Parmenides utilizes in two instances the verb εἰδέναι, "to know," which is incompatible with all the verbs referred to in the δόξαι, and in the same fragment, uses the verb πείθομαι in relation with πειθώ, a notion always reserved for the way of truth.

This cohabitation of "true" statements that are susceptible to an authentic "knowledge," with an implausible hypothesis, clearly shows that the texts that *traditionally* compose the Parmenidean δόξα were not originally in the same section.[7]

Consequently, I propose to reduce the δόξα to those passages in which Parmenides exposes what *he* considers to be δόξα, and to the examples he gives of this notion. For Parmenides, the δόξα is what he considers δόξα, and he is quite explicit when he uses the term. What Parmenides considers as δόξα has nothing to do with what Plato considers "appearances." Parmenides is innocent of this anachronistic inference.

## The δόξαι do not expound the "appearances"

Perhaps the origin of the misunderstanding is this: as Parmenides is an author who is difficult to comprehend not only for us post-modern scholars, but also for the post-Parmenidean philosophers, there has been the temptation since Plato's time to interpret his philosophy according to the schemes of thought of the time. In the passage of the *Theaetetus* that is the subject of this Symposium, Plato said that Parmenides is "venerable and awesome" (183e), but he confesses his fear that he is "not to understand Parmenides' words and, even more, not to understand the underlying thought." Moreover, if this were the case, the most natural attitude would be to attempt to explain the philosopher's thought according to the interpreter's schemes. That is why, in the *Sophist*, Parmenides seems to adopt a 100%

[7] In a desperate attempt to conserve the positive value of the δόξαι, Panagiotis Thanassas proposes to find a good δόξα, the divine δόξα, and a bad δόξα, the δόξα described as something ἀπατηλόν (P. Thanassas, "How many δόξαι are there in Parmenides?," *Rhizai* III:2 [2006], passim).

platonic dichotomy (appearances vs. real being) but only to deny one of the elements of the dichotomy, appearances (237a). In another passage, Parmenides unexpectedly seems to belong to a monist group (242d), but only because Plato is interested in classifying the previous philosophers into monists or pluralists, another anachronistic dichotomy.

It is evident that among the so-called pre-Socratic philosophers one can find "polar" schemes of thought.[8] It is enough to evoke the perhaps later list of Pythagorean oppositions (Aristotle, *Metaphysics* 986a) or the Heraclitean references to the visible and the invisible harmony (fr. 54). However, in all of those cases, *both* parts of the dichotomy have a real existence. It is not that one is "being" and the other is "appearance." The whole thing is different in Plato, to whom, in order to reject sophistry, everything that belongs to the realm of sensation (i.e., all "physical" realities) belong to the realm of "appearances," which can only be grasped through sensations and therefore are the object of "opinions."

When platonic schemes are employed to interpret Parmenides (a pre-sophistic philosopher), it is easy to apply to his philosophy a dangerous dualism. According to this dualism, whatever Parmenides affirms about "being" corresponds to the "truth" (the equivalent of the platonic ἐπιστήμη), and all that concerns "physical" questions (equivalent to the "sensible universe" in Plato) need to be relegated to the world of appearances (appearances justified or denied according to the interpreters' wishes) and therefore are objects only of δόξαι. The Poem of Parmenides is thus taken as an antecedent of the divided line of the *Republic.*

However, nothing assures that the philosophers who were also interested in physical phenomena (and who elaborated cosmological, medicinal or anthropological theories) considered that the physical objects of their study were merely "appearances." Parmenides was seemingly a medical doctor, and a doctor—in older and in present times—cannot consider a patient as something purely "apparent." Indeed, in Parmenides, only the

8 See G. E. R. Lloyd, *Polarity and Analogy* (Cambridge: Cambridge University Press, 1966).

discourse is "like" (ἐοικότα, 8.60): it is similar to the true speech. But the discourse is only a set of words (κόσμον ἐπέων, 8.52; διάκοσμον, 8.60); *the subject* of the discourse ("physical" realities) is not "apparent." The authors who "platonize" Parmenides prefer to believe that the subject of the δόξα is an antecedent of the εἰκασία of the *Republic*. In fact, a discourse can be deceptive even when it refers to what is real. That is the case with the δόξαι.

## What does Parmenides understand by "δόξα"?

Let us now try to understand what Parmenides—and not his commentators—could possibly understand by *doxa*. Leaving aside line 30 of the Proemium, in which Parmenides only says that there is no true conviction in the opinions, the word δόξα appears again in line 8.51 (in plural) and in fragment 19 (in singular). In 8.51, as announced in the Proemium, the δόξαι belong to the mortals: "they establish two points of view to name the forms." Moreover, this activity of mortals was previously presented in lines 38–39 of the same fragment 8: "they are just names that men have established, believing that they are true things." This relation between δόξα and naming reappears once again in fr. 19, "to every thing men have given a particular name." *Therefore, δόξα, for Parmenides, is a human activity in relation to naming.* Most probably, this kind of activity corresponds to some specific philosophical school, one I would call Nominalism *avant la lettre,* although as of today we have no concrete evidence pointing to it.

Nevertheless, *for Parmenides,* opinions seem to be a question of words, but of deceptive, empty words that pretend to impose a sense to reality instead of reflecting it. Fragment 9 describes this process through an example. "Men" name (cf. ὀνόμασται, 9.1) *all* things light and night (and affirm that nothing exists apart from them), but this naming gives "powers" (δυνάμεις, 9.2) to each thing, and these powers, for mortals, are of an opposing nature. As a result of this arbitrary nomination, mortals "are convinced" (πεποιθότες, 8.39) that these names are true (8.44), and accordingly, they interpret reality as composed of opposites that exist simultaneously, for example, to be born and to die, and even to be and not to be (8.40). The only possible naming consists, for Parmenides, of saying "what is," and "what is" does not have a contrary. The expression of any thought, that is, naming, is only possible *thanks* (ἐφ' ᾧ[9]) to being.

However, what would be the object about which mortals forge opinions, or empty words? From the few examples offered by Parmenides, there is an obvious answer. The coupled "to be *and* not to be" is the key to the solution, because both notions also constitute the nucleus of the true *logos*. This means that the object of study of the true discourse and that of the "ordering of words" of the opinions *is the same:* reality, everything that is, πάντα τὰ ὄντα. For Parmenides, there is a single reality, looked at in two different ways. We must not forget that the word "ὁδός" already had in Parmenides' time the double sense of "way": a route, and a manner of doing. The essential difference that exists between both ways of studying the same object is this: one way goes from reality (the "being") to the human being who needs to accept the necessity of "being"; the other way takes as a point of departure the human being and imposes their rules on reality. The first way "grasps" (as Heraclitus would say) the absolute character of the fact of being, which becomes necessary because it is impossible not to be. But as the real presence of the fact of being is attested "now," "ἔστι" is the ideal word to name this "present presence."

However, the elements that characterize what Parmenides himself calls the δόξα (a speech elaborated by mortals, in relation to naming or with words that assume a contradictory cohabitation of principles) are found *only in five passages* of the Poem: (1) in lines 38–40 of fragment 8, where Parmenides affirms that mortals establish names that they take to correspond to reality (and, in consequence, are "true" . . . for them); (2) in lines 52–59 of fragment 8, which contains a summary of the deceitful speech of opinions; (3) in fragment 9, where, once again, Parmenides affirms that opinions "name" a couple of opposite realities, and outside of them, nothing exists; (4) in fragment 12, where an anonymous goddess (and not necessity) governs all things; and (5) in fragment

[9] I adopt ἐφ' ᾧ (Proclus) instead of ἐν ᾧ (Simplicius). On this choice, cf. N.-L. Cordero, "La Pensée s'exprime 'grâce' à l'être: Parménide, fr. 8.35," *La Revue Philosophique de la France et de l'Étranger* 129 (2004, 1), 5–13.

19 (the conclusion of the presentation of the δόξα): "thus, these things occur according to the δόξα," and "to each thing men have given a particular name."

## The content of fragments 10–11 and 13–18 is neither "deceitful" nor is it not true

None of the specific elements that Parmenides considers "doxastic" can be found in the rest of the texts that have been abusively placed since ancient times in the *dossier* "the δόξα of Parmenides." Only the adoption of post-Parmenidean schemes that connect "appearances" to "physical" entities could justify that fragments 10–11 and 13–18 form part of the δόξαι. Consequently, in an attempt to give more coherence to Parmenides' text, I propose to move fragments 10–11 and 13–18 and place fragment 19 immediately after fragments 8, 9, and 12, which exposes an erroneous and deceptive theory of reality that is nothing but a summary of the deceitful discourse that Parmenides himself calls "the δόξαι of mortals."

I repeat once again: it is not fair to interpret the δόξα of Parmenides in an anachronistic way, in the sense of "appearances." M. Heidegger, disciple of K. Reinhardt (the "father" of this misleading interpretation[10]), utilized his poetic-demagogical style to contribute to this task of disinformation in Parmenidean studies: "this way [that is, the way exposed in fr. 6] is the way of δόξα in the sense of appearance."[11] We owe also to Heidegger the most anti-Parmenidean statement possible: "in Parmenides, being reveals itself through appearance and against appearance."[12] This statement forgets that in the so-called pre-Socratic philosophy, at least until the atomists, δόξα was always related to knowledge and never meant "appearance." Y. Lafrance, who in his work on Plato's δόξα resented a complete *status quaestionis,* wrote that

[10] "Die Stelle, an der Parmenides das Verhältnis zwischen Sein und Schein . . ." (K. Reinhardt, *Parmenides und die Geschichte der Griechischen Philosophie,* 2nd edition [Frankfurt am Main: V. Klostermann, 1959], p. 5).

[11] M. Heidegger, *Einführung in die Metaphysik* (Tübingen: Niemeyer, 1953), p. 85.

[12] "[. . .] im Schein und dagegen den Schein das Sein sich enthüllte," M. Heidegger, loc. cit.

"in pre-Socratic thought, the use of the terms δόξα, δοκεῖν and δοξάζειν appear in a context of criticism to human knowledge,"[13] which can already be observed in Xenophanes (fr. 34) and in Heraclitus (fr. 28).

According to my interpretation, in fragments 10–11 and 13–18, we face theories that Parmenides considers not only "true," but also worthy "to be known" (forms of the verb *εἴδω appear twice in fragment 10), because they are presented in a "persuasive" speech (fragment 10.4). The Goddess speaks in her own name; she is not the spokeswoman for the two-headed mortals, and nothing is "deceptive" in this set of texts. In consequence, we can affirm without any doubt that fragments 10–11 and 13–18 belong to the "trustworthy reasoning (λόγος) and thought (νόημα) about the truth" (fragment 8.50–51). Accordingly, this set of texts originally belonged *before* the sentence where the Goddess says that "I finish here the true speech," that is, before line 8.51, because in the last lines of fr. 8 (52–61) (as in fr. 9, fr. 12 and fr. 19), the Goddess exposes the deceitful speech of the δόξαι βροτῶν.

Since Parmenides says in a clear and distinct manner, that there are only two "ways" (ὁδοί) to explain reality, and as the *doxa* is deceptive and not true, fragments 10–11 and 13–18 can only be located *in the way of truth.* The hypothetical "third way," originated by an unfortunate conjecture of H. Diels for line 3 of fragment 6, which was deemed officially sacred by Reinhardt[14] and poetically promoted by Heidegger, is in fact a fading ghost.[15] Some scholars, even if they disapprove of Diels's conjecture, think nevertheless that a third subject of research appears in the formula τὰ δοκοῦντα of line 1.31. However, this is not the case. In lines 1.28–32, the Goddess presents only two possibilities, not three, because τὰ δοκοῦντα is synonymous with δόξαι βροτῶν. After ordering the listener to be informed about the heart of the truth and the δόξαι, the Goddess does not say that "you will learn *also*

[13] Y. Lafrance, *La Théorie Platonicienne de la δόξα* (Montréal/Paris: Les Belles Lettres, 1981), p. 393.

[14] K. Reinhardt, op. cit., p. 36.

[15] Cf. N.-L. Cordero, "Pour en finir avec la *troisième voie* chez Parménide," *Elenchos* 27 (2006, 1), 5–33.

these things (τά δοκοῦντα)"; rather, she says: "but, however (ἀλλ' ἔμπης), you will learn also these things [the δόξαι]." The formula ἀλλ' ἔμπης is only justified if it refers to the previous phrase. The necessity to be informed of the δόξαι is so strange that Parmenides needs to justify this need. There is no true conviction in opinions, "but, however, you will also learn them."

There is another reason to reject the association of τὰ δοκοῦντα with "appearances." The verb δοκέω, in conjunction with δοκοῦντα, means "to seem to somebody, to have a point of view," that is to say, "to have an opinion." This sense is very obvious in a central passage of the *Theaetetus,* where Plato makes a link between the verb and the participle: "What seems (τὸ δοκοῦν) to someone, also exists to the person to whom it seems (δοκεῖ)" (162d). In pre-Socratic philosophers, δοκοῦντα always means "opinion," or "fame," as in fr. 28 of Heraclitus: δοκέοντα γὰρ ὁ δοκιμώτατος γινώσκει: "the most famous man [that is, he about whom one has the best opinion] knows [only] opinions." In Parmenides, δοκοῦντα is "what it seems to the mortals," not "what appears to them." Moreover, only "points of view" (τὰ δοκοῦντα) would exist *if there were no truth.* This is the sense of both last lines of the Proemium.

## Can "physical" questions be a part of the true speech of the Goddess?

Before suggesting in what passage of the discourse on truth we must relocate these fragments, we must respond to an earlier question: is it possible to find in the way of truth a speech about "physical" questions, such as the birth of the universe, the constitution of things, the stars, the union of sexes, procreation, etc.? Obviously, yes. It is precisely the absence of these subjects that would have been unusual for a philosopher of the time. Parmenides is a pre-Sophistic philosopher. His originality consisted of going beyond the answers presented by previous philosophers and, probably, this aspect of his philosophy—which, for us, is of exceptional importance—might not have been fully understood in its time. But *in addition* to a complete explanation of reality—which, we may say, is not very original, according to the summaries presented by the ancient doxographers—Parmenides discovered that if any theory about πάντα τὰ ὄντα can be proposed, it is because they exist, and that is possible because τὰ ὄντα "have" being. Moreover, the central point of Parmenides' philosophy is the analysis of the "fact or state of being," whose main character is necessity. *It is necessary to be because it is impossible not to be.* The reality is a coherent totality because it is dominated by the necessity of being. Being keeps all within its limits, thereby preventing all from not being.

In this sense, the plural used in the first line of fragment 7 is very explicit: it is inadmissible that there are "beings that are not." This formula, "[οὐκ] εἶναι μὴ ἐόντα" is certainly the most important of Parmenides' Poem because it is a summary of his philosophy. Once both negations are suppressed, the phrase "εἶναι ἐόντα" comes to justify what Parmenides says explicitly on at least two occasions: being cannot be separated from what is being; "it is impossible to force that which is, not to be connected with that which is" (fr. 4.2), since "that which is being touches that which is being" (fr. 8.25).

Only a reductive perspective of Parmenides' philosophy can affirm that his originality consisted merely of a sort of "shout"—"ἔστι!!!"—and nothing else. "ἔστι" (present tense) is the basic *axiom* from which a series of statements are deduced, the first of them, that "there is being." And, logically, the fact of being (which is characterized by a series of σήματα presented in fr. 8: the singularity, the a-temporality, etc.) confers being to all that is being. The σήματα are valid for the fact of being, and nothing impedes Parmenides from explaining all that is in the ether (specially his φύσις, that is, his way of *being*), as he does in fragments 10 and 11, and also from saying how the Earth, the Sun and the Moon were produced. In fact, everything that exists obeys the same law: the *necessity* that maintains the fact of being within the chains of limit (πείρατος). This is the task of Moira (according to the true speech, fr. 8.30–31) that "forces" (ἐπέδησεν) being to remain total and immovable (fr. 8.37–38), ideas that reappear in fragment 10 by way of the same verb, "to force" (ἐπέδησεν, fr. 10.6), which, in this case, alludes to the "limits" (πείρατ', 10.7) of the stars. According to fragment 12, the Goddess guarantees that this rule governs the cosmos.

Indeed, the great innovation of Parmenides is the justification and promotion of the notion of Necessity. For Anaximander, for example, alternating (cosmic, human and social) between justice and injustice was carried out "κατὰ τὸ χρεών," necessarily (fr. 1), but he did not say why. For Parmenides, the fact of being is necessary (because it is not possible not to be), and wherever there is being, there is necessity. It is indeed the notion of necessity that proves to us that the "physical" universe exhibits the necessary and absolute character of the fact of being, as is demonstrated in the true discourse. The pseudo-cosmologies elaborated by mortals who "know nothing" ignore this necessary character of the fact of being and explain reality using capricious principles, generally with a couple of opposites that mysteriously decide to be roommates. Necessity is the distinguishing character of the fact of being, and it dominates and controls being (fr. 8.30–31).

I have said that fragments 10–11 and 13–18 expose what could be termed "the Parmenidean physics." However, it is not the purpose of my paper to analyze the "physical" theories exposed in these fragments (which are completed by some doxographical testimonies, in particular, a very important text of Aëtius, II, 7, 1), because very respectable authors have already done it. My intention is to separate these texts from the so-called "δόξα of Parmenides," because the content of fragments 10–11 and 13–18 have nothing to do with the section of the Poem dedicated to the δόξα. *Parmenides exposes δόξαι that are proposed by mortals (other philosophers, or naïve thinkers), and as he does not share these "opinions," he criticizes them.*

## The placement of fragments 10–11 and 13–18

However, the question of where these fragments belong remains. We may never know in what part of the Poem they were located originally, but they were certainly not in the section called "δόξα" by Parmenides himself. In these texts we find not deceptive theories but true knowledge. Therefore, I propose they be placed before line 51 of fragment 8, where Parmenides finishes the true speech. However, as fragments 7 and 8 form a unity, we only can locate fragments 10–11 and 13–18 *before* fragment 7. But is this possible? It most certainly is.

In fragment 10, the Goddess invites the listener to know (εἴσῃ, line 1) how the present cosmic order originated (ἐξεγένοντο, line 3) and how it was born (ἔφυ, line 6). Fragment 11 exposes the generation (ὡρμήθησαν γίγνεσθαι) of the Earth, the Sun and the Moon. And the remaining fragments of this group (if we leave aside some "medical" texts) add cosmological elements without precise details. All these events can be the object of knowledge (that is, they are "thinkable"), since they can *be known*, although they happened in very distant times. Happily, thought can make "absent" events "present," and, thanks to the νόος (which is able to detect its structure, if a suitable method is followed), they may be "known." This possibility appears in the enigmatic fragment 4, which I propose to identify as a sort of "introduction" to the "physical" texts of Parmenides. We can observe, by the way, that fragment 4 begins with an exhortation, as does fragment 10: "you must observe," λεῦσσε.

Fragment 4 confirms the capacity of thought (νόος) to explain realities that are not present. However, thought is not infallible: in fragment 6, the Goddess affirms that not only can sensations be mistaken when they try to explain reality, but the intellect can also "drift." Consequently, before maintaining that νόος is able to explain "everything," not only present but also absent things, Parmenides must justify the origin of the "deviation" of thinking attested in fragment 6. We find this explanation in fragment 16.

In fact, there is a conflict in Parmenides between a "present" state of things, in which the mortals are slaves to routine, and a way of learning that will produce a "man who knows" (cf. εἰδότα φῶτα, fr. 1.3). The "present" state of things (and of the means to know it) is described in fragment 16. In this text, Parmenides (through the intermediation of the Goddess) explains why the intellect can make a mistake: because it is located in the chest (στήθεσιν), which is a set of "members."[16] And the chest, in the case of mortals who have not yet achieved the *status* of "men who know," is a mixture of "wandering"

[16] M. Conche cites a text of Aeschylus (*Persians*, 991–992) where μελέων, "members" (the term used by Parmenides) is synonymous with the inner side of the body, that is, the chest (*Parménide. Le Poème: Fragments* [Paris: Presses Universitaires de France, 1996], p. 245).

elements (πολυπλάγκτων, fr. 16.1). Therefore, in the majority of people (φῦλα, 6.7) it is the φύσις of the members that thinks; that is why their νόος is πλακτός (fr. 6.6).

I propose to place fragment 16, where Parmenides explains the origin of the error of mortals, immediately after fragment 6. Finally, the last line of fragment 16 (although its interpretation is not universally agreed upon) opens a new perspective. There is a new reference to thought, "τὸ γὰρ πλέον ἐστὶ νόημα" (16.4). These words, according to my interpretation, show that *all that is real* can be the object of thought. Thus, I interpret line 16.4 in the following way: the "whole" (synonymous with the totality, because "being touches being") is a νόημα, an object of thought. A well-educated νόος must go beyond the constraints of its own constitution to see in reality more than a mere union of light and of nonluminous night (fragment 9). The νόος knows that "it is impossible to force that which is, not to be connected with that which is, neither scattering it completely in regular order, nor gathering it" (fr. 4.2–4). This fr. 4 (which I propose to place after fragment 16) is an excellent introduction to the eight "physical" texts that we have set aside (fr. 10–11, 13–15 and 17–18).

Fragment 4 begins with an exhortation (similar to that in fragment 10) that would be impossible to imagine if the context proposed a "deceitful" knowledge, and this exhortation repeats the notion of νόος presented in fragment 16. The Goddess (and not the human δόξαι) explains that, thanks to the νόος, "absent" events are "present," because the νόος has the capacity to explain them. And between these "absent" events, which possess their own φύσις (fr. 10.1, 10.5) (that is, their "being"), we can certainly include the origin of the universe and of the celestial bodies (the subject of fragments 10 and 11).

In this set of fragments (in a detailed way in fr. 10 and 11 and in a fragmentary way in fr. 13–15 and 17), we find the essence of Parmenidean "physics," and any notion is "deceptive." Fragment 10 shows how necessity (the same necessity that maintains the fact of being in its limits in fragment 8) also maintains the universe in its limits, and fragment 11 invites the listener to know (or is the conclusion of an explanation: the fragmentary state of the text prevents us from giving a precise answer) the origin of some celestial bodies. Fragment 18, known only in its Latin version, certainly belongs to a positive teaching, from which we can obtain the notion of "proportion" ("*temperiem servans,*" line 3) which optimistically could make an allusion to a "necessary" stability. Eventually, once it is specified that the νόος is able to rationalize absent events, fragment 7 confirms that a "mortal who knows" must take away his thought (νόημα) from the way that upholds that "there are things (ὄντα) that do not exist" (fr. 7.1).

## A new arrangement of Parmenides' fragments

As a summary of my interpretation, I propose the following rearrangement of Parmenidean "fragments": fr. 1, 2, 3, 5, 6, 16, 4, 10, 11, 13, 14, 15, 17, 18, 7, 8, 9, 12, 19. According to this scheme, the enigmatic expression that alludes to a "πολύδηριν ἔλεγχον" *already exposed* (the verb is in past tense, ῥηθέντα) (fr. 7.5) acquires a clear and distinct sense. In the present ordering, *before* fragment 7, there is no ἔλεγχος, controversial or not. According to my rearrangement, the ἔλεγχος (that is to say, a set of arguments), which would certainly be controversial (because it is not usual to affirm that the νόος is able to grasp real things, but can also wander) would allude to the "physical" arguments of fragments 10–11 and 13–18.

My interpretation aims to demonstrate, once again, that for Parmenides there are only two ways to conceive any type of research: either the νόος, in a good way (using method and manner), admits the necessary and absolute character of the fact of being and then the knowledge acquired is "persuasive"; or it is engaged in a nomadic course, guided by sensations and by a wandering thought producing only contradictory names, that is, opinions (δόξαι), deceitful and untrue. This nomadic method is a vicious circle that gets out of it just what it puts in it. Parmenides calls the two methods ἀλήθεια and δόξα, and, among them, *tertium non datur.*

# Thought and Body in Parmenides[1]

Patricia Curd

**Summary**

Parmenides' fragment B16 is a puzzle: it seems to be about thought, but Theophrastus uses it in his account of Parmenides' views on perception. Scholars have disagreed about its proper place in Parmenides' poem: does it belong to *Alētheia* or to *Doxa?* I suggest that the fragment indeed belongs to *Doxa,* and in it Parmenides claims that mortals, who fail to use *noos* correctly, mistake the passive experiences of sense perception for genuine thought about what-is, and hence fail to understand the true nature of what-is. I argue that genuine thought (the correct use of *noos*) must go beyond sense experience and grasp what is truly intelligible; in doing so I explore the question of immateriality in Presocratic thinking.

Theophrastus places Parmenides among those who "let perception come about by similarity." One paragraph later, Theophrastus is complaining that Parmenides gives no clear account at all of perception and merely said "that there are two elements and that knowing (γνῶσις) depends on the dominating one," and that

[1] This is a fragment of a larger project (a book in progress in 2007–2008 and beyond) on divinity, intelligibility, and human thought in Presocratic philosophy. I have been working on other parts of the project (on Empedocles and on Heraclitus and Anaxagoras) at the same time as this paper, and there is some overlap in the interim publications that have resulted from this work. It is a pleasure to thank Néstor Cordero and Estela Erausquin, the Centro de Estudios de Filosofía Antigua, and the Universidad Nacional de San Martín for the wonderful conference in Buenos Aires and their gracious hospitality. I am grateful to all the participants for their friendly criticisms and suggestions, and especially to José Trindade Santos. Thanks also to Richard McKirahan for his helpful comments.

if the hot predominates, thought (διάνοια) becomes better and purer (A46). He then gives us B16:

> As on each occasion there is a mixture of the much-wandering limbs, so is mind (νόος) present to (παρέστηκεν[2]) human beings (ἀνθρώποισι); for the same (τὸ αὐτό) is what the nature of the limbs thinks in humans (φρονέει μελέων φύσις ἀνθρώποισιν), both in all (πᾶσιν) and in each (παντί). For the full is thought (νόημα).

Then, perhaps noting the oddity of this evidence for his claim about perception, Theophrastus adds: "For he speaks of perceiving and thinking as the same thing (τὸ γὰρ αἰσθάνεσθαι καὶ τὸ φρονεῖν ὡς ταὐτὸ λέγει) . . ."[3] He goes on to say that Parmenides also attributes sense perception to the opposite "in its own right" and that "this is clear in the places" where Parmenides claims that "a corpse does not perceive light, heat, or sound because of the lack of fire, but it perceives cold, and silence, and such opposites." André Laks has pointed out that Theophrastus seems to have had difficulty in finding evidence for a clear account of perception in Parmenides, and that what survives as B16 (and whatever text Theophrastus used to support his account of *aisthēsis* in corpses) is all he had to go on.

What is odd about the evidence is that fragment 16 is *not* about perception (although the remark about corpses seems to be). It is about νόος and *noēma*, and despite Theophrastus' claim to the contrary, Parmenides does not identify genuine thought with perception (see B6 and B7). Yet B16 clearly wants to say something about human thought and to connect it in some way with states of the body. In this paper, I try to untangle some problems about thought that arise from what seem to be

[2] Text (from Theophrastus *de Sensu*) as in Tarán and Coxon who canvass the philological considerations for accepting Theophrastus' text rather than that given by Aristotle in *Met.* IV.

[3] For discussion, especially of the last line, see Laks, "'The More' and 'The Full.'" For an account of the layers of ambiguity that can be found in B16, see Mourelatos, *Route*, pp. 253–260.

conflicts between B16 and the claims of the *Alētheia* section of Parmenides' poem. Briefly, my claims are these:

(1) Genuine (true, trustworthy) thought has as its object what-is (τὸ ἐόν: that which genuinely is).
(2) Thought about what-is (τὸ ἐόν) is not mediated through sensation or perception.
(3) Mortals, who stray from the path of what-is, suppose that they are thinking when they are not, because the object of this false (non-genuine) thought is what is other than what-is (i.e., what-is-not; what is not genuinely real).
(4) Purported thinking is merely affection of the body by light and night; this is experience misunderstood as "thought." It is aimless and undirected, and cannot be equated with the understanding or knowledge gained by one whose νόος has traveled the correct route of inquiry.
(5) Geniune thought (and its object) are not to be identified with states of the body.

An immediate objection to my claims is that there is a false presupposition underlying claims (2) and (5), and lurking behind (4). This objection claims that there is no notion of the incorporeal or immaterial in the Presocratics; therefore, Parmenides *could not* have supposed that genuine thought and its object are not bodily states. I think that this objection is misguided; here I want to examine it in order to show that claims (2) and (5) remain at least an open possibility in Parmenides. Then I shall turn to a fuller discussion of B16, with a few suggestions about how to interpret it.[4] My conclusion is that B16 does not belong to the *Alētheia* section of the poem, but that nevertheless, it tells us something important about the difference between mortal thinking and the

[4] B16 has been the subject of much debate. I will not discuss other interpretations in detail, hoping that my agreements and disagreements with these will become clear as I proceed. Among those whose views I have been thinking about are Finkelberg, Hershbell, Laks, Mourelatos, Tarán, and Vlastos.

divine-like insight of the man who knows.[5] It is connected with the closing lines of B1, where the contrast between what can be known and what mortals take to be true is introduced and (somewhat) developed. More pessimistically, I doubt that a complete understanding of B16 is possible, given the state of the evidence.

## I. Parmenides on Thought and its Object

It is clear that there is an intimate connection between genuine thought and what-is (see B3, B6.1, B8.34–37). What I want to focus on here is how Parmenides treats the power of thinking. A good place to begin is B4:

> Gaze on things which though absent are nevertheless present firmly to mind (νόῳ); for it [νόος] will not cut off[6] what-is from holding to what-is, neither dispersing everywhere in every way in order nor gathering together.

Mind (or understanding) has the power to conceive of things that are not actively present to and stimulating the senses. While perception is limited to what happens to be present to and acting on the sensing organs, νόος can move beyond perception altogether to grasp the reality of what-is. For Parmenides, successful thought is insight achieved and this is a mental process entirely different from perceiving.[7] It is complete at a moment ("complete" both in the sense of "finished" and in the sense of "perfected"), and it may or may not be connected with what one is sensing at that moment.

---

[5] Hershbell argues that B16 belongs to *Truth* rather than *Doxa*.

[6] This translation follows Coxon, who says, "The ground given for asserting that the exercise of reason puts the philosopher in the presence of absent things is that, if it is directed (as it must be . . .) upon Being, it will not divide this by regarding it as dispersing or gathering, like the divine primary substances of Anaximenes and Heraclitus, and can then contemplate it steadily. The argument is about the activity of mind, and is destroyed if ἀποτμήξει is taken as a second person singular middle instead of as active with νόος understood as subject. The verb is construed with an infinitive as expressing prevention: 'the mind will not sever Being from holding fast to Being.'" (Coxon, *Fragments*, 1986: p. 188; Revised and Expanded Edition, 2009: p. 307.)

[7] The notion of insight that I have in mind here is developed by Graham in his article on Heraclitus in the *Oxford Handbook of Presocratic Philosophy*.

One reason for this is surely the monogeneity of what-is, its perspectival neutrality. Because any thing that genuinely is maintains the same character all through, to grasp any of it in thought is to grasp all of it. Yet there is more to this than just a claim about the unity of the object of thought. Any Parmenidean being or entity (leaving open the question of numerical monism) must be both unchanging and not subject to change (these requirements are consequences of the proofs of B8). The objects of sense perception fail to meet the requirements of B8, and so they cannot qualify as what-is. Further, these objects of sense perception cannot be the objects of genuine thought: what-is-not cannot be genuinely said or thought (B8.8–9; B2.7–8), although what-is is indeed what mortals (wrongly) suppose that they are thinking of and naming when they engage in the activities that they (wrongly) suppose constitute genuine thought. This opens the question of the nature of thought and its object. I suggest that in some cases these are immaterial [non-corporeal]; they are not part of the world as mortals experience it at all, though they are certainly part of what-is. It is this non-material character of thought and its object that allows Parmenides to exploit the present-while-absent image of B4. Even though what-is is not present to the perceiver through the senses, it can be present to a νόος that is properly directed: thought can grasp non-sensible being.

To justify this assertion, we need to distinguish between real/genuine thought (the activity of the knowing insightful νόος) and what may seem to be but is not genuine thought. Further, we need to examine the very possibility of the conception of non-material or incorporeal reality. I begin with the first problem.

In the closing arguments of Book V of the *Republic* (arguments that are full of Parmenidean influence[8]), Plato claims that knowledge (ἐπιστήμη) always concerns what-is (478a6), while opinion (δόξα) is connected with that which "rolls between being and not-being" (479d3–5). He uses this argument to show that the lovers of spectacle, who acknowledge and appreciate beautiful sensible particulars, but deny the reality of the Form of Beauty Itself, are not qualified to rule in the ideal city. Later, in the discussion of

[8] See Crystal, "Parmenidean," among others.

the Divided Line, Plato restricts the highest levels of cognition, thought (διάνοια) and understanding (νόησις), to the realm of the intelligible (τὸ γένος τοῦ νοουμένου) and claims that they are not concerned with the perceptible (τὸ γένος τοῦ ὁρωμένου); 509c6ff. This means that "thought" and "knowledge" or "understanding" are technically and formally restricted to the realm of being and denied to the realm of becoming. Claims about "knowing" particulars must rely on secondary, dependent, or informal uses of the relevant terms. That is because the faculties of knowing and opining are restricted to certain objects. I can perhaps justifiably claim to know that Helen is beautiful, but my claim must be backed up by reference to my knowledge of what Beauty itself is (and that may require that I have actually seen the form of the Good); such a justified claim is not impossible, but it is fairly difficult to make. Parmenides is not so strict about terminology and not so profligate in commitments to human faculties. (Whether these are philosophical virtues or vices is an open question.) Parmenides allows human νόος to cross borders. What qualifies as knowing is the result of the correct use of νόος: restricting it to apprehending genuine realities, using the proper tests, and so judging correctly. When used correctly, νόος will be limited and contained, aimed at what-is, rather than undirected and straying towards what-is-not. Parmenides usually signals the difference between successful and unsuccessful uses of νόος by pointing out that it is mortals (or human beings) who fail to use νόος properly. The implication is that the control of νόος, and hence its successful use, is something divine (or quasi-divine).[9] Mortals (βροτοί) are mentioned at B1.30, where the beliefs of mortals are contrasted with the "unshaking heart of well-persuasive truth"; and at B6.4, where know-nothing mortals are said to wander on the forbidden route. At B8.39 mortals are said to posit names, (falsely) supposing them to be true; mortal

---

[9] My thinking on this has been much influenced by Lesher and Mogyorodi. The goal is enunciated in the title of Hermann's *To Think like God*. In a discussion of B16, Finkelberg explicitly links the divine and what-is and offers this account of knowing: "Being (the divinity in its self-cognition) is . . . cognized by the 'like', i.e., by a being which is a self-cognizing human individual: through his own self the mortal cognizes the self of the deity, i.e., cognizes the universe as unspecified existence, Being" ("Reality in Parmenides," p. 407).

opinions reappear at B8.51, and at B8.61 the *kouros* is assured that he is being told the tale by the goddess so that "no mortal opinion (βροτῶν γνώμη) will ever outstrip" him. In all these cases, mortal thought or thinking is contrasted with genuine thought about what-is; mortals are unsuccessful in thinking because they try to *think about* the wrong sort of thing.

Similarly, human beings (ἄνθρωποι) are contrasted with the goddess, with respect to both her haunts and her views. At B1.27, the route the *kouros* has traveled is said to be "far from the beaten track of human beings (ἀπ' ἀνθρώπων ἐκτὸς πάτου ἐστίν)." At B19.3 human beings have given a name and sign for each thing that, according to opinion, has sprung up and grown. Finally, there are two occurrences of *anthrōpos* in B16, which I shall postpone discussing for the moment.

Thinking like a mortal is something that one can overcome: indeed, the story the goddess tells is directed at just that goal.[10] The *kouros* will be able to leave mortal thought processes behind, once he learns the lesson the goddess teaches, evaluates her story (B7.5) and applies the criterion of B8.15–16 in order to test his own thoughts. The test is of the object: is it or is it not? (Answering that question will require application of the criteria given in B8.1–6.) Mortals' feeble attempts to grasp what is not fail to count as genuine thinking. Hapless mortals do not judge, they suppose. The goddess describes their plight:

> . . . [this route] on which mortals (βροτοί), knowing nothing wander, two headed; for helplessness in their breasts rules their wandering νόος (πλακτὸν νόον); they are carried along equally deaf and blind, amazed, uncritical (ἄκριτα) hordes by whom to be and not to be (τὸ πέλειν τε καὶ οὐκ εἶναι) are supposed (νενόμισται) both the same and not the same, and the path of all is backward-turning.

Note that here the goddess does not deny that mortals have νόος. The problem is that they fail to control it; thus mortal νόος

[10] I have argued for this in my book, *The Legacy of Parmenides.*

wanders rather than heading straight along the correct path of inquiry (for thinking).[11] Further, as B7 shows, the incorrect path of inquiry is identified with uncritical reliance on sense experience rather than judicious trust in *logos* (argument, reason, reasoning):

> For never shall this be forced through: that things that are not are;
> but you hold back your thought (νόημα) from this route of inquiry (ἀφ' ὁδοῦ διζήσιος), nor let habit force you along this much-experienced path (πολύπειρον ὁδόν), to ply an aimless eye and resounding ear and tongue, but judge by reasoning (λόγος) the much-contested testing spoken by me.

What-is, the intensional content of genuine thought, cannot be identical with the content of sense experience. Thus, genuine thought must concern itself solely with grasping the intelligible.

## II. Objection

So far, what I have said about thought and its object in Parmenides is fairly unobjectionable to many scholars who study the Presocratics. What is perhaps odd is my claim that the intelligible is immaterial in Parmenides. We have no difficulty in believing this about Plato; for many scholars, it is Plato who first introduces the notion that the intelligible is immaterial.[12] Although a number of people believe that there is a notion of the immaterial in Parmenides (or wish that were the case[13]), there is little discussion of this claim. Rather more often we find the assertion that not only is there no immaterial reality in Parmenides, there is no conception of the immaterial at all in

[11] See Lesher, "Critique on Thinking," on controlling one's νόος.

[12] Melissus says that the One has no body (B9); there are disagreements about whether this means it is immaterial. The problem is how to interpret B3 and B9 together. See, for instance, Palmer.

[13] This assertion is the result of an informal survey among my colleagues in ancient philosophy.

the Presocratics (unless, perhaps in post-Parmenidean thinkers). Let us call this the matterist view.[14]

Here is an example. This is J. E. Raven:

> Quite the most striking aspect of the whole history of pre-Socratic speculation is, to my mind, just this: that whereas, with the exceptions of the Milesians at one end of the story and the Atomists at the other, every single one of the pre-Socratics was striving after an incorporeal principle, their minds were yet so firmly possessed by the preconception that the only criterion of reality was extension in space that one and all they ended in failure.[15]

What particularly interests me in discussions about Presocratic materialism, as we might call it, is the claim that the early Greek thinkers could not have conceived of something immaterial. In discussing the Pythagoreans, Guthrie makes this claim briefly and forcefully: "the only form of existence so far *conceivable* is bodily substance; hence it [void or air in Pythagoreanism] is thought of as a particularly tenuous form of matter" (italics mine).[16] Guthrie's claims about early Greek thought have been echoed by others[17] (for instance, Burkert, Inwood, Nussbaum, Palmer, Sedley) and extended to all the Presocratics.

How do we know whether or not early Greek thinkers could *conceive* of something?[18] The authority to which many have pointed recently are Robert Renehan's arguments about the concepts of soul and immateriality, and it is to his thesis that I now turn.[19] Put roughly, the argument is this: the notion

---

14 My vocabulary needs to be more complicated here. See for instance, Cooper, "Chrysippus on Physical Elements."

15 Raven, "Cosmology," p. 133.

16 Guthrie, *A History of Greek Philosophy*, Vol. I, p. 280. It should be noted that Guthrie thinks that Anaxagoras' *Nous* is not corporeal, though he does attribute material natures to Love and to Strife. His claims about Parmenides are more complex, but similar.

17 In articles and in discussion.

18 This section is taken from my forthcoming article, "Where are Love and Strife? Incorporeality in Empedocles."

19 See Renehan's articles: "ΣΩΜΑ" and "Incorporeality."

of soul before Plato must be that of a corporeal thing. Why? The reasons are these: We have no good evidence for the use of ἀσώματος or related terms in any context before Plato; ὕλη (matter) is Aristotelian (although there may be hints about it in the *Timaeus*). No one before Plato explicitly says that *soul* is immaterial (ἀσώματος). All existence (for the early Greeks) is bodily existence, so the soul must be something bodily. This is because the Greeks did not and could not have conceived of something other than body.

A first statement of this view can be found in Renehan's "The Meaning of ΣΩΜΑ in Homer" (the particular details of his argument need not detain us at the moment). What is relevant is that, in arguing for his own view, Renehan cites Guthrie on the absence of a word for "matter" in early Greek thought: Guthrie says that the Milesians had no word for matter "since they knew of no other form of existence . . ." Renehan's approving comment is, "Here is a concept for which the early Greeks had no word precisely because it never occurred to them to question the concept. It was taken for granted."[20] This is basically the same view as that of Raven, quoted above. In a later paper, "On the Greek Origins of the Concepts of Incorporeality and Immateriality," Renehan expands his argument, but it depends crucially on these two claims.[21]

There are, I argue, three flaws in the argument. First, a general point about the strategy of Renehan's claim: it seems to stress the wrong thing and so miss the point. While it may be the case that early Greek thinkers did not think of soul as immaterial, nothing at all follows about the general conceivability of something that is not corporeal.

Second, there is the claim that early Greek lacked a word for *matter*. In response, we might look no farther than Renehan himself. In disagreeing with Snell about the Greek body (σῶμα), Renehan rebukes Snell for using just such an argument. Snell

[20] ΣΩΜΑ, p. 274; the words quoted from Guthrie are a parenthetical comment on p. 82 of *A History of Greek Philosophy*, Vol. I.

[21] Renehan's specific target in one part of the paper is the claim (by Gomperz) that both the word and concept ἀσώματος go back as far as the sixth century. I do not dispute Renehan's philological reasons for rejecting Gomperz's claim.

had claimed that in Homer, σώματα must be *dead* bodies because there are no uses of σῶμα in Homer to mean living body. Renehan himself correctly points out that we cannot decide that something is or is not the case because of the absence of a word, or a set of words.[22] In reply to Snell, Renehan says that "It is very questionable whether absence of a word necessarily implies a total absence of the corresponding concept. Language lags."[23] Yet Renehan's own claims about immateriality and incorporeality are ultimately based on the absence of certain words in early Greek texts.

Finally, like Raven and Guthrie, Renehan assumes that "the Greek mind" accepted unquestioningly the idea that existence entails extension in space:

> . . . the Greeks considered it [the notion of extension in space] so natural and essential an attribute of all reality that it simply did not occur to them at first to deny spatial extension to Being even when they were struggling to divest it of body. Since in ordinary thought bodily matter is that which is extended in space, this attitude was one potent source of confusion when speculation about non-material Being began.[24]

This is where the problem really lies. The culprit is the presumption that for the early Greek thinkers, to be is to be matter or body extended in space.[25] It is this that buttresses the

---

22 In discussions at a conference on the *Timaeus* in September, 2007, both Sarah Broadie and Anthony Long questioned how much weight we should give to the presence or absence of a word; Broadie suggested that the attempt to portray notions for which there is not yet vocabulary is not a rare occurrence in early philosophy (including Classical and Hellenistic Greek philosophy).

23 Renehan, "ΣΩΜΑ," p. 274.

24 Renehan, "Incorporeality," p. 118.

25 Again Renehan uses a linguistic support. He writes, "σῶμα was responsible for another confusion of thought, in my judgment the decisive one. All physical bodies . . . partake of such sensible properties as weight, shape, extension in space, not insofar as they are *bodies*, but insofar as they are *matter*. In the fifth century σῶμα still bore a predominantly literal meaning—human or animal figure; at the same time the nature of matter was imperfectly understood. There was as yet not even a word for it. The consequence of this state of things was that it

assertion that Parmenides' what-is must be a solid sphere, that supports the claim that Love and Strife are corporeal entities, and that leads scholars to claim that Anaxagoras' *Nous* must be corporeal or material in some sense. I claim that we have no good reason to assume that this presupposition is correct. What we have to do is examine the evidence and see where it leads us; but that evidence must be examined as impartially as possible.

What is misleading is the idea that *matter* or *extension* is such an obvious notion to the early Greeks, and that their problem lay in learning how to think of the immaterial. Look again at this claim: "their minds were . . . firmly possessed by the preconception that the only criterion of reality was extension in space" (Raven); this makes the early Greek thinkers Cartesians without Cartesian souls. Many discussions of the Milesians make a similar point. The Milesians are supposed to be material monists who conceive of some matter (water, the indefinite, air) as an underlying reality (substance) that transforms into other things while somehow maintaining its own special watery or airy character.[26] This is an Aristotelian interpretation: on this view, the Presocratics suppose that there is an underlying subject that gains or loses properties. These subjects occupy space and are moved through it by the action of matter itself (this is the hylozoism that Guthrie, for instance, attributes to the pre-Parmenidean thinkers). Thinking of things as subjects in this way already involves conceiving them as combinations of matter and form—first, the subject which is to be enformed, and then the properties enforming the subject in certain ways. This matter/form view holds at every level: whether of Aristotelian primary substances (ensouled bodies), or simple alterations as when the man becomes musical by, as "matter," taking on a new "form."[27] For Aristotle, *form* and *matter* are congruent

was possible to conceive of Body and Matter as two distinct entities. So long as σῶμα had a rather restricted meaning and matter was both vaguely conceived and nameless, no thinker was in a position, either linguistically or conceptually, to perceive clearly that a denial of Body necessarily involved a denial of properties which Body had not *qua* Body but *qua* Matter" ("Incorporeality," p. 119).

[26] This view is criticized by Graham in *Explaining the Cosmos*.

[27] See Frede, "Categories," on individuals and substances in Aristotle; his views are further developed and the point expanded by Mann.

terms: matter is co-extensive with form.[28] Thinking this way invites one to study these notions in their own right—to write the *Metaphysics*, perhaps. But this is not what the Presocratics did. Rather, Presocratic basic things generally are stuffs and powers: the hot, earth, the cold, fire, water, the moist, etc., all mixed up together. There will be certain differences among the theories (for Xenophanes earth and water are basic at the level of earthly phenomena, cloud plays this special role in meteorological phenomena; for Heraclitus the opposites and their processes, as controlled by *Logos*, are basic). Parmenides offers an example: his cosmological model is the mixing of ingredients to produce the natural world.[29] This example stands, whether or not one takes the *Doxa* as serious cosmology, a critique of cosmology, or an extended jest; and once Parmenides offers mixture as a model, it becomes the standard explanation of the coming-to-be and changing of the things that the world presents to our senses. The problems that post-Parmenidean thinkers face are (1) how to explain the processes of mixture and separation, and (2) how to produce structure from mixture.[30] This is not to deny that these stuffs (and perhaps even the opposites) are corporeal, but I deny that these are to be thought of as matter, in the sense of an uncharacterized extended something that is to be characterized.

Further, it is not clear that the Presocratics think of their stuffs as things in space. The very concept of space is one that both Plato and Aristotle wrestle with as something new and very difficult, and not at all intuitively obvious. The empty (τὸ κενόν) is not space. In pre-Platonic atomism, the void is what separates atoms, it is not a container for atoms. It is moved just as the atoms are, like the interstices in a sponge or, as Sedley suggests, the vacuum in a flask.[31] Rather, the stuffs (whichever

---

[28] Ryan suggests that form without matter is impossible in Aristotle. The unmoved mover is *ousia*, pure actuality. As unmattered it cannot *have* form, much less *be* pure form.

[29] Consider B12 and the goddess who supervises mixture.

[30] See Mourelatos, "Quality, Structure, and Emergence" and Curd, "Metaphysics." There are similar questions to be asked about the status of Platonic particulars (see Mann and also Silverman).

[31] Sedley, "Two Conceptions of Vacuum," Algra, pp. 46–51. Sedley seems to say that there is space in Democritus, and that both atoms and void occupy space.

stuffs a theory requires) are what is real, and their mixtures produce the world that we perceive. An excellent example of this is to be found in Anaxagoras B17:

> Anaxagoras says clearly in the first book of the Physics that coming-to-be and passing-away are combining and dissociating, writing this: "The Greeks do not think correctly about coming-to-be and passing-away; for no thing comes to be or passes away, but is mixed together and dissociated from the things that are. And thus they would be correct to call coming-to-be mixing-together and passing-away dissociating." (59B17; Simplicius *in Phys.* 163.18)

The two problems, of process and of structure, are faced by all later thinkers (including Plato) before Aristotle, who finally introduces specific sorts of causes to explain them. These problems become particularly acute after Parmenides, but I think that they are present in theories before Parmenides, and that devices like Xenophanes' god and Heraclitus' *Logos* are their attempts to deal with them. Early thinkers (and here I mean Heraclitus, Anaxagoras, Empedocles, and the pre-Platonic atomists) see structure as a function of ratios and proportions of ingredient stuffs. If this is so, their theories are going to be concerned with problems of the arrangement of stuffs in appropriate proportions, rather than questions about matter as such. Thus, the germ of the idea of the immaterial in the Presocratics will be found in their accounts of process, change, and structure, rather than in their accounts of soul. Concentrating primarily on immaterial or incorporeal soul as the source of this notion takes us in the wrong direction. To be sure, in those theories that do include the soul, soul might be thought of as a (corporeal or incorporeal) source of change and arrangement; but as such soul is an instance of the larger questions about the sources of change, arrangement, and organization.[32]

[32] For instance, the single use of *psychē* in Empedocles (B138) is a reference to life, which is "drawn off" or ended, with a bronze knife, presumably by causing loss of blood (Wright, *Empedocles: the Extant Fragments,* p. 288); the shedding of blood is the terrible source of the fall of *daimōns*; see Osborne, "Sin." Empedocles

The brief claims I have made here cannot prove that Parmenides thinks that the intelligible is the immaterial; but I hope to have given some reasons for denying that he could not have thought this. I wish to give one more indirect argument: Parmenides B16, with its apparently matterist analysis of human thought, contrasts mortal thinking (dependent on the stuffs of experience) with the genuine thought of the one who knows, who is able to grasp what-is with νόος unencumbered by the bodily forms of light and night.

## III. Back to B16

What the goddess promises the *kouros* is that he will have a view like that of the divine. He will be able to conceive of and think the truth of all things. A mortal who fails to learn the Goddess's lesson, and fails to control νόος, misses the truth altogether. Consider again the claims about mind/thought in the *Doxa*:

> As on each occasion there is a mixture of the much-wandering limbs,
>
> so is mind (νόος) present to (παρέστηκεν) human beings (ἀνθρώποισι); for the same (τὸ αὐτό)
>
> is what the nature of the limbs thinks in humans (φρονέει μελέων φύσις ἀνθρώποισιν),
>
> both in all (πᾶσιν) and in each (παντί). For the full is thought (νόημα).

I have long taken this to be one of the most confounding passages in Presocratic thought; I might add that I find most attempts to translate and explain it (including my own) equally perplexing. The choices for each of the disputed notions in the fragment are wide. In line 1: mixture or temper? Bodily limbs or mortal posits such as day and night or hot and cold (Theophrastus' choice)? In the final line: is the full to be equated with the fullness of what-is (which underlies attempts to make

apparently does not treat soul as the source of organization, motion, or character (as motivating actions), but he is certainly interested in all of these problems.

B16 part of the *Alētheia*) or is it the preponderance of the stuffs in a particular human mixture which causes a particular thought in a human being?[33]

Lines 2b–4 have been compared to B8.34–41. On this line of interpretation, all human beings have what-is as the referent of their thought, although they do not recognize this.[34] One of the striking things about the passage is its echoing of Homeric views on mortal thought. Like Homer on the claim that the mind of man is as the day Zeus sends, this passage seems to insist that this sort of thinking is something that happens to humans, over which they have no control. This is a pessimistic view of human cognition, and those who want to see B16 as explicating Parmenides' own positive view of thought (and even more so for those who place it in *Alētheia*) must explain this. Moreover, while B16 presents the (κρᾶσις μελέων) as an account of the mind (νόος) of human beings, in line 3, rather than the expected νοεῖ, we have the verb φρονέει ("thinks"). Parmenides nowhere else uses this word, and I suggest it is because what we are being told here is that mortals take the content of their perceptual experience (the state of their bodies) to be thought. In the case of human beings (as mortal thinkers), the state of the body is taken to be the same[35] condition as thinking: as the body is, of such a mind is a human being. On this (incorrect) view, the content of mortal thought is reduced to material components—a mixture of light and night.[36] The commensurability of light and night in the sensed object and in the sense organs produces certain sensations.[37] Mortals, as described in B6 and B7, are wanderers just because there is nothing on which to fix their thought, given that they take the passing world of experience to be all that there is and real (see the end of B1). They are passive: carried, forced

[33] For alternatives, see Mourelatos, Robinson, Finkelberg, and Coxon.

[34] See especially Robinson ("Parmenides," pp. 631–632), who cites Mourelatos's *Route*, pp. 256–257.

[35] On this sense of "the same," see Mourelatos: "the correct paraphrase of the direct meaning is 'same state' or 'same condition'." (*Route*, p. 256)

[36] See Laks, "'The More' and 'The Full'," who argues that the limbs of line 1 are the forms light and night. This view is also discussed in Hershbell, "Way of Truth"; see also Tarán, *Parmenides*.

[37] See Laks, "'The More' and 'The Full'," and also Vlastos, "Theory."

along the much-experienced route of inquiry that goes nowhere and never gets there.[38] This passive account is at odds with the active exercise of νόος required by the goddess, and leaves no room for connection between human and the divine thought.[39] (Recall Theophrastus' comment that corpses perceive cold and dark—passive mortal experience if ever there was any!)

The overarching story of the fragments of Parmenides is the message of the goddess to the *kouros*: not all human beings must remain mortal thinkers; we can learn how to stop thinking like mortals. Once we do this, we have it in our power to grasp the divine truth about things that the knowledge of what-is can give us. On the evidence of B16, all human beings must begin by thinking like mortals; yet this need not be our fate. To gain that knowledge we must actively think, taking our own thought on the journey of the path of what-is, to what is true and intelligible. The key to this, I think is the following: we must not mistake the stuffs that constitute our limbs and our physiological processes for what-is. The intelligible is not to be found in the stuffs of the sensible world.[40] I have not argued for this here (although I shall in the next part of this project), but I think that Parmenides takes it to be true. What I want to say here is that there is no conceptual reason to deny that Parmenides could suppose it to be true.

---

38 I take the "much-experienced" route to be both a route that relies on experience, and the route that is "normal" for human beings, the one that they usually experience.

39 See Mansfeld, "Minima Parmenidea" (though he is not discussing B16 here, what he says is relevant): "People believe that what they see every day and night is real; they even believe that the moon shines with its own light. They are doubly wrong" (p. 559).

40 Because Parmenides leaves open what will qualify as a genuinely basic metaphysical entity, it might be that some such entities are material: Anaxagorean stuffs and Empedocles' earth, water, air, and fire, for instance. One could argue that the genuine natures of these are not perceptible by human beings, i.e., that phenomenal stuffs are already mixtures (both Anaxagoras and Empedocles endorse this view), but that need not impugn the corporeal aspect of these basic things. Nevertheless, there are good reasons to think that the moving forces in Anaxagorean and Empedoclean physics are not corporeal. Anaxagoras' *Nous* and Empedocles' Love and Strife do not have corporeal or material natures. Like the stuffs and the roots, these forces are basic parts of the theory of each, and all are intended to be Parmenidean basic entities, meeting the requirements of B8, and as such, objects of genuine thought.

## Bibliography


Algra, Keimpe. *Concepts of Space in Greek Thought.* Leiden: Brill, 1995.

Crystal, Ian. "Parmenidean Allusions in *Republic* V." *Ancient Philosophy* 16 (1996): 351–363.

Cooper, John M. "Chrysippus on Physical Elements." In Richard Salles, ed., *God and Cosmos in Stoicism.* Oxford: Oxford University Press, 2009: 93–117.

Coxon, A. H. *The Fragments of Parmenides.* Assen: Van Gorcum, 1986. Revised and Expanded Edition edited by R. McKirahan with a new Preface by M. Scholfield, Las Vegas: Parmenides Publishing, 2009.

Crane, Tim and Meller, D. H. "There is no Question of Physicalism." *Mind* 99 (1990): 185–206.

Curd, Patricia. *The Legacy of Parmenides: Eleatic Monism and Later Presocratic Thought.* Revised paperback edition with new introduction, Las Vegas: Parmenides Publishing, 2004.

_____. "The Metaphysics of Physics: Mixture and Separation in Anaxagoras and Empedocles." In V. Caston and D. Graham, eds. *Presocratic Philosophy: Essays in Honor of A. P. D. Mourelatos.* Ashgate Publishing Co., 2002: 139–158.

_____. "Where are Love and Strife? Incorporeality in Empedocles." Forthcoming in the Proceedings of the 2007 Fall Lecture Series, Catholic University of America: Early Greek Philosophy: Reason at the Beginning of Philosophy.

Finkelberg, Aryeh. "'Like by Like' and Two Reflections of Reality in Parmenides." *Hermes* 114 (1986): 405–412.

Frede, Michael. "Categories in Aristotle." In M. Frede, *Essays in Ancient Philosophy.* Minneapolis: University of Minnesota Press, 1987: 29–48.

_____. "Individuals in Aristotle." In M. Frede, *Essays in Ancient Philosophy.* Minneapolis: University of Minnesota Press, 1987: 49–71.

Graham, Daniel W. *Explaining the Cosmos: The Ionian Tradition of Scientific Philosophy.* Princeton: Princeton University Press, 2006.

_____. "Heraclitus: Flux, Order, and Knowledge." In *The Oxford Handbook of Presocratic Philosophy.* New York: Oxford University Press, 2008: 169–188.

Guthrie, W. K. C. *A History of Greek Philosophy*, Vols. I and II. Cambridge: Cambridge University Press, Vol. I, 1962; Vol. II, 1965.

Hershbell, Jackson P. "Parmenides' Way of Truth and B16." *Apeiron* 4.2 (1970): 1–23.

Inwood, B. *The Poem of Empedocles: A Text and Translation with an Introduction*. Toronto: University of Toronto Press, 1992; 2nd edition, 2001.

Laks, André. "'The More' and 'The Full': On the Reconstruction of Parmenides' Theory of Sensation in Theophrastus, *De Sensibus*, 3–4." *Oxford Studies in Ancient Philosophy* 8 (1990): 1–18.

Lesher, James H. "Parmenides' Critique of Thinking: The *poludêris elenchos* of Fragment 7." *Oxford Studies in Ancient Philosophy* 2 (1984): 1–30.

Mann, Wolfgang-Rainer. *The Discovery of Things: Aristotle's Categories and their Context*. Princeton: Princeton University Press, 2000.

Mansfeld, Jaap. "Minima Parmenidea." *Mnemosyne* 58 (2005): 554–560.

Mourelatos, Alexander P. D. "Quality, Structure, and Emergence in Later Presocratic Philosophy." In J. Cleary, ed., *Proceedings of the Boston Area Colloquium in Ancient Philosophy*, Vol. 2. Lanham: University Press of America, 1987: 127–194.

_____. *The Route of Parmenides*. Revised and Expanded edition, Las Vegas: Parmenides Publishing, 2008.

Osborne, Catherine. "Sin and Moral Responsibility in Empedocles' Cosmic Cycle." In A. Pierris, ed. *The Empedoclean Kosmos: Structure, Process and the Question of Cyclicity*. Proceedings of the Symposium Philosophiae Antiquae Tertium Myconense. Patras: Institute for Philosophical Research, 2005: 283–308.

Palmer, John. "On the Alleged Incorporeality of What Is in Melissus." *Ancient Philosophy* 23 (2003): 1–10.

Raven, J. E. "The Basis of Anaxagoras' Cosmology." *Classical Quarterly* n.s. 4 (1954): 123–137.

Renahan, Robert F. "The Meaning of ΣΩΜΑ in Homer." *California Studies in Classical Antiquity* 12 (1980): 269–282.

_____. "On the Greek Origins of the Concepts Incorporeality and Immateriality." *Greek, Roman and Byzantine Studies* 21 (1980): 105–138.

Robinson, Thomas M. "Parmenides on the Ascertainment of the Real." *Canadian Journal of Philosophy* 4 (1975): 623–633.

Ryan, Eugene G. "Pure Form in Aristotle." *Phronesis* 18 (1973): 209–224.

Sedley, David. "Parmenides and Melissus." In A. A. Long, ed., *The Cambridge Companion to Early Greek Philosophy*. Cambridge: Cambridge University Press, 1999: 113–133.

_____. "Two Conceptions of Vacuum." *Phronesis* 27 (1982): 175–193.

Silverman, Allan. "Timaean Particulars." *Classical Quarterly* n.s. 42 (1992): 87–113.

Tarán, Leonardo. *Parmenides.* Princeton: Princeton University Press, 1965.

Vlastos, Gregory. "Parmenides' Theory of Knowledge." In G. Vlastos, *Studies in Greek Philosophy*, Vol. I. Edited by Baneil W. Graham. Princeton: Princeton University Press, 1995: 153–163.

# Mortals (βροτοί) According to Parmenides

Jean Frère

**Summary**

It is a common opinion that when Parmenides refers to "mortals," he is referring to all human beings. But in fact, when he talks of "mortals," he implies only a limited fraction of humanity: those thinkers who have elaborated clever but nevertheless insufficient or misleading theories about the origin of things and the cosmos. This can be observed in fragment 6, where the formula "mortals who know nothing," far from implying all humanity, refers only to Heraclitus and his disciples. In the same way, in fragment 8.53–61, "mortals" who acknowledge two separate types of light and night to apprehend the structure of the cosmos are only the Pythagoreans, not all humans.

It is often claimed that Parmenides uses the word "mortals" (βροτοί), to designate the hordes of human multitude. However, is it not the case, when Parmenides speaks of the βροτοί, that he refers only to a limited group of men, that is, the thinkers who elaborated insufficient or erroneous theories about ἀρχή and cosmos?

To get a better grasp of Parmenides' conception of the βροτοί, one has to take into account all the words he uses to designate men as living beings subject to death. This will allow us to grasp the part played by the βροτοί.

In fact, Parmenides uses three different words to designate men as living beings subject to death: φώς (1.3), ἄνθρωποι (1.27;

16.2–3; 19.3), and βροτοί (1.30; 6.4; 8.39; 8.61).[1] My first point will be an analysis of the meaning of these three designations of mortal men.

Two of these words may be found primarily in poetry, namely φώς and βροτοί. Ἄνθρωπος is frequently used in Heraclitus' texts as well as in poetry. The term θνητός may be found in Homer, is frequent in Hesiod and may also be found in Heraclitus, but it never occurs in the remaining fragments of Parmenides.

## Mortal men: φώς, ἄνθρωποι, βροτοί

The βροτοί, who are referred to at the end of fragment 8 and previously mentioned in fragments 1 and 6, are similar neither to the philosopher-man who knows (1.3) nor to the ἄνθρωποι (16). How can we distinguish those three designations in the *Poem*?

## Φώς

Φώς is the man who knows, the young male companion of the "immortal" female drivers (1.24). He differs from the men-ἄνθρωποι (1.27) by the fact that he is progressing along the Way (ὁδός, 1.27), which is the Way of Right and Justice (*Themis, Dikē*, 1.28). He is also distinct from the kind of "mortals" (βροτοί) whose judgments (δόξαι) include no true conviction (πίστις ἀληθής, 1.30).

It is possible to evoke the assonance linking the term φώς with φάος, "light" (φῶς, 14: the light from somewhere else, the moon; φάος, 1.10: to pass into the light; 9.1: all things have been named light and night; 9.3: everything is full of light and of night). According to this sense, φώς is a radiant man, the kind of man who is illuminated by the goddess.

## Ἄνθρωπος

Ἄνθρωπος refers to human beings in general. The "Way" to Being is separated from the road of men (1), that is, from the beaten track (2). The word ἄνθρωπος is frequently found before Parmenides' time in Heraclitus, where it refers either to

[1] Βρότειος is the adjective used to designate the mortality of mankind (8.51).

an ignorant man or to men in general. When they are criticized, the ἄνθρωποι in Heraclitus are designated as the multitude (οἱ πολλοί).

In Parmenides, ἄνθρωποι are not criticized. When he wishes to evoke a pejorative connotation, Parmenides uses the word βροτοί. The ἄνθρωπος-man is the man who perceives and knows (16) and is the name-giver (19). He is the man who dedicates himself to everyday needs, who does not care about the eternal things that constitute Being as a divine being, and who gives names only to the sensible realities inside the cosmos (19.3: "To them men have assigned a name, peculiar to <and distinctive of> each <and every> one" [trans.: O' Brien]).

## Βροτοί

On the other hand, mortals (βροτοί) are defined in Parmenides with reference to the ways leading to the immortal divinity: the goddesses (θεαί), children of the sun (1.9, 24); Justice with its keys (1.14); the speaking Goddess (θεά) (1.22); the divinity (δαίμων) (1.3). Βροτοί are men who think but who are ignorant of the true Way, which is illuminated by immortal divinities and by the immortal Word-Goddess. Does βροτοί, then, designate the multitude of men? Certainly not. It designates only some mortals. Which ones? Those among mortals whose judgments (δόξαι) concerning the double Way of knowledge (the way of Being and the way of knowledge of the cosmos) are insufficiently grounded. Βροτοί are not all mortals, but some "mortal thinkers." And who are these thinkers? Some poets and philosophers.

Why is it certain that βροτοί cannot mean men in general? Because in the passages where Parmenides mentions them, it is not banal opinions that are at stake, but a highly elaborated doctrine.

Therefore, there are in Parmenides three distinct aspects of mortal man: the wise man (φώς), man as a mortal living being (ἄνθρωπος), and men as mortal thinkers whose knowledge is erroneous (βροτοί).

## The Homeric starting-point: the relationship between mortal men and Gods

In Homer, βροτός is employed alternatively in the singular and in the plural. The word frequently designates a heroic mortal man related to a divinity, and less often a human hero confronted by other human heroes. A βροτός is not a thinker, but he is a human mortal being insofar as he is related to some immortal God. The opposite adjectives ἄμβροτος and ἀμβρόσιος (cf. ambrosia) are used only as adjectives to qualify the immortal Gods, the θεοί.

*Βροτός in the singular.* One may read in *Iliad* II, 821: "Aeneas, whom the divine Aphrodite conceived from Anchises, a goddess couched to a mortal man (θεὰ βροτῷ)." It is true that βροτός may sometimes refer to all mortals as opposed to Gods, but in many cases βροτός refers to a singular mortal hero and not to all mortals; thus one may read, in XXIV, 565 (Achilles to Priam): "Some god led you to the ships of the Achaeans. For no mortal man (βροτός) would dare to come into our camp."

*Βροτός in the plural.* One may read in *Iliad* XXIV, 67: "Hector too was dearest to the gods of all mortals (φίλτατος . . . βροτῶν)." One may also read in XXIV, 464: "It would cause anger that an immortal god should thus openly be entertained by mortals (βροτούς)." And again, in *Odyssey* II, 216: "I may ask any mortal man (βροτῶν), or I may hear a rumour from Zeus." Or in *Odyssey* IV, 78: "With Zeus no mortal man (βροτῶν . . . τις) may compare himself."

In Homer, when βροτοί designates the whole of mankind without any reference to the Gods, "mortals" is in almost every case associated with "all" (πάντες βροτοί).

Thus, in *Odyssey* VIII, 487 (Odysseus): "Demodocos, truly above all mortal men (βροτῶν . . . ἁπάντων), do I praise you." Another example is *Odyssey* XI, 216–218 (Anticleia to Odysseus): "Alas, my son, ill-fated above all mortal men (πάντων . . . φωτῶν)." And similarly in XI, 287: "Noble Pero, a wonder to all mortal men (θαῦμα βροτοῖσι) sought in marriage by all (πάντες) her neighbours."

Hence, it is clear that, when the word βροτοί refers to the whole of mankind, it is accompanied by πάντες. Otherwise, βροτοί in Homer implies a relationship between one living mortal human hero and one immortal divine being. The βροτοί are not living beings insofar as they are subject to death (to designate them, Homer uses ἄνθρωπος or θνητός), but mortal heroes insofar as they are opposed to divine beings. The same kind of relationship between individual mortals and immortal Gods is found in Parmenides, but applied to such and such a mortal thinker.

## An erroneous interpretation of the opinions of the mortals: D. O'Brien, *Parménide*, I, 147–151

As a result of the previous considerations, the interpretation endorsed by D. O'Brien appears to be partial—in both senses of the word.[2] O'Brien writes: "Comment *les* mortels en sont-ils venus à affirmer l'existence des non-êtres" ("How mortals finally asserted the existence of non-beings") (6.1)? According to him, "this is due to the fact that they have been abused by their senses, which make them believe in birth and death" ("c'est parce qu'ils ont été abusés par les sens qui leur font croire à la naissance et à la mort"). He quotes fragment 8.38–41: "<They> will therefore be <no more than a> name—all <things> so ever that mortals, convinced they were true, laid down as coming into being and passing away, as being and not <being>, and as changing place and as altering <their> bright color" (p. 147). Later, referring to the "conviction of the mortals," O'Brien adds, "they believe that the objects they perceive through their senses come to be and disappear; they believe that the objects of sense-perception both are and are not" ("ils croient que les objets qu'ils perçoivent par les sens viennent au jour et disparaissent; ils croient que les objets perçus par les sens sont et ne sont pas," pp. 148–149).

However, when Parmenides speaks of mortals, contrary to what O'Brien maintains, he never refers to the multitude of mortals. His mortals talk about non-beings, not-Being and Being. Therefore, when Parmenides criticizes "mortals," he criticizes solely those among mortals who maintain elaborate but unsustainable doctrines.

[2] *Études sur Parménide* (Paris: Vrin, 1987), p. 147–151.

Furthermore—and this is something omitted by O'Brien—these mortals are mistaken in more areas than just the ontological issues related to Being, not-Being and not-beings. Parmenides' "mortals," namely, those mortals who are "mortal thinkers," are mistaken about the structure of the cosmos, as may be seen at the end of fragment 8 and in fragments 9 to 19 of the *Poem.*

Moreover, when some of those mortal thinkers are mistaken in other matters than the dual structure of the cosmos (light and night, 8.51ff.), their mistake does not consist of using sense-perception, namely in exercising "an aimless eye, an echoing ear and tongue." On the contrary, from fragment 9 to fragment 19, Parmenides examines the genesis and structure of the cosmos with the help of sense-perception coupled with reason. Parmenides vigorously rejects in fragment 7 the use of sense-perception to grasp the nature of the principle. The rules contained in verses 1 to 5 of fragment 7, pertain solely to the erroneous use of sense-perception when the knowledge of Being is at stake.

## The βροτοί and their erroneous thoughts about the order of the cosmos: Fragment 8.53–61

According to this passage of Parmenides, the βροτοί are mistaken concerning the organization of the cosmos. To point out this mistake, Parmenides uses two significant words that both refer to a highly elaborate thought, γνώμη and κρίσις. Therefore, we have to criticize some translators who have not given sufficient attention to Parmenides' vocabulary.

## Γνώμη

In the description of the erroneous thoughts of the mortals, Parmenides twice uses the keyword γνώμη (8.53; 8.61), but this word is often mistranslated or misunderstood by translators.

O'Brien's translation of 8.53 is the following: "For <mortals> have set their minds (γνώμη) on naming two forms" ("Les mortels ont pris la décision (γνώμη) de nommer deux formes"); M. Conche translates: "Les mortels ont jugé bon (γνώμη) de nommer deux formes"; B. Cassin translates: "Ils ont pris le parti (γνώμη) de nommer deux formes." J. Bollack is the only French translator who translates γνώμη, but he rephrases the construction of the sentence and wrongly introduces the word "principle": "Ils ont posé des formes, pour donner nom à deux principes (γνώμη)."[3]

One can find attempts to translate γνώμη in 8.61, but these attempts are approximate. Thus, M. Conche: "Afin qu'aucune sagesse de mortels (βροτῶν γνώμη) ne l'emporte sur toi"; B. Cassin: "Afin qu'aucun jugement de mortels ne te dépasse."[4]

However, in all these passages, γνώμη refers to a philosophical doctrine. This erroneous doctrine consists of a dualist and separatist conception of the structure of the cosmos. To this, Parmenides opposes his mono-dualist conception of cosmos: two great Bodies or Forms (δέμας, μορφαί) that are inseparable. Therefore, γνώμη is an illusory doctrine that is opposed to Parmenides' own γνώμη, which relies on rational foundations.

## Κρίσις

Mortal thinkers asserted erroneous "doctrines"; their "judgments" (κρίσις) are no less mistaken (8.55). Therefore, the Goddess urges them to express a different "judgment" (7.5; 8.16).

The authors of these erroneous doctrines and judgments that are reported or outlined in Heraclitus are some "mortal thinkers." These doctrines and judgments are highly elaborated, so they have nothing to do with the vagueness of the instable imagination of the multitude reacting to the multiplicity of sensible bodies. The multitude is radically far from being familiar with the precision that is distinctive of this kind of thought. Such elaborate doctrines belong solely to those mortal thinkers who are partially enlightened by reason but who are not illuminated by the Goddess's Speech, which refers to some likely Truth enabling us to grasp the structure of the cosmos (διάκοσμος, 8.60).

Who, among the multitude of human beings, ever thought the structure of the cosmos as built upon the opposition of Light and Night? Noboby; that can be said for sure. When some mortal

[3] D. O'Brien, ibid., pp. 44; M. Conche, *Parménide* (Paris: Presses Universitaires de France, 1996), p. 187; B. Cassin, *Parménide* (Paris: Seuil, 1998), p. 89; J. Bollack, *Parménide* (Paris: Verdier, 2006), p. 208.

[4] M. Conche, ibid., p. 188; B. Cassin, ibid., p. 91.

men refer to Night and Light as two separate entities, they display the insufficient knowledge of some mortal thinkers. This partial knowledge is reasonably practicable and may be completely transformed into a certain knowledge, asserted by the Goddess and legitimized by her as a true Likeness. Parmenides contrasts these illusory doctrines with the physical doctrine of mixture (κρᾶσις), as the union of Night and Light juxtaposed to each other.

To whom does Parmenides refer in his analysis of cosmic principles? On the one hand, when he mentions Fire and Night as the first principles, he alludes to the Pythagoreans, and on the other hand, when he mentions Primitive Night, he alludes to Hesiod and Orphic thinkers. When he describes the attributes of cosmic principles, Parmenides employs the vocabulary used by some poets and philosophers. Such is the case of ἤπιος (gentle), which is frequently used by Homer, with its double meaning, both ethical ("favorable," "kind") and physical ("soothing," "assuaging"), as in *Iliad*, IV, 218; XI, 515; XXIV, 770. Such is also the case with ἀραιός—"thin" (*Iliad* V, 425) or "narrow" (Hesiod, *Works and Days*, 807; Anaximenes, 95, 5)—ἐλαφρός ("light," "easy to bear," *Iliad* XXII, 287).

When, in verse 61, Parmenides mentions these mortals who may never surpass him, he does not speak of the opinions produced by the imagination of individuals belonging to the multitude. He refers solely to the doctrine and elaborate thought of a particular thinker, philosopher or poet. He is reacting to some conceptions—either fully elaborated or even just roughly sketched out—about the structure of the cosmos, but he does not refer to the opinion of the multitude. Therefore, one should not translate βροτοί as "mortals," but as "some mortals."

## The erroneous thought of the βροτοί about not-Being and not-beings in the cosmos: Fragment 6

6.2–3: "While it is not possible for <what is> nothing (μηδέν) <to be>. These <things> I command you to turn over in your mind."

6.4–5: "and then next from the <way> which *some* mortals fabricate, knowing nothing (βροτοὶ εἰδότες οὐδέν), double headed."

6.5–9: "For helplessness guides in their hearts and mind astray, as they are carried along, unhearing and no less unseeing <all> agape, hordes incapable of discernment, by whom the fact of being and not to be are reckoned as the same—and not the same; of all these <these people> the path is one that turns back upon itself."

Two unacceptable conceptions are juxtaposed here. Neither of them is either a possible logical conception or a popular thought widespread among ordinary people. These are two precise philosophical theses that have been maintained and expressed by "the mortal thinkers," not by *all* the mortals. In addition, it is worth noting that these two theses do not apply to the same realm of reality.

The first thesis is that the existence of what is nothing is impossible. This prefigures what is found in fragment 8.7–9: "For what origin will you look for of it? Where would it have increased to? Where <would it have increased> from? I shall not let you think that <it comes> out of not-being; for it cannot be said, not thought, that 'is not.'" In fact, this is a criticism of Hesiod's primordial Chaos. "First of all Chasm (Χάος) came to be; and then broad-breasted Earth . . ." (*Theogony* 116–117). Not-Being in Parmenides is not not-being in a logical sense. It is a primitive Not-Being, a real Nothingness, so to speak, out of which God and Cosmos come to existence. This first critic, encapsulated in fragment 6.1–2, aims at the Hesiodic myth of the existence of Nothingness, out of which the first divinity is supposed to emerge.

The second thesis (Fragment 6.4ff.) concerns the beings of the cosmos for which "the fact of being" and "not being" are thought to be "the same" and "not the same." Here Parmenides refers to the moving realities of the sensible world as described by Heraclitus. It is not possible for "not being" to be associated with "being" in the realm of changing realities (τὰ πάντα, from 9 to 19).

It follows that, in 6.7, the ἄκριτα φῦλα are not "hordes incapable of discernment" but the "races" such as the race of the Heracliteans, who misconceived the cosmos. What is at stake here is not primitive Not-Being, but not-beings located inside the cosmos. One may refer to Heraclitus (49a, DK): "We enter and we do not enter into the same river. We are (εἶμεν) and we are not (οὐκ εἶμεν)." The "double headed" (δίκρανοι, 6.5) creatures, "knowing nothing" (εἰδότες οὐδέν, 6.4), "unhearing and no less unseeing" (6.7), who are mauled by Parmenides are not, contrary to what was the case in verses 1–2, thinkers who entertain erroneous beliefs about the origins, but thinkers who entertain erroneous beliefs about the structure of the cosmos, since the cosmos may contain solely beings, and not non-beings. In this context, Parmenides objects to the Heraclitean doctrines relating to the cosmos, and not to the "hordes" who ignore such distinctions.

## The βροτοί and their erroneous use of the verbs "to come into being" and "to pass away": Fragment 8.38–40

"Concerning Being (τῷ), they will therefore be <mere> names, all things that some mortals suppose to be true: things coming into being and passing away."

My translation differs radically from traditional translations, for traditional translations do not grasp that here Parmenides is not at all criticizing perceptive knowledge as such. Parmenides solely maintains that perceptive knowledge is not apt to grasp what is Being. Moreover, these verses (8.38–39) reassess the criticism of sense-perception contained in fragment 7, which consists not of a general criticism of sense-perception but of its use in any attempt at grasping Being: "For never shall this <wild saying> be tamed, <namely> that things that are not, are; but do you turn away your thought from this way of inquiry. Let not habit, <too> full of experiences, drag you along this way <and force you> to exercise an aimless eye, an echoing ear and tongue; but judge by reason (λόγος) the refutation that has been uttered by me, <a refutation> arousing much controversy" (7.1–5).

Contrary to the opinion of many readers of Parmenides, he does not deny that one could use sense-perception when one tries to gain knowledge of the cosmos. To exercise a lucid eye and an echoing ear and tongue is an indispensable starting-point, when the knowledge of the cosmos is at stake. However, if one tries to grasp what Being is, using such a method is completely foolish. Therefore, sense-perception is to be rejected solely when one tries to ascend to the knowledge of Being.

Consequently, it is erroneous to translate 8.38–39, the way Denis O'Brien does: "<They> will therefore be <no more than a> name, all things so ever that mortals, convinced they were true, laid down as coming into being and passing away, as being and not <being>, and as changing place and altering <their> bright color."

According to Parmenides, many things "come into being," many things remain and "are" for the time being (fragments 9–19). However, Being itself does not come into being, does not change, has no color, does not move around. According to Parmenides, "birth" and "temporal existence" are key notions to grasp the nature of the cosmos. Thus 10.6–7: "You will know too the heaven that holds <them> round about: where it grew from (ἔνθεν ἔφυ)"; 11.1, 2: "[You will know] how were impelled to come into being (ὡρμήθησαν γίγνεσθαι) earth and sun and moon, aether common <to all>"; 19.1, 2: "That then, I tell you, is how these things were born to be (ἔφυ), and now are (νῦν ἔασι), and shall from this <time> onwards grow and perish." Thus, for Parmenides, "coming into being" and "perishing" are essential to the understanding of the nature of the cosmos. On the other hand, in order to grasp Being in its everlasting being and in the sphericity of its being, such concepts are misplaced. Who, precisely, are the thinkers who have used such concepts in order to grasp the divine principle of the cosmos?

Parmenides aims at traditional theology as his target. The engendered gods of Hesiod's *Theogony* fall victim to the criticism of Parmenidean rationalism, and such is also the case of the glistening multiplicity of Homeric gods and their endless courses. It is when ontology is at stake, and only in that case, that being born, moving from one place to another, having shining colors—all of which are godly attributes in mythology and in philosophical poetry—should be banned. In fact, Hesiod is attacked, for instance in *Theogony* 116–127: "In truth, first of all Chasm, and then broad-breasted Earth [. . .] and Eros. [. . .] From Chasm, Erebos and Black Night came to be; and then Aether and Day came forth from Night, who conceived and bore them after mingling in love with Erebos. Earth first of all bore starry Sky, equal to herself . . ." (Most transl.)

## The βροτοί and their illusions: Fragment 1.28–32

1.28–30: "You must hear about all things, both the still heart of persuasive truth and the opinions of mortals, in which there is no true conviction (πίστις ἀληθής)." 1.31–32: "But even so, these things too you shall learn: how the things that appear would have to have real existence."

Parmenides here is mapping the inquiries to appear in the course of the *Poem* during the progression of his critiques of mortal thinkers. After a brief assessment of Parmenides' own thesis about Being, which anticipates the content of fragment 8, comes the necessity of studying and rebuking mistakes—not the mistakes of the multitude, since that would be a very strange study, but the mistakes of philosophers and poets among mortals: the γνώμη of mortal thinkers misunderstands what is Being (29–30), and what is cosmos as well (31–32). In this proem, the hordes of mortals are not involved, no more than they are in any other passage of the *Poem*. Several great thinkers, though unnamed, are virulently criticized: Hesiod and Heraclitus above all.

Translated by Jean-Baptiste Gourinat

# Parricide or Heir? Plato's Uncertain Relationship to Parmenides

Arnold Hermann

## Summary

Most scholars view Plato's critique of Parmenides in the *Sophist*, particularly the observations surrounding the "parricide" remark, as quite apt and justified. The theory is that Parmenides deserves to be rebuked for failing to recognize that "What Is Not" can be understood in more ways than one, namely, not only in an existential sense, but also predicatively or, in the language of the *Sophist*, as indicating "difference." I aim to show, nevertheless, that Plato's indictment of Parmenides misses the mark in significant ways, allowing Parmenides to escape the so-called threat of parricide not once but twice.

For example, Parmenides' abundant use of *alpha*-privatives (e.g., ἀγένητον)—as well as the negative οὐ (or οὐκ) when there is no *a*-privative form available—indicates that he was well aware of the difference between indicating "is not" predicatively versus existentially. Moreover, the Poem nowhere suggests that his strictures regarding the use of What Is Not are to be taken in the broadest possible sense, disallowing, in effect, the discrimination between the existential and the predicative case. Only when sought after as a "way of inquiry" does What Is Not—in contrast to the Way of What Is—fail to provide us with a graspable, expressible object. After all, the "Way of What Is Not," lacks any sort of *sēmata*, or signs, that can be used to navigate it. As a "way of inquiry for thinking" (B2), it leads nowhere, lacking any sort of expressible or knowable object or goal. The complete absence of an object or result, however, does not hinder us from making statements to this effect, nor from uttering the words "What Is Not" or "Not Being." Yet this fine distinction is lost to many who have criticized Parmenides for being inconsistent, careless, or simply ignorant. The move from the intellectual unavailability of an object that marks a defunct way of inquiry, to the claim that to even speak of such a "way" is both illegitimate and impossible—all the while insisting that Parmenides himself is to be blamed for such a monstrous fallacy—seems an egregious gloss-over, even if the perpetrator is someone of Plato's stature. If my arguments prove sound, then Parmenides should be absolved of the charges leveled against him.

---

Was Plato a supporter of Parmenides of Elea, or an opponent? Considering that he seems to view Parmenides as a "father" of sorts, perhaps the more appropriate question should be: was Plato a "prodigal son" as opposed to a faithful one, and if he was indeed prodigal, did he maintain his opposition, unwavering, even throughout the "Eleatic" dialogues? Is this the message we should glean from the figurative parricide alluded to in Plato's *Sophist* dialogue?[1] Arguably, the question—like many others deriving from Plato's often opaque stance on the Eleatics—is not easily resolved. Its solution depends largely on a scholar's personal interpretation of the available text. Nonetheless, I shall attempt here a somewhat atypical approach, a comparison of positions and methods that, hopefully, will shed some further light on Plato's relationship to Parmenides.

Let us grant for the sake of argument that Plato aimed to refute Parmenides in the *Sophist,* particularly the Eleatic's claims regarding the unintelligibility and inexpressibility of Not-Being[2]—an act that, as Plato also suggests, might be construed as "trying to kill one's father." If we accept the above as true, we then must ask whether Plato succeeded at this. Did he actually refute Parmenides?

To tackle this question effectively, we also need to ask whether he had sufficient grounds or motives for such an act; in other words, was parricide justified? First, we must determine whether Parmenides' actual position on Not-Being deserved to be repudiated by Plato; secondly, we will want to ask whether Plato reproduced Parmenides' position accurately in the *Sophist.*[3] To date, mainstream scholarship has provided largely affirmative

[1] Plato, *Sophist*, 241d.
[2] Cf. Parmenides, B2.6–8, 6.1–2, 7.1–2, 8. 15ff.
[3] We must also include the *Parmenides* in our considerations.

answers to these questions, in so far as it has claimed that Plato uncovered a major error or inconsistency in Parmenides, to which he supplied the necessary correction.[4] My aim here is to dispute these claims. It is also my position that only when these matters are sufficiently clarified can we even attempt to tackle the underlying issue, that is, did Plato really *intend* to commit the alleged parricide? Or did his scheme serve a different purpose?

First, we should restate the charges advanced against Parmenides in the *Sophist,* and determine why the subject of parricide became an issue at all. In this particular dialogue, we find Plato pursuing a rather unusual form of philosophical investigation: he is embarking on a hunt. The quarry, or prospective prey, is the (generic) Sophist—an adherent of the likes of Protagoras or Gorgias, we may assume—a "many-headed" deceiver of the public, as Plato has it, who masks his falsehoods with misleading arguments. The Sophist's ruse, as we are told, is largely founded on a distortion of Parmenides' warnings that "What Is Not cannot be thought or spoken" and that "one should turn away from such a way of inquiry" (B2; 7.1–2). Plato describes how the Sophist recasts Parmenides' statements in such a way that to claim that falsehoods are possible is tantamount to asserting that "What Is Not" exists. Even to bring up the subject of "What Is Not"—if only to deny its existence—is to call it a singular concept or thing, meaning we treat it as a "something" that *is.* This, of course, would be a direct violation of Parmenides' injunction against thinking or expressing "What Is Not." The slippery Sophist manages to protect himself from being exposed by retaliating with the following conundrum: "Is a false image the image of something that *is,* or of something that *is not*?" And, if we are forced to concede that a false image is a depiction of "what is not," the Sophist will triumphantly exclaim, "Gotcha!" and immediately accuse us of transgressing

4 Cf. Guthrie, *A History of Greek Philosophy* V, 56, 123, 135–36; Scolnicov, *Plato's* Parmenides, 8. However, Palmer argues that the *Sophist* aims to defend Parmenides against attempts by the Sophists to misuse his ideas (*Plato's Reception of Parmenides,* 16).

against Parmenides[5] ("you cannot know that which Is Not [*ouk estin*], nor can you express it," B2.7–8).[6]

It appears that the only way to counter the machinations of the devious Sophist was by means of a drastic, if not desperate, maneuver: Plato had to "slay" his philosophical "father" Parmenides by disproving his claims. Only in this way could he deprive the Sophist of his favorite hiding place, the Eleatic's teaching on Not-Being.[7] I quote here what amounts to a slightly abbreviated version of Plato's strategy (both the enigmatic figure of the Eleatic Stranger and Theaetetus are the dialogue's protagonists). We join the dialogue at a point where the elusiveness of the Sophist is being debated:

> THEAETETUS: If so, then it seems it would be impossible to catch him.
> STRANGER: What, then? Are we going to go soft and give up?
> THEAETETUS: I say we shouldn't, if there's even the smallest chance that we can catch him.
> STRANGER: Then I've got something even more urgent to request.
> THEAETETUS: What?
> STRANGER: Not to think that I'm turning into some kind of parricide.
> THEAETETUS: What do you mean?
> STRANGER: In order to defend ourselves, we're going to have to subject father Parmenides' saying to further examination, and insist by brute force both that *that which is not* somehow is, and then again that *that which is* somehow is not.
> THEAETETUS: It does seem that in what we're going to say, we'll to [*sic*] have to fight through that issue.
> STRANGER: That's obvious even to a blind man, as they say. We'll never be able to avoid having to make

[5] *Sophist*, 236e–239c, 240d–241b, 261a–b.

[6] See *Sophist*, 237a and 258d, which reproduces Parmenides, B7.1–2 (with slight textual differences).

[7] *Sophist*, 254a.

> ourselves ridiculous by saying conflicting things whenever we talk about false statements and beliefs, either as copies or likeness or imitations or appearances, or about whatever sorts of expertise there are concerning those things—unless, that is, we either refute Parmenides' claims or else agree to accept them.
> THEAETETUS: That is true.
> STRANGER: So that's why we have to be bold enough to attack what our father says. Or, if fear keeps us from doing that, then we'll have to leave it alone completely.[8]

Subsequently, and only after a variety of related issues are discussed, Plato achieves what is conventionally considered a significant breakthrough: The notion of the so-called *interweaving of Forms,* which clarifies how one concept can participate in a multitude of Forms, even opposing ones, at the same time.[9] Among these Forms we should also distinguish a particularly important one, namely the Form of Difference. It is subsequently raised to the level of a "Master Form."[10] Now a thing can be said *to be* in an existential fashion, and, at the same time be said *not to be* some other thing in character. In this way the Sophist cannot accuse us of illegitimately verbalizing "Is Not" and thereby attempting to do the impossible. A cat can both exist and *not be* black. It both "is" something and "is not" something at the same time.[11] Hence, as the dialogue contends, Parmenides has been proven wrong and the Sophist is finally caught.[12] This, at least, is the conventional interpretation of the narrative.

But I have put forth only a crude version of the prevailing theory. I quote here a key passage (in redacted form) from W. K. C. Guthrie's *A History of Greek Philosophy* V. He offers, in my view, a most apt representation of the mainline thinking on the issue:

[8] *Sophist*, 241c–e. Translation White, *Plato Complete Works*, ed. Cooper.
[9] *Sophist*, 250eff., 253a, 254c, 259a, e.
[10] *Sophist*, 254c–255e.
[11] *Sophist*, 258b–c, 259a–b.
[12] *Sophist*, 261a, 268c.

> Perhaps the great contribution of the *Sophist* to philosophy lies in the statements that I have italicized, that a word can be used in more than one sense:
>
> > "We can say Motion is both the same and not the same because *we are not using the word in the same sense in both cases*" (256a11).[13]
>
> The whole challenge of Parmenides, and many of the arguments of Sophistic, rested on the assumption that the verb "to be" meant one thing and one thing only. Once it had been shown that the same word was not always used to express the same concept—that for instance existence, identity and attribution were not the same, though expressed by the same word "is"—Greek thought was freed from a whole host of unreal problems.
>
> By noting the all-pervading nature of Difference Plato has been able to maintain against Parmenides that what is not really *is,* though contrasted with what also is, as the non-Beautiful is contrasted with the Beautiful but exists no less than it (258d–e). Non-being need not mean absolute non-existence, but simply Difference in relation to *x* . . . "And this is the non-being which our concern with the Sophist led us to seek" (258b6). When we accuse him of creating misleading copies that "are not" the originals, we only mean that they differ from them.[14]

Perhaps the Sophist got caught in Plato's web, but what about Parmenides? Technically, to be "killed" by Plato, the Eleatic would first have to be caught in that very same trap—even if he were innocent of the misdeeds of the Sophist, and merely ignorant of the many uses of "Is Not" (existential, predicative, etc.). The critical question here is this: was Parmenides, in actual fact, as unaware of the critical issues as Plato wanted him to be?

---

[13] This particular passage occurs earlier in Guthrie's text (he is here referring back to it). I have moved it to this position to provide the necessary context.
[14] Guthrie, *HGP* V, 152–154.

For my part, I think not. In fact, I believe that there is more than one way for Parmenides to evade both the trap *and* the parricide.[15]

## The First Escape

The Premise:

*Parmenides holds* ouk estin (*"is not"*) *to be both inexpressible and unthinkable.*

The Charge:

(a) *Whenever "Not-Being" and "Is Not" are used in the Poem, they are used strictly in an existential sense.*
(b) *Parmenides does not realize he is transgressing his own rule regarding inexpressibility whenever he employs the terms "Not-Being" and "Is Not."*

There are two schools of thought on these points: either Parmenides was unaware that "is" and "be," and therefore "is not" and "not be," can be used in more ways than one—that is, not only in a strictly existential sense[16]—or he intentionally avoided making a clear distinction on these issues and thus ignored the difficulties and paradoxes that might ensue and adhered unyieldingly to his rigid scheme (for purposes that still escape us).[17] Yet a straightforward survey of the relevant terms used in his Poem reveals that he did indeed recognize the difference between the predicative and existential use of Is and Is Not. Particularly in regard to the latter—as revealed by the list of key words and locutions below—Parmenides was quite liberal in his use of *alpha* privatives (also referred to as *a*-negatives) in the Poem. These indicate a negative quality or

[15] Cf. Austin, who also attempts to let Parmenides off the hook in ways (more elegant than mine) that complement and indeed even support my first attempt ("Parmenides, Double-Negation, and Dialectic," in *Presocratic Philosophy*, ed. Caston and Graham, 95ff).
[16] E.g., Aristotle, *Metaphysics*, 984a29.
[17] Cf. Furth, "Elements of Eleatic Ontology," in *The Pre-Socratics*, ed. Mourelatos, 241ff. (see, especially, 268–270).

condition.[18] (I have here restricted myself to the word "using" on Parmenides' behalf, as I want to avoid commenting at this point on his level of awareness in such matters. That issue will be addressed later.) As noted, terms with an *a*-prefix can generally mean a loss or absence of a quality or attribute, in much the same way as we use "un-" or "non-" or "in-" or "im-" in English. The privative form is also employed with nouns to indicate a "lack of," an "absence," or simply the negation "not." (For obvious reasons, I have not listed *a*-privative terms occurring in the Doxa. Also included in the list is one example in which *ouk* is used to denote the negative.)

ἀπεόντα = absent/things absent 4.1
ἀμηχανίη = helplessness 6.5
ἄκριτα φῦλα = uncritical hordes 6.7
ἄσκοπον = unseeing 7.4
ἀγένητον = ungenerated 8.3
ἀνώλεθρον = imperishable 8.3
ἀτρεμές = unshakeable 8.4
ἀνόητον = not thinkable 8.17
ἀνώνυμον = unnameable 8.17
ἄπυστος = not heard of 8.21
ἀκίνητον = not moving 8.26; 8.38
ἄναρχον = without beginning 8.27
ἄπαυστον = without end, unceasing 8.27
ἀτελεύτητον = incomplete 8.32
οὐκ ἐπιδευές = not lacking 8.33
ἄσυλον = inviolate 8.48[19]

The Poem offers no indication that Parmenides would judge the use of such terms to be a breach of his own injunction against speaking and thinking "is not." Moreover, to claim that he could only conceive of "is" or "is not" in a strictly

[18] Also noted by Austin, *Parmenides, Being, Bounds, and Logic.*

[19] For a similar listing and a thorough venting of the issues, see Mourelatos, *The Route of Parmenides* (revised edition), under "Determinacy and Indeterminacy," 344–345, and Austin, *Parmenides, Being, Bounds, and Logic*, 44–45; "Parmenides, Double-Negation, and Dialectic," in *Presocratic Philosophy*, 96–97.

existential sense is to say that he was unaware or ignorant of the fact that when the *a*-prefix is added to words indicating attributes—adjectives, to us—it is meant as an indication of the absence of a quality or state.[20] What would Parmenides have thought, for example, of his own use of the term *akinēton*? Did he believe what he was expressing was mere gibberish, or rather "*not* moving"? And why would "*not* moving" be legitimate, but not "*not* being"? In fact, Parmenides had no choice but to use "*not* being" to effect an unbridgeable gap between it and "being," if only to protect the latter from being spoken of in both ways indiscriminately. This, after all, appears to be his main charge against Mortals, "for whom," as he says, "'to be' and 'not to be' are deemed the same and not the same" (B6.8–9). He seems much more vexed by the possibility that Mortals are persuading themselves to call Being both "to be" and "not to be" (B8.39–41), rather than simply going about uttering the phrases "not being" or "is not," arbitrarily.[21]

But there is a larger question here: could a writer possess the necessary skill to frame such a difficult subject as the one dealt with in the Poem—in strenuous hexameter verses, no less—and still be as unaware of non-existential uses of "not," as some have claimed? If the suggestion is that for some reason Parmenides has failed to notice that the *a*-privative denotes "lack of" or "not," we find him in 8.35–36 pairing *ouk* with *heurēseis* ("**not** find"), which has no privative Form preceded by *alpha*; and, in 8.33, we find him using ouk *epideues* for "**not** lacking." These are solid instances of what even Plato seems to have missed: a non-existential use of *ouk* together with a character or property, one that does not immediately force upon us an *existential ouk estin* (or Is Not).

I am aware that Alex Mourelatos and Scott Austin have dealt with the issue of *a*-privatives quite thoroughly in their works on Parmenides, and certainly in greater detail than I am able to in

[20] This is a critical detail in Parmenides' work completely missed by both Plato and Aristotle. (See, e.g., *Sophist*, 256a, also 259c–d; *Physics*, 185a21, 185b6, b19, b30, 186a22ff.; *Metaphysics*, 1028a10, 1089a7ff.)

[21] Again, this major point is missed by Plato and Aristotle, as well as by subsequent scholarship, I am sorry to say.

this limited format.[22] However, unless I have missed something, I have found no discussion in the general literature (commentaries on the *Sophist, Parmenides,* and the like) on what Plato might have made of such predicative use of negatives in Parmenides' Poem. Would the question of parricide still be of import?

In this sense, I find it rather difficult to believe that Parmenides did not know what he was doing, or that he was a careless or sloppy thinker who continued to use negatives even though he made the ban on *all* negative statements the hallmark of his doctrine.[23]

Below are some further examples of the occurrence of "not" in the Poem, used not in the existential sense (i.e., adding *ouk* to a subject not for the purpose of indicating that it does not exist):

> οὕνεκεν οὐκ ἀτελεύτητον τὸ ἐὸν θέμις εἶναι
> because it is not right [or lawful] for What Is to be incomplete (8.32)

> οὐ γὰρ ἄνευ τοῦ ἐόντος, ἐν ᾧ πεφατισμένον ἐστίν, εὑρήσεις τὸ νοεῖν
> For without What IS, in which it is expressed [or revealed], you will not find thinking/knowing (8.35–36, also mentioned above)[24]

> οὔτε γὰρ ἂν γνοίης τό γε μὴ ἐόν (οὐ γὰρ ἀνυστόν)
> for you cannot know that which Is Not (for this cannot be accomplished) (2.7)

And, an example of the existential use:

> ἠδὲ βροτῶν δόξας, ταῖς οὐκ ἔνι πίστις ἀληθής

[22] Mourelatos, *Route*, 333ff; Austin, *Parmenides, Being, Bounds, and Logic*, 11ff, 16–17, 18, 22, and especially 45ff; and "Parmenides, Double-Negation, and Dialectic," 95ff.

[23] Cf. Mourelatos, *Route*, 338–339, on Negative Predication and "Parmenides' predicament." But see Furth's remarks, "Elements of Eleatic Ontology," 268–270; and Owen, "Eleatic Questions," in *Studies in Presocratic Philosophy*, ed. Allen and Furley, 72n44.

[24] Cf. also Austin, *Parmenides, Being, Bounds, and Logic*, 45, 49.

> as well as the opinions of mortals, for which there is
> no true conviction (1.30)

If my observations are correct, we should grant Parmenides this initial escape from parricide. This constitutes ample proof not only that he allowed the use of the negative form (both *ouk* and *a*-privative) when dealing with attributes, but also that he was capable of distinguishing existential from predicative use.[25] Moreover, it is also clear that he did not forbid the use of the existential Is Not indiscriminately, but accepted it where absence, or the impossibility of existence in a specific context, was to be expressed.[26] "True conviction" or "evidence"[27] is obviously incompatible with the "opinions of mortals."

Parmenides may have had something different in mind with his strictures on *ouk estin*, perhaps something not quite as simplistic as the notion mangled by the (generic) Sophist. But he was certainly not as one-sided or naïve as Plato and Aristotle made him out to be.

## The Second Escape

What follows is based in part on some ideas introduced in other papers, as well as in *To Think Like God*. First, I will attempt to explain the function of the *sēmata*, or "signs," in Parmenides' Poem, and show how they serve as proofs.[28] They appear to function as viable indicators—which when taken together, act as proofs—and so allow us to establish a reliable pathway to *estin*, or "What Is." However, this approach, as presented in the first few lines of Fragment 8, appears insufficient. Why would Parmenides have thought to accompany these positive proofs with a challenge or a method of disproof, also known as the

---

[25] Contra Aristotle et al., *Metaphysics*, 984a29. Furth, on the other hand, believes that Parmenides tends to "fuse" the existential with the predicative ("Elements of Eleatic Ontology," 258).

[26] Cf. Cordero: "In Parmenides the negation is the rejection of the statement" (*By Being, It Is*, 75).

[27] Cf. Heitsch, *Parmenides, Die Fragmente*, 13, 29, "evidenter Beweiss." Also Hermann, *To Think Like God*, 156n464 and passim.

[28] Similarly, Cordero, *By Being, It Is*, 168ff.

*elenchus* (7.6)? It seems that, for him, assertions should ideally be juxtaposed against a counterargument.[29] If a statement or claim survives the challenge, we may deem it a Reliable Account (cf. πιστὸν λόγον, B8.50). In short, positive proof must be accompanied by a negative approach, and the latter must be overcome if truth is to be attained. Otherwise, we are dealing with nothing more than *ta dokounta*—popular opinion.[30] Here is a sample of the *sēmata* for what I call the positive route:

> "ungenerated," "imperishable," "whole," "of one kind," "unshakeable" and "complete," "nor was it before," "nor will it be," "since it is now," "all together," "one" and "continuous" (B8.4–6)

What is "whole" is "complete"; what is "complete" is "now, all together"; what is "now, all together" is "one"—and finally, what is "one" is "whole," and the discursive circle is closed. Now, if Parmenides is attacked at any point—whether on account of his use of circular reasoning[31] or his inadvertently introducing "plurality" by assigning *estin* a multitude of *sēmata* (see critique of the "advocates of the many" in the *Parmenides*, 128d)—the Eleatic could easily sidestep the issue by showing that having a multitude of characteristics does not cause the object of inquiry to be more than one thing. Clearly (as B8.38–41 demonstrates), the multitude of names bestowed upon Being by Mortals does not affect it at all.[32] Moreover, the kind of naïve "plurality" appealed to by the young Socrates in the *Parmenides* dialogue—"I am both one and many" (129c)—misses its mark in the Poem. For example, in order to be "one," What Is does not need to be one among several things, in the way that Socrates is one man among

---

[29] Cf. B8.6–10, on generation.

[30] Cf. Parmenides, B1.30–32, especially the contrast between τὰ δοκοῦντα and δοκίμως εἶναι.

[31] See also B5. Cf. Jameson, "Well-Rounded Truth and Circular Thought in Parmenides," *Phronesis* 3 (1958): 15–30; Stannard, "Parmenidean Logic," *The Philosophical Review* 69 (1960): 526–533.

[32] Cf. also Vlastos, "'Names' in Parmenides," in Mourelatos, *Route*, 367–388; Woodbury, "Parmenides on Names," *Harvard Studies in Classical Philology* 63 (1958): 145–160.

seven men (129d). There are no other What Ises. We are not dealing here with the same conceptual dependency as that raised by the *Parmenides* and the *Sophist* dialogues (in respect to the object of inquiry *itself-by-itself*). Without a contrary or a part in the "weaving together" of concepts, what is by itself must remain unthinkable and unnamable.[33]

But Parmenides can also point to a different sort of proof or corroboration, one that employs the *sēmata* cleverly in an evidentiary way, if only to distinguish What Is categorically from What Is Not. This critical distinction, after all, is the one Mortals fail to make, being "hordes without judgment, for whom to be and not to be is the same and not the same" (B6.7–9). The proof is this: whatever is "now, all together, one, and continuous" need never be generated nor must it perish, as there is never a "now" in the absence of all the other *sēmata*. Indeed, we cannot, it seems, attribute one *sēma* to *estin* without taking into account all other *sēmata* that belong to it. That is what makes the Way or the *Method* of What Is so reliable. If only one *sēma* is missing, then it is incomplete; if it is incomplete, it is not *estin*. Instead, it would be *ouk estin*:

> 8.29 Remaining the same in the same it lies by itself
>
> 8.30 and thus fixed in [its] place, for mighty Necessity
>
> 8.31 holds it within the bonds of the limit which encloses it all around,
>
> 8.32 because it is not right [or lawful] for What Is to be incomplete
>
> 8.33 for it is not lacking—but Not-Being would lack everything.

Accordingly, only What Is Not can lack anything. In fact, it lacks everything. What is this everything that it lacks? It must lack precisely those characteristics that would make it thinkable, namable, and speakable, namely the *sēmata*. Indeed, the Poem

[33] *Parmenides*, 142a; *Sophist*, 259e.

forces us to recognize that What Is Not cannot have any sort of *sēmata* whatsoever. In contrast, when Necessity holds What Is "within the bonds of the limit which encloses it all around" (B8.31), it must be that all the *sēmata* are enclosed within this precise limit. What else is there to be held? And obviously, if the bonds of Justice prevent "coming-to-be" and "passing away" (B8.13), it is only because both "generation" and "corruption" are incompatible with the other *sēmata*. To include them would create injustice. Accordingly, not a single legitimate *sēma* can escape, because again, it would not be right or lawful for *estin*, or What Is, to be incomplete (B8.32). If any of them did escape, *estin* would be lacking. But that would go against what it *is*, hence it would be what it *is not*. And as What Is Not, it would lack everything, which of course must mean all *sēmata* (B8.33). So, by losing one, we lose all (B8.11, 8.33).

It is not necessary to detail the *sēmata* of Doxa at this point. It suffices to point to Doxa's dual groupings of *sēmata* to recognize that no matter how contradictory they may seem, they do not yield Not-Being, because again, Not-Being has no *sēmata*. And we see also in B9.4 that "nothing has no share in neither Form of Light and Night." Why? Having just stressed that the Forms have *sēmata* and that the Mortals have allocated all things to them in "accordance to their powers" (B9.2) (which can only mean in accordance with the *sēmata* that the Mortals recognize in them), Parmenides raises the issue of "nothing" (*meden*) if only to exclude it from a cosmology based on Light and Night. Obviously, the latter two have *sēmata;* the former does not. So in the context of the ability to think something or to speak it, it does not matter whether the *sēmata* are homogeneous like *estin*'s or heterogeneous like Doxa's. What matters is whether there is an utter lack of *sēmata*. Only this complete absence of names (hence, characteristics) gives us the unthinkable and unspeakable that Parmenides emphasizes.

Accordingly, the difference between the various approaches must be distinguished as follows, giving us three approaches but only two objects of inquiry:[34]

[34] *Pace* both Cordero and O'Brien.

1. An object whose account consists of homogeneous or non-conflicting *sēmata*
2. An object whose account is made up of a combination of heterogeneous or antonymic *sēmata*
3. And Is Not, which lacks an object, hence, all *sēmata,* and for that reason cannot be an account of anything[35]

In summary, if the Parmenidean What Is Not possesses no *sēmata* whatsoever, it cannot serve as an object of inquiry—not even as an object of thought and speech. Without defining characteristics, there is nothing to be objectified. Therefore, the Parmenidean What Is Not should not be confused with the sort of Not-Being the Sophist was trying to use as a ruse. Much less can it be equated to the Not-Being distinction that Plato recast into a predicative claim based on the Form of Difference. After all, the Parmenidean Is Not is so radically "not there" or "not available" to be thought or expressed that even Mortals, who can get away with all kinds of errors and self-deception, are not actually capable of naming it, even if they desire to do so. What indeed ends up being named by Mortals in this case is nothing other than What Is or *estin,* which they name both "to be" *and* "not to be." Try as they might, Mortals never succeed in assigning any name whatsoever to What Is Not. In Parmenides' words:

> Which is why *it* [*estin*] has been named all things, that mortals have established, persuaded that they are true: "coming-to-be" and "passing-away," "to be" and "not [to be]," "to change place," and "to alter bright color." (8.38–41)

[35] The notion of Is Not as an objectless approach—based on its utter lack of *sēmata* (a significant detail largely ignored by other interpretations)—is a mainstay of my own research into Parmenides' methodology. I have explored the subject in a number of papers, either directly or tangentially; see, for example, "Negative Proof and Circular Reasoning," in Néstor-Luis Cordero et al. *Eleatica 2006: Parmenide scienziato?*, ed. Rossetti and Marcacci; and "Parmenides' Methodology: The Unity of Formula," Symposium Megarense, 2005 (publication forthcoming).

This important statement is part of the so-called Reliable Account, thus there is nothing deceptive about it. The truth is that Mortals can assign a name only to the Is—including contradictory ones—because only it is *available for naming,* while its contrary is not.[36] The Is must be the most tolerant thing there is, particularly if it has no competition. On this account alone (namely, that *it is the Mortals* who are inadvertently plastering the Is with all kinds of designations, including the label "Is Not"—the gist of Parmenides' criticism [cf. B6.8–9]), we must give Parmenides a pass and admit that he has once again escaped. The Eleatic turns out to be a real Houdini.

Are there further ways in which Parmenides can escape from the threat of parricide? Yes, a few, so it seems. And they are largely owing to Plato's lack of consistency in dealing with the Parmenidean object of inquiry. One such example is the *Parmenides* dialogue. In contrast to the *Sophist,* where this object is reproduced as Being in a strictly existential sense, the *Parmenides* presents it as "the One." The latter is a poorly disguised attempt to match the Parmenidean object to Zeno of Elea's alleged endorsement of his teacher's doctrine.[37] Zeno's work, as depicted in this dialogue, is both a defense of Parmenides and an attack on plurality. The Parmenidean object is conveniently recast to signify the contrary of Zeno's target, the One is thus taken as the opposite of the Many. Plato simply selects that particular *sēma* ("one")—which is only referred to once (B.8.6)—to serve exclusively as the opposite of "the Many," and the myth of Parmenidean Monism is born. Yet, the Poem repeatedly posits only What Is Not as the contrary to What Is (cf. 8.16, as the most celebrated example); it never equates Not-Being with "the Many," or with plurality. How could this be, if Not-Being lacks all *sēmata?* Regrettably, Plato overlooks these details when they

[36] Both Woodbury and Vlastos come close to this realization. However, while they allow the Is "to be named all things" because it is *all* that *is,* they miss Is Not's utter lack of *sēmata,* which reinforces the fact that it is unthinkable and unspeakable. Plus, Woodbury equates What Is with the name of the world, a read that has become untenable. (See Woodbury, "Parmenides on Names," *Harvard Studies in Classical Philology,* Vol. LXIII [1958], 145–160, particularly 153, 156; Vlastos, "'Names' in Parmenides," 367–388.)

[37] Plato, *Parmenides,* 128c–d.

are at odds with his prevailing strategy. Thus, in the *Sophist* (if, in fact, it was written after the *Parmenides*), when Plato shifts positions, it is only because he needs What Is to be read existentially. "Why here?" one may ask. Because Plato's fictional Sophist *takes it that way*—as, apparently, do those who are fooled by him. Still, the question of whether anyone was in actual fact misusing Parmenides' teachings precisely in the way portrayed by the *Sophist* remains largely unresolved.[38] In the end, the whole scheme—in tandem with the perilous scent of "parricide"—may have been nothing more than an effective plot device.

[38] Guthrie mentions Protagoras and Antisthenes as advocates of the impossibility of speaking falsely, linking their "thesis" to Parmenides, B2.7–8 (*HGP* III, 218), but the association is Guthrie's own. Aristotle, for example, who had ample motive and opportunity to criticize Antisthenes and his followers (*Topics*, 104b21; *Metaphysics*, 1024b33, 1043b23), fails to make a similar link between Antisthenes and Parmenides. Whether it was Euthydemus or Dionysodorus, as also argued by Guthrie (*HGP* IV, 135), remains just as inconclusive. Aristotle attributes a different type of fallacious argument to Euthydemus (*Sophistical Refutations*, 177b12; *Rhetoric*, 1401a27). But above all, it is not easy to comprehend why lightweights like Euthydemus and Dionysodorus would pose such a tremendous threat to Plato that he would be willing to sacrifice "father" Parmenides in order to defeat them.

## Bibliography

Austin, Scott. *Parmenides: Being, Bounds, and Logic.* New Haven: Yale University Press, 1986.

_____. "Parmenides, Double-Negation, and Dialectic." In V. Caston and D. Graham, eds., *Presocratic Philosophy: Essays in Honour of Alexander P. D. Mourelatos* (pp. 95–99). Aldershot: Ashgate, 2002:

Cooper, John M., ed. *Plato Complete Works.* Indianapolis: Hackett Publishing Company, 1997.

Cordero, Néstor-Luis. *By Being, It Is: The Thesis of Parmenides.* Las Vegas: Parmenides Publishing, 2004.

Diels, Hermann. *Parmenides Lehrgedicht.* Berlin: G. Reimer, 1897; 2nd edition, Sankt Augustin: Academia Verlag, 2003.

Furth, Montgomery. "Elements of Eleatic Ontology." *Journal of the History of Philosophy* 6 (1968): 111–132. Reprinted in Alexander P. D. Mourelatos, ed., *The Presocratics: A Collection of Critical Essays.* Garden City, NY: Anchor Press, 1974. Reprinted, Princeton: Princeton University Press, 1993.

Guthrie, W. K. C. *A History of Greek Philosophy*, Vols. III, IV, V. Cambridge: Cambridge University Press, Vol. III, 1969; Vol. IV, 1986: Vol. V, 1986.

Heitsch, Ernst. *Parmenides: Die Fragmente.* Munich: Heimeran, 1974. 3rd ed. Zurich: Artemis & Winkler, 1995.

Hermann, Arnold. *To Think Like God: Pythagoras and Parmenides. The Origins of Philosophy.* Las Vegas: Parmenides Publishing, 2004.

_____. "Parmenides' Methodology: The Unity of Formula." Proceedings of the Symposium Megarense, 2005 (publication forthcoming).

_____. "Negative Proof and Circular Reasoning." In Néstor-Luis Cordero et al. *Eleatica 2006: Parmenide scienziato?* Edited by Livio Rossetti and Flavia Marcacci. Sankt Augustin: Academia Verlag, 2008: 103–112.

_____. *Plato's* Parmenides*: Text, Translation & Introductory Essay.* Translation in collaboration with Sylvana Chrysakopoulou. Foreword by Douglas Hedley. Las Vegas: Parmenides Publishing, 2010.

Jameson, G. "'Well-rounded Truth' and Circular Thought in Parmenides." *Phronesis* 3 (1958): 15–30.

Mourelatos, Alexander P. D. *The Route of Parmenides.* Revised and Expanded Edition, with a new introduction, three supplemental essays, and an essay by Gregory Vlastos. Las Vegas: Parmenides Publishing, 2008.

O'Brien, Denis. "The Poem of Parmenides." In *Le Poème de Parménide: Texte, Traduction, Essay Critique. Études sur Parménide* (sous la direction de Pierre Aubenque) Vol. 1. Paris: Librairie Philosophique J. Vrin, 1987.

Owen, G. E. L. "Eleatic Questions." *Classical Quarterly* 10 (1960): 84–102. Reprinted in R. E. Allen and David J. Furley, eds., *Studies in Presocratic Philosophy, Vol. 2: Eleatics and Pluralists* (pp. 48–81). London: Routledge & Kegan Paul, 1975.

Reale, Giovanni, and Luigi Ruggiu. *Parmenide: Poema sulla natura: I frammenti e le testimonianze indirette.* Presentazione, traduzione con testo greco a fronte dei frammenti del poema e note di Giovanni Reale. Saggio introduttivo e Commentario filosofico di Luigi Ruggiu. Milano: Bompiani, 2003.

Reinhardt, Karl. "The Relation between the Two Parts of Parmenides' Poem." In Alexander P. D. Mourelatos, ed., *The Presocratics: A Collection of Critical Essays*. Garden City, NY: Anchor Press, 1974 (pp. 293–311). Reprinted, Princeton: Princeton University Press, 1993.

Scolnicov, Samuel. *Plato's* Parmenides. Berkeley, CA: University of California Press, 2003.

Stannard, Jerry. "Parmenidean Logic." *The Philosophical Review* 69 (1960): 526–533.

Tarán, Leonardo. *Parmenides: A Text with Translation, Commentary and Critical Essays*. Princeton: Princeton University Press, 1965.

Vlastos, Gregory. "Names of Being in Parmenides." In Alexander P. D. Mourelatos. *The Route of Parmenides*: 367–390.

Woodbury, Leonard. "Parmenides on Names." *Harvard Studies in Classical Philology* 63 (1958): 145–169.

# Parmenides, Early Greek Astronomy, and Modern Scientific Realism*

Alexander P. D. Mourelatos

## Summary

"Doxa," the second part of Parmenides' poem, is expressly disparaged by Parmenides himself as "off-track," "deceptive," and "lacking genuine credence." Nonetheless, there is good evidence that "Doxa" included some astronomical breakthroughs. The study presented here dwells on fragments B10, B14, and B15 from the "Doxa," and especially on the term *aidēla,* interpreted as "causing disappearance," in B10.3. The aim is to bring out the full astronomical import of Parmenides' realization of four related and conceptually fundamental facts: (i) that it is the sun's reflected light on the moon that explains lunar phases; (ii) that it is the sun's glare which, as the sun moves in its annual circuit, causes the gradual seasonal disappearance of stars and constellations, and that the absence of such glare explains their seasonal reappearance; (iii) that it is likewise the sun's glare which causes the periodic disappearance, alternately, of the Morning Star and the Evening Star, and it is the absence of such glare that allows, alternately and respectively, for the reappearance of each of these stars; and (iv), a ready inference from (iii), the realization that the latter supposedly two stars are an identical planet.

In seeking to make sense of the paradoxical antithesis of "Truth" vs. a disparaged yet scientifically informed "Doxa," the present study explores two modern analogues: Kant's doctrine of the antithesis of "things-in-themselves" (or "noumena") vs. "appearances" (*Erscheinungen* or "phaenomena"); and the twentieth-century doctrine of scientific realism, notably propounded by Wilfrid Sellars. The latter model is judged as more apt and conceptually more fruitful in providing an analogue for the relation between "Truth" and "Doxa."

---

By the middle of the last century, serious challenges had already been posed, and then continued being posed in subsequent decades, to older estimates by historians of science and historians of philosophy concerning the extent and depth of astronomical knowledge attained by Parmenides' predecessors, i.e., by the Milesians, by Pythagoras, and by the early Pythagoreans. In the light of these challenges,[1] the older estimates of the contributions of pre-Parmenidean philosophers to astronomy now appear rather sanguine and exaggerated. The exaggeration has had an unfortunate impact on the scholarship concerning the immediate successor to the Milesians, Xenophanes of Colophon, and likewise on the analysis of Parmenides' "Doxa." For if, as some scholars have argued, the sixth-century BCE natural philosophers had already achieved some major astronomical breakthroughs—such as articulating a spherical model of the universe, knowledge that the moon is illuminated by the sun, some inkling of the optical mechanism of solar eclipses, understanding the distinction between the celestial equator and

---

* This is a revised version of the paper that was presented at the 2007 conference, "Parménides: venerable y temible," in Buenos Aires. Other presentations in paper/lecture form were as follows: September 2007 at the Catholic University of America, Washington, D.C.; December 2007, at the University of Naples, Italy; February 2008, at the University of Crete, Rethimno (for the latter in my own Modern Greek translation). I thank the audiences on the four occasions of oral presentation for their helpful comments and questions. I also thank Patricia Curd for written comments on an earlier draft. Both in its present form and in its four oral presentations, the study incorporates, with revisions, material excerpted from *The Route of Parmenides,* 2nd edition, revised and expanded (Las Vegas: Parmenides Publishing, 2008), pp. xxxvii–xlviii, as well as from my article "Xenophanes' Contribution to the Explanation of the Moon's Light," *Philosophia* (Athens), 32 (2002), 48 and 52–54. I acknowledge the kind permissions, by Parmenides Publishing and by the Academy of Athens, for use of the excerpted material in the present venue.

[1] For Pythagoras and his schools, see Walter Burkert, *Lore and Science in Early Pythagoreanism*, translated by E. L. Minar, Jr. (Cambridge, MA: Harvard University Press, 1972; original German edition, 1962); for the early Ionians and more generally, see D. R. Dicks, *Early Greek Astronomy* (London: Thames & Hudson, 1970. Reprinted Ithaca: Cornell University Press, 1985), especially chs. 1–4. The accounts both by Burkert and by Dicks have been criticized as hyper-skeptical in one or another respect; but the new standard—established in the second half of the twentieth century by these and other historians of early Greek science—a standard of cautious-critical canvassing of the sources for early Ionian philosophy and for Pythagoras and early Pythagoreanism, is no doubt salutary and has generally prevailed: cf. n4, below.

the ecliptic—the ostensibly more primitive "cloud-astrophysics" of Xenophanes was bound to appear, at best, as a scientifically irrelevant exercise in philosophical satire, or, at worst, as absurdly retrograde.[2] Correspondingly, the higher the estimates were of Milesian and Pythagorean scientific accomplishments, the lower was the motivation to search Parmenides' "Doxa" for content of significance for the history of science. Moreover, given Parmenides' explicit disparagement of the content of the "Doxa" as "deceitful" (B8.52 *apatēlon*),[3] it could readily be assumed that any scientifically fecund elements found in the "Doxa" represented doctrines that had already been established by Parmenides' predecessors.

By the standard, however, of today's more cautious assay of pre-Parmenidean science,[4] both the cloud-astrophysics of Xenophanes and the "Doxa" in Parmenides' poem ought to be viewed as constituting part of the record of early exploratory thrusts and gradual conceptual gains that ultimately led, in the second half of the fifth century, to the more sophisticated grasp of the fundamentals of astronomy attributed (among natural philosophers) to Anaxagoras and Philolaus, and (among astronomers) to Meton and Euctemon of Athens and to Oinopides of

---

[2] For an interpretatively more sympathetic account of the natural philosophy of Xenophanes, see my studies: "'X Is Really Y': Ionian Origins of a Thought Pattern," in K. J. Boudouris, ed., *Ionian Philosophy* (Athens: International Association for Greek Philosophy, 1989), pp. 280–290; "La Terre et les étoiles dans la cosmologie de Xénophane" [Earth and Stars in the Cosmology of Xenophanes; translated from the English by C. Louguet], in A. Laks and C. Louguet, eds., *Qu'est ce que la philosophie présocratique?* (Lille: Presses Universitaires du Septentrion, 2002), pp. 331–350; "Xenophanes' Contribution to the Explanation of the Moon's Light," *Philosophia* (Athens), 32 (2002), 47–59; "The Cloud-Astrophysics of Xenophanes and Ionian Material Monism," in Patricia Curd and Daniel W. Graham, eds., *The Oxford Guide to Presocratic Philosophy* (Oxford and New York: Oxford University Press, 2008), pp. 134–168.

[3] References to the fragments of the pre-Socratics are, as standardly, to the B (fragments) or A (testimony) sections of Hermann Diels, *Die Fragmente der Vorsokratiker*, 6th ed., revised by W. Kranz, 3 vols. (Berlin: Weidmann, 1951–1952) [cited as DK].

[4] For a fine example of balanced approach (neither sanguine nor hyper-skeptical) to the accomplishments of earliest Greek science, see Stephen White, "Thales and the Stars," in Victor Caston and Daniel W. Graham, eds., *Presocratic Philosophy* (Aldershot: Ashgate Publishing Co., 2002), pp. 3–18. For another example, in this instance of wider compass, see Daniel W. Graham, *Explaining the Cosmos: The Ionian Tradition of Scientific Philosophy* (Princeton and Oxford: Princeton University Press, 2006), passim.

Chios.[5] Accordingly, the "Doxa" may no longer be taken as merely polemical. Rather it now appears more likely that its astronomical tenets either represent scientific discoveries made by Parmenides himself or reflect his own engaged grappling with quite recent discoveries made by others.[6] To be sure, Parmenides had fundamental philosophical reasons—which I discuss in the final two sections of this paper—that motivated his marking these tenets as "deceitful" and as not worthy of "genuine credence" (B1.30 *tais ouk eni pistis alēthēs*). But as I shall show in what follows, there is impressive inferential nexus in the astronomical tenets of "Doxa"; and this nexus is something Parmenides, philosophical enthusiast for strict logic that he was, must have found enthralling and even congenial.

## The Clue in *erga aidēla*

When Parmenides has the goddess announce that she will explain (cf. B10.3 *hoppothen exegenonto*) the "works (*erga*) of the sun," he puts in her mouth the rare and curious adjective *aidēlos, -on*. Pierre Chantraine, in his definitive *Dictionnaire étymologique*,[7] lists, s.v., three senses, already found in Homer and also attested for later authors:

(a) "not to be countenanced" ("dont on ne peut supporter la vue");

(b) the active sense, "causing disappearance, destructive" ("qui fait disparaitre, qui détruit"), which is supported by the ancient commentators with glosses such as

---

[5] See Dicks, *Early Greek Astronomy*, pp. 55–59, 66–71, 87–89; Gregory Vlastos, *Plato's Universe* (Seattle: University of Washington Press, 1975. Reprinted Las Vegas: Parmenides Publishing, 2005), pp. 36–40.

[6] In ch. 9 of the original edition (1970) of *The Route of Parmenides* (see n[*] above), I emphasized the aspects of irony and ambiguity, both literary and philosophical, that allow "Doxa" to provide an important semantic commentary on potentially misleading terms used in "Truth." (For example, the sense in which "what-is" is *pleon*, "full," in "Truth" must not be equated with the sense of "full" in "everything is full of Light and Night" in "Doxa." See *Route*, p. 261.) I still think that the play of ambiguity and irony is relevant and important. But I now find that I had greatly underestimated the proto-scientific (especially astronomical) content in "Doxa."

[7] *Dictionnaire étymologique de la langue grecque: histoire des mots* (Paris: Klincksieck, 1968).

*aphanistikos*, *olethreutikos*), and which is the required sense ("le sens qui s' impose") when the adjective qualifies *pyr*, "fire";

(c) the passive sense, "what cannot be seen" ("secret, obscur").

In the Parmenides context, both senses (a) and (c) may be contributing subdued nuances. The sun's brilliant light is "not to be countenanced"; it blinds. And there may well be something "secret, obscure" in the effects (*erga*) at issue. Semantic-rhetorical-poetic play involving "foreground" and "background" meanings is precisely what we should expect in the "Doxa."[8] There can be little doubt, however, given both the general use of the adjective and the context in which it occurs in Parmenides, that the foreground meaning is active: "*making* unseen, i.e., causing disappearance," hence even "destructive, annihilating"—the sense well-attested in Homer when the adjective is paired with *pyr*, "fire," in the latter's function of "consuming" things. Certainly in Parmenides' use of the adjective at B10.3, the active sense is corroborated and reinforced by the term *erga*, "works."[9] It would seem that the unusual adjective keys here on its subject as an *explanans*, not as an *explanandum*, as a cause, not as an effect. Let us look at the full context. For the moment I leave the word at issue untranslated in its plural form *aidēla*:

> You shall learn the *aidēla* works of the pure torch (*katharas lampados*) of the brilliantly shining sun (*euageos*

[8] See my *Route*, ch. 9. The latter chapter also appears, in condensed version, as "The Deceptive Words of Parmenides' 'Doxa'," in the volume I have edited, *The Pre-Socratics: A Collection of Critical Essays*, Modern Studies in Philosophy (Garden City: Doubleday and Company, 1974); second printing, with revised introduction and bibliography (Princeton: Princeton University Press, 1993), pp. 312–349.

[9] I judge it quite unlikely that the adjective can bear the sense of "always bright" or of "very bright" ("toujours clair," "bien clair"), as is proposed and argued for by Jean Bollack in *Parménide: De l'Étant au Monde* (Lagrasse: Verdier, 2006), pp. 264 and 266–267. Bollack leans on either of two rather remote possibilities: that *aidēlos* might stand for *aeidēlos* (*ai* for *aei*: as in *aidios*, "eternal"; or in *aizēos*, "robust"); or that it should somehow bear the sense of *arizēlos* or *aridēlos*, "clear, easy to recognize." Besides, there would be pointless redundancy in having "very bright" (*aidēla*, B10.3) just four words after "brilliantly shining" (*euageos*, B10.2).

> *ēelioio*), and how they came about (*hoppothen exegenonto*). (B10.2–3)

Or, because *euageos* might be taken either as masculine, and thus attaching to "sun" (which is how it is construed in the translation just given), or as feminine, attaching to "the torch," the translation might be slightly different:

> You shall learn the *aidēla* works of the pure, brilliantly shining torch (*euageos katharas lampados*) of the sun (*ēelioio*), etc. (B10.2–3)

The ambiguous syntax is unproblematic, and it may be viewed as another instance of that rhetorically charged ambiguity which characterizes this part of the poem. Still, on either syntax, how does the sun's action result in "making things unseen"?

The noun "torch" firmly points us in the direction of Homer's *pyr aidēlon*, a fire that consumes and annihilates—notably "the torch of war," fire used as a weapon. Accordingly, it has been suggested, and I too entertained that possibility previously, that the reference is to the scorching, parching, withering action of the sun either in a catastrophic event (one thinks of the sun's running off-course in the Phaethon myth), or simply in the worst of a Mediterranean heat wave.[10] But the adjectives "pure" and "brilliantly shining" would be incongruously mild in references to catastrophes. Indeed, before the advent of modern physics, observers and natural philosophers would hardly have viewed the scorching and parching involved in a heat wave as a process that is "secret, obscure." Rather, they would have seen it as a transparently obvious process: one in which both explanandum and explanans are manifest; not as one that calls for "explanations"—whereas it is precisely "explanations" (cf. *hoppothen exegenonto*) the goddess promises to deliver.

There is, however, a way in which the "torch of the sun," unlike ordinary fire, "renders things unseen" without physically burning them. And since the wider context in this same fragment

[10] See *Route*, p. 239.

is one of astronomy (the stars, the sun, the moon), it is unlikely that the explanandum (the effect) envisages catastrophic and extreme occurrences, whether experienced or mythical; it is more likely that it envisages events of celestial periodicity. The question asked shortly before can now be asked with greater precision. What is the action of the sun that is significantly tied with effects of stellar periodicity? The answer is obvious: it is the sun's "making unseen" in the course of blotting out, successively and periodically, other heavenly bodies by virtue of its glare.

There is a manifold of such *erga*. First, and most obviously, there is the diurnal disappearance of the stars. Immediately before Parmenides, Xenophanes had thought stars smolder by day and then flare up by night.[11] The "Doxa" offers the more sophisticated explanation: the disappearance is an illusion; the stars become invisible because of the sun's glare. Then, too, there is a corresponding effect of dimming that is seasonal rather than diurnal. From remote prehistoric times, humans had noticed that constellations and conspicuously bright single stars rise earlier and earlier, and set earlier and earlier, from week to week (indeed from one night to the next). This is the slow change in the appearance of the night sky that allows us to speak of the stars of winter, of spring, of summer, of fall. It is also the phenomenon that provides the oldest and most reliable method of marking the seasons and the span of a full year: by noting the first appearances or disappearances of prominent stars or constellations—the method familiar to the ancient Greeks from Hesiod's *Works and Days*. This slow westward advance of all the fixed stars (a motion different from that of their nightly passage from east to west) is, so the "Doxa" tells us, another illusion. It results from the annual progression of the sun in the *opposite* direction, eastward, through the band of the zodiac. It is not that the stars constantly outpace the sun in their common diurnal course. No, it is rather the dazzling fire of the sun which, day-by-day, and season-by-season, "makes unseen, blots out, dims" successively new (longitudinal) bands of the sky as the sun drifts eastward in its annual circuit through the zodiac.

11 See my essay, "La Terre et les étoiles," pp. 331–350, especially p. 346.

And there are more such *erg' aidēla*, more dimmings by the sun's overwhelming glare, that have explanatory implications in astronomy. The Evening Star's eastward movement, away from the sun, makes that star periodically visible; its subsequent retrograde westward drift, toward the sun, eventually and once again renders it invisible. Correspondingly, it is the Morning Star's movement ahead of the sun (westward, retrograde) which, at some stage, makes it visible; and subsequently it is the drift back toward the sun (eastward) that once again renders the Morning Star invisible. Quite obviously, these *aidēla erga*, "acts of dimming," are inferentially connected with the realization—first attested for Parmenides—that the Evening Star and the Morning Star are the same celestial body (DK A40a).

Of course, there are also other bright stars in the sky that are lost in the sun's glare and which, like the Morning and Evening Star, fail to reappear with that unfailing regularity with which the fixed stars make their seasonal re-appearance. Could it not be the case that identical stars may also be the subjects at issue in such seemingly irregular appearances and disappearances? Thus the identifying of Morning Star and Evening Star brought Parmenides to the threshold (and I leave it open as to whether he did or did not cross that threshold) of the identification of the other four "planets" (sun and moon being the first two) known to the ancients.

## The Moon and Its Light

The sun's glare—obviously for us, but not as obviously before Parmenides—affects the visibility of the moon. In this case the dimming is very closely connected with the great discovery, for which the "Doxa" offers the first secure attestation, that the moon gets its light from the sun. In the Aëtius doxography we are told expressly that Parmenides held that the moon is illuminated by the sun (DK 28A42). The same is stated indirectly, in poetic yet fairly transparent terms, in fragments 14 and 15:

> νυκτὶ φάος περὶ γαῖαν ἀλώμενον ἀλλότριον φῶς
> Daylight into the night [or "for the night"], a light from somewhere else, wandering around the earth

[with the reading νυκτὶ φάος of the MSS, rather than the venerable emendation νυκτιφαές introduced by the Renaissance scholar Joseph Scaliger]. (DK 28B14)

αἰεὶ παπταίνουσα πρὸς αὐγὰς ἠελίοιο
Always gazing toward the shining beams of the sun . . . (DK 28B14)

Once again, it is worth dwelling on the wording of these two fragments.[12] The fact that in B14 Parmenides does not say *hyper gaian*, "above the earth," but rather *peri gaian*, "around the earth," is highly significant. It indicates that he has grasped that the moon's complete diurnal course, and, by implication the sun's diurnal course as well, take these two bodies on loops that lie partly above and partly below the earth. And though I do not wish to suggest that he has understood the distinction between the sidereal and synodic periods of the moon,[13] his choice of the adjective *alōmenon*, "wandering," highlights his awareness of a distinct and important aspect in the variability of the "inconstant moon": its shifting of points of moonrise and moonset from one diurnal period to the next.

Another striking detail in this fragment is the metrical effect of two spondees before the main caesura (– – | – – | – ⏑). Unmistakably, this puts heavy emphasis on the lengthened first syllable in the adverb of time *aiei* (normally *aei*), "always," in the first foot of the hexameter line. Given this metrical reinforcement, *aiei* serves to encapsulate seven crucial facts about the orientation of the moon vis-à-vis the sun. I list these here, marking them for subsequent reference with Greek letters, and using italics to highlight the component of each observation that corresponds directly to the "always" of B15:

(α) When, at first crescent, the moon reappears after its two-three days of monthly disappearance, it does so in the western sky, soon after sunset. In its relatively

[12] In what follows here I incorporate remarks I have offered in "Xenophanes' Contribution to the Explanation of the Moon's Light," pp. 48 and 52–54.

[13] The sidereal period is the time it takes the moon to complete a full revolution in its eastward movement through the zodiac (27.3 days); the synodic period is the familiar month of lunar phases (29.5), New Moon to New Moon, or Full Moon to Full Moon.

short time of visibility, the horns of the crescent point eastward, i.e., *the convex edge of the thin crescent faces the setting sun*.

(β) As the moon waxes into first quarter, it is seen progressively higher in the sky at dusk, and it shines progressively longer before moonset. But the *convex side* of the waxing crescent *continues to be oriented in the direction of the sun*, toward the region of the horizon in which the sun has disappeared.

(γ) Later yet in the waxing phase, in the days before and after half-moon, the moon is now far enough from the sun and large enough to be visible even before the sun has set. The non-waxing edge of the moon, opposite the direction in which the moon is growing, continues to be oriented toward the sun. The effect of *facing the sun is maintained*.

(δ) Full Moon rises as the sun sets; Full Moon sets as the sun rises. The disks of the two luminaries are *in direct opposition*, "*face-to-face*," an impression that is heightened at moonrise by the familiar intuition (for observers at middle-northern latitudes) of a human face on the moon.

(ε) As the moon wanes, rising later and later in the night during the early days of third quarter, the effect of facing the sun is not as obvious after sunset and for most of the night. Toward the end of third quarter, however, by night, it is evident that the non-waning edge of the moon is now facing east, "longingly anticipating" (cf. *paptainousa*), as it were, the sun's return to the sky at the end of night.[14] In the absence of the sun, the

[14] Karl Popper has very perceptively detected a hint of erotic sentiment in the participle *paptainousa*, "gazing." See *The World of Parmenides: Essays on the Presocratic Enlightenment*, Arne F. Petersen and Jørgen Mejer, eds. (London and New York: Routledge, 1998), p. 68. In Greek, as in many other Indo-European languages (though not in Popper's mother tongue, German), *Selēne* or *selēne*, "Moon-goddess/moon," is feminine, and *Hēlios* or *hēlios*, "Sun god/sun," is masculine. If I may elaborate on Popper's astute observation by referring to the scheme of seven lunar phases distinguished above, the strongest "longing" occurs twice in the course of the synodic month: first, as the moon is being pulled away from her "lover," after astronomical conjunction (New Moon) in first quarter ([α] and [β]); and then again

"always" in B15 now assumes primarily extrapolative rather than observational character.

(ζ) After sunrise, however, during third quarter, the moon is still visible in the sky; and for the rest of the day till moonset the luminous part is *again on that side of the lunar disk which faces the sun.*

(η) In the last days of last quarter, the waning meniscus rises toward the end of the night or at dawn, just ahead of the sun. In its progressively diminishing time of visibility, before the risen sun's glare blots the moon out, the horns of the crescent point away from the sun, i.e., the convex edge of the thin crescent is *oriented toward* the region of the horizon *where the sun has just risen or will be rising.*

A modern manual for navigators and outdoorsmen records the same facts, with none of Parmenides' poetic conceits, through prosaic repetition of the word "always":

> New crescent moon (waxing) *always* close behind the sun . . . . When full moon is rising the sun is *always* setting . . . . When the full moon is setting the sun is *always* rising.[15]

Of special interest is the contrast between (ε) and what is recorded for the other six phases. As noted above, (ε) constitutes an extrapolation, based on the observations made in (α)–(δ) and in (ζ)–(η): through the dark part of the night, well after sunset and long before dawn, the moon is still "gazing" at the sun. Anyone who has realized that these six observations and the one extrapolation admit of no exception has either grasped, or is on the way to grasping, the fact that the moon gets its light from the sun.

The connection between B14 and B15, on the one side, and the *erg' aidēla* of B10 is now clear. Just as the sun makes the moon

as reunion with her lover (astronomical conjunction) is increasingly anticipated, in late third quarter and in fourth quarter ([ε] to [ζ]). For other insightful aspects of Popper's highly original discussion of Parmenides B14 and B15, see below.

[15] Harold Gatty, *Nature Is Your Guide: How to find your way on land and sea* (Harmondsworth: Penguin Books, 1979), p. 218. I have added the italics.

visible by casting its light on it, that very same *ergon* makes it impossible—certainly for ancient observers—to see the moon under the following conditions (and for modern observers, who can avail themselves of binoculars and telescopes, we would have to say not "impossible" but utterly difficult with naked eyes):

(1) one or two days either before or after New Moon;
(2) when the sun is still high in the sky before dusk, in the early days of first quarter;
(3) at moonrise during the first quarter;
(4) for about the first half of the gibbous phase before Full Moon;[16]
(5) after sunrise in the late days of fourth quarter;
(6) at moonset in the fourth quarter.

Xenophanes had departed only slightly from the naïve pre-scientific belief that the moon from time to time dies and is subsequently reborn. Indeed, he appears to have exploited both the aspects of variability of the "inconstant moon" and the six circumstances noted immediately above, under which the moon is absent from the sky, to argue that there is no single moon but a plurality, successively, of "moons." Each "token" of the moon-"type" is a special cloud-formation which either congeals out of vapors into visibility or is dissipated and thus lost from view. By contrast, Parmenides' "Doxa" connects facts about the moon's non-visibility (observations cited here under [1]–[6], above) with that very trenchant observation recorded in B15: "[The moon] always gazing at the bright beams of the sun."

[16] On a clear day, a sharp-eyed and systematic observer may be able to spot moonrise already in the afternoon of the earlier days of second quarter. But even on a cloudless day, the combination of strong sunlight and the inevitable haze low in the eastern horizon makes this observation difficult and unlikely. Before the last days of second quarter, for a "naked eye" observer, the moon first comes into view—or, as Xenophanes theorized, is constituted out of vapor—somewhere above the eastern horizon.

## The Full Astronomical Import of B14 and B15

Karl Popper[17] and Daniel W. Graham[18] have rightly hailed the tremendous conceptual import of Parmenides' realization that the moon gets its light from the sun. For, as both these authors have shown, the discovery is logically tied up not only with the twin inferences I have already mentioned (viz., the passage of both moon and sun under the earth) but with a cluster of another six, or even eight, powerful such inferences:

- (i) the moon has spherical shape;
- (ii) the moon is a solid, inherently dark (opaque) body;
- (iii) the moon passes under the earth;
- (iv) the sun passes under the earth;
- (v) the orbits of both luminaries are not arcs (let alone straight lines, as Xenophanes had thought) but complete circles;
- (vi) the orbit of the sun is higher than that of the moon.

And this cluster of logically tied inferences invites and encourages two further hypotheses and extrapolations:

- (vii) the earth too is a sphere;
- (viii) the universe is spherical.

For there is credible evidence in the testimonia that the latter doctrines too, (vii) and (viii), were featured in "Doxa."[19] What is more, once (i)–(vi) are connected with the observation that the moon's path across the heavens stays close to that of the sun's annual eastward drift (the ecliptic), the correct explanation of solar and lunar eclipses is nearly inevitable. (We have no testimony, however, that the correct explanation of eclipses was offered by Parmenides; that honor, according to our sources, goes to Anaxagoras.[20])

---

[17] *World of Parmenides*, pp. 68–145 passim, especially pp. 68–70, 80, 84–85.

[18] *Explaining the Cosmos*, pp. 180–181; cf. also his "La Lumière de la lune dans la pensée grecque archaïque," trans. Létitia Mouze, in Laks and Louguet, eds., *Philosophie présocratique*, pp. 351–380, especially pp. 366–370.

[19] See Diogenes Laertius IX.21–22 (DK28A1). Cf. Charles H. Kahn, *Anaximander and the Origins of Greek Cosmology* (New York and London: Columbia University Press, 1960. Reprinted Philadelphia: Centrum, 1985. Reprinted Indianapolis: Hackett Publishing Co., 1994), pp. 115–116; Graham, *Cosmos*, pp. 181–182.

[20] Anaxagoras A42. Cf. Graham, *Cosmos*, p. 221.

This complex of astronomical doctrines is no potpourri of views held by predecessors; the doctrines constitute a well-woven inferential fabric. Even more remarkably—this time with credit to Popper alone for having noticed and exploited this feature of "Doxa"[21]—the two constitutive forms, Light and Night, are the warp and woof that run through that inferential fabric. The whole world of "Doxa" is indeed one of play of Light and Night. On the side of Night, we have solid, opaque, inherently invisible bodies. Light that is cast upon them makes such bodies extrinsically visible, as light is reflected. And yet, paradoxically, Light also produces effects of extrinsic invisibility, in two ways. First, it casts shadows as it is blocked by opaque bodies, the congeners of Night, thus restoring other such opaque bodies to their intrinsic invisibility. And, second, even on the side of pure, unmixed (cf. *katharon*) Light, the glaring strongest light (that of the sun) blots out lesser lights, thus rendering them invisible.

## Reprise on the Relation of "Doxa" to "Truth": the Relevance of Kant

Given the explanatory potential of the observational astronomy in "Doxa," the topic of the relation between the two parts of Parmenides' poem needs to be re-examined, specifically from the angle of scientific content. Nothing that I have said in what precedes, and nothing that will be said in what follows, should be taken as mitigating the very sharp contrast Parmenides posits between "Doxa" and "Truth." In the latter, he deduces a set of at least four "constraints" on the *eon*, "being, what-is, the real"—otherwise put, four criteria that *eon*, the subject at issue, must meet, or four formal or defining attributes it must bear: (a) "unborn and imperishable"; (b) "indivisible," "all-of-it-together-one" (*homou pan/hen*), "continuous" or "cohesive" (*syneches*); (c) "motionless" or "unchanging," or (what is more likely) "immovable, unchangeable"; (d) "fully actualized, perfect." Some readings of Parmenides would add one or more of three additional constraints or specifications: (e) non-temporal, outside time; (f) unique, solitary; (g) spherical. And yet, in spite of the famous

[21] See above n14.

or notorious attempts by his pluralist successors in cosmology to reconcile the world-image that is prompted by the familiar ordinary intuitions that draw on the testimony of the senses, it is evident that no entities of that familiar world-image could possibly meet even the first four of the constraints. The contrast between "Truth" and "Doxa" is stark; the gulf that separates them logically insuperable.

In speaking of a "world-image prompted by familiar intuitions," I am deliberately avoiding the language of "appearances." It is of paramount importance to note that the "Doxa" is not intended as a phenomenology of the "given," as a purely descriptive account of appearances.[22] And even though "Light" and "Night," the primary constituents in "Doxa," are referred to as *morphai*, "forms, (visual) aspects," Parmenides nowhere says or suggests that he intends these as *morphai tou eontos*, "(perceptible) forms of what-is/of the real." Most strikingly, he does not speak of *phainomena* but rather of *dokounta* (B1.31). The latter term, has a deep logical connection with the verb phrase *dokei moi*, "it is acceptable/appeals to me," hence "it seems to me," and also with that phrase's etymological ancestor, the verb *dechomai* or *dekomai*, "I accept." The *dokounta*, accordingly, must be things that are "*taken* (to be thus and so)," or things "deemed *acceptable*," or "approved," or "assumed"—not things simply "given" to our senses.

Indeed, the *dokounta* of Parmenides have something of the conceptual richness of Kant's "phaenomena" (note the Latinizing transliteration, with "-ae," used by Kant) or *Erscheinungen*. There is some danger that the general use of the English term "phenomena" may prove misleading, both in the immediate context of my comments here and also in the comments I offer in what follows. For we find the term "phenomena" used both in translations of the Greek term *phainomena* (in the standard modern transliteration of alpha iota), for contexts in which that Greek term could bear a purely phenomenological or phenomenalistic sense, but

[22] I stress this point in ch. 8 of *The Route of Parmenides*. Others have made the same point: most recently Néstor-Luis Cordero in *By Being, It Is: The Thesis of Parmenides* (Las Vegas: Parmenides Publishing, 2004), pp. 33 and 152–154.

also in translation of Kantian "Phaenomena"/*Erscheinungen*. The latter is a theory-laden term, thus properly corresponding in Greek to *dokounta*, "things deemed to be so."[23] To avoid confusion I shall henceforth use the spelling "phaenomena" (without capitalization, and with quotation marks omitted) when I refer to Kant.

Comparisons between Parmenides and Kant have at various times been introduced in discussions of Parmenides—though sometimes only so that any such comparison be ruled out or discouraged, as "anachronistic."[24] In the second half of the twentieth century, the relevance and suggestiveness of the Parmenides-Kant comparison was strongly promoted by Karl Popper, in connection with his appreciative reading of the scientific content of the "Doxa."[25] The comparison is in several respects quite apt:

(a) In Kant we have a sharp contrast between the realm of "noumena" or "things-in-themselves" and the world of phaenomena (*Erscheinungen*). In Parmenides we have a similarly sharp contrast between the realm of "what-is" or "the real" and the world of "Doxa."

(b) The world of phaenomena in Kant is conceptually structured: it constitutes a system; and it affords the possibility of empirically based science. Similar comments apply to the *diakosmos*, "world order," of the "Doxa."

(c) Mis-handling the distinction between noumena and phaenomena gives rise, according to Kant, to contradictions, "paralogisms," "antinomies." There is more than a little resemblance here with the predicament of Parmenidean "mortals" who wander on a *palintropos keleuthos*, "a route that turns back on itself" (B6.9).

---

[23] And, of course, as students of Kant know well, the ordinary use of *Erscheinungen* in German shows the same ambiguity that is found in the general use in English of "phenomena" (as distinct from Kant's quite technical use of "Phaenomena").

[24] John Burnet, *Early Greek Philosophy*, 4th edition (London: McMillan, 1930), pp. 182–183.

[25] *World of Parmenides*, pp. 143–144: "Burnet once said . . . that we must not (as Th. Gomperz did) interpret Parmenides as a Kant before Kant: . . . . But this is exactly what we must do." Cf. pp. 81–82, 98–99, 128n26, 134n76.

(d) The Kantian realm of phaenomena is constituted by forms, structures, and categories that are projected by human sensibility and human understanding. An act of human projection is likewise the source and origin of "Doxa": B8.53 "They resolved (*gnōmas . . . katethento*) to name two forms."

But there are also some major disanalogies. For Kant, noumena are altogether unknowable and beyond understanding, whereas for Parmenides "what-is" is pre-eminently the object of knowledge and understanding. Moreover, nothing that applies to the realm of noumena could serve to explain or make intelligible the structures or features that characterize the world of Kantian phaenomena. Parmenides, by contrast, does invite—albeit programmatically—a transfer of properties from "what-is," his counterpart of Kantian noumena, to *dokounta*, his counterpart of Kantian phaenomena, the very move that is prohibited by Kant. The deductions of B8 are specifically intended to serve as criteria of reality, as constraints on any project of cosmological inquiry.[26] So understood, these constraints do function rather like Kantian "categories," which for Kant apply exclusively to the world of phaenomena. In Parmenides, again by contrast, the criteria and constraints apply in the first instance and primarily to the counterpart of Kantian noumena, to the "what-is"; but they also apply programmatically to the *dokounta*. This is what I take to be the import of B1.31–32:

> . . . how it would have been right [*chrēn* counterfactual, as most commonly in the imperfect] for *dokounta* to be *dokimōs* [by the best of tests and criteria], if only they just had being in every way [I read *per onta*, not *perōnta*, and I construe the participle as hypothetical].[27]

[26] This is not a universally accepted interpretation of Parmenides; but it is one that I have supported in *The Route of Parmenides* and in other studies. See especially *Route*, pp. 134–135; also references in next note.

[27] *Route*, pp. 203–218. Cf. my comment on B1.31–32 in my review of Patricia Curd, *The Legacy of Parmenides* (Princeton: Princeton University Press,

It is also of paramount importance that in Kant there is no "rivalry" between phaenomena and noumena. Even though Kant speaks of the latter as "transcendent" (i.e., transcending human sensibility and cognition), he envisages no evolutionary, historical, epistemological, or idealized circumstances in which noumena may come to "replace" phaenomena. In Parmenides, by contrast, we have a strong sense that the realm of "what-is" revealed by the goddess goes beyond—ontologically and epistemologically—the world of "Doxa."

## A Better Modern Analogue

If the comparison with Kant fails in these respects, there is at least one other modern philosophical model that lends itself for comparison with Parmenides; and in this case I find the comparison even closer and more successful. I have in mind a system from the latter half of the twentieth century, one significantly inspired by Kant: the "scientific realism" of Wilfrid Sellars. Corresponding to Kant's contrast between noumena and phaenomena, and to Parmenides' contrast between "Truth" and "Doxa," we have in Sellars the contrast between the "Scientific Image" and the "Manifest Image."[28] The Scientific Image presents the world as the latter is revealed and exhibited by the latest and best-defended scientific theories. Saliently characteristic of the Scientific Image is that it "postulates *imperceptible* [my emphasis] objects and events for the purpose of explaining correlations among perceptibles," and may therefore also be referred to as the "postulational" or "theoretical" image.[29] The Manifest Image, the Sellarsian foil to the Scientific Image, is no primitive world-view; nor is it a phenomenalist scheme of sense-contents that are immediately "given"—Sellars famously attacked the "Myth of the Given."[30] Prominent categories in the Manifest Image are "persons, animals, lower forms of life

---

1998. Reprinted Las Vegas: Parmenides Publishing, 2004): "Parmenides and the Pluralists," *Apeiron* 32 (1999), 125.

[28] Wilfrid Sellars, *Science, Perception and Reality* (London: Routledge & Kegan Paul/New York: Humanities Press, 1963; hereafter "*SPR*"), ch. 1, passim.

[29] *SPR*, pp. 19, 7.

[30] *SPR*, chs. 3 and 5.

and 'merely material things' like rivers and stones." The original and fundamental category in the Manifest Image is that of persons; and "impersonal things and impersonal processes" are conceptualized as persons "in a pruned or truncated form."[31] Moreover, most of what Sellars refers to as "merely material things" (what, in his lectures I heard as student, he spoke of as the "stuffing" components of reality, in contrast to structuring principles or to structured or configured objects) present themselves within the Manifest Image as "ultimately homogeneous." By way of example, "[t]he manifest [pink] ice cube," Sellars writes, "presents itself as something which is pink through and through, as a pink continuum, all the regions of which, however small, are pink." Indeed, he generalizes, "colour expanses in the manifest world consist of regions which are themselves colour expanses, and these consist in their turn of regions which are colour expanses, and so on."[32] This is in stark contrast to the theoretical objects postulated by the Scientific Image, for which the governing principle is one of non-homogeneity: the parts or regions of a theoretical object T are not themselves Ts (e.g., atoms are not made of atoms, electrons are not made of electrons, genes are not made of genes).

With strong emphasis and with much repetition, Sellars proclaims that there is an inevitable "clash" between the two images. (And the words or phrases I quote from Sellars, in this paragraph and all others that follow, are the ones that bear the stress in their original context, even when Sellars does not mark them with italics.) Sellars states specifically that the Scientific Image is a "rival" to the Manifest Image; that the Scientific Image is "superior" to the Manifest Image and has "primacy" over it; that only the Scientific Image affords a "complete" explanation; that the Scientific Image gradually "replaces" the Manifest Image; that ultimately, and in principle (i.e., except for practical purposes) the Scientific Image is destined to replace in all respects the Manifest Image, so that the latter (again in principle) totally

[31] *SPR*, pp. 9, 13.

[32] *SPR*, pp. 26 and 35. In place of "ultimately homogeneous," in characterizing this pervasive feature of the Manifest Image, many philosophers today would prefer the more precise Aristotelian term "homoeomerous."

"disappears"; and that the Manifest Image may properly be judged as "false" or "unreal."[33] Even more remarkably, à propos the comparison I am drawing here with Parmenides,[34] Sellars makes statements such as the following:

> On the view I propose, the assertion that the micro-entities of physical theory really exist goes hand in hand with the assertion that *the macro-entities of the perceptible world do not really exist* . . . .
> [T]he objects of the observational framework *do not really exist—there really are no such things* [italics in the original].[35]

Kant, then, was right, for Sellars, to this extent: beyond the world of phaenomena, transcending it, is the ultimate reality of the noumena. But the latter, Sellars insists, are not "unknowable things in themselves, but simply the world as constructed by scientific theory,"[36] a world comprising "scientific objects about which, barring catastrophe, we shall know more and more as the years go by."[37]

I find the analogy between "Doxa" and the Manifest Image quite striking. Persons or "truncated persons" populate the world of "Doxa"; and the "merely material things" (to borrow the phrase used by Sellars) that are the prime constituents of the world of "Doxa," Light and Night, are marked by that property of "ultimate homogeneity" which signals the clash between the Scientific Image and the Manifest Image in Sellars. And here is another significant point of the comparison. At the start of her

---

[33] *SPR*, pp. 14, 20, 25, 27, 29, 32, 38.

[34] Without referring to Sellars, Cordero comes at one point remarkably close to this Sellars-inspired conception of the relation between "Truth" and "Doxa." Bringing forward the example of water, Cordero remarks: "only the scientist grasps its inner structure, its *logos* . . . and expresses it in a formula: $H_2O$ . . . . A lay, nonscientific viewpoint believes that water is 'just' a liquid, colorless, tasteless, and odorless element" (*By Being*, p. 155).

[35] *SPR*, pp. 96, 126.

[36] *SPR*, p. 97.

[37] Wilfrid Sellars, *Science and Metaphysics: Variations on Kantian Themes* (London: Routledge & Kegan Paul / New York: Humanities Press, 1968), p. 173.

expounding of the "Doxa," Parmenides' goddess states that she will "disclose/declare (*phatizō*) this whole truth-like framework (*diakosmon eoikota*), so that no mortal may outstrip (*parelassēi*) you in knowledge [reading dative, *gnōmēi*]" (B8.60–61). The implication, as many students of Parmenides have rightly noted, is that there are better and worse ways of articulating the framework of "Doxa," and that what the goddess offers is (presumably) the best. Sellars correspondingly observes that "there is a correct and incorrect way to describe this objective image which we have of the world in which we live, and it is possible to evaluate the correctness or incorrectness of such a description." He also observes that "much of academic philosophy can be interpreted as an attempt by individual thinkers to delineate the manifest image."[38] Finally, and most importantly, he stresses that the Manifest Image is, like the Scientific Image, an "idealization," and that "the conceptual framework [of] the manifest image is, in an appropriate sense, itself a scientific image." For "[i]t is not only disciplined and critical; it also makes use of . . . aspects of scientific method," notably "correlational induction."[39] The crucial difference, of course, is that the Scientific Image is "postulational": the entities it introduces (like the entity or entities introduced by Parmenides in "Truth") have wholly and purely theoretical character and status.

Anachronism has a bad name in the history of philosophy, because its practice often serves the purpose of making extravagant and gratuitous claims of anticipation of modern theories by ancient ones. But in the present instance, the comparison between Parmenides and either Kant or Sellars has a more modest heuristic purpose and function: to explore conceptual structure by modeling an ancient theory on a modern one. I believe that there is more of potential gain and benefit than of loss and harm in this sort of comparative analysis. The

---

38 *SPR*, p. 14. He also notes that "the so-called 'analytic' tradition . . . under the influence of the later Wittgenstein, has done increasing justice to the manifest image, . . . isolating it in something like its pure form" (p. 15). He adds that this exhibits continuity with the tradition of "perennial philosophy" (sc. Aristotelianism, Thomism, common-sense realism).

39 *SPR*, pp. 14, 15, 19, 7.

disparaging, even condemnatory, language Parmenides' goddess uses in reference to the "Doxa" comes across as incomprehensibly paradoxical. How could the same philosopher, we may ask, who gave us "Truth" expound in detail and with earnest engagement the cosmology of "Doxa"? After branding "Doxa" as shaped by opinions "in which there is no true/genuine trust/credence" (B1.30 *pistis alēthēs*), after warning that "Doxa" is formulated in "a deceptive scheme of words" (B8.52 *kosmon . . . epeōn apatēlon*), how could Parmenides make "Doxa" the vehicle either of his own scientific doctrine or of the best scientific thinking of his day? I, for one, find that the comparison with Sellars' scientific realism can serve to remove the paradox and to make the relation between "Truth" and "Doxa" intelligible. Sellars characterizes the Manifest Image as the product of millennia of conceptual sophistication, and he recognizes it as "scientific" strictly within its empirical ambit. In fact, a large part (perhaps the largest) of Sellars' philosophical oeuvre aims at doing "increasing justice to the manifest image." And yet, the same Sellars does not hesitate to dismiss the latter with such words as "false," "unreal," "disappearing," "non-existent" when what is at issue is not its "refinement," or "increased sophistication" but rather the global comparison and the ontological choice between the Manifest Image and the Scientific Image.

In our own time, the scientific realism of Sellars prepares us for the extraordinary, truly mind-bending, developments that have unfolded and continue to unfold in the physical and biological sciences and in mathematics—in the twentieth century and beyond it. The more the Scientific Image gains in scope and explanatory power, the more unfamiliar, strange, counterintuitive, imagination-defying, and even thought-defying come to be the theoretical objects and principles the Scientific Image postulates. Like the route that leads to the "what-is" in Parmenides, these theoretical objects and principles of the Scientific Image are "indeed outside the beaten track of men" (B1.27). And here is what I see today, in the perspective of 2011, as Parmenides' greatest bequest, not only to his contemporaries and Greek successors, but more broadly to philosophy, to science, to humanity. For all the achievements and glories of *historiē*, of empirical investigation, we must prepare ourselves for the outcome that the *eon*, the really and ultimately real, is something that defies human imagination and ordinary modes of thought. No entity we are familiar with, no entity of the manifest world, satisfies even the initial four—the ones generally accepted by interpreters—of the requirements deduced in B8.[40] All the same, as Parmenides reasoned, these are precisely the attributes the real must possess.

[40] See above, pp. 180–181.

# Parmenides and the Forms

Massimo Pulpito

## Summary

Historians of Greek thought have often described the Parmenidean doctrine as a sort of philosophical exception, hostile to the prevalent naturalist interests of earlier philosophers. The structure of the Parmenidean poem itself, juxtaposing a section on Truth, concerned with an entity displaying characteristics incompatible with those of Nature, to a section on Opinion, concerned with physical theories, seems to support that interpretation. A re-examination of the relationship between these two sections, however, and their authentic internal articulation, can help to understand the Parmenidean position on physics, thus restoring him to his historical-philosophical context. The alleged tension between the two sections is contained mainly in verse B8.53. The verse is traditionally understood as referring to the decision of mortals to name two forms (μορφάς) corresponding to Fire and Night. However, a more careful reading of the verse (as proposed by some scholars) leads us to the conclusion that the "two" are not the forms but the mortal points of view (γνώμας). So what are the forms then? A reading of verse B9.1 allows us to stipulate that, for Parmenides, the forms are all the visible things and thus the physical objects. If we identify these exterior forms with τὰ δοκοῦντα from verse B1.31 (translated as "the objects of opinion") it becomes possible to recompose the poem's structure. We can recognize three sections: the first, on Truth, dedicated to existence in oneness and homogeneity; the third, on physical forms, providing a description of the world from a morphological standpoint. Between these two lies the second section, dedicated to mortal Opinions which, like the cosmogonies, confuse the ontological status of Everything with the morphological and mereological status of particular objects. Nonetheless, in the section on correct physical theories (the third one) Parmenides attempts to recuperate the two principles recognized by mortals, accepting their δυνάμεις (most likely identified with Hot and Cold) as elements of which the cosmos consists. This reading allows us to place Parmenides inside the development of Pre-Socratic thought, connecting him to earlier thinkers and, more importantly, to the later ones. The idea that the physical world consists of forms both visible and mutable, as manifestations of a reality fundamentally invisible and immutable, perceivable only through reason, will become a cliché of natural philosophy after Parmenides; at least until Plato, who will go on to recognize in the invisible and immutable forms the paradigm of the world.

## 1. The bipolar structure of the forms

In the history of Parmenides studies there is no shortage of readings that have philosophically decontextualized (sometimes unintentionally) the great Eleatic philosopher. Parmenides has often been described as an exception within the tradition of Pre-Socratic philosophy: in recent times, the idea of an epistemological exception, according to which Parmenides was concerned with the way in which we should speak about the cosmos and not with the cosmos itself, has gradually replaced the classical thesis of the ontological exception, which holds that Parmenides did not concern himself with the cosmos at all. In either case, Parmenides emerges not so much as a perfect Pre-Socratic, fully immersed in the intellectual climate of his times, but as an intelligent digression, while at the same time recognizing his enormous influence on subsequent thought.

It is in the description of the relationship between the two parts of the poem that Parmenides, the Pre-Socratic philosopher, may be found, by bringing to the fore the connections with his predecessors and successors, without losing sight of his philosophical originality in the process. The problem consists in understanding how these two parts come to be reconciled and, more radically, if they can be reconciled at all.

The passage in which the tension between the two sections is greatest occurs where they are linked, that is the last verses of fragment B8 (Diels-Kranz numbering system). Here, the Goddess states that she has reached the end of her speech on truth and will now describe the opinions of mortals. Every verse of this passage poses a problem and our understanding of the whole piece can even depend on the correct interpretation of single words. In any case, the most important verses in this passage are B8.53–54:

> μορφὰς γὰρ κατέθεντο δύο γνώμας ὀνομάζειν,
> τῶν μίαν οὐ χρεών ἐστιν—ἐν ᾧ πεπλανημένοι εἰσίν.

Here, Parmenides makes clear what mortals' beliefs consist of, which he will then develop in the following verses. While scholars have focused their attention on verse B8.54, due to its vagueness and consequent variety of possible meanings,[1] there is an almost unanimous consensus about verse B8.53. Here, too, different approaches have been used, but nearly all these have been variations that did not modify the meaning of the verse. The fact that a notion acting as a counterpart to the ἐόν of the speech on Truth appears here would seem to indicate that verse B8.53 is a crucial juncture: this is the concept of "form," μορφή. Like ἐόν, μορφή appears quite unexpectedly, without the Goddess dwelling on its meaning. Just as ἐόν was the protagonist in the veridical speech, μορφή appears to play a central role in the doxastic and physical one. Evidence of the difference between the two notions first appears as a difference of number: while ἐόν is singular, μορφή is presented in the plural, μορφάς. This is the main difference. Moreover the verse contains a δύο, which scholars link to μορφάς and in which some have identified the point of divergence between Truth and Opinion: ontological monism seems opposed to morphological dualism. In fact, this verse is generally understood in this way: "for they [sc. mortals] decided to name two forms."[2] These two forms would be the elements that the Goddess presents a few verses later: Fire (then, in fragment B9, Light) and Night. In contrast to a reading that appears so clear and suited to the context, the enigmatic vagueness of the next verse, B8.54, has attracted the interest

[1] Furley wrote: "That [sc. B8.53], however, is less important than the next line, which has probably aroused more comment than any other from Elea" ("Notes on Parmenides," 5).

[2] This is the classical translation by Tarán, *Parmenides,* p. 86.

of scholars. However, if we shift our attention away from the difficulties of verse B8.54 and concentrate on B8.53, we notice something strange about the translation:

> μορφὰς γὰρ κατέθεντο δύο γνώμας ὀνομάζειν

At first sight, the verse seems to link δύο to the word immediately following it: γνώμας. As already said, however, we usually refer δύο to the more distant μορφάς, on the other side of the caesura. If this really were the correct reading, we would have to admit that the verse is very ambiguous. This fact is generally undervalued, also on the basis of the idea for which γνώμας constitutes a semantic unit together with κατέθεντο (with μορφὰς δύο being a direct object of ὀνομάζειν). Diels[3] found this usage in Theognis, with the meaning "to take a decision," thus discarding the variant found in some Simplician manuscripts, γνώμαις.[4] It should be said, however, that Parmenides uses κατατίθεσθαι at other points,[5] without linking it to γνώμην, with a similar meaning (as the context always confirms): "to establish," which offers a plausible meaning for B8.53 as well. Also, Mourelatos[6] reminds us that the examples adopted by Diels link the verb exclusively to the singular γνώμην. The presence of the plural γνώμας, then, is evidence for the link with δύο. If we read verse B8.53 as most scholars do, we have to admit that there is a connection between κατέθεντο and γνώμας, which intersects that between μορφάς and δύο. Woodbury's comment on this point (in a posthumous article of 1986) is very incisive: "Yet verse 53, as it is usually read, assumes an aspect of intricate interlacing [. . .]. Meanwhile, the usual rendering of the line must give it the appearance of an artificial puzzle such as those invented for intelligence-tests, rather than that of a piece of actual com-

[3] Diels, *Parmenides Lehrgedicht,* p. 92.
[4] Among those who adopted this variant: Patin, "Parmenides," 592; Loew, "Lehrgedicht des Parmenides," 159n1; Furley, "Notes on Parmenides," 5; Gallop, *Parmenides of Elea,* p. 74.
[5] B8.39, B19.3.
[6] Mourelatos, *Route*, p. 229.

munication within a functioning society."[7] Also Mourelatos[8] (as Falus[9] had in certain ways) observed that, if this were the meaning of the verse, one would not be able to understand why Parmenides had inverted the positions of μορφάς and γνώμας.

Well, the idea of Fire and Night as two forms named by mortals is based on this bizarre translation. This however is not founded on any evidence whatsoever. Our ancient sources actually speak anachronistically of two "principles," "causes," "elements" or even of two "gods."[10] None of these refer to two "forms." In itself, this does not mean anything, because the same sources say nothing about a possible alternative meaning for μορφάς. This means that everything we can know of this notion is to be found in the passage of Parmenides' poem. The point is that Fire and Night seem to lend themselves to being two physical forms established by mortals: the great attraction of this reading has led scholars to read the verse in such a contorted way.

As I have mentioned, there is no shortage of alternative readings, often differing only in matters of detail. For example, Joël[11] proposed the reading γνώμης (on the basis of Democritus 68 B11 DK), understanding that the verse indicated the naming of two forms of knowledge, and therefore accepting the reference to Light and Night as forms, but not in the material sense. For Deichgräber,[12] κατέθεντο would support both μορφὰς δύο and γνώμας. For Falus,[13] however, μορφὰς δύο should be read as an object of κατέθεντο, and γνώμας as an object of ὀνομάζειν (Cerri[14] has suggested a similar reading). Recently Guarracino[15] has suggested interpreting μορφάς as a predicate of the object δύο γνώμας: "essi infatti stabilirono di chiamare forme due opinioni"; this position reminds us of that of Deichgräber, but is distinguished from it by the role of

[7] Woodbury, "Parmenides," 2.
[8] Mourelatos, *Route,* pp. 228–229.
[9] Falus, "Parmenides-Interpretationen," 287.
[10] 28 A1, A7, A23, A24, A33, A34, A45 DK.
[11] Joël, *Antiken Philosophie,* p. 437n1.
[12] Deichgräber, *Parmenides' Auffahrt,* p. 54n1.
[13] Falus, "Parmenides-Interpretationen," 287.
[14] Cerri, *Parmenide,* pp. 245–246. Cf. Furley, "Notes on Parmenides," 5.
[15] Guarracino, *Parmenide,* pp. 88–89.

ὀνομάζειν (in place of κατέθεντο) assumed as the verb governing the double object, and above all for the interesting reference of δύο to γνώμας instead of to μορφάς.

Actually, the link between δύο and γνώμας, according to a more natural reading of the verse, had already been sensed by other scholars. Mourelatos[16] imagined the possibility of a double reading of the verse, as the Goddess's purpose was ironic. The first, immediate reading corresponds to the traditional interpretation; the second reading, and that preferred by a more careful audience, interprets the verse on a different level, one which connects δύο to γνώμας. Cordero, in the critical edition of 1984, also links δύο to γνώμας by suggesting a reading of the verse that follows the most obvious and probable translation: "Ils ont établi deux points de vue pour donner des noms aux apparences extérieures."[17] This reading was proposed by Woodbury two years later in the article cited earlier: "for, as to forms, they came to two decisions (put themselves into two minds) concerning their naming."[18] (If the dative γνώμαις were maintained, the reading would become: "they established in fact that the forms should be named from two points of view.")[19]

In this case, the verse's structure seems to be better articulated, organized almost into concentric circles. Μορφάς lies at one extreme of the verse and is the object of the verb ὀνομάζειν, which lies at the other. They are divided by a dense nucleus on which ὀνομάζειν depends: κατέθεντο δύο γνώμας. In Woodbury's view, this structure is closer to that which was usual at the time of Parmenides. The simplification and immediacy are due to the disappearance of the dispersion and entanglement of the semantic units (μορφὰς . . . δύο—κατέθεντο . . . γνώμας).

If this reading is correct, and I believe it is, γνώμας, and not μορφάς, are δύο. I think Cordero has given the best interpretation

---

16 Mourelatos, *Route,* pp. 228–230.

17 Cordero, *Deux Chemins,* p. 40.

18 Woodbury, "Parmenides," 3.

19 Bollack also translated the verse linking δύο to γνώμας, but inverting the governing verbs with respect to the reading suggested by Mourelatos, Cordero, and Woodbury, and hence putting forward the structure recognized by Falus and Cerri, but in an innovative way: "Car ils ont posé des formes, pour donner nom à deux principes" (*Parménide,* p. 208).

of γνώμας, understanding them to be mere "viewpoints"[20]: in this way mortals show that they do not have a μία γνώμη, but are split (duplicitous as they are, B6.5) by two different conjectures. This means that Fire and Night are not forms, but points of view, conjectures (in the non-propositional sense of conjectural objects), or rather two signs corresponding to two different interpretations of the physical world. So, when the Goddess in verse B8.61 states that she wishes to explain cosmology so that Parmenides will not be led astray by a βροτῶν γνώμη, she is referring to the opinions of mortals, in the sense of their points of view on the cosmos, which are precisely the Fire and Night principles.

However, if Fire and Night are only γνώμας, what then are the μορφάς? As we have seen, Cordero translates it as "apparences extérieures."[21] Despite that, this scholar ended by returning to the classical reading, as he understood the position of the two points of view on external forms to be a way of affirming the duality of the forms: "Le resultat est une conception dualiste de la réalité qui conçoit l'existence de formes opposées."[22] Evidence for this is found in verse B8.55, with its reference to ἀντία . . . δέμας: following on from Bormann, Cordero identifies μορφάς with δέμας. Having conceived external appearances from two points of view, mortals would surely admit two opposite forms. However, Cordero has recently clarified the word's meaning, reconnecting it to Homeric usage[23]: external forms are only empty verbal forms, a fact that seems to be confirmed by the presence of ὀνομάζειν. Woodbury has also interpreted the verse by giving particular emphasis to the question of naming. Similarly, Cerri[24] has understood Fire and Night to mean "due forme della nominazione," or more exactly as two "aree semantiche generalissime, due strutture categoriali."

I believe that we have to return to the earlier Cordero, but draw quite different conclusions, in order to find a convincing interpretation of this passage. That is, I think we should understand μορφάς in its eminently physical sense, as

20 Cordero, *By Being*, p. 156.
21 Cordero, *Deux Chemins*, p. 194.
22 Ibid.
23 Cordero, *By Being*, p. 156.
24 Cerri, *Parmenide*, pp. 245–246.

the classical reading had already supposed. For this reason, "external appearances," "exterior aspects," and hence simply "forms," seem to me to be the best interpretation of the word's meaning. The passage is, in fact, clearly physical in character and would be without sense if the verse only had a linguistic meaning. Take fragment B19: at verse B19.3 the Goddess states that men established names for every thing. However, this follows on from two verses dealing with birth, growth, and ending, that is the affirmation of change, therefore a purely physical content. In B8.53, Parmenides announces what are probably two cosmological principles, which he then goes on to describe. He tells us what they are and what they are like; but if he had reduced them to purely verbal expressions in verse B8.53, he would not have told us their function in the cosmology of mortals. This irrelevance, on closer examination, is the same as the problem posed by the traditional reading. In this case, in fact, the Goddess would say that mortals had proposed two forms, Fire and Night, and that they had opposing characteristics. She would not say what they are for, or rather, what function they have in the cosmology of mortals: in other words, she would not say that they are two principles with which mortals claim to explain the cosmos, that is *everything*. This situation is, of course, aggravated by a purely linguistic reading: it is supposed, in fact, that mortals named many things. Why did Parmenides concentrate specifically on the naming of Fire and Night? Certainly, because they are two cosmological principles. Where does Parmenides say this? In verse B8.52 (that is just before) the Goddess evokes κόσμος. Now that we are dealing with "cosmos," we might believe that to describe what mortals have established means to declare implicitly how they have interpreted this cosmos: that is, through two forms or two expressions that are empty. The point is, of course, that κόσμος is accompanied by ἐμῶν ἐπέων. If you really want to find a Homeric value, you can find it here, where κόσμος seems to communicate just that expressive external appearance that one looks for in μορφή. One could almost say that κόσμον ἐπέων catalyses that purely expressive, external value that one expects to find in the following verse, because it reminds us strongly of the Homeric μορφὴ ἐπέων (*Od.* XI.367). Instead, the following verse seems to add something new, which can only be the expression of the cosmological function of the two points of view which, as we have seen, κόσμος can in no way provide. Moreover, verses B8.50 to B8.61 in the passage handed down to us by Simplicius have a compactness and autonomy of their own. Even if, after B8.61, the doxastic speech continues, these verses seem to give a concise presentation of the two principles. Now, what would have been the sense if Parmenides had not already clarified what was being referred to? To present Fire and Night's characteristics and affirm that they are in opposition is not the same as to express their function as constitutive of the cosmos. Sweet and bitter or wet and dry also have opposing characteristics. I should point out that to assume that μορφάς are mere expressive forms would probably mean to misunderstand ὀνομάζειν: in B8.53 the verb appears to have the same naming value (that is, of attribution of a name) that it has in B9.1, and not merely that of expression. To understand it to mean "to name the forms of words" is the same as reducing "to name" simply to "to say" or "to utter."

What, then, are the μορφαί? I believe the answer can be found in verse B9.1, which I have just mentioned.

αὐτὰρ ἐπειδὴ πάντα φάος καὶ νὺξ ὀνόμασται

We find here, it could be said, the squaring of the circle: "but as all things have been called Light and Night." Parmenides here seems to recall something he has already said, rather than something new. As he is now referring again to Fire and Night, the philosopher is probably affirming something already anticipated in the last verses of our fragment B8. This, we should recall, closes with the Goddess who has already presented the two principles and justifies her wish to dwell on cosmology.

If, then, the relationship in B9.1 is thus: mortals *(A)* called all things *(B)* Light and Night *(C)*,[25] it seems to me that this logical structure may have been anticipated in B8.53: mortals *(A)*

[25] Cf. Mourelatos, *Route*, pp. 183–184.

established two points of view *(C)* in order to name the forms *(B)*. Otherwise, in B8.53, we would have the predicate of the object (they gave this name: Fire and Night, that is they established the two points of view from which, or the two signs with which, to give a name: κατέθεντο δύο γνώμας ὀνομάζειν) but a true object would be missing (to what did they give this name?).

Now, if all this is true, then the "external forms" Parmenides refers to here must be "all things": if πῦρ-φάος and νύξ are the two γνῶμαι, then μορφάς must stand for πάντα. We then deduce that the μορφαί are the visible forms, the external appearances of things. If this is so, and the forms are not two but innumerably many (or rather, as many as there are things in the world), what is the meaning of ἀντία . . . δέμας in B8.55 which, in foreseeing an opposition, can only imply a duality? I believe that B8.53 and B8.55 hold together only if, *pace* Bormann, μορφάς is not identified with δέμας. It is clear that, when using δέμας, Parmenides refers to two opposing principles, Fire and Night, and hence to something different from μορφάς. Therefore, if in B8.53 the Goddess states that mortals have established two points of view on the totality of physical forms (and therefore expresses their cosmological function), it is in B8.55 that she starts telling us in what these points of view consist (and therefore expresses their nature), before calling them by their name: so, in B8.55 the Goddess tells us that these are not two external forms (μορφάς), but two different "material structures." The meaning of δέμας is, in fact, bodily frame. Moreover δέμας is related to δέμω, which expresses the idea of constitution, construction, or manufacture. In this sense, δέμας suggests itself as an extremely effective lexical choice, because on the one hand it always refers to figure or shape, just as μορφή does (and in fact, for the Goddess, Fire-Light and Night are always "forms" of being, and this, as we may see, is the Trojan horse by which the mortals' deception will be insinuated); on the other hand, it does not just have that exterior character possessed by μορφή, but also implies a structural and constitutive aspect, as befits two cosmological principles. Therefore, in B8.55, we have the true proclamation of δύο γνώμας, either with "they distinguished opposing structures" (or rather, opposite in structure, with δέμας as relative accusative) or "they judged the structure (inference: of the forms) oppositely" (with δέμας as direct object and ἀντία understood in its adverbial sense) making a distinction between form and structure even more clearly.

In this way μορφή assumes full physical value (as, for that matter, already occurred in the majority reading) which adheres more closely to the context and is not extraneous to its primary meanings (for an example contemporary with Parmenides of μορφή as exterior form, or real aspect, see Aeschylus, *Prometheus Bound*, v. 210). This does not take away the fact that in μορφάς we can recognize a Homeric nuance, that of superficial appearance and vacuity of expression. For the Goddess, Truth always means fundamental Being, but not that of worldly things of course, with their partiality and mutability. On the other hand, it cannot be excluded that Parmenides is introducing here a philosophical use of the word, as I shall later suggest.

## 2. Order of words and order of the world

This interpretation of the verse in question seems to me to provide the key to a correct understanding of the relationship between the ontological and physical sections of the poem. I maintain, in fact, that there is a possible connection between the μορφαί and τὰ δοκοῦντα of verse B1.31.[26] By τὰ δοκοῦντα we should understand not opinions, nor appearances, but "objects of opinions."[27] If we interpret the notion in this way, not only does it explain the meaning of couplet B1.31–32, but also what is in my view a sub-articulation of the second part of the poem. On the one hand, in fact, there are the opinions without certainty upheld by mortals; on the other hand, there are correct theories about the being δοκίμως (B1.32) of the objects of opinions. The fact that opinions are incorrect does not imply that the objects they refer to do not exist. So, according to the interpretative

---

26 The couplet B1.31–32 is one of the most hotly debated passages in Parmenides' poem. I limit myself here to citing Brague, "La vraisemblance du faux," pp. 44–68. In the following section I shall briefly deal with some of the conclusions found in my article, "*Ta dokounta*."

27 Cf. Mourelatos, *Route*, p. 210.

hypothesis I mean to put forward here, these objects correspond to the μορφαί, the visible forms of the single ἐόν. These forms may, in fact, be interpreted in an inadequate manner, and hence generate false opinions; but they may also be the object of correct theories. The correctness of these theories is not, naturally, to be confused with the axiomatic truth of being, the discussion of which is organized like a real theorem. Instead they are theories that are to be proven, verified from time to time (δοκίμως is related to δοκιμασία, which means "examination or test"). So this is not a conflict between infallible reason and the necessarily deceptive senses. There is, instead, the opposition between right reason and a "wandering mind" (B6.6) which interprets objects of the senses (in themselves neutral) in an incorrect way. The senses do not deceive, but they *can* deceive, if not accompanied by right reason. One can not stop at sensible data, which are in themselves dumb. In this sense, Cordero is right to say that δόξα is not appearance.[28] A correct description of that which appears (that is, in my view, of the forms) is developed in the physics expounded by the Goddess. It is correct because it describes the forms for what they are, without drawing incorrect conclusions, without introducing non-being, because it does not mistake the forms for ἐόν and therefore does not transfer that which is valid on the physical plane on to the ontological plane, as happens with δόξα.

We must therefore recognize that there is a sub-articulation in the second section of the poem: on the one hand, a *pars destruens* (opinions of mortals), on the other hand, a *pars construens* (correct theories).[29] In the first, the Goddess rails against the ideas of "mortals who know nothing" (B6.4), referring to that which mortals established; in the second, instead, mortals leave the scene and the Goddess deals directly with sensible beings (in fragment B10.1, we read "You will know the nature of the ether . . ."). As has been said, both sub-sections have forms as their object, but they are distinguished by an important

---

[28] Cordero, *By Being*, pp. 152–154.

[29] Thanassas, "Doxai," 199–218, is in agreement with this, although he understands these two sections to be two δόξαι of different kind.

difference, which we should explain trying to grasp the general meaning of the doctrine.

In the first part of the poem Parmenides argued for the coherence of beings (in verse B8.25 he affirms that ἐὸν ἐόντι πελάζει, i.e., "being adheres to being," since no non-being can separate them). That is not all, for he also affirms that beings are all the same, or equivalent. It is not possible to *be* more or less: being is identical for all. There is a real *ontological indifference* among beings. Now, this being is not only conceptually equivalent, but really is the same thing. It is one and the same for all. For this reason one can speak of only one ἐόν.[30] To illustrate this idea I shall make use of a simile. The ἐόν of Parmenides may be likened to a mirror. If a mirror is smashed, its pieces do not lose the essential characteristic of the original mirror. While pieces of a table are not tables, fragments of a mirror are still mirrors because they continue to reflect. In this sense the whole is in every part.[31] Being-a-mirror is shared by all the fragments. Now, if the fragments of the mirror were put together and fit together perfectly, they would only make one large mirror. So when Parmenides presents ἐόν, he actually refers to the totality of beings, considered on the basis of their common ground, which thus renders them one large being, without denying their multiplicity. But this multiplicity is now purely formal: just as fragments are only mirrors in different *forms*, that together constitute one large mirror, in the same way beings are only formally diverse, partial, and mutable, while together they constitute a single, complete, and immutable ἐόν.[32]

At the formal level, in fact, things are not only partial and isolated from one another, but come and go. In reality, from an ontological point of view, nothing changes in substance. If a tree burns and becomes ash, this does not mean it becomes a non-

[30] The same line of reasoning can be found in Furth, "Eleatic Ontology," 128: "Betathon: Trees are. —Parmenides: [silent]. —Betathon: Lizards are. —Parmenides: You're repeating yourself."

[31] Aristotle would speak of ὁμοιομέρειαι.

[32] That ἐόν is the All, is the view adopted by, for instance, Woodbury, "Parmenides on Names," 145–169; Robinson, "Parmenides," 623–633; Casertano, *Parmenide*; Finkelberg, "Reality in Parmenides," 405–412.

being. The tree-form disappears, but in its place a being always remains: the ash. Therefore, first there was a being, then there is a being again. From an ontological point of view, for the single ἐόν nothing has changed. As long as we do not question the fact that these are only formal changes, as long as we describe the physical world for what it is, that is, in its partiality, we shall not fall into error. Error occurs whenever we transfer partiality and precariousness of the forms to the All; in other words, when we confuse the mereological and morphological plane with the ontological one. This, then, is where mortals have erred.

When the Goddess presents the duality of Fire and Night, she probably refers to a popular cosmogony, widespread also in Elea, and presented in philosophical terms (take, for example, the Orphic cosmogony whose protagonists are Night, on the one hand, and Φάνης, the Inflamed, on the other[33]). Δόξα, moreover, not only refers to belief or opinion, but also to fame and popularity: by considering both things together, we understand that the notion expresses the "commonplace."[34] Here, however, we are not referring to ordinary commonplaces: Parmenides is concerned with the All, and is therefore speaking about a popular opinion regarding the cosmos. Well, mortals committed this very error: by not placing unity or coherence at the basis of everything, they have maintained that the All can be explained by making use of a duality of opposing principles. It is clear that to trust the constitution of the cosmos to a polarity between the principles of Light and Night means to attribute the existential precariousness of particular beings to the totality of existence. It is not so much the characters' enantiomorphic opposition that poses the problem (as has been subtly proposed by the predicational perspective[35]), as the complete existential exclusivity of the two elements: when *there is* light, *there is not* darkness; when *there is* darkness, *there is not* light.[36] However, as we know, non-being is banished from the space of the All, so this duality is not allowed. So Parmenides denies that the world is founded on this

[33] *Orph. Arg.* 15.
[34] Cf. Calvo, "Truth and Doxa," 258.
[35] Curd, *Legacy*, pp. 107–109.
[36] Cf. Furley, "Notes on Parmenides," 8.

intermittency, the alternation between being and non-being. The alternation of Light and Night, the periodic exchange of roles, only has *formal* meaning for the Goddess, because it reveals all its partiality and therefore cannot constitute the All.

For this reason, what mortals say is empty and deceptive. Parmenides counterposes a physical order to this order of words with the *pars construens*. This does not deceive, but is valid, being suited to its object: not a κόσμος ἐπέων ἀπατηλός (B8.52), "a deceptive order of words," but a διάκοσμος ἐοικώς (B8.60), "a correct cosmic order." In this way we move from the purely verbal plane into the physical one.

Parmenides demonstrated the error of mortals in verse B8.54: they have not recognized the necessary unity of the two principles (or have asserted that each, taken one at a time, does not necessarily exist). Parmenides takes up a dialectical position towards these incorrect opinions. He seems disposed to admit them, as long as the error is corrected by recognizing the unity of the principles. In this way, coexistence is opposed to alternation: in fragment B9 Parmenides says that, as all things have been called Light and Night, this duality may be maintained, as long as the fundamental error is removed by recognizing that the two principles, to remain such, must coexist: all must be equally filled with Light and Night (B9.3). Neither of the two should overcome the other and annihilate it. If they are to be considered cosmological principles, and hence placed on the constitutive plane and not on the formal one, we must admit that neither may be annulled, but may at most mix or separate.

## 3. Forces and forms

Parmenides also seems to indicate the sense in which this mythic duality might be recuperated, and here we come to the *pars construens*. He mentions the δυνάμεις (B9.2) of Fire-Light and Night, their *forces*, powers, and activities, as they are attributed to (or operate on) this or that thing in the world. I would hold that a further hypothesis may be formulated, that is to interpret the two constitutive principles found in Parmenides as two opposing forces: the Eleatic refers to them by pointing out the activity or power of the two elements imagined by mortals.

We have a trace of what these δυνάμεις might be. We find them in Aristotle,[37] a writer whose testimony (as with any ancient writer) should be questioned: neither accepted uncritically, nor rejected hypercritically. It is therefore possible that Aristotle, who I think misinterpreted the meaning of the two principles (by recognizing being and non-being as fixed identities of opposites—Fire as being and Night as non-being—and not as alternating roles), is right when he identifies their opposition with the ancient one between hot and cold. Alcmaeon testifies that hot and cold are δυνάμεις when he speaks of ἰσονομία τῶν δυνάμεων, among which he also lists ψυχρόν and θερμόν (cf. 24 B4 DK). If this is so, hot and cold may also be thought of as opposite elements constituting the cosmos of Parmenides, in so far as they generate forms of existence that are differentiated on the basis of their distribution and mixture. It is clear that from a partial perspective in which there is the hot, there is not the cold (even though, in the mixture, this total exclusiveness is questionable). From a global viewpoint, however, which is that of Truth, ἐόν is always perfectly and immutably isothermic. In the All, the equilibrium of the δυνάμεις (just that equilibrium which mortals had, erroneously, not proposed) is perfect and unchanging, because they are coexistent and equal: equal in both force and quantity. It is in the particular that purely formal variations exist, which do not affect the whole Being. The unequal distribution of the two forces in the particular produces the different forms of the single ἐόν: that is, physical objects. So Parmenides not only reduces objects to mere external forms of a single Being that is the same everywhere, but explains their genesis by imagining a hot-cold dynamic within an unchanging and unitary cosmos.[38]

---

[37] *Metaph.* A5, 986b18 = 28 A24 DK.

[38] This interpretation allows us to imagine a more specific hypothesis on the identity of τὰ δοκοῦντα, which is an alternative to that suggested above, although without conflicting results. In fact, while continuing to admit the division of the second part of the poem as a separation between one section devoted to the deceptive δόξαι and another devoted to the correct theories on forms, we can recognize in τὰ δοκοῦντα not the μορφαί, but the two γνῶμαι, πῦρ, and νύξ, objects of opinion in that they are structurally opposed cosmological principles, but then correctly described as simple δυνάμεις. As I think both alternatives are

As we see, then, a different interpretation of B8.53 can have important consequences for the comprehension of the whole poem. It can, certainly, leave us perplexed regarding the fact that the reference to μορφάς is oblique and is limited, furthermore, to a passage in which the Goddess presents the incorrect opinions of mortals. At the same time, however, it should be said that while ἐόν in its nakedness is the constant object of the ontological discourse, in the physical discourse the focus is placed on single forms: the Sun, the rings, seed, etc. This perhaps justifies the eclipse of this notion in the few passages from the physical section that have come down to us. Above all, though, I believe a further consideration is due: that the ideas of Light and Night represent two γνῶμαι is not the view of mortals, but that of the Goddess. The Goddess uses *her own language* to express what mortals have established (as Cordero writes: "We must not forget that it is not mortals who are speaking, but the Goddess, and therefore she expounds in 'her' terms."[39]). This is not about the truth: they are just two γνῶμαι, two points of view. For this reason, it is probable that μορφάς also belongs to the Goddess's language and not that of mortals: in other words, it is probable that this word expresses the way in which the Goddess, in the physical section, names the various beings of which she will then give a complete cosmological picture (διάκοσμον ἐοικότα, B8.60). It is the Goddess, therefore, who understands the Light and Night principles to be *points of view* on the totality of *forms.*

I believe this reading can help us reinstate Parmenides in a precise line of development of Pre-Socratic thought, perhaps helping us to reach a new understanding of this historical process, starting from the relationship between Parmenides and Ionic philosophy. As is common knowledge, the idea that visible things derive from a common, invisible and eternal ἀρχή is older than Parmenides. Similarly, the idea that at the basis of ἀρχή there is a pair of opposites that determines the structure of things (in Anaximander the principal pair of opposites is *hot-cold*) is

possible (δοκοῦντα as μορφαί in general or as the two γνῶμαι in particular), I leave this question open here.

[39] Cordero, *By Being*, p. 156.

ancient. Parmenides, however, will surpass this vision by maintaining that conflicts cannot consist in the existential negation of opposites. In Anaximander, for example, this oppositional dynamic is interpreted as an injustice that should be expiated in the order of time by means of an atonement. The reintegration of ἀλλήλοις, absent from the Aldine edition of fragment 12 B1 DK, has led scholars increasingly to recognize injustice in the reciprocal opposition of contraries, probably deriving from the principal opposition between hot and cold. Each thing commits an injustice towards its opposite, negating it with its presence, and pays the penalty for its offence, destroying itself and giving up its place to it. Parmenides recognized the same injustice in the mortals' Light-Night opposition. However (and herein lies his originality), Parmenides substituted the overbearing ἄπειρον in which the inexorable τάξις τοῦ χρόνου is realized, condemning the guilty being to death, with a more virtuous ἐόν, in which injustice is never done (or, if you prefer, an even more totalitarian ἐόν: the ἀδικία of annihilation is not fulfilled because Δίκη does not loosen the "chains," but "keeps them tight" and prevents destruction—B8.14–15). However, if opposites can only coexist, Parmenides ends up depriving himself of an effective explanatory model of the cosmos that was successful for the preceding philosophies. Contraries, in fact, are at the basis not only of Anaximander's cosmology, but also of the Pythagoreans' and Heraclitus' view of reality. Although Parmenides proposes an approach that is analogous to that of these thinkers (consider Heraclitus' unity of opposites), he excludes the alternation of opposites. Parmenides substitutes for this a model which, although in a developed form, would be very popular in later philosophy. This is the model based on the mixture-separation dynamic, a model that does not imply the destruction of the elements involved. The visible forms therefore result from the mixture and separation of Fire and Night, that is of hot and cold.

We have noted that just as there is no direct testimony to the concept of Fire and Night as forms, there is none for physical objects as forms either. This, however, is not completely true. Even though it is true that nobody explicitly attributes this idea to Parmenides, we have evidence for the fact that, after

Parmenides, the theory according to which worldly things are visible forms, resultants of a mixture of fundamentally invisible elements, became a guiding concept in natural philosophy. This explanatory model, as mentioned above, found great resonance in post-Parmenidean pluralist philosophy. The central idea is always the same: to counterpose substantial, immutable, and permanent beings to unstable and impermanent appearances. The fact that this theoretical model comes from Parmenides has always been acknowledged. We could be even more radical and ask ourselves whether it was Parmenides who initiated not just this philosophical theme, but also a certain technical vocabulary.[40] Consider Empedocles, a "Parmenidean" philosopher. At fragment B137.1 (in the Καθαρμοί) he uses the expression μορφὴν ἀλλάξαντα and refers to the son who has "changed form" and, having probably become a ruminant (for a recomposition of the "roots," naturally), has his throat cut by his unwitting father (this is the famous and dramatic argument for Empedocles' propaganda in favor of vegetarianism). As for Περὶ φύσεως, for example in fragment B21, the word appears twice: at verse 2, we find μορφή, which refers to the "form of the elements," but from the following list those forms seem to consist in the things that correspond to those elements (celestial bodies, compact, and solid things . . .); at verse 7, we find διάμορφα which indicates the diversity of things in the Conflict. The concept of form returns at other times in Empedocles. In Anaxagoras there is a similar concept, but expressed by a different term, ὄψις: consider the famous fragment B21a, ὄψις γὰρ τῶν ἀδήλων τὰ φαινόμενα. With the atomists, who also maintained the model of physical reality as a play of visible appearances constituted of invisible elements, the notion of form was retraced to the fundamental structure itself: atoms are distinguished, in reality, also by their shape (μορφή or σχῆμα, e.g., 67 A9 DK). This new idea (partly Anaxagorean), according to which external forms may be justified by appealing to invisible forms, was not without consequences.

[40] A. H. Coxon, *Philosophy of Forms*, p. 3 (who even continues to maintain that the forms are Fire and Night) writes: "Parmenides' ontology had given rise to a philosophical controversy about the concept of form itself."

If we consider that, already in Empedocles, in addition to μορφή we sometimes find the word εἶδος, a word that was to have some philosophical importance, we can perhaps guess that the idea of pure, fundamental, invisible, and eternal forms, as a justification of the exterior appearance of sensible reality, is the version that Plato proposed of this ancient Pre-Socratic theory, first conceived by Parmenides.

# Bibliography


Bollack, Jean. *Parménide: De l'étant au monde*. Paris: Verdier, 2006.

Brague, Rémi. "La vraisemblance du faux." *Études sur Parménide*, Vol. II. Edited by P. Aubenque. Paris: Vrin, 1987: 44–68.

Calvo, Tomás. "Truth and Doxa in Parmenides." *Archiv für Geschichte der Philosophie* 59 (1977): 245–260.

Casertano, Giovanni. *Parmenide: Il metodo, la scienza, l'esperienza*. Naples: Guida, 1978.

Cerri, Giovanni. *Parmenide: Poema sulla natura*. Milan: Rizzoli, 1999.

Cordero, Néstor-Luis. *Le deux chemins de Parménide*. Paris/Bruxelles: Vrin/Ousia, 1984; 2nd Edition, augmented and corrected, 1997.

_____. *By Being, It Is: The Thesis of Parmenides*. Las Vegas: Parmenides Publishing, 2004.

Coxon, A. H. *The Philosophy of Forms: An Analytical and Historical Commentary on Plato's Parmenides*. Assen: Van Gorcum, 1999.

Curd, Patricia. *The Legacy of Parmenides: Eleatic Monism and Later Pre-Socratic Thought*. Princeton: Princeton University Press, 1997; 2nd Edition with new introduction, Las Vegas: Parmenides Publishing, 2004.

Deichgräber, Karl. *Parmenides' Auffahrt zur Göttin des Rechts*. Wiesbaden: Akademie der Wissenschaften und der Literatur in Mainz, 1959.

Diels, Hermann. *Parmenides Lehrgedicht*. Berlin: G. Reimer, 1897; 2nd Edition, Sankt Augustin: Academia Verlag, 2003.

Falus, R. "Parmenides-Interpretationen." *Acta Antiqua Academiae Scientiarum Hungaricae* 8 (1960): 267–294.

Finkelberg, Aryeh. "'Like by Like' and Two Reflections of Reality in Parmenides." *Hermes* 114 (1986): 405–412.

Furley, David. J. "Notes on Parmenides." In E. N. Lee, A. P. D. Mourelatos, and R. M. Rorty, eds., *Exegesis and Argument: Studies in Greek Philosophy Presented to Gregory Vlastos*. Assen: Van Gorcum, 1973: 1–15.

Furth, Montgomery. "Elements of Eleatic Ontology." *Journal of the History of Philosophy* 6 (1968): 111–132.

Gallop, David. *Parmenides of Elea: Fragments*. Toronto: Phoenix, 1984.

Guarracino, V. *Parmenide: Poema sulla natura*. Milan: Medusa, 2006.

Joël, Karl. *Geschichte der antiken Philosophie*. Tübingen: Mohr, 1921.

Loew, E. "Das Lehrgedicht des Parmenides: Gliederung und Gedankengang." *Rheinisches Museum* 78 (1929): 148–165.

Mourelatos, Alexander P. D. *The Route of Parmenides*. New Haven: Yale University Press, 1970; Revised and Expanded Edition, Las Vegas: Parmenides Publishing, 2008.

Patin, Alois. "Parmenides im Kampfe gegen Heraklit." *Jahrbücher für classische Philologie*, Supplementband 25 (1899): 489–660.

Pulpito, Massimo. "*Ta dokounta*: Oggetti Reali di Opinioni False." In L. Rossetti and F. Marcacci, eds., *Parmenide scienziato?* Sankt Augustin: Academia Verlag, 2008: 113–122.

Robinson, Thomas M. "Parmenides on the Ascertainment of the Real." *Canadian Journal of Philosophy* 4 (1975): 622–633.

Tarán, Leonardo. *Parmenides*. Princeton: Princeton University Press, 1965.

Thanassas, Panagiotis. "How Many Doxai Are There in Parmenides?" *Rhizai* 3 (2006): 199–218.

Woodbury, Leonard. "Parmenides on Names." *Harvard Studies in Classical Philology* 63 (1958): 145–169.

_____. "Parmenides on Naming by Mortal Men: fr. B8, 53–56." *Ancient Philosophy* 6 (1986): 1–13.

# What is Parmenides' Being?

Chiara Robbiano


## Summary

Nobody could know what ἐόν meant before listening to the Poem: even native speakers of Ancient Greek needed to acquire new mental categories and form this new concept, ἐόν, which is usually translated as "Being." Throughout his Poem, Parmenides teaches his audience to form this concept. One of the means he uses are the signs (σήματα) given by the goddess to the traveler in fr. B8. I focus here on the fourth σῆμα, where Parmenides gives hints about the special relation between Being and those who understand Being. I will show that Being is the fundamental unity of what-is (what is stable, without differences, development, needs) and what-understands. This perfect unity is what the audience is encouraged to understand. This unity is also the condition of the possibility of human understanding. Human beings can, in fact, understand this unity, directly, with an act of νοεῖν, since νοεῖν and Being are not separate but are one.


## 1. The starting point and the sketch of the project

There are questions that have become traditional in the history of Parmenides scholarship and that continue to be asked. One of them is "What is Parmenides' Being?" Many different suggestions have been made in order to shed light on this issue:[1] e.g., Being is the result of a law of thought;[2] it is the world regarded as

[1] See also Robbiano, *Becoming Being,* ch. 3, section 3.4.
[2] Cf. e.g., Owen, "Eleatic Questions"; Tarán, *Parmenides.*

its totality and unity;[3] it is one;[4] it is many;[5] it is the being of the world without the world;[6] the nature of Being can be discovered by looking at the value of the verb "to be," which is predicative;[7] existential;[8] veridical.[9]

My starting point, in order to give a new answer to the old question about Parmenides' Being, is the following. Parmenides' audience, when listening to the Poem for the first time, could not possibly have guessed to what Parmenides was referring when he used the words ἐόν and εἶναι in the Poem. They could not possibly have guessed it just by reflecting on the meaning of the verb εἶναι: the fact that they were native speakers of Greek was not enough. They could only understand what Parmenides meant by εἶναι and ἐόν *after* having succesfully taken the perspective on reality that is encouraged by the Poem. The Poem makes, in fact, a call on its audience and tries to persuade them to accept its guidance, which will lead them to a new understanding of reality. In order to achieve this understanding, the audience needs to acquire new mental categories so that they can look at reality in a new way. They will need to form a new concept, which, in the course of the Poem, will often be referred to as ἐόν, which is usually translated "Being." Being is what can be understood by the ones who, after listening to the words of the goddess, have acquired a *specific perspective.* The audience will acquire such a perspective if they follow the guidance of the goddess, made up of encouragements, warnings, alternatives, and, as we shall see below, signs (σήματα).

---

3 Cf. e.g., Casertano, *Parmenide.*

4 Cf. e.g., Mackenzie, "Parmenides Dilemma"; Sedley's "Parmenides" and "Parmenides and Melissus."

5 Cf. e.g., Curd, *Legacy.*

6 Cf. Reale, *Storia Delle Filosofia Antica,* p. 126: ". . . è chiaro che l'essere parmenideo è l'essere del cosmo, immobilizzato e in parte purificato, ma ancora chiaramente riconoscibile: è, per quanto possa suonare paradossale, l'essere del cosmo senza il cosmo . . . . "

7 E.g., Calogero's *Studi Sull'eleatismo* and *Storia Della Logica Antica*; Mourelatos, *Route*; Austin, *Parmenides.*

8 E.g., Owen, "Eleatic Questions"; Tarán, *Parmenides*; Gallop's "'Is' or 'Is Not'?" and *Parmenides of Elea;* Gómez-Lobo, *Parménides;* Gadamer, "Parmenides."

9 E.g., Kahn, "Thesis"; Jantzen, "Parmenides"; Aubenque, "Syntaxe"; Kahn, "Being."

It is important to realize that my claim that Being can be understood only if one looks in a certain way, i.e., from a certain perspective, does *not* imply that such a perspective (or the minds of the audience who look from that perspective) *originates* (is the source of) Being. I do not attribute any idealism or postmodernism to Parmenides: I rather claim that Being is both *real* and that it is what one can see if one looks *at reality* in a certain way. "To look at reality in a certain way," implies focussing on what does *not* change, what is always and everywhere the same, does not have differences and does not lack anything.

One may well choose to look, on the contrary, on what *does* change and on the differences one sees around: this enterprise, even if it can be useful, will never bring one to the truth, as the goddess explains in the second part of the Poem about the opinions of the mortals. Parmenides is a realist and according to him there is just *one* reality[10] that can be looked at in *two* ways, which are different in that they focus on different aspects of reality.[11]

Even less postmodern is Parmenides when it comes to epistemology. Parmenides is not only a realist, but also a full-blood epistemological optimist who wants to help his audience, by means of the Poem, to look at reality in such a way as to understand it, i.e., so as to grasp nothing less than the truth about it.

In the first place, we shall turn to some instruments that Parmenides has in order to guide his audience toward understanding. These instruments are σήματα, signs. I will first make it clear that σήματα are always instruments of communication that require an interpretative effort on the part of the addressee. I will argue that three layers of interpretation can be given to what I regard as the 4 σήματα of B8: the σήματα that say in the first place that ἐόν is 1. without birth and death, 2. homogeneous, 3. immobile and unchangeable, and 4. without development. Then I will focus on the fourth σῆμα, where we

10 For the explanation of the fact that Parmenides is not Plato and does not postulate two "worlds" but only one reality, looked at in different ways, see Cordero, *By Being*, p. 155: "... the genuine philosopher ... and the mortals who know nothing ... share the same object of study ... But the same object of study can be looked at in a deeper or shallower away."

11 For my interpretation of the Δόξαι, see my book, *Becoming Being*, ch. 7.

shall find Parmenides' suggestion about the relation between Being and those who understand Being. In this suggestion lies the founding stone of Western philosophy: the conviction that there is homogeneity between human mind and truth. Western philosophers have cherished this Parmenidean gift for millennia.

Thus, what is Being? I will argue that Being is the fundamental unity of what-is (what is stable, without differences, development, needs) and what-understands. This perfect unity is what the apprentice philosophers, who have trained to disregard every kind of what-is-not (or not-being), are encouraged to understand. This unity is also the condition of the possibility of human understanding. The apprentice philosophers can, in fact, understand it, directly, with an act of νοεῖν, which can understand Being since νοεῖν and Being are not separate but are one.

## 2. The σήματα

At the beginning of B8 the goddess uses the word σήματα to introduce what follows.

> B8.1–3: . . . μόνος δ' ἔτι μῦθος ὁδοῖο
> λείπεται ὡς ἔστιν· ταύτῃ δ' ἐπὶ σήματ' ἔασι
> πολλὰ μάλ', ὡς . . .
>
> Only one story still remains of the way
> that-is: on that way there are very many signs
> that . . .

On using the word σήματα she suggests a lot to the audience about the status of what she will say and about how the audience should deal with what has been referred to as σήματα. As van Ophuijsen[12] has shown, the presence of an addressee belongs to the very core of the verb σημαίνειν which has more to do with communication than with description:

> . . . *sēmainein* is best understood in the strict sense of providing a *sēma* (σῆμα), a mark or signpost pointing

[12] Ophuijsen, "Parts," p. 84.

> the recipient addressed to the thing, fact or state of affairs envisaged; in other words, that it applies not so much to expression pure and simple as, more specifically, to *communication*. It is not just that *vox significat rem*, but rather that *ego voce tibi*, or *vobis*, *significo rem*.

Moreover, we can assume that the word σήματα in the mouth of the goddess at B8.2 evokes the frame of reference of a god or a goddess giving or showing signs (think of e.g., birds, lightnings, dreams or oracles) to mortals in order to let them know things usually out of their reach, i.e., gods offer mortals a glance upon reality from the divine point of view. This frame suggests what kind of behavior the words of the goddess require from the ones who hear them: σήματα are such things that must be interpreted.

The awareness of the need to interpret signs in order to grasp the truth at which they point can be found in other fragments of the Presocratics, e.g., in Heraclitus (DK22 B93).[13] Heraclitus reminds his readers that the oracle does not conceal or say, but gives signs (σημαίνει).[14] One of the most important implications of this is that an oracle requires an interpretation. By saying this Heraclitus stresses a property that belongs not only to oracles but also to the language of his own book. The truth does not lie on the surface of the words; and yet words—if they are fully interpreted—can show the way to the truth.

Parmenides and Heraclitus' audiences are, at the beginning of the fifth century, already familiar with texts about gods who give signs to mortals (dreams, oracles, birds . . .) that can be interpreted in *different* ways. They are familiar with the fact that the poets, the fundamental source of education, need to be interpreted and can be interpreted in different ways.[15] At the beginning of the fifth century, the audience might well know that literal and allegorical

13 Diels-Kranz, *Fragmente*.

14 Kahn, *Art*, p. 123. See also Morgan, *Myth*, pp. 55ff.

15 About the awareness of the need of interpretation in Ancient Greece and the practice of interpreting oracles and of explaining what poets meant, by means of glosses, paraphrase, and allegory, see Sluiter, "Part Three," pp. 163–168.

interpretations of Homer on the one hand differed very much and on the other hand could live next to each other.[16]

Whereas scholars[17] usually identify the σήματα announced at B8.2 with the predicates of Being enumerated at B8.2–6, I agree with Cerri (214) in identifying the σήματα rather with the *arguments* that follow (B8.6–B8.49). These arguments—just as every sign given by a god—must be interpreted.

In the first place, the goddess herself anticipates one "interpretation" of her own signs, by suggesting that they point at the fact that Being is: 1. not generated and imperishable; 2. homogeneous; 3. immobile; 4. complete. This is what I call "the first layer of interpretation."

> B8.1–6: . . . μόνος δ' ἔτι μῦθος ὁδοῖο
> λείπεται ὡς ἔστιν· ταύτῃ δ' ἐπὶ σήματ' ἔασι
> πολλὰ μάλ', ὡς ἀγένητον ἐὸν καὶ ἀνώλεθρόν ἐστιν,
> οὖλον μουνογενές τε καὶ ἀτρεμὲς ἠδ' ἀτέλεστον
> οὐδέ ποτ' ἦν οὐδ' ἔσται, ἐπεὶ νῦν ἔστιν ὁμοῦ πᾶν,
> ἕν, συνεχές . . .
>
> Only one story still remains of the way
> that-is: on that way there are very many signs
> that Being [1.] is not generated and imperishable
> [2.] entire, unique and [3.] immobile; and [4.] incomplete [it]
> never was nor will be, since [it] is now all together,
> one, continuous . . .

[16] Theagenes of Rhegium, at the end of the sixth century, had already tried, by means of allegory, to find a kind of truth in Homer that was different from the one about what happened in front of the rock of Troy in a far past. Theagenes interprets, for instance, a pair of warriors fighting as the conflict between opposite principles in nature. About the practice of allegoric interpretation of Homer from the sixth century, see Most, "Poetics."

[17] Cf. e.g., Coxon, *Fragments*, p. 193 [2009: p. 312]: "On this [way], she proceeds, there are many monuments or landmarks (σήματα), which (or some of which) she at once enumerates; they appear as predicates of 'Being,' the applicability of which is then established deductively."

As we have seen, the context of a god giving σήματα—e.g., oracles—suggests that the interpretation is sometimes not as transparent and one-sided as it may seem.[18] To realize this can enhance our understanding of Parmenides' B8 and Parmenides' ideas about the achievement of knowledge. What the goddess says in B8 is not the whole story: even if one hears all the words of B8 and understands what one hears, one still has not walked the way of truth—just like the one who has read the travel guide to a faraway land but has not made the journey. The journey will be the real experience, whereas the travel guide is just the preparation.

I submit that the σήματα of B8 can tell us much more than that Being, on the way ὡς ἔστιν, is without birth and death, homogeneous, immobile, and without development.

## 3. The fourth σῆμα. 1st layer of interpretation: Being is complete; 2nd layer of interpretation: theories of development do not lead to understanding

Elsewhere[19] I have shown in detail that every one of the σήματα can also be interpreted as part of an ἔλεγχος that dissuades the audience from engaging in the traditional ways of explaining reality: 1. cosmogony, 2. theory of differentiation, 3. theory of change, and 4. theory of development. For instance, the first sign, the one about the impossibility of an origin for Being, must (also) be interpreted as offering this advice: "do not go and look for an origin: do not engage in cosmogonies! If you do so you exit this way and take another way: the one 'that-is-not.'"

According to this second, elenctic, interpretation, the fourth σῆμα (on which I concentrate in this paper) warns the audience

[18] I have another reason for supposing a plurality of levels of meaning in the words of the goddess in what we know as B8. Mourelatos describes the language of the goddess in the second part of the Poem (the Δόξα) in terms of ambiguity (of *amphilogia*). Mourelatos regards this as a very powerful and effective instrument in communicating various levels of meaning to the ones in the audience who could understand them. Parmenides had, thus, a very powerful instrument at his disposal: it would have been strange if he had not used it in the first part of the Poem, but only in the second one. See Mourelatos, *Route*, ch. 9.

[19] Robbiano, *Becoming Being*, ch. 4 and, more recently, "Duas Fases Parmenídeas."

that no theory about the *development* of the universe can be trustworthy, since it would involve not-being. Theories including development were popular among Parmenides' contemporaries and predecessors, some of whom saw the universe in continuous motion or development towards a next state or condition (think of both Anaximander and Heraclitus). Such models of the universe cannot lead one to understanding, according to Parmenides.

According to the first layer of interpretation of this fourth σῆμα, Being is not incomplete, as the goddess had claimed at B8.4–6: "incomplete [it] never was nor will be, since [it] is now all together, one, continuous." Being is not on its way to become something different, it is not at a certain stage in its development. The goddess explains throughout B8.32–44 that Being is complete, not in development and not lacking anything (B8.32–37); that it is not split in any of the oppositions suggested by the words of mortals (B8.38–41), but safely guarded in its unity by Μοῖρα (B8.38–39); that, whereas the boundaries that mortals draw between opposites are not true, the only boundary is the extreme one that encloses Being as a perfect sphere (B8.42–44). Then (B8.44–49), the argumentation proceeds in order to show that only the presence of not-being inside Being would produce internal differences; which would have to be overcome at a later stage, e.g., by developing in such a way as to become smaller here and bigger there. Within Being there is no room for development, since there is no not-being that could prevent it from being perfect. Indeed, development presupposes, for instance, a "not being yet": a child develops since it is not yet an adult; in a child there is room for development: he or she will become bigger, whereas Being does not behave like that. Being does not lack anything and always remains the same.

## 4. The fourth σῆμα. 3rd layer of interpretation: the complete Being does not lack νοεῖν; mortals understand Being

A third layer of interpretation will reveal to the audience that the σήματα do not only point at characteristics of Being and do not only contain methodological advice about approaches that one should avoid if one is looking for understanding. The σήματα also point (for the one who is capable of interpreting them) at those human beings who understand Being, i.e., at their relation (at the relation of their minds) with Being, i.e., the object that they (try to) understand, and at the right approach in order to understand it.

By discussing this layer of interpretation of the σήματα, especially of the fourth σῆμα, I will discuss what I have called the Parmenidean gift to Western Philosophy, which can also be described as an antidote against the impossibility for mortals to know the truth. This impossibility was held as unbridgeable for normal mortals, both by the tradition—who attributed either no mind, νόος, to mortals or a νόος completely dependent on the gods[20]— and, more recently, by Xenophanes.[21] Parmenides roots his gift in the perspective of the one who, after abandoning the way that involves not-being, becomes committed to the way that-is. One of the signs of the goddess on the way that-is—the fourth sign—points in the direction of "no lack" (B8.32–33).

While arguing that Being is complete and not in need of anything else in order to become perfect, the goddess explains that "no need" and "no lack" also involve no lack of νοεῖν: νοεῖν is also "part" of Being, i.e., an undifferentiated part of it, which is to say that νοεῖν is Being, as the goddess already stated at B3;

---

20 Mansfeld, *Die Offenbarung*, explores throughout in his first chapter the theme, very popular in lyric poetry and in other kinds of poetry before Parmenides, of the impotence (ἀμηκανία) and dependence of the human νόος on the gods: e.g., Semonides Fr. 1. D., vv. 3–5: νόος δ' οὐκ ἐπ' ἀνθρώποισιν· ἀλλ' ἐφήμεροι/ ἃ δὴ βοτὰ ζώομεν οὐδὲν εἰδότες,/ ὅκως ἕκαστον ἐκτελευτήσει θεός. *There is no intelligence among men, but we live like grazing animals, subject to what the day brings with no knowledge of how the god will bring each day to pass*, Gerber, *Greek Iambic Poetry*; Theognis 141–142: ἄνθρωποι δὲ μάταια νομίζομεν εἰδότες οὐδέν·/ θεοὶ δὲ κατὰ σφέτερον πάντα τελοῦσι νόον. Palmer, "Indo-European."

21 Bodnár's essay, "Reason," calls "archaic 'epistemology,'" the "doctrine about the (im)possibility of human knowledge," (p. 61) and shows how this doctrine has been integrated into the systems of the philosophers before Parmenides, especially Xenophanes and Alcmaeon, who accepted archaic epistemology "to limit the certainty of what they assert themselves" (p. 63). As Bodnár argues, the effects of implanting this anthropological paradigm into philosophy could have been devastating. About Parmenides' rescue of philosophy's pretensions to reaching the truth from this impasse, see also Hermann, *To Think Like God*, 132ff. and Robbiano, *Becoming Being*, ch. 2.

and that neither νοεῖν nor anything else can be something next to Being, as she will observe in B8.36–37:

> B8.36–37: . . . οὐδὲν γὰρ <ἦ> ἔστιν ἢ ἔσται
> ἄλλο πάρεξ τοῦ ἐόντος . . .
> . . . for nothing else is or will be
> apart from Being . . .

But first the goddess says that to understand is one and the same with what causes the understanding—i.e., the object of understanding.

> B8.34: ταὐτόν δ' ἔστὶ νοεῖν τε καὶ οὕνεκεν ἔστι νόημα
> to understand is the same as what causes the understanding

The identification seems to be between the understanding and what prompts, causes or fulfills understanding,[22] which, in verse B8.35, turns out to be Being. The other possible way of interpreting this verse, that is, that νοεῖν is the same as the thought "that-is," is not to be excluded;[23] however I am not willing to accept that the *only* purpose of these lines is to explain something about the *content* of understanding, by saying that what one must understand is "that-is." I assume that the goddess, in the context of the argumentation about the completeness of Being, also clarifies here something crucial about Parmenides' monism, and about the one who adopts the perspective that leads to monism. Thus, what we

---

[22] This verse has been interpreted as the identification of νοεῖν and the reason, (cf. Fritz, "Nous, Noein," 237–238; Vlastos, "Parmenides' Theory," p. 68) or the goal (Diels, p. 85: "Denken und des Gedankens Ziel ist eins," in Tarán, *Parmenides*) of understanding. Cerri, *Parmenide Di Elea*, p. 235 observes about οὕνεκεν: "qui l'espressione non ha, come al v. 37 [32], valore di congiunzione, ma conserva in tutta la sua pienezza il significato originario di pronome neutro relativo al caso genitivo + preposizione; occorre anzi aggiungere che, sul piano semantico, il pronome relativo sottintende e ingloba in sé il pronome dimostrativo neutro al caso nominativo, al quale si riferisce: intendi τὸ οὗ ἕνεκεν, 'ciò a causa del quale.'" Cf. also Cerri, *Parmenide Di Elea*, p. 232.

[23] Cf. scholars who take οὕνεκεν to mean ὅτι, e.g., Tarán, *Parmenides*, pp. 121–122.

learn from verse B8.34 may well be, *both* that the successful νοεῖν is the one that focuses on the thought or understanding "that-is": the successful νοεῖν is the one of the person who chooses the right way towards truth i.e., the right perspective; *and* that νοεῖν is the same as τὸ οὗ ἕνεκεν (that which causes) that the understanding "is" (occurs). We should not try to define too strictly what οὕνεκεν, i.e., τὸ οὗ ἕνεκεν, suggests at this stage: it is the cause, the reason, the goal, the subject, the object of understanding: what can originate understanding, something without which there is no understanding. This vague οὕνεκεν ἔστι νόημα (34) is immediately specified as τὸ ἐόν: the "thing" without which (35) no understanding can be found:

> B8.35–36: οὐ γὰρ ἄνευ τοῦ ἐόντος ἐν ᾧ πεφατισμένον ἐστίν
> εὑρήσεις τὸ νοεῖν . . .
> for without Being you will not find understanding in what has been said (by me, i.e., the goddess) . . .

According to my interpretation, ἐν ᾧ refers[24] *to an implied antecedent such as "my words, the verses of the Poem"*: "in what has been said," i.e., "in the words that have been said by me." I do not agree with the majority of scholars who take ἐν ᾧ to refer anaphorically to τοῦ ἐόντος.[25]

---

[24] Cf. Sedley who translates: "for in what has been said [i.e., the preceding arguments (sc. in the fragments)] you will not find thinking separate from Being" (Sedley, "Parmenides"). My doubts about the possibility of this grammatical construction (which had prevented me from adopting it in my book, *Becoming Being*) have been dispelled after David Sedley kindly drew my attention to the virtual exact grammatical parallel of it in Plato, *Phaedo* 69a3. As the majority of the scholars, the message that Sedley sees in the passage is monism. He interprets this one and a half verse as expressing this monistic thought: "thought and being are one single thing—as I have explained in the fragments." It certainly makes sense to interpret these verses as repeating once more the idea that νοεῖν is not separated from Being. However, these verses seem to express more than only monism, namely something about the words and arguments of the goddess (see below).

[25] Cf. e.g., DK vol. 1, 238: "denn nicht ohne das Seiende, in dem es als Ausgesprochenes ist, kannst du das Denken antreffen." Cf. also e.g., Aubenque, *Études Sur Parménide,* 2 Volumes, p. 40: "Car tu ne trouveras pas le penser sans l'être, dans lequel <le penser> est exprimé [For you will not find thinking

In their interpretation it is difficult to reconcile the idea that νοεῖν is *expressed in Being* with what the Poem says about *words*. The majority of scholars focus on the—of course crucial—message that νοεῖν will not be found without Being—so far so good—but then they interpret ἐν ᾧ πεφατισμένον ἐστιν, as the claim that νοεῖν also belongs to Being, *in the form of expression / argumentation*. That means that they regard *words* and arguments that express νοεῖν as belonging to Being. What would be the point of suggesting the location of words in Being, while the passage closely following B8.35–36 states that words are something that mortals have instituted, that they are not true, since they draw oppositions that seem to split Being?

It is much more coherent with the rest of the Poem to see two complementary indications in the words of the goddess addressed to the one who wants to find νοεῖν. How to find νοεῖν? In the goddess' own words, ἐν ᾧ πεφατισμένον ἐστίν and also οὐ ἄνευ τοῦ ἐόντος, that is to say, in her words that reveal or express[26] νοεῖν, but not without Being. Thus, the goddess explains that one will not find νοεῖν in what expresses or reveals νοεῖν (= in all the words and arguments that help one achieve νοεῖν), if one lacks Being: in order to achieve understanding, it is not enough to listen to the words of the goddess, but one must find Being as well. One cannot achieve understanding just by listening

without the being in which <the thinking> has been given expression].”; Cerri, *Parmenide Di Elea,* p. 153: “senza l’ “essere” mai, in cui diviene parola, puoi trovare l’intelletto,” and p. 58: “Non troverai mai il capire (. . .) al di fuori dell’ essere (. . .) nel quale il capire risulta espresso (. . .)”; Collobert, *L’être De Parménide,* p. 19: “Car sans l’étant, dans lequel il est exprimé, tu ne trouveras pas le penser.” For discussions of B8.34–35 see Mourelatos, *Route,* pp. 170–172.

[26] There are only 5 occurrences of πεφατισμένος in the full corpus of Greek literature, besides the quotations of Parmenides B8.35 (3 by Simplicius, 1 by Proclus). Two are in the *Scholia in Pindarum* and three in Hesychius. πεφατισμένος occurs in the *Scholia*: 1. ἐν δὲ Πυθῶνι χρησθέν/ παλαίφατον (*Olympian* 2, 39–40) is explained as the oracle long ago “ordained, predestined” (πεφατισμένον) by Apollo and told to Laius; 2. παλαίφατον ἀγορά (*Nemean* 3, 14) is explained as the *agora* with much tradition (πεφατισμένην), hence the *agora* about which many positive things have been handed down and sung since long ago. It occurs in Hesychius always in relation with a god or an oracle; we might translate “ordained by a god” / “foretold by an oracle.” It seems, thus, appropriate for the goddess to refer to her speech with this word, which could possibly suggest once more that her speech that tells of νοεῖν, like the expressions of oracles, must be interpreted.

to words that explain something about understanding or give directions how to find it: one must go beyond those words and seek Being at which the words point. These words of the goddess encourage the audience to regard the given σήματα as *signs* pointing to something else and not as elements of a definitive, absolute, description of Being. After listening to her words, the audience must accept that her words *alone* will not bring them to understanding.

B8.34–36 are, thus, no diversion from the discussion about Being:[27] these verses are embedded in the discussion of its fourth sign: its completeness, the fact that it does not lack anything. This characteristic excludes both the possibility of something next to Being and the possibility of its development. What has been regarded as an excursus is actually a part of the argument about the completeness of Being: Being also includes νοεῖν: thought / mind / understanding.[28]

Moreover, as we have seen, the fourth sign can give information about the minds of apprentice philosophers (and their relations to Being) to the one who tries not to miss any layer of meaning in the signs of the goddess. In fact, what the goddess says about νοεῖν is something that can be applied to subjects that are endowed with the capacity of νοεῖν. Parmenides does not follow the tradition that denies νόος to mortals: mortals do have a νόος. Therefore this completeness of Being must be put in relation with an understanding in which human beings share. The audience who is willing to interpret the signs of the goddess will realize that the signs also say something about the knowing subject (the audience) and not only about the object (to be) known, i.e., the signs of the goddess reveal to the audience that they *can* understand Being with their νόος.

---

[27] E.g., Coxon, *Fragments*, pp. 208–209 [2009: p. 330 n40] maintains that at B8.34–41 Parmenides "diverges from his discussion of the nature of Being in order to consider that of human experience."

[28] For the elaboration of this conclusion see my book, *Becoming Being*, ch. 5, where I develop A. A. Long's suggestion that: "when we are thinking Being with Parmenides we are (in) Being and at least momentarily lose our phenomenal identities as two-headed mortals (Long, "Parmenides," p. 147). On this issue see also Crystal, "Scope."

## 5. The treatment of words in the last σῆμα

Unfortunately habit, i.e., the normal way of looking at reality of which the words that they use are witnesses, lets their νόος wander and prevents it from focusing on Being and understanding it.

After dealing with νοεῖν, the so-called "excursus" deals with human names; however, it is now easy for us to see that also what the goddess says about human names can be integrated in the argument:

> B8.38–41: . . . τῷ πάντ' ὄνομ(α) ἔσται,[29]
> ὅσσα βροτοὶ κατέθεντο πεποιθότες εἶναι ἀληθῆ,
> γίγνεσθαί τε καὶ ὄλλυσθαι, εἶναί τε καὶ οὐχί,
> καὶ τόπον ἀλλάσσειν διά τε χρόα φανὸν ἀμείβειν.

> Therefore all those things will be named
> that mortals have established, persuaded that they are true
> to be born and to die, to be and not to be
> to change place and bright complexion.

What human words point to are not things or processes that could challenge the completeness or the perfection of Being: they are just names. All names that mortals use—B8.40–41: 1. *to be born and to die,* 2. *to be and not to be*, 3. *to change place and* 4. *change bright complexion*—seem to refer to the characteristics that have been denied to Being throughout B8 and that might well be summed up here. The idea may be that, once one finally—when listening to the fourth σῆμα—accepts that Being is not in development and not incomplete, one will have successfully rejected both birth and death, as argued in the first σῆμα; and differentiation, as argued in the second; and movement and change, as argued in the third, and, indeed development, which the fourth σῆμα rejects. In fact, what is complete and not in development

[29] Coxon, *Fragments,* p. 211 [2009: p. 334] observes: "ὄνομ' ἔσται ["will be a name"] is preserved by the ms. F at p. 87 of Simplicius . . .," whereas Woodbury, "Parmenides on Names," defends ὀνόμασται, instead of ὄνομ' ἔσται. For the argument against Woodbury's choice see Meijer, *Parmenides,* p. 176.

has no birth and no death (γίγνεσθαί τε καὶ ὄλλυσθαι, first σῆμα); what is not in development has no internal differences between something that is and something that is not (yet) (εἶναί τε καὶ οὐχί, second σῆμα); it will not change place, as opposed to, for instance, animals who are looking for something that they do not yet have (καὶ τόπον ἀλλάσσειν, third σῆμα); it will not change bright color or complexion, which can imply a sort of development (διά τε χρόα φανὸν ἀμείβειν, fourth σῆμα), like the one of animals that grow up, mature and then grow old.[30]

It is important to notice that even *to be* and *not to be* are regarded as mere names: truth is one homogeneous unity, whereas even the most useful names always split this unity: even the word Being is just a name, since it suggests the reality of its opposite, not-being. Therefore also Being (and not-being) are just names, words: σήματα that one must interpret in order to find the truth.

## 6. Conclusion

Words like those of B8 offer guidance on the journey towards the truth. And the truth is to be found by interpreting the persuasive words of the goddess that lead to the understanding of a new concept: ἐόν, Being. To the one who is willing to interpret the signs of the goddess they will *not only* (1st layer of interpretation) point at characteristics of the trustworthy object of understanding, Being, and *not only* (2nd layer of interpretation) at the methods the apprentice philosophers should not adopt in order to reach the truth. Her signs, while pointing at Being, *also* (3rd layer of interpretation) give hints about the understanding (νοεῖν) that is directed towards Being. The signs of the goddess, especially the fourth one, point, in fact at the fundamental unity of νοεῖν and Being. Being is the unity of what is (stable, unchangeable, homogenous and perfect) and what understands.

This unity called Being assures to every mortal the possibility of grasping the truth. In fact this unity implies, on the one hand, that understanding (νοεῖν) is not possible without Being: therefore this guided journey toward the formation of

[30] Coxon, *Fragments*, pp. 211–212 [2009: p. 335] observes: "the noun *chrôs* is not used of inanimate things."

the concept of Being is the only way left to the one who really seeks the truth and is not content with opinions.

On the other hand, Being would not be complete without understanding: therefore, when one realizes what this Being is, one will also realize that it includes the possibility of being understood directly by this "instrument," νοεῖν, that mortals possess.

This complete Being which includes understanding is the founding stone of Western Philosophy.

# Bibliography


Aubenque, Pierre, ed. *Études sur Parménide,* 2 Volumes. Paris: Vrin, 1987.

_____. "Syntaxe et Sémantique de l'être dans le Poème de Parménide." In P. Aubenque, ed., *Études sur Parménide,* Vol. 2. Paris: Vrin, 1987: 102–134.

Austin, Scott. *Parmenides: Being, Bounds and Logic.* New Haven: Yale University Press, 1986.

Bodnár, Istvan M. "Reason and Revelation in Parmenides." *Doxa* 17 (1989): 61–67.

Calogero, Guido. *Storia Della Logica Antica, Vol. 1.: L'età Arcaica.* Bari: Laterza, 1967.

_____. *Studi sull'eleatismo.* Roma: Tipografia del senato, 1932.

Casertano, Giovanni. *Parmenide, il Metodo, la Scienza, l'Esperienza.* Napels: Guida, 1978.

Cerri, Giovanni. *Parmenide di Elea, Poema sulla Natura.* Introduzione, testo, traduzione, e note; testo greco a fronte. Milan: Biblioteca Universale Rizzoli, 1999. 2nd Edition, 2000.

Collobert, Catherine. *L'Être de Parménide ou le Refus du Temps.* Paris: Kimé, 1993.

Cordero, Néstor-Luis. *By Being, It is: The Thesis of Parmenides.* Las Vegas: Parmenides Publishing, 2004.

Coxon, A. H. *The Fragments of Parmenides: A Critical Text with Introduction, the Ancient Testimonia and a Commentary.* Assen: Van Gorcum, 1986. Revised and Expanded Edition, Las Vegas: Parmenides Publishing, 2009.

Crystal, Ian. "The Scope of Thought in Parmenides." *Classical Quarterly* 52 (2002): 207–219.

Curd, Patricia. *The Legacy of Parmenides: Eleatic Monism and Later Presocratic Thought.* Princeton: Princeton University Press, 1998. Reprinted with new introduction, Las Vegas: Parmenides Publishing, 2004.

Diels, Hermann and Walter Kranz. *Die Fragmente der Vorsokratiker,* 3 Volumes. Berlin: Weidmann, 1903. 6th Edition with final editing and revisions by W. Kranz, 1952. Editions after the 6th are mainly reprints with little or no change. Reprinted, 1996.

Gadamer, Hans-Georg. "Parmenides oder das Diesseits des Seins." *La Parola del Passato* 43 (1988): 143–176.

Gallop, David. "'Is' or 'Is not'?" *The Monist* 62 (1979): 61–80.

_____. *Parmenides of Elea: Fragments.* A text and translation with an Introduction. Toronto: University of Toronto Press, 1984. Paperback Edition, 1991. Reprinted, 2000.

Gerber, Douglas E. *Greek Iambic Poetry.* Edited and translated by D. E. Gerber. *The Loeb Classical Library* No. 259. Cambridge, MA: Harvard University Press, 1999.

Gómez-Lobo, Alfonso. *Parménides: Texto Griego, Traducción y Comentario.* Buenos Aires: Editorial Charcas, 1985.

Hermann, Arnold. *To Think Like God: Pythagoras and Parmenides. The Origins of Philosophy.* Scholarly and Illustrated Editions. Las Vegas: Parmenides Publishing, 2004.

Jantzen, Jörg. "Parmenides zum Verhältnis von Sprache und Wirklichkeit." *Zetemata* 63 (1976): 1–135.

Kahn, Charles H. "Being in Parmenides and Plato." *La Parola del Passato* 43 (1988): 237–261.

_____. *The Art and Thought of Heraclitus: An edition of the fragments with translation and commentary.* Cambridge: Cambridge University Press, 1979. First Paperback Edition, 1981. Reprinted 1999.

_____. "The Thesis of Parmenides." *The Review of Metaphysics* 22 (1968): 700–724.

Long, Anthony A. "Parmenides on Thinking Being." In J. J. Cleary and W. C. Wians, eds., *Proceedings of The Boston Area Colloquium in Ancient Philosophy* 12. Lanham: University Press of America, 1996: 125–151.

Mackenzie, Mary M. "Parmenides' Dilemma." *Phronesis* 27 (1982): 1–12.

Mansfeld, Jaap. *Die Offenbarung des Parmenides und die Menschlische Welt.* Assen: Van Gorcum, 1964.

Meijer, P. A. *Parmenides Beyond the Gates: The Divine Revelation on Being, Thinking and the Doxa.* Amsterdam: J. C. Gieben, 1997.

Morgan, Kathryn A. *Myth and Philosophy from the Presocratics to Plato.* Cambridge: Cambridge University Press, 2000.

Most, Glenn W. "The Poetics of Early Greek Philosophy." In A. A. Long, ed., *The Cambridge Companion to Early Greek Philosophy.* Cambridge: Cambridge University Press, 1999.

Mourelatos, Alexander P. D. *The Route of Parmenides.* New Haven and London: Yale University Press, 1970. Revised and Expanded Edition, Las Vegas: Parmenides Publishing, 2008.

Ophuijsen, Johannes M. van. "Parts of what speech? Stoic notions of statement and sentence; or, how the dialectician knew voice and begat syntax." In P. Swiggers and A. Wouters, eds., *Syntax in Antiquity.* Louvain (Belgium): Peeters Publishing, 2003: 77–94.

Owen, G. E. L. "Eleatic Questions." *The Classical Quarterly* 10 (1960): 84–102.

Palmer, Leonard R. "The Indo-European Origins of Greek Justice." *Transactions of the Philological Society* (1950): 149–168.

Reale, Giovanni. *Storia Delle Filosofia Antica.* Milano: Vita e Pensiero, 1975.

Robbiano, Chiara. *Becoming Being: On Parmenides' transformative philosophy.* St. Augustin: Academia Verlag, 2006.

_____. "Duas Fases Parmenídeas ao longo da Via para a verdade: Elenchos e Ananke." In *Acerca do Poema de Parmênides: Estudos apresentados no I Simpósio Internacional OUSÍA de Estudos Clássicos*, Rio de Janeiro (2006). *Anais de Filosofia Clássica,* Vol. 1, No. 2 (2007): *www.ifcs.ufrj.br/~afc.*

Sedley, David. "Parmenides." In E. Craig, ed., *Routledge Encyclopedia of Philosophy,* Vol. 7. New York: Routledge, 1998: 229–235.

_____. "Parmenides and Melissus." In A. A. Long, ed., *The Cambridge Companion To Early Greek Philosophy.* Cambridge: Cambridge University Press, 1999: 113–133.

Sluiter, Ineke. "Part Three: The Greek Tradition." In W. J. van Bekkum [et al.], *The Emergence Of Semantics In Four Linguistic Traditions: Hebrew, Sanskrit, Greek, Arabic.* Amsterdam: John Benjamins Publishing Co., 1997: 147–224.

Tarán, Leonardo. *Parmenides. A Text with Translation, Commentary and Critical Essays.* Princeton: Princeton University Press, 1965.

Vlastos, Gregory. "Parmenides' Theory of Knowledge." *Transactions and Proceedings of the American Philological Association* 77 (1946): 66–77.

von Fritz, Kurt. "Nous, Noein, and Their Derivatives in Pre-Socratic Philosophy (Excluding Anaxagoras): Part I. From the Beginnings to Parmenides." *Classical Philology* 40:4 (1945): 223–242.

Woodbury, Leonard. "Parmenides on Names." *Harvard Studies in Classical Philology* 63 (1958): 145–160. Reprinted in a slightly revised version in J. P. Anton and G. L. Kustas, eds., *Essays in Ancient Greek Philosophy.* Albany: State University of New York Press, 1971: 145–162.

# *Ta Sēmata*: On a Genealogy of the Idea of Ontological Categories

Fernando Santoro

**Summary**

My hypothesis is that some figures of speech, like catalogs, present in the sapient epics of Hesiod and Homer, as well as figures emerging from a discursive field of veracity belonging to the newborn fifth century forensic rhetoric, helped build the originality of Parmenides' categorical ontological language. Especially for the characteristics of Being, presented in fragment B8 as *signals:* σήματα. I would also like to add to these elements of language, the early physicists' (φυσικῶν) interest in limits (περάτων). With these genealogic views, we can speculate about some important parameters of ontological categories such as subordination, attribution, and opposition.

Parmenides belongs to a family of thinkers who founded philosophy, since philosophy would not exist the way it does for us if both Parmenides' Being and his metaphysical and parricidal sons, Plato and Aristotle, had not existed. Like it or not, we are a legacy emerging from his decisions. But I am less interested in the motivations that Parmenides had than in the decisions that, in spite of himself, the language in his text exposes. Not the decisions that he wisely took, but the decisions that, unaware of whether he was taking them or not, nevertheless appear in his venerable words, and especially appear in his truly terrifying syntax. Although I run the risk of being taken for an intruder in this conference, I confess that my exotic viewpoint intends to focus less on the wise statements and assumptions of a philosopher than on the well-succeeding creations of an unusual poet, even knowing that we are talking about a poet who poetized philosophy itself.

It is precisely this poet of a very special genre called "philosophy" who captivates me. Not Parmenides, the maker of monumental allegories, like his mares, his chariots and his detailed portals, but the properly categorical Parmenides, with no images and no allegories—the one who divinely exposes the barest truth about Being; Parmenides, the teller of the conceptual signals belonging to the bright fragment B8, who exposes in his absolutely demystified way his ontological thesis about the unity and immobility of Being.

In sequence, I intend to briefly present my starting points as well as my genealogical point of view, which governs my reading of fragment B8. As everyone knows, this fragment itself majestically encloses *the intrepid heart of persuasive truth*.

I believe that language is a living organism, functioning with autonomous processes and producing itself through us, its human hosts. For this reason, I neither question our philosopher's intentions, however explicit they are, nor am I concerned with apprehending them. I am properly interested in the position of his poem both as a deed and an effect of language, and as a thought that emerges in the history of literature and in the legacy of our tradition. Parmenides' Poem is unquestionably one of the most creative and original deeds belonging to this tradition, since it creates at once the philosophical science of Being, named Ontology, and also creates its very object, method, semantics and syntax. But this creation does not come from nowhere; such a thing does not exist. Being, as is well known, comes from what already is. Therefore, I intend to search for the elements that Parmenides takes from the documented deeds of Greek language, in order to examine how these elements are understood in their original context, until the next moment, when they come to appear as knowledge of reality that is expressed in an almost categorical way through conceptual signals of Being. I do not intend to proceed endlessly with my genealogies; I will restrain myself to what appears immediately relevant to the

Poem, coming both before and after it, and I will focus on the elements that can clarify the Poem's very originality concerning its linguistic usages.

My hypothesis is that some figures of speech present in the sapient epics of Hesiod and Homer, as well as figures emerging from a discursive field of veracity belonging to the newborn forensic rhetoric, help to build the originality of Parmenides' categorical ontological language. I would also like to add to these elements of language the early tradition of the physicists (φυσικῶν). Advancing cautiously, let us begin with an exposition of the cognitive resources inherent to epics.

One preliminary note: this genetic hypothesis is not sustained in an understanding of any kind of evolution from primitive forms of knowledge to more developed ones; this genealogical perspective aims to understand the unfolding of a historical process, not necessarily an evolutionary one, which would evaluate the following as something better. Nor will it evaluate it as something worse. Concerning forms of understanding like the categories, my intention is simply to analyze the creative spontaneity of language which, in its free play of experiments, finds multifarious ways of intertwining words and of weaving with them the fabric in which the world is comprehended.

## 1) The trace of Epic poetry: genealogies and catalogs

Hesiod's *Theogony* is a classical text usually presented as dwelling on the border between mythic and oral forms of knowledge on the one hand, and the categorical, conceptual philosophical way of articulating language on the other hand. It is a genealogic narrative about Greek gods, from Chaos to the poet's own time. At the same time it begets gods, the poem begets a whole world, endowing it with its own elements and natural forces, its values and tensions, as well as with the harmonies and conflicts that these elements entail. *Theogony* is thus clearly a cosmogony in which the entire world expresses itself; it also represents to us, its readers, the expression of a well-articulated worldview. The elements and constitutive forces of this worldview are the very gods who act and interact similarly to human beings: loving, begetting, fighting for power, making alliances, committing violent deeds, making war. Since this worldview gives a human form to the gods, who constitute the structural elements of the world, it is usually understood as allegory, in which anthropomorphic gods function as metaphoric images of natural elements like heaven and earth, or of abstract values like love and justice.

In *Theogony*, to a stronger degree than in other epic poems, we may already find a certain articulation of words that form relations close to the categorical relations belonging to both scientific cosmologic and philosophical speeches. This resemblance leads us to suppose that such articulation of words may operate in Hesiod as a proto-categorical scheme. The cognitive scheme of cosmologies is not Hesiod's privilege, as it can be found in many sapient narratives, including in the second part of Parmenides' poem. Robbiano, showing good feeling for the Hellenic spirit, suggested that the first part of the poem could be read as a refuting of some cosmogonic speeches.[1] Thus, if Parmenides strives to remain apart from these speeches, would not that be precisely because he feels they are too close to his own, and he would have to dispute with their authors over a common space?

Because it constitutes a genealogy, *Theogony* presents a recurring relationship among the divine entities, namely filial kinship. This recurrent relationship engenders groups and subgroups identified by the bonds shared by their members, who are all brothers or sisters and also the offspring of a certain mother or father. (It is notable that the gods do not need to have both father and mother, and the absence of one of them is very frequent.). These groups make up the so-called "catalogs" of gods, the sometimes very long lists of a god's descendants.

Cataloging, from the Greek καταλέγω, means reporting, step by step and in detail, a certain subject or event. In *Odyssey* III, 69–80, when Nestor addresses a list of questions to Telemachus ("Who art thou? Where dost thou come from? What dost thou do?"), the latter says he will answer the questions one by one: ἐγὼ δέ κέ τοι καταλέξω. These detailed catalogs seem to me to

1 Robbiano, "Duas Fases Parmenídeas."

function as categorical proto-schemes, already apart from narrative and coming closer to a predicative, declarative or apophantic discourse. It is necessary to underline that this notion cannot be applied to every catalog as such: there are catalogs in epic poetry that do not fulfill the conditions that bring a catalog close to the categorical scheme.

I would like to underline two features appearing in a more or less explicit way in the catalogs that can help us to understand the relationship between essence and categories that is inherent to the categorical scheme: Subordination and Attribution. Not every catalog presents these features; most of them operate merely as a list of elements belonging to a single kind or class; for instance, the list of the ships, tribes and chiefs presented in the *Iliad*'s second chant is a detailed inventory of the Greeks who took part in the assault on Troy. It is a kind of inventory, like most texts composed in pre-alphabetic writing found on tablets by archeologists. It is not the case of describing the Greek through their features or any other predicate; it is a matter of gathering all the Greeks by pointing them out one by one, or one hundred by one hundred, which has the same effect. Beside the list of names and tribes, the relevant information is circumscribed to geographical descriptions of the regions where the tribes dwell—although from a perspective at once genealogical and ethnological, the region and the homeland have an important meaning in characterizing someone, especially for war purposes.

*Theogony*'s catalogs of gods present other characteristics that cause them to resemble categorical speech. First, and differently from other enumerating catalogs, it presents a relationship of subordination between parents and offspring; on many occasions the parent's name is an ordinary one that gains the status of an Anthroponym, like Earth, Heaven, Ocean; in addition, the offspring often have names that embrace the semantic field opened by the parent's. The offsprings' names are very often explicitly adjectives of quality and the attributive relation between them and the names of the parents, can be easily traced. In these moments, we find a very clear proto-scheme of the categorical relation between an underlying entity and its predicates.

There is a catalog that is especially interesting to our present study: the Catalog of Nereids, which appears in *Theogony* 240–264, and in *Iliad*, Chant XVIII, 37–49. I would like to draw attention to the anthroponyms of these marine goddesses:

Νηρῆος δ' ἐγένοντο μεγήρατα τέκνα θεάων
πόντῳ ἐν ἀτρυγέτῳ καὶ Δωρίδος ἠυκόμοιο,
κούρης Ὠκεανοῖο, τελήεντος ποταμοῖο,
Πλωτώ τ' Εὐκράντη τε Σαώ τ' Ἀμφιτρίτη τε
Εὐδώρη τε Θέτις τε Γαλήνη τε Γλαύκη τε
Κυμοθόη Σπειώ τε Θόη θ' Ἁλίη τ' ἐρόεσσα
Πασιθέη τ' Ἐρατώ τε καὶ Εὐνίκη ῥοδόπηχυς
καὶ Μελίτη χαρίεσσα καὶ Εὐλιμένη καὶ Ἀγαυὴ
Δωτώ τε Πρωτώ τε Φέρουσά τε Δυναμένη τε
Νησαίη τε καὶ Ἀκταίη καὶ Πρωτομέδεια
Δωρὶς καὶ Πανόπεια καὶ εὐειδὴς Γαλάτεια
Ἱπποθόη τ' ἐρόεσσα καὶ Ἱππονόη ῥοδόπηχυς
Κυμοδόκη θ', ἣ κύματ' ἐν ἠεροειδέι πόντῳ
πνοιάς τε ζαέων ἀνέμων σὺν Κυματολήγη
ῥεῖα πρηΰνει καὶ ἐυσφύρῳ Ἀμφιτρίτη,
Κυμώ τ' Ἠιόνη τε ἐυστέφανός θ' Ἁλιμήδη
Γλαυκονόμη τε φιλομμειδὴς καὶ Ποντοπόρεια
Ληαγόρη τε καὶ Εὐαγόρη καὶ Λαομέδεια
Πουλυνόη τε καὶ Αὐτονόη καὶ Λυσιάνασσα
[Εὐάρνη τε φυήν τ' ἐρατὴ καὶ εἶδος ἄμωμος]
καὶ Ψαμάθη χαρίεσσα δέμας δίη τε Μενίππη
Νησώ τ' Εὐπόμπη τε Θεμιστώ τε Προνόη τε
Νημερτής θ', ἣ πατρὸς ἔχει νόον ἀθανάτοιο.
Αὗται μὲν Νηρῆος ἀμύμονος ἐξεγένοντο
κοῦραι πεντήκοντα, ἀμύμονα ἔργα ἰδυῖαι.

And of Nereus and rich-haired Doris, daughter of Ocean the perfect river, were born children, passing lovely amongst goddesses, Ploto, Eucrante, Sao, and Amphitrite, and Eudora, and Thetis, Galene and Glauce, Cymothoe, Speo, Thoe and lovely Halie, and Pasithea, and Erato, and rosy-armed Eunice, and gracious Melite, and Eulimene, and Agaue, Doto, Proto,

> Pherusa, and Dynamene, and Nisaea, and Actaea, and Protomedea, Doris, Panopea, and comely Galatea, and lovely Hippothoe, and rosy-armed Hipponoe, and Cymodoce who with Cymatolege and Amphitrite easily calms the waves upon the misty sea and the blasts of raging winds, and Cymo, and Eione, and rich-crowned Alimede, and Glauconome, fond of laughter, and Pontoporea, Leagore, Euagore, and Laomedea, and Polynoe, and Autonoe, and Lysianassa, and Euarne, lovely of shape and without blemish of form, and Psamathe of charming figure and divine Menippe, Neso, Eupompe, Themisto, Pronoe, and Nemertes who has the nature of her deathless father. These fifty daughters sprang from blameless Nereus, skilled in excellent crafts.[2]

Nearly all the goddess's names express marine qualities, and almost all of them are morphologically feminine adjectives. All of them could be taken for characteristics of the sea, or of some region of it. By the toponyms that are presented here (I can single out at least four: *Melite* from Malta; *Doris,* the Doryan one; *Panopea* from Panopee; and *Galatea* from Galate), the region focused on by the poem would be the Aegean Sea. Nereus could be thought of as an ancient god from this place, or perhaps an ancient name for "sea."

But there is a small syntactic discrepancy in this interpretation, since Nereus is a masculine name and the names of all of his daughters are feminine adjectives. It does not seem such a serious problem, because they could be thought of as the Old Man of the Sea's virtues (ἀρεταί), just as in the same *Theogony,* Zeus brings together the virtues he needs in order to rule: Cunning (Μῆτις), Justice (Θέμις), Magnanimity (Εὐρυνόμη), Fertility (Δημήτηρ), Memory (Μνημοσύνη), Splendor (Λητώ), Zeal (Ἥρα), and so on. But I would like to venture another hypothesis, based on a detail proper to the Nereids' catalog. This catalog, which has the typical structure of Hesiodic genealogies,

2 Translation by Evelyn-White, *Hesiod.*

also maintains a certain independence from *Theogony* itself, since it has already appeared in another poem, Homer's *Iliad*, and may be echoing a tradition earlier than both. It may come not from an oral tradition, like the one that encompasses the Homeric chants, but perhaps from an already written tradition, since the structure of lists and inventories appears in vestiges of pre-alphabetic syllabaries.

Here I present the more reduced version of the Catalog (with 33 instead of 50 Nereids) in *Iliad*, Chant XVIII:

κώκυσέν τ' ἄρ' ἔπειτα· θεαὶ δέ μιν ἀμφαγέροντο,
πᾶσαι ὅσαι κατὰ βένθος ἁλὸς Νηρηΐδες ἦσαν.
ἔνθ' ἄρ' ἔην Γλαύκη τε Θάλειά τε Κυμοδόκη τε,
Νησαίη Σπειώ τε Θόη θ' Ἁλίη τε βοῶπις,
Κυμοθόη τε καὶ Ἀκταίη καὶ Λιμνώρεια
καὶ Μελίτη καὶ Ἴαιρα καὶ Ἀμφιθόη καὶ Ἀγαυή,
Δωτώ τε Πρωτώ τε Φέρουσά τε Δυναμένη τε,
Δεξαμένη τε καὶ Ἀμφινόμη καὶ Καλλιάνειρα,
Δωρὶς καὶ Πανόπη καὶ ἀγακλειτὴ Γαλάτεια,
Νημερτής τε καὶ Ἀψευδὴς καὶ Καλλιάνασσα·
ἔνθα δ' ἔην Κλυμένη Ἰάνειρά τε καὶ Ἰάνασσα,
Μαῖρα καὶ Ὠρείθυια ἐϋπλόκαμός τ' Ἀμάθεια,
ἄλλαι θ' αἳ κατὰ βένθος ἁλὸς Νηρηΐδες ἦσαν.

Then around her gathered all the divine daughters of Nereus deep in the sea—Glauce, Thaleia, Cymodoce, Nesaea, Speio, Thoe, ox-eyed Haliё, Cymothoë, Actaia, Limnoreia, Melite, Iaera, Amphithoe, Agave, Doto, Proto, Pherousa, Dynamene, Dexamene, Amphinome, Callianeira, Doris, Panope, lovely Galatea, Nemertes, Apseudes, Callianassa. Also there were Clymene, Ianeira, Ianassa, Maera, Orithyia, Amatheia with her

lovely hair, and others, Nereus' daughters living
in the ocean depths.[3]

*Iliad's* catalog has a more restrained and consistent semantic field than the Hesiodic one, in which other feminine and marine names seem to have been added to make up a round number (50). Chant XVIII, in its turn, does not have a name for a Nereid that cannot function as a vessel's name; thus it becomes clear why all of them are qualities in the feminine gender. According to this hypothesis, the names of the goddesses would be predicates of each vessel and neither qualities of Nereus nor of a region of the sea. But the semantic field of a fleet of Aegean vessels in the end brings up indirectly a statement about life, activities, cities, and hiding places of the sea. Who would Nereus, the father of these vessels, be? An old shipowner, a constructor of vessels, the owner or commander of a fleet? Nereus appears in the *Theogony* as a venerable old man "with neither forgetfulness nor lie." Would his claimed truth be the result of a great skill?

If we think of the painful context of Tethys' mourning while consoling her son Achilles, who cries for the death of his lover Patroclus—in whose context the Nereids appear—could we not think that it denotes a funeral rite in which some shipwrecked vessels were liturgically invoked in a farewell chant, like a litany? Nereus, the father of these vessels, could be the inevitable destination (νημερτής) that drags them into the depths of the sea? Just conjectures . . .

But we attest the literal fact that a list of predicates is indeed established, these predicates on the whole being subordinate to a substantive through relationships that come close to attribution. It is this structure of knowledge's exposition that we tend to see as a categorical proto-scheme.

This scheme will reach philosophy later through Parmenides' Poem, in which (in fragment B8) the signals of being (σήματα) will be displayed.

[3] Translation by Ian Johnston at *http://records.viu.ca/~johnstoi/homer/iliad18.htm* (11/20/2008).

2 . . . ταύτῃ δ' ἐπὶ σήματ' ἔασι
πολλὰ μάλ', ὡς ἀγένητον ἐὸν καὶ ἀνώλεθρόν ἐστιν,
οὖλον μουνογενές[4] τε καὶ ἀτρεμὲς ἠδ' ἀτέλεστον·
5 οὐδέ ποτ' ἦν οὐδ' ἔσται, ἐπεὶ νῦν ἔστιν ὁμοῦ πᾶν,
ἕν, συνεχές·
[. . .]
22 οὐδὲ διαιρετόν ἐστιν, ἐπεὶ πᾶν ἐστιν ὁμοῖον·
οὐδέ τι τῆι μᾶλλον, τό κεν εἴργοι μιν συνέχεσθαι,
οὐδέ τι χειρότερον, πᾶν δ' ἔμπλεόν ἐστιν ἐόντος.
25 τῳ ξυνεχὲς πᾶν ἐστιν· ἐὸν γὰρ ἐόντι πελάζει.
αὐτὰρ ἀκίνητον μεγάλων ἐν πείρασι δεσμῶν
ἔστιν ἄναρχον ἄπαυστον, ἐπεὶ γένεσις καὶ ὄλεθρος
τῆλε μάλ' ἐπλάχθησαν, ἀπῶσε δὲ πίστις ἀληθής.

2 In it are very many signals that what being
is, unborn it is and incorruptible, complete,
unique, intrepid and without aim.
5 Nor was it ever, nor will it be; for now it is, all
alike, one, continuous.
[. . .]
22 Nor is it divisible, since it is all alike:
there is no more of it, to hinder it from holding
together, nor less of it: it is totally full of what
is being.
25 Wherefore all holds together; for what is; is in
contact with what is.
Moreover, it is immovable in the bonds of
mighty chains, without beginning and without
end; since coming into being and passing away
have been driven afar: so true belief has cast
them away.

[4] οὖλον μονογενές Simplicius; μοῦνον μουνογενές Clemens, Plutarch [pseudo]; ἔστι γὰρ οὐλομελές Plutarch, Proclus (Diels).

The influence of epic sapient poetry in Parmenides is exceedingly well-known. Many aspects of it have already been exhaustively explored, starting from his verses—dactylic hexameters as Homer's, making the verses memorable and audible, like the ones belonging to all the perennial poets—to the solemn presence of the goddesses, like Dike and Moira, which makes his word become equally sacred and venerable. Even the reference to heroic episodes, like the one about Odysseus and the mermaids, confer to his poem at once enchantment and drama—which is so well illustrated by the filtering of palimpsests done by Barbara Cassin.[5]

However, among all the epic elements, what will remain as the proper trace of this promising philosophical speech about Being—a trace that will demarcate every ontological reading of our Metaphysical Occident from then on—is this cascading structure that belongs to Epic catalogs, a structure that pours from original Being the whole of its manifestations of "what this being is." And it substitutes, in the discursive field belonging to knowledge, the narrative's sequential diachrony, in which facts succeed one after another, due to the synchrony of a subject's constituent attributes. Scientific investigation thus appropriates a figure of speech whose scheme reproduces in the word the genealogical relation between a father and his offspring, which now becomes the essential hierarchy between a noun, "being," and its attributes, "the signals." However, this succession of predicates is already connected by the verbal form "is," which declaredly assumes the previously occult relation of attribution, as is proper for the categorical predicative function.

Now I would like to examine the semantic and topic fields that present themselves in fragment B8's "sēmata."

## 2) The accusation topics: the natural categories of the defendant

Aristotle, as the philosopher who stated the many ways in which being is enunciated in a tradition starting from Parmenides and passing through Plato, assumed and clarified, like nobody

---

5 Cassin, *Parménide,* pp. 48ff.

did until then, the structure of knowledge whose linguistic scheme is already illustrated in both Hesiodic and Homeric catalogs. But his categories did not occur to him at random, as Immanuel Kant assumed when he wrote commentaries on them in order to introduce his own idea and table of categories.[6] On the contrary, they follow a topic listing whose record belongs to the first written speeches (λόγοι)—the speeches of accusation and defense in courts.

Thus Aristotle can be said to be very coherent when he describes the multiple forms of saying "being" with the term κατηγορία. And what is a category in ancient Greek language's colloquial usage? It is an accusation, a public declaration of hostility (κατά+ἀγορέυω). In fifth-century colloquial classic Greek, the word "category" is the effecting of the accusing action: κατηγορέω, an action done by a prosecutor: ὁ κατήγορος. The accusation, besides the noun "category" (κατήγορία), is also usually and simply assigned as "speech" (λόγος). In an article published in 1984, Richard Bodéüs noticed that the origin of philosophical categories, either in Aristotle or in the lists of the Pythagorean Archytas of Tarentum, can be found in this precise field of ancient forensic speech.[7] I believe that it must also be applied to the model of discursive figuring found in the presentation of the signals of being (σήματα) that is displayed by the goddess in Parmenides' Poem.

In judicial practice, all accusation relies on proofs, its trustworthy indications, signals by which one can hold a true conviction (πίστις ἀληθής). Σήματα means signals of being, signals in which one can trust. In Parmenides' Poem, the signals of being are therefore not just a catalog, like a cataract of adjectives; instead, they are qualities that are faithfully attributed to being, to something that is. Σήματα, πίστεις, signals, proofs: we are still in exactly the same semantic field of forensic figures of speech. Such figures aim to create a sensation of trust, denoting credibility and veracity.

---

6 Kant, *Kritik,* B107 / A81.

7 Bodeüs, "Origines," 121–137.

We can find an exemplary usage of this model of forensic figures of speech in still another author immediately subsequent to Parmenides who is known to share a kinship with Eleatic dialectics, and who also resumes one of Homeric character's lines. (We will not use it as proof of the genealogy, however, because it would be an anachronistic inversion; instead, it is the trace of a usage that is contemporary to the philosopher's.) It is the *Apology of Palamedes* by Gorgias of Leontini, the fifth century's great Greek rhetorician. Literally taken, an "apology" is "a speech (λόγος) starting from something (ἀπό)." It is a counter-speech, a defense against, which also means a defense *from* an accusation. In this work, Gorgias has Palamedes repel the treason accusation leveled at him during the campaign against Troy. This defense is effectively a deconstruction of his plaintiff's logos (of his κατηγόρου), in which he must answer to each topic and address, one by one, the charges handed down by the prosecution. In one of his apologetical deconstructions, Gorgias interrogates the plaintiff in his very accusing capacity:

> εἰ μὲν οὖν ἰδών, φράσον τούτοις <τὸν τρόπον>, τὸν τόπον, τὸν χρόνον, πότε, ποῦ, πῶς εἶδες[8]

> If you really saw it, then point at these ones: the way, the place, the time, when, where, how you've seen it.

What does he demand from the plaintiff but the categories themselves, the accusation topics, in the same terms that will be employed by Aristotle: πότε, ποῦ, πῶς—"when," "where," "how"?! To accuse is therefore to point at categories! It is nothing but pointing and showing the signals, the trustworthy indications that characterize the defendant's guilt (αἰτία).

Then what does it mean to know the effect of these discoursive figures? It is a matter of enumerating and showing the signals of being which being, then pouring out these signals in a cascade of attributes. The verb "to be" is not a mere copulative particle, it develops the concrete action of pointing at, of

[8] 82 B 11a, 22 (DK).

designating, of showing something—and of joining attributes in a sequence without narrative. The pragmatic and concrete ground of the ontological syntactic articulation derives from somebody's act (the speaker) when he or she points at *signals* in someone else (the "defendant"), signals that disclose his or her characteristics (and that require someone to be what he or she is—his or her cause, his or her "guilt"—αἰτία). However, when talking about knowledge, it is not just the defendant who is the defendant-listener (*res*, the object), but it is the very underlying being, the substance, the essence that has the function of subject in the sentence. This is the way we find the categorical proposition, which is the sentence par excellence in philosophy and in sciences.

However, what are the kinds of signifiers that being receives in Parmenides' Poem? These types are inherited both by its main subject, nature (φύσις), and by the speeches about nature, the speeches of the "physical" sages, of the "φυσικοί."

The first philosophical subject known to us is about limits, "πέρας," which already appears in the sentences of Anaximander, and is the first item in the Pythagorean lists. It is a traditional subject of moral wisdom, especially in the case of problems related to moderation. However, in the thinking of the physiologoi, it applies to the universal question of the world's generation, cosmogony. According to Anaximander, if we trust Simplicius' interpretative testimony, despite all things having generation and corruption, the principle of cosmos must have neither beginning nor end; therefore, it should be without limits, ἄπειρον. Parmenides unfolds this problem of limit through several points: vital or existential limits (unborn it is and incorruptible), quantitative limits (complete, unique), space limits (intrepid and without aim), time limits (nor was it ever, nor will it be; for now it is), qualitative limits (all alike), or comparative one (there is no more of it, nor less of it).

These are precisely the categories and the accusation terms applied in demonstrating a defendant's guilt (αἰτία). First, the defendant is asked whether the cause is mortal or immortal (if the cause is divine, the defendant is innocent) and proof of responsibility is presented; then the presence of accomplices when the crime occurred is quentioned, and quantitative proofs are brought; then where the fact occurred is questioned, and the precise place is pointed out; then they are asked when the fact occurred and proof of which moment it was done is brought; then the intensity of the crime is questioned in order to evaluate its relative gravity and to determine the penalties.

If the defendant is pronounced guilty, he or she is condemned to stay totally *immovable in the bonds of mighty chains.*

Let us add some historical or genealogical comments on this subject. It should be clear that we are not simply implying that Parmenides takes the figures of his ontological speech from the forensic language. Even when we are talking about forms that were instituted by the city's laws or about a philosopher's text, the ways of attributing proofs by means of a public speech must certainly be said to be posterior and derivative of colloquial uses. But the fact that the philosopher is employing figures of speech that are so similar in both circumstances is especially significant to understand the functions that they perform in each context. In the case of Parmenides' Poem, this proximity highlights the deictic effect of indicating and pointing, an effect which is present through the whole sapient speech belonging to the Goddess. Stating that being is so and so is to accuse being of being so and so. And if the categorical predication's particle "is" performs this function, why could we not assume that when the Goddess herself simply says, without adding any predicate, "is" or "there is" being, she would be simply pointing at reality, launching the language so that it effectively jumps outside itself to what is ahead, either in terms of space, as the objective world, or in terms of time, as the present?

Moreover, the context of litigious speech in courts provides another detail of the discursive configuration of ontological and categorical speech. Beyond the topics of accusation or meaning about nature, we also find the division of each subject into aspects that oppose each other. The ontological speech appears in the form of litigations as antilogical speech. Let us see how it appears in the text.

Parmenidean being shows itself in Fragment B8 as "unbegotten, imperishable, intrepid and without aim; something that never was nor will be, indivisible, neither something more, nor something less, intrepid, immovable, without beginning or end." It is sufficiently evident that a great part of the signals of being appear in privative form. In this group of adjectives, there is evident abundance of privative alphas as well as of negative adverbs. They had already appeared in the Poem, in the interdiction of the way of not being—unthinkable, unspeakable, unnamable, unknowable, without confidence, not true—but we find them again now in an opposite context: the way of what is. The signals of being are also characterized as privative. They are positions unfolded in clearly opposing relations. This is why Parmenides calls them "polemical proofs," since they are proofs presented in the context of an ἔλεγχος.

The polemical way of presenting proofs is the shape that λόγος takes in Greek courts. This is the same shape that will stimulate the practical and theoretical inquiries of Oratorical Science, Rhetorics, Sophistics, and, without a doubt, Greek Dialectics, which is eminently agonistic. In the knowledge speech, this opposition will figure first as the opposition between firm and vacillating knowledge (or as the opposition between truth and opinion) and later as the one between true and false.

The polemic-argumentative shapes taken by the figures of speech in Greek philosophers' thinking can also lead us to assume a delirious hypothesis concerning the sense of privative alpha in the word "ἀλήθεια": the truth is not what is seen when the daughters of the sun remove with their hands the veils that hide their heads. The truth is instead the firm position detached from a polemical, vacillating, bicephalous opposition. The truth is the intrepid position of Being itself.[9]

[9] I gratefully acknowledge the financial assistance of CAPES, Brazil.

# Bibliography

Aristotle. *Categoriae et Liber de Interpretatione.* Edited by L. Minio-Paluello. Oxford: Clarendon Press, 1949; 1989.

Aubenque, Pierre. *Le Problème de l'être Chez Aristote.* Paris: Presses Universitaires de France, 1962. 5th edition, 1983.

_____, ed. *Concepts et Catégories dans la Pensée Antique.* Paris: Vrin, 1980.

Baratin, Marc and Françoise Desbordes. *L'analyse Linguistique dans l'Antiquité Classique I: Les Théories.* Paris: Klincksieck, 1981.

Benveniste, Émile. *Problèmes de Linguistique Générale,* 2 volumes. Paris: Gallimard, 1992.

Bodeüs, Richard. "Aux Origines de la Doctrine Aristotélicienne des Catégories." *Revue de Philosophie Ancienne* 1 (1984): 121–137.

Cassin, Barbara. *Aristote et le Logos.* Paris: Presses Universitaires de France, 1997.

_____. *Sur la Nature ou sur l'étant. La Langue de l'être?* Paris: Seuil, 1998.

Chantraine, Pierre. *Dictionnaire Étymologique de la Langue Grecque: Histoire des Mots.* Paris: Klincksieck, 1968. 2nd edition, 1999.

Cordero, Néstor-Luis. *Les Deux Chemins de Parménide.* Paris: Vrin, 1984. 2nd edition, 1997.

_____. *Siendo Se Es: La Tesis de Parménides.* Buenos Aires: Biblos, 2006. English edition: *By Being, It Is: The Thesis of Parmenides.* Las Vegas: Parmenides Publishing, 2004.

Couloubaritsis, Lambros. "Fécondité des Pratiques Catalogiques." *Kernos* 19 (2006): 249–266.

Diels, Hermann and Walther Kranz. *Die Fragmente der Vorsokratiker,* 3 volumes. Berlin: Weidmann, 1903; 6th edition with final editing and revisions by W. Kranz, 1952; editions after the 6th are mainly reprints with little or no change. References to the 1996 reprint.

Evelyn-White, Hugh G. *Hesiod. The Homeric Hymns, Epic Cycle and Homerica.* English translations by H. G. Evelyn-White. The Loeb Classical Library No. 57. Cambridge, MA: Harvard University Press and London: Heinemann, 1914. Reprinted 1936 and 1995.

Havelock, Eric A. *A Revolução da Escrita na Grécia e suas Conseqüências Culturais.* Translated by Ordep J. Serra. São Paulo: Paz e Terra, 1994.

Hesiod, *Teogonia.* Translated and edited by Ana Lucia Silveira Cerqueira and Maria Therezinha Arêas Lyra. Niterói: Editora da Universidade Federal Fluminense, 1996.

____. *Teogonia. A Origem dos Deuses.* Translated and edited by Jaa Torrano. São Paulo: Iluminuras, 1992.

Homer. *Opera,* Vol. 3 and Vol 4. Edited by Thomas W. Allen. Oxford: Clarendon Press, 1990.

____. *Iliade.* Translated and edited by Paul Mazon. Paris: Gallimard, 1987.

____. *Iliade.* Translated and edited by Pierre A. Pierron. Paris: Hachette, 1869.

____. *Odisséia.* Translated and edited by Haroldo de Campos. São Paulo: Mandarim, 2001.

____. *Odissée.* Translated and edited by Victor Bérard. Paris: Belles Lettres, 1947.

Kant, Immanuel. *Kritik der reinen Vernunft,* Vol. 3. Darmstadt: Wissenschaftliche Buchgesellschaft, 1956–1983.

Mattéi, Jean-François, ed. *La Naissance de la Raison en Grèce.* Actes du Congrès de Nice 1987. Paris: Presses Universitaires de France, 1990.

Porphyrius. *Isagoge.* Edited by P. Gomes. Lisbon: Guimarães, 1994.

____. *On Aristotle's Categories.* Edited by Richard Sorabji. Ithaca: Cornell, 1992.

Robbiano, Chiara. *Becoming Being: On Parmenides' Transformative Philosophy.* Sankt Augustin: Academia Verlag, 2006.

____. "Duas Fases Parmenídeas ao longo da Via para a verdade: Elenchos e Ananke." In *Acerca do Poema de Parmênides: Estudos apresentados no I Simpósio Internacional OUSÍA de Estudos Clássicos.* Rio de Janeiro (2006). *Anais de Filosofia Clássica,* Vol. 1, No. 2 (2007): *www.ifcs.ufrj.br/~afc.*

# The Role of "Thought" in the Argument of Parmenides' Poem[1]

José Trindade Santos

**Summary**

It is my aim in this paper to analyze the role played by "thought" in the argument of Parmenides' Poem. The relevance of the "thought" theme in Greek philosophical tradition has long been recognized. In Parmenides it implies approaching the study of reality through the experience of thought in language. As knowledge is to the known, thought is to being. Their identity dominates Parmenides' argument in the Way of Truth, persisting in later relevant conceptions as Platonic ἐπιστήμη and Aristotelian "active intellect."

In Greek tradition, in addition to Parmenides, Heraclitus concentrated on "thought." His approach to "thought" pervades a rather substantial number of his fragments, weaving a net of significant relations connected with the concepts bearing on cognition and its terminology.[2] Nevertheless, as much as these concepts show an undeniable interest in the cognitive approach to reality—enough to establish a significant tie among thought, cognition and the world outside—they did not capture the

---

1 I am deeply indebted to Patricia Curd for having read this paper and offering her comments on it.

2 Cf. Von Fritz, "*Nous, Noein* and Their Derivatives in Pre-Socratic Philosophy," *Classical Philology* 40 (1945), 41; (1946) reprinted in A. P. D. Mourelatos, ed., *The Pre-Socratics* (New York: Anchor Press/Doubleday, 1974), pp. 23–85. See also J. H. Lesher's criticisms of von Fritz in his "Perceiving and Knowing in the *Iliad* and the *Odyssey*," *Phronesis* 26 (1981), 2–24.

attention of Plato and Aristotle, who focused their appraisal of Heraclitus' contribution to philosophy on the theme of "change."

The resurgence of the cosmological trend in Greek philosophical tradition through its insertion in a strong epistemological context was Parmenides' task, achieved in *On Nature.* I sustain that this objective was attained mainly through the identification of thought and being.

## The argument of the Poem

The dissimilarities between Heraclitus' "Book" and Parmenides' Poem are immediately obvious. Not only does *On Nature* allow the reader to sense a textual unity that is absent from the Ephesian's collection of maxims, the frequent inclusion of connectives is revealing of the logical form of the argument.

Indeed, the setting of the Poem as a voyage metaphorically suggests it should be read as an argument. Thought travels along a route (2.2 passim) marked by a succession of crossroads at which the protagonist must choose avoiding the wrong "path" (2.6), the "regressive track" (6.9), or the "worn out road" (7.3).

I take my main task as an interpreter to uncover this argument by showing what it intends to propose, and what it manages to propose. In the current fragmentary status of the poem, I divide the argument into three main steps. Its final scope is to show that being is the condition and purpose of thought (8.34–36),[3] unveiling the manifold consequences of the acceptance of the premise: "is."

## B2–B3

In the first step, an alternative is presented between two possible ways for thinking: "is" and "is not."[4] Although no

[3] A. P. D. Mourelatos, *The Route of Parmenides: A Study of Word, Image, and Argument in the Fragments* (New Haven & London: Yale University Press, 1970. Revised and Expanded Edition, Las Vegas: Parmenides Publishing, 2008), pp. 165–175, underlines the affinity of οὕνεκεν with words expressing "goal" or "consummation." It is my contention that this view reinforces the amplitude of the causal nuances of the expression, through the connection of an antecedent (being) with its consummation in thought (op. cit., pp. 121; cf. 30–31; 168–169, 189).

[4] The lack of a subject in "is" and "is not" seems to be a deliberate choice. Only through the course of the argument will the referent of each way become clear. After the elimination of "is not," B3 establishes the identity of the elided terms.

explicit recommendation is made, the impossibility of knowing "[what] is not"—that is, "not being" (B2.7)—offers the identity of "thinking" and "being"[5] (B3) as the resolution of the disjunction. On this identity depends the whole argument of the Way of Truth.[6]

Like many other arguments springing from an oral source, this one is extremely concentrated. We can conceive a suppressed hypothetical premise—"if there be thinking"—out of which come the only two possible alternatives, interconnected by modal clauses:

"is" = "cannot not be"
"is not" = "necessarily is not"

Given that there are only these two possibilities,[7] and the fact that one of them is found impossible (5–7[8]), the other one remains as the sole possibility for thinking. The lack of reference

The several readings of the Greek verb "be" will be discussed presently. Suffice it to say for now that I fully agree with the considerations of D. Sedley on the Greek verb "to be" in "Parmenides and Melissus," in A. A. Long, ed., *The Cambridge Companion to Early Greek Philosophy* (from now on, *CCEGrPh*) (Cambridge: Cambridge University Press, 1999), pp. 114–115.

[5] Being "the same," "thinking" and "being" are one and identical. I will offer more on this later.

[6] The identity of thinking and being—"the same is to think and to be"—is not the only reading of the fragment. Other translations connect the form of the Greek verb "is" to the infinitives, importing to B3 the construction expressed in B2.2, 3, 5, 6.1: "for it is the same *thing* that can be thought and can be." Cf. W. Guthrie, *A History of Greek Philosophy* II (Cambridge: Cambridge University Press, 1965), p. 14. The parallel with B2.2, "are for thinking," etc., seems unjustified. First, in none of these cases do we find a copula connecting two active infinitives. Second, this translation destroys the parallel with B8.34 (where "is thinking"—in the active—cannot exhibit the dative reading of the infinitive; cf. *The Route of Parmenides*, p. 165). In the potential translation of "is" in B3, only rendering "the same" as a noun (= "the same thing") may change it into a subject.

[7] "Possibility" is expressed by the potential construction: "the only two ways that are for thinking." There is no other path besides those two, established in 2.3b and 2.5b, for the negation of each one calls for the other.

[8] Not being is "a path utterly indiscernible," for it is not possible to know whatever it names. Or, since thought is unable to grasp whatever "not being" names, they cannot be "the same."

of "is not" concentrates all possible reference in the opposite alternative: "is" is the thought that asserts being.

At this stage of the argument, there is no other mystery besides the obvious conclusion that only "[what] is," implicitly designated as "being,"[9] can be thought. But difficulties lie ahead.

## B6–B7

The second step starts opposing the conjunction of thinking, saying and being[10] to the equation of not-being with nothing. Both bring up something new. The conjunction broadens the previous identity (B3), making it inclusive of saying. The objective of this move is to legitimate the strategy supporting the argument: the use of language to investigate thinking and being.

In addition to that first identity, the ontological commitment of thought is then positively asserted (B6.1a), opposing the possibility of being (6.1b) to the second identity, of "is not" with "nothing" (B6.2a). If "nothing" is the referent of "is not," the identity to which it is opposed must necessarily be. That is, the very possibility of thinking "is" is made into a necessity by the corresponding impossibility of thinking "[what] is not" (B61–2a).

Though the gap at the end of B6.3 does not allow any clear reading of this verse,[11] B6.4 undeniably launches an attack on the road where ignorant two-headed mortals wander, to whom

---

9 Once one assumes the parallel between B2.5 and B2.7, if the name "not-being" reveals the subject of "is not" (2.5–7), "being" should be chosen as subject for "is."

10 "It is necessary that saying, thinking and being are." By uniting the two infinitives to the participle, 6.1a acknowledges their identity in being, sealed by the statement that it is necessary that they are. This formulation establishes one aspect of the "ontological commitment" of thought.

11 Néstor-Luis Cordero (*Les Deux Chemins de Parménide* [Paris: J. Vrin, 1984]) is definitely right in pointing out that Diels's conjecture, despite its parallel in 7.2, seems too weak to support such a strong turn of the argument, particularly because it should be noted that the parallel is not so obvious when it is noticed that B7.2 clearly points to what follows (7.3–4), and not to what precedes the gap (6.2a). Alexander Nehamas, "On Parmenides' Three Ways of Inquiry," reprinted in A. Nehamas, *Virtues of Authenticity: Essays on Plato and Socrates* (Princeton: Princeton University Press, 1999), pp. 125–137, is sympathetic to Cordero's reading of the gap rejecting as well a third road in B6. Persuasive as these interpretations are, I do not think that they are strong enough to cancel the vehemence with which the goddess condemns the thought of mortals.

several insults are addressed (B6.4–7). This road, either introducing a new disjunction or reinstating the first one (B2.3–8a), approaches thinking as the conflation of "is" and "is not," conducive to the belief that "to be and not to be" are "the same and not the same" (B6.8–9a).

The figurative association of such practice to perception ("deaf and blind," 6.7) will be reinforced in B7.3–5a by the condemnation of "wandering eye," "resounding ear or tongue" (7.4–5a). Against the "habit" of using such "worn out path," the goddess sternly advises the young man to decide by argument the "much contested" challenge (7.5b) she has uttered: "is."

With this turn, the didactic program of the Poem begins to come to light, pointing to two goals that are complementary yet distinct:

1. The focus on the ontological commitment of thought.
2. The task of correcting "human thought."

The reception of Parmenides by Greek philosophical tradition can be appreciated in the way in which, from different perspectives, both these goals are accepted by all those who follow him. Parmenides exerts a direct influence on Zeno and Melissus; structures the work of later Presocratic thinkers; provokes the reaction of Sophists, especially Protagoras and Gorgias; and is extensively adopted by Plato, while Aristotle prefers to elect him as a target of criticism. Questionable as it is that the two positions above encapsulate the main goals of the Poem, the fact that Parmenides' descendents thought so is beyond doubt.

## Thought and opinion

From B6–B7 on, the several fronts of the conflict opposing perception with reasoning argument[12] are defined, impacting

[12] Lacking in the Poem is the characterization of each of these as "potencies" or "faculties," a characterization that is found only in Plato and Aristotle. It is consequently difficult to consider them opposed to one another, or even maybe to separate them. The Poem suggests one should be seen as the complement of the other, sometimes taken as a contraposition that is hopefully changeable into cooperation. It is, however, obvious that the formal approach of thought is not corresponded by the syncretism of opinion, involving senses and language in

the negative value conferred to the "thinking of mortals." By believing that "being and not being are the same and not the same" (B6.8–9a), mortals infringe on the rule forbidding that "things that are not are" (B7.1).

The impact of B7.1 on Plato's written work would be immense. Several dialogues approach the fallacy inherent in reading the prohibition of the goddess as a statement of fact.[13] On the other hand, Parmenides' denunciation of the inconsistency of mortal thinking would bear important consequences on Greek culture and tradition. Three unexpected results are produced.

The first one is the immediate and irrevocable eradication of the mythical approach to the cosmos, through the story of its origins. Not only does argument surpasse narrative[14] as a method of research, but the fact that "is" is a thought forbids, even before the confirmation brought about by B8, each and every possibility of "coming to be."

Connected with the former, the second result would have to wait some time to be noticeable in the gradual transference of research from a cosmological into an onto-epistemological context. More than a century passes before Plato states that there is no way to investigate the cosmos without asserting that "it is" (*Soph.* 243d–e).

This shift of research from cosmology to epistemology provokes the emergence of a new type of σοφός, covertly guided by the ideal of infallible ἐπιστήμη. Complying with the injunction to defend by λόγος the premise "is" (B7.1), Plato's Socrates engages in the practice of the *elenchus* setting his conception of knowledge against the paradigm of "technical/practical" experience,

---

a complex of cognitive functions. On the other hand, despite the fact that the translation of λόγος in 7.5a into "reason" is an anachronism, there is no doubt that the basis for preferring "is" is argumentatively presented and asserted in a strong cognitive context.

13 If one cannot possibly say that "things that are not are," no statement can be contradicted once it is uttered. Besides the direct quotation in the *Sophist* 237a, the rule forbidding contradiction is echoed in each passage in which the problem of falsity and contradiction is raised (*Cra.* 429d; *Euthd.* 283e–284c, 286c–e; *Theat.* 167d).

14 Notice Simmias' preference for "demonstration" when judging anamnesis and soul-harmony against each other in the *Phaedo* 92c–d.

traditionally framed by those concerned with "the service and tendance of the things that grow or are put together" (Plato, *Republic* VII 533b[15]).

If we take each disjunction of the Poem as a paradigmatic *elenchus*, the methodology of the Socratic dialogues, as well as the concept of knowledge associated with it, are obviously respectful of the injunction of the goddess (B7.5). The successive confrontations of Socrates with the representatives of public "knowledge" show how much his reasoning depends on Parmenides' argument.

From it stems the argument of *Republic* V 476e7ff. If both oppositions—"knowing"/"not knowing" and "being"/"not being"—are exactly parallel, only the infallibility of knowledge can match the consistency of being. This is one possible explanation for the request that each and every investigation aiming at knowledge should begin with an answer to the "what is?" question (*Men.* 71b), as well as a consensus on the infallibility of ἐπιστήμη (*Gorg.* 454d; *R.* V 477e6; *Theaet.* 152c5).

These are proofs that the tautological consistency of the argument of the goddess aims higher than truth at the requirement that knowledge is infallible. And this requirement will, henceforward, characterize all efforts to attain knowledge, while the evidence of contradiction will not imply the falsity of the opinions stated, though it proves its bearer failed in his pretence to wisdom.

## The value of opinion

The synthesis of all these effects suggests a reevaluation of opinion. By tradition, far from taking it as false, few philosophers have been blind to the circumstance that opinion is the only access to knowledge.[16] This being so, the most impressive challenge the programmatic section of the proem presents to the reader is the goddess's promise to teach him:

---

15 Translation by Paul Shorey (Cambridge & London: Loeb Classical Library, 1980).

16 Notice the *ad hominem* way in which the criticism of opinion is generally addressed in the Platonic dialogues. There seems to be nothing wrong with opinions as long as they are supported by argument and not accepted as ultimate truths.

> . . . as appearances[17]
> need acceptably be, all of them permeating everything (B1.31–32).

The assimilation of opinion to falsehood is therefore a serious mistake, as Parmenides' Poem never asserts that all opinions are false. It is known that they do not sustain themselves, that they lack sufficient strength to impose on men as long as they cannot offer the consistency of proof. Those deficiencies do not, however, force us to let them drown in the ocean of falsehood and irrelevancy.

Thus, mortal men may be right when they accept the "errancy" (6.5–6; 16.1) into which they are forced by their own nature (16.3). They are wrong if they ignore the injunction to decide by reasoning argument the "much contested challenge" (7.5a), setting "is" against the "worn out road" of "eyes, ears, and tongue" (7.3–5a), that is, their own opinions.

## B8–B9

The third main step of the argument links a sequence of disjunctions, explicit as well as implicit, from which the terms contaminated by "is not" (already disposed of in the first disjunction) are subsequently rejected. The starting moment of the sequence points once again to the identity of thought and being.

Among the four dominant disjunctions of this third step of the argument, two of them have an over-determining position over the other two: the ones establishing being as one and unchangeable. It is because being is one and unchangeable that it cannot come to be or pass away, that it is indivisible and complete.

---

17 More than a correction of human opinions, the sentence denounces the fact that "appearances" are contrived by human perceptions/opinions. The complex of opinion presents in Parmenides an onto-epistemological sense: there are no "things" outside men's perceptions (cf. Gorgias B3.77–86).

The translation of τὰ δοκοῦντα into "appearances" seems anachronistic. Discounting the dualistic context in which it will come to appear in Plato, it is justified by the parallel with Xenophanes' fragments 34–36. The affinity of the δοκ-terms in B1.30–32 with the δόξα complex seems indisputable (A. P. D. Mourelatos, *Route*, pp. 203–205).

All of those predicates negated in B8 stem from the conjunction of the opposed roads—"is and is not"—explicit in B6.7–8 and harshly condemned by B7.1–2. On the contrary, the affirmed predicates reinstate the uniqueness, authenticity and unchangeable character of being recalled in 8.34–38a. Confronted with the only two possible alternatives—being and not-being—thought is "promised" (8.35) to the first one, because "it cannot not be" (2.3b). But "be" what?

## The verb "be" and the fusion of readings

This question cannot be answered without an inquiry into the meaning of the Greek verb "be," which clarifies its mode of operation in language, for if thinking, saying and being are, necessarily, language reveals thought and what is.

Being is one and unchangeable (in all the senses enumerated in B8[18]). Being unchangeable, it is always the same. Being one, it exists. This is confirmed by the "authenticity" of the "true way" (B8.15b–16a). If these are the predicates of being, these are the readings the Greek verb "be" exhibits: predicative, identitative, veridical and existential.

The relevant linguistic fact to be taken into account is that these readings are inseparable. They simultaneously express the semantic unity of the Greek verb "be" and its ambiguity, all of them resting on the thought: "is."[19]

In current everyday language, the verb "be" has two syntactically distinct uses: complete and incomplete. At 2.3, the "naked copula" neither reveals "what" is nor "what is it" that "is." However, after B3 it is clear that either "being" or "thinking" can be placed in the positions of subject or predicate, thus immediately establishing the identitative and predicative readings in the incomplete use of the verb.

This claim in no way implies the exclusion of the existential reading of the verb εἶναι, though it seems impossible to find a single form of the Greek verb presenting the reader with an unambiguous existential use in the Poem. This situation is

[18] That is, "ungenerable," "incorruptible," "indivisible," and "complete."

[19] A. P. D. Mourelatos, *Route*, pp. 47–73, cf. pp. 51–61.

explained by C. H. Kahn when, addressing Parmenides and the beginnings of ontology, he recognized "that the copula use is implicitly existential, and that most if not all existential uses of *einai* are potentially predicative."[20]

The interpretation here set forth displays the semantic unity of εἶναι, what Kahn has called its "conceptual system" (op. cit., VIII). The verb "be" has only one sense, covering a diversity of readings, conveyed through the propositions in which the verb appears, bespeaking the comprehension of the Eleatic notion of being. But it also acknowledges its ambiguity as caused by the diversity of readings the verb shelters in the unity of its semantic field.

A significant number of texts[21] show that, up until Aristotle,[22] Greek speakers impose the semantic unity of the verb "be" on the diversity of readings it allows for, making possible fallacies that explore the equivocal senses of those same readings in order to obtain paradoxes and contradictions.

However, particularly in philosophical contexts, classical Greek presents the translator with one unavoidable problem. How can he decide on an existential rendering of the Greek verb, in its complete reading, without excluding all the others implicit in the inseparable semantic unity of the verb?[23]

The simple answer to this query is he cannot. For, if Kahn is right—as I believe he is—many uses of the Greek verb "be"

---

[20] C. F. Kahn, "Introduction," in *The Verb "BE" in Ancient Greek,* (Indianapolis: Hackett, 2003), p. ix.

[21] From the Sophists (Gorgias B3, B3a), or attributed to them by Plato in the *Cratylus, Euthydemus,* and *Theaetetus.*

[22] Aristotle seems to be making two different points when he contends that "being is said in many ways." The first one, taking being as a subject, is that there are lots of things that we call "being," and that is a simple countenance of pluralism (*Physics* I 3,187a11). The second point, taking being as a predicate, sustains that we can talk about being from several points of view: according to the categories (*Phys.* I 2,185a20–30), activity and potentiality, etc. (*Phys.* I 2,186a1–3).

[23] It is illustrative to observe the strategies recurrently applied by Plato in the *Parmenides* (see, for instance, the second hypothesis) and the *Sophist* to attack the ambiguity of the Greek verb "be." In order to isolate each one of its relevant readings, he resorts to paraphrases (e.g., "participates in being," *Soph.* 251a1, 256d, e) or else inserts the verb in unambiguous contexts (e.g., "is the same and not the same," *Soph.* 256a5).

While the predicative reading is approached as a problem in itself (251a–c), the veridical one is dismissed by presenting "truth/falsity" as "qualities" of sentences (263b).

display incomplete *and* complete uses fused in its semantic unity.[24] Both readings are allowed. However, if the translation of "is" is rendered as "exists," automatically all the other readings of the Greek verb are cancelled.[25] Thus the reader is deprived of grasping most philosophical problems implicit in its ambiguous translations, like "be" or "is."

## The unity of being and names

This is not the only problem caused by the unity of the verb "be" and the nature of "being." Constantly stressed on par with other signs, unity is explicitly attributed to being in 8.4–6a.[26] Though it would be the focus of increasing attention from all sections of tradition, from the Eleatics to Aristotle, in B8 no attention is paid to the opposition between one and many. The problem does, however, show up indirectly in the contraposition of being with names:

> . . . with reference to it are spoken[27] all
> [the names[28]] which mortals posited convinced that they
> were true" (8.39)

[24] Lesley Brown, "Being in the *Sophist:* A Syntactical Enquiry," in Gale Fine, ed., *Plato 1: Metaphysics and Epistomology* (Oxford: Oxford University Press, 1999), pp. 455–478, proposes to interpret "the complete use of ἐστι as a use where there is no complement (explicit or elided) but which allows a complement" (p. 459). It seems to me that such interpretation supports Kahn's statement that any use of the Greek verb "be" "potentially" or "implicitly" contains its complement.

[25] For example, only allowing a complete reading of εἶναι, its possible complement, makes εἶναι μὴ ἐόντα compatible with the argument in B8, for "existence" is completely alien to the "unchangeability," "indivisibility," and "completeness" of being. However, the argument would make no sense if it is admitted that "what is" does not exist.

[26] The series of signs condensed in B8.4–6a—"compact," "homogeneous," "one," "continuous"—confirms the setting, in B2–B3, of the unity, as well as the "uniqueness," of being. On the basis of the identity of thinking and being, "is" is presented as the only thought about the only thinkable entity: "being" (B8.34–36).

[27] Reading πάντ' ὀνόμασται, and partially accepting the reading of this verse suggested by L. Woodbury, "Parmenides on Names," in J. Anton and G. Kustas, eds., *Essays in Ancient Greek Philosophy,* (Albany: State University of New York Press, 1971), pp. 145–162; cf. Mourelatos, *Route*, pp. 181–183.

[28] I assume that "names" is the implied object of the verb.

Is it possible that what "comes to be" is not what "passes away," that what "changes place or color" is not the same as that which does not "change," thus "being and not being" (8.41–42; cf. B6.8–9a)? If it is "to it [being]" (B8.38b)—to which the preceding verses have just attached thought—that "are called all the names which mortals posited" (8.39), this single referent is at variance with the positing of distinct names, particularly those expressing contrary views.

After the end of the Way of Truth, the concentration of these same verbs in the diagnostic of "mortal opinions" (8.51) suggests that such spreading of names should be related to the later positing of two forms, "called notions" (8.53), through which "everything is called light and night"[29] (9.1). Finally, at what is taken to be the end of the Way of Opinion, again "opinion" (19.1) consists of having "posited a name marking each one" (19.3) of the things that were born, will grow and come to an end (19.1–2).

It seems obvious that such diverse nomination is misleading, for it is attributed either to a single being or to anything "besides it" (B8.13, 37a) that "is not." Since these names show no respect for the unity of being,[30] the verb cannot express all its readings. For how can many different names be identical to a single being (be the names of the one being)? How can so many names be predicated of it? How can they "truly" name it? What kind of existence can be attributed to whatever they are the names of?

The interpreter is led to conclude that, by pointing out the dangers of equivocation (B8.39b) or nonreferentiality of all names, the goddess warns him against considering these names "true"[31] (B8.39b). The question lies in appraising the effect this naming may have on the relation of the Way of Opinion to the

[29] Notice the "dissociating" effect brought about by the repetitions of ὀνομάζειν at B8.38, 53 and B9.1 and κατέθεντο at B8.39 and B19.3.

[30] In the *Cratylus*, Socrates attributes to Euthydemus the fallacy of stating that "everything is in the same way for everyone at the same time and ever" (386d; cf. *Euthd.* 294a, 296a). The statement may aim at vindicating the unity of being against the attribution of many names to a single referent.

[31] The ability to tell "true" from "false" names is certainly respected by Cratylus' naturalistic theory on naming (*Cra.* 429b–430a). Alternatively, another solution to this difficulty might lie in submitting all forms of predication to identity (cf. Plato's criticism of the "late comers to knowledge" in the *Sophist* 251b–c).

argument in the Way of Truth. This question calls for a brief summary of the conclusions so far attained.

### What does the "commitment of thought to being" amount to?

The thesis that, in the Way of Truth, Parmenides expresses the commitment of thought to being incorporates the three steps of the argument sketched above:

1. If only being can be thought, thinking and being are the same (B2, B3).
2. "It is necessary that saying, thinking and being are" (B6.1a).
3. Thinking and what is thought ["being"] are the same (B8.34–36a).

In these three concepts, the commitment of thought to being amounts to the statement that "being" is the thought "is." As for the meaning of "is" in these sentences, the argument in B8 allows the interpreter the readings listed above.

The question that cannot be evaded concerns the meaning of "the same" in B3 and B8.34 and the basis for asserting the identity of "saying, thinking and being" in B6.1. How can one or two human capabilities, namely "thought" and λόγος, be identical to reality? It seems obvious that they cannot.

However, nothing forces us to consider Parmenidean "thought" a human capability and take "reality" to be the referent of "being." Leaving the second item to be addressed in a moment, I concentrate now on "thinking" and "thought."

No one doubts that, throughout the Poem, "thinking" and "thought" display a definite cognitive value, making them equivalent to "knowing" and "knowledge." If this equivalence is accepted, the question above may be rhetorically rephrased in the negative as "how can knowledge not be the same as the known? How can these two not be identical?" They have to be, if "what-is-not . . . (known)" cannot be[32] (known, thought of or said).

[32] Patricia Curd, "Eleatic Arguments," in Jyl Gentler, ed., *Method in Ancient Philosophy* (Oxford: Oxford Clarendon Press, 1998), p. 22, rejects "identity" and regards thought and being "as essentially connected" (p. 19).

I think that the claim asserting the identity of thought with being left an enduring mark on the work of several Greek thinkers. Gorgias targets it in his "What is not" (B3.77–86[33]), arguing for the unknowability and unintelligibility of "whatever may be" (B3.77.1). But identity returns in Plato in a number of capital theses, either in the constitutive power of Forms on the structure of soul[34] (*Men.* 81d1; *Ti.* 35a–37c) or in the original Platonic version of the rhetorical question above: "how could that which is not be known?" (*R.* V 477a1). I also suggest that on this intuition ultimately rests Aristotle's notion of the active intellect, which "produces everything" (*On the Soul* III 5,413a13), and without which "nothing thinks" (ibid., 25).

In Parmenides, this "sameness" constitutes the basis for the claim, repeatedly asserted here, of the identity of thought and being. Its price may, however, be deemed too high by many interpreters, for on this ground, such identity must be purely formal. "Being" cannot be related to this world, thereby remaining the pure thought "is."[35]

This explains the new disjunction presented at B8.34–41. The reference of τῷ (B8.38b) to being rests on the identity of thought to "what it is the thought of" reasserted in the preceding verses. But mortals posit names that violate the signs posted through B8. This is dutifully noted by the goddess who later will comment on the positing of more than one form: "in this they erred" (B8.54b).

The *crux* lies in this "errancy," for since the very moment it enters the argument (B6.1a), language shows two opposing connections: through saying and λόγος (B6.1, B7.5) to thinking and being; through "the tongue" and "names" to the thinking of mortals as expressed by their opinions.

---

[33] The sophist approaches "existing things" either as "things thought" (pp. 77–80) or as perceived, as "things seen, heard and uttered" (pp. 81–86). Naturally, he concludes that these cannot be identical.

[34] Notice in the VII *Epistle* (342a–343d) the gradual ascent of knowledge from name, definition, image, and knowledge itself, to the known in itself.

[35] This interpretation of the identity of thought and being was first stressed by G. Calogero, "Parmenide," in *Studi sull'eleatismo* (Firenze: La nuova Italia, 1970; originally 1932), pp. 6–67.

Taking human thought for "divine" thought seems to be the fault that the injunction of the goddess at B7.5 aims at correcting when she commands mortals to use argument to stand for "is,"[36] following in B8 with the enumeration of the correct predicates: "unchangeable," etc.

The fact that an inspection of Greek tradition shows that this instruction has been well understood and dutifully obeyed by every relevant thinker from Empedocles to Aristotle cannot pass unnoticed. In their theories, "being" emerged as the focal problem in philosophy by being related to the world in which mortals live. No longer as a thought but connected to reality, as mortals experience and describe it,[37] being and the verb "be" robbed cosmology of the leading position it had in Greek tradition.

No one doubts that this effect was brought about by the argument in the Way of Truth. More subtle, however, is the way Parmenides himself reinforced this effect by unequivocally relating the δόξα section of his Poem to the outside world.

## How may the two Ways be related?

The question lies in understanding what possible relation there is between Parmenides' being and the external world. A series of points have to be taken into consideration when looking for an answer to this question. I start with the nature of what is. According to the interpretation proposed, being is what is thought.

Mortal men err when they forget the evidence stressed by the argument in B8. And they err when they submit thought and

---

[36] Patricia Curd, op. cit., pp. 14–15, sustains that "the *kouros* must judge by *logos*." It seems to me that this commandment may be addressed to mankind, advising the use of "argument" or "reason" in the much-contested challenge she has uttered and shortly will address.

[37] Certainly in the *Sophist*, Plato is guilty of anachronism when the Eleatic Guest evaluates past Greek cosmological conceptions as theories on being (242c–243a). But soon afterwards, the Guest presses his point when he asks: "Come now, all you who say that hot and cold or any two such principles are the universe, what is this that you attribute to both of them when you say that both and each of them are?" (243d–e; translation: H. N. Fowler, Loeb Classical Library, 1921).

language to the complex experience of perception and naming, thus making allowances for the "is not" thought.

The argument of the Poem looks deceptively simple: if it "is," it "cannot not be" (B2.3). Does it follow from this that what is perceived "is not"? In one sense, yes, for perception is "regressive" (B6.9b). On the other hand, nothing imposes the belief that, because it "is and is not," "what is perceived" does not exist, "is not this or that," and "is not (true)." Yet given that it cannot be "what is"—which is "one" and "unchangeable," etc.—it cannot be identified with being and thought.[38]

As Gorgias has shown, what is thought, what is perceived and "what is" are completely different: one is a thought consistent with itself, the other an inconsistent web of manifold reflections of the world outside. Such difference explains why, despite the fact that only being is thought, the δόξα complex shows something, namely that

> . . . things sprouted, and now are,
> and then will grow and come to an end (B19.1–2)

If only "being is," any violation of the signs listed in B8.1–49 necessarily "is not." However, appearances do still "permeate everything" (B1.31–32); they are perceived, but cannot consistently be thought.

It does not follow, from the fact that they "are not," that mortal opinions as a mode of capturing whatever is outside are false, mistaken, illusive, and so on, because they are and they are not. However, all notions supposing that whatever is captured through perception *is*, as if "to be" could be used to describe what is sense, will be false, mistaken and illusive, because they are refutable and therefore inconsistent.

As has already been suggested, I do not think this criticism implies a condemnation of the "two forms" and the "notions" referred to by them, as long as humans—having to live with both—understand that none of them "is" without the other or

[38] Notice that the goddess does not state that mortal names are wrong. Mortals "err" by being at variance with being when they are convinced that they are true.

in opposition to the other.[39] Whatever is thought must be what is. Men, however, "believe" (B6.8) their eyes, ears, and tongue (B6.7, B7.4–5a), experiencing what is and is not (B6.8–9a).

Therefore, there are not two worlds. The identity of thinking and being provides men with a standard against which all opinions must be judged. However, judgment on opinion requires using argument to appraise human experience, that is, man's perception of the outside world.

The resulting debate inevitably brings two complementary ways of thinking face-to-face. One of them, the "true" one, is thought; the other, the "acceptable" one, is the complex of perception and language, the "erring mind" (B6.6) or "human thought" (B16.1–4a). But these two ways do not relate to two opposing worlds.

What really matters is not their differences, but what happens when they are brought together. As perception is subjected to rational argument, two consequences follow. In one, debate and criticism arise. In the other, being will inevitably be transposed to the world created by the submission of sense experience to thought.

This program was carried on by Parmenides' followers. They were the ones who compelled "being" to address the nature of "what is."[40] But the first steps of the program are already noticeable in two consecutive moves in the Poem. The first one, B8, presents the reader with a two-edged critique of language: "being" and the verb "be" are given a rationale, while the deceptiveness of human names is denounced by their being aptly referred to what is.

The second move presents the Way of Opinion as a proposed description of our world construed on two of those names, made into paradigmatic contrary notions, and confirmed through rather elaborate biological, physiological and astronomical research.

---

39 After all, how could mortals perceive the outside world as a unity if their "mixed" nature (B16.1) makes them think that that is the way it is? B16.2 is in flat contradiction of B4.

40 To say "what is" is indifferent to the content of "what is," to the "thing" that is, not only because only being "is," but also because "is" expresses thought and what it is about, not that there must be some one "thing" thought.

The apparent discontinuity of both parts of the Poem should probably be seen as the synthesis of all the previous disjunctions—the crossroads—presented in the Way of Truth, alternatively proposing two complementary approaches to thinking.[41]

But they were read as if they proposed two opposite worlds. Δόξα was considered wrong, and Parmenides was taken for a monist, not paying attention to the fact that the cosmic order referred to in B8.50–61ff. cannot be explained by a substance out of which the others are generated.[42] Despite the fact that this conception does not attribute any material character to the world perceived through δόξα, the ontological commitment of thought has been given an ontological turn by bestowing a material character to whatever is thought.

However, "what is" is alien to material/immaterial categories, because it does not exist as a "thing" that is or is not this or that. It is what is "common" (B5) to what "is," not by virtue of any of its physical properties, but only because it "is firmly present in thought" (B4) and because it must be thought, said and be (B6.1a). As a result of thought, it "necessarily is" (B6.1a), "similar

[41] The solution to the discontinuity (present in the dualistic theory presented by the "friends of forms," 248a) may be found in the conception of "being" suggested by the Eleatic Guest: the ". . . power . . . to produce a change . . . or to be affected . . ." (247d–e). Being is not a property of things, but the power that causes these properties to be and change into one another. That is the very problem Aristotle addressed with his theory on hylomorphism.

[42] D. H. Graham, "Empedocles and Anaxagoras: Responses to Parmenides," doubts Parmenides' defense of monism (*CCEGrPh*, p. 66; cf. 179n19, n20), quoting Mourelatos, *Route*, pp. 130–133; J. Barnes, *The Presocratic Philosophers* (London and New York: Routledge & Kegan Paul, 1979); P. Curd, "Parmenidean Monism," *Phronesis* 36 (1991); and P. Curd, *The Legacy of Parmenides: Eleatic Monism and Later Presocratic Thought* (Princeton: Princeton University Press, 1998. Reprinted with new introduction, Las Vegas: Parmenides Publishing, 2004). (Cf. also R. D. McKirahan Jr., "Zeno," *CCEGrPh*, p. 157n15. On the contrary, D. Sedley, op. cit., p.121, apparently takes the reference to only one entity as proof of monism.

Arguments against monism were systematically developed by Aristotle, targeting either the Eleatics (*Phys.* I, 2–3, 184b15–187a11) or *physiologoi* (*Met.* I, 3, 983b6–19; *On Generation and Corruption* I, 1, 314b1ff.). In particular, the argument in *On Generation and Corruption* I, 1, referred to in *On the Soul* II, 5, 416b34–417a2; II, 11, 424a6–11, shows the relevance of the difficulty above to the defense of hylomorphism, in Aristotle.

to a sphere" (B8.43–44). But it neither "is a sphere" nor looks like one,[43] without having to be either material or immaterial.[44]

From my point of view, δόξα has an epistemological rather than an ontological bearing on reality, showing how speech is used to describe perceptual experience[45] and how it should be used in connection with thought. Therefore, perceptions should not be seen as true or false but as attempts to reach the world outside.[46]

## Conclusion

I want to emphasize the point presented above. Besides falsity, there is also truth on the Way of Opinion, even if it is not possible to distinguish one from the other or to choose one

---

43 Whatever Empedocles and Plato think it is, in Parmenides, the sphere is an analogy. Like the Sun Analogy in *Republic* VI, it allows for the understanding of a certain nature that is inaccessible to common perceptual experience: the invisible being as it is represented by a visible image.

D. Sedley, "Parmenides and Melissus," *CCEGrPh*, pp. 121–123, argues for the spatial sense of what is from arguments in B8 ("larger/smaller," "here/there"). I do not think, however, that the negation of the fact that being *is not* larger or smaller here or there implies that being *exists* in or *is* this world.

44 I do not think that Greek tradition allows for a notion—much less a concept—of matter before Aristotle. On the contrary, Anaxagoras' fragments 11 and 12 provide unquestionable proof that νοῦς is incorporeal either in the event that it is mixed or that it is mixed only with a few things (cf. Melissus B9: Simplicius in *Phys.* 109, 34).

As Aristotle's arguments in *On Generation and Corruption* I 1 suggest, the notion of "matter" as a constituent of reality arises only in a pluralistic context, when there are "things" to be perceived and thought. This is hardly possible in the *Timaeus*. But notice the entanglement Aristotle falls into when he mistakenly states that Plato had the creator "fashioning soul out of the elements" (*On the Soul* I, 3, 406b29) or stating that "matter and χώρα were the same" (*Phys.* IV, 2, 209b11–17).

45 See B14, B15 for a suggestion as to how the complex of opinion works. Though the moon is seen shining by night, it does so by a "foreign light," for it is "always looking at the rays of the Sun." But this conclusion cannot come out of perception, but through the scrutiny of thought, so that it takes both sensation/perception and reflection/thought to understand what is perceived.

Such endeavor is congenial to philosophers. Notice Heraclitus' fragment 3 about the sun ("broad as human foot") and Aristotle's reflections on it ("the sun appears to measure a foot across, but we are convinced that it is greater than the inhabited globe" [*On the Soul* III, 3, 428b4–9], ". . . but something else contradicts this impression" [*On Dreams* 460b18–19]).

46 See some possible interpretations of the role the "δόξα section" plays in the Poem, listed by J. H. Lesher, "Early Interest in Knowledge," *CCEGrPh*, pp. 239–241. The suggestion of trying within Parmenides' Poem "to distinguish *a priori* from empirical knowledge" (241) sounds convincing.

of them correctly. Only by paying attention to the lesson which states that being is thought is it possible to correct those partial, transitory or contrary visions expressed by human opinions, relating them to "what is."

Thought and perception must not be taken as two opposed "faculties"—and neither should being or cosmos be seen as conflicting realities—but they should rather be examined based on the contrasting results they provide.

That is the enduring lesson to be extracted from *On Nature*. Parmenides suggests a method that he hopes will allow men to find knowledge from the experience they acquire, either on their own or through discourse with others and the study of their works.

If this is the lesson that the goddess addresses to mankind, then everyone in Greek tradition has understood it perfectly and taken it seriously, even though, again and again, each personal interpretation of the argument has always remained "mortal." But no human being can aspire to more than that privilege, as any philosopher will agree.

# Parmenides: Logic and Ontology

José Solana Dueso


## Summary

Many scholars (especially Calogero) affirm that in the age of Parmenides, a theoretical treatment of logic and ontology was not clearly differentiated. Accepting this thesis, valid as well for Plato and Aristotle to some extent, this paper provides arguments for a primarily logical and only secondarily ontological interpretation of the ἀλήθεια of Parmenides (fr. 2–fr. 8.50). An interpretation of this type allows us to solve the arduous problem of the relationship between both parts of the poem, the ἀλήθεια and the δόξα, in a satisfactory way. Besides the internal arguments from Parmenides' own text, there are two external references that support the proposed interpretation: firstly, some data of the philosophical-poetic context, and secondly, an insistent thesis of Aristotle according to which some Presocratic philosophers (Parmenides among them) supposed that reality is confined to sensible things.


Before starting with the argument itself, I would do well to make two points that clearly establish the guidelines of my position from the beginning.

First, I would like to call attention to the chronological fact, along with Xenophanes and Heraclitus, that Parmenides belongs to the second generation of thinkers, after the Milesians and the Pythagoreans and, of course, after the great poets Homer and Hesiod. The sense of criticism we observe in those philosophers is a peculiar characteristic of their fragments that can be better understood from their position in the sequence of the history of philosophy. Thus Xenophanes (fr. 11 and 12) dares to question

Homer and Hesiod's theological vision, and Heraclitus includes in his criticism not just poets and philosophers, but also ordinary people as well as his own fellow citizens. In Parmenides, the criticism has become normal practice (fr. 6, 7 and 8) derived from an order of the goddess (fr. 7.5), and this criticism takes place to such an extent that it is a particular feature of the Eleatic school. Those who ignore the goddess's order will be "a horde incapable of judgement" (ἄκριτα φῦλα).

The immediate stimulus for this critical exercise is to be found in the plurality of accounts (μῦθοι) from philosophers and poets, showing a clear disagreement (διαφωνία) about the φύσις, the gods and the men. Parmenides took an additional step by setting aside φύσις, gods and men, and trying to resolve the διαφωνία by means of a previous investigation, developed in analogy with the investigations of physicists: because they had started by studying the ἀρχή or ἀρχαί of the natural beings, he would start by establishing the principles of language (λόγος), the logical principles. If physicists meant to discover natural order and legality, he meant to discover the order and legality of language, the order of speech, even the order of thought.

Parmenides' experience was different from that of Xenophanes and Heraclitus because of his knowledge of the mathematical tradition developed among the Pythagoreans in Magna Graecia.[1] Parmenides was the first to understand the contradiction between the change of the *physis*, as explained by the Ionian physicists, and the logical demands of thought. He tried to overcome the *aporia* through the mathematical method for demonstration. As Cornford states (*Platón y Parménides*, p. 72), Parmenides is the man who thinks, the first man to argue, deducing conclusions from premises instead of making dogmatic affirmations. The fact that the dialectic had its origin in the Eleatic school, with Zeno, confirms this point of view.

[1] Contact between Parmenides and the Pythagoreans, from whom he could have derived his demonstrative method, (in particular the *reductio ad absurdum*), is commonly admitted. The influence of the mathematical tradition in Parmenides is recognized by, among others, Tarán (*Parmenides*, p. 201), Vernant (*Mito y Pensamiento*, p. 362) and Cornford (*Platón y Parménides*, p. 72).

With regard to Parmenides, the key issue is the goddess's order in the first part of the poem: "Judge with reason the much contested argument which has been given by me" (fr. 7.5). His own poem is a result of this kind of proceeding, relying on the argument and accepting every consequence, even the most exasperating one, on the condition that they derive from strict reasoning. This methodology, which would become commonplace[2] in Greek thought, had its first expression in the mentioned passage of Parmenides.

The second reference has to do with the Aristotelian[3] thesis according to which some Presocratic philosophers, Parmenides among them, "although they studied the truth about reality, they supposed that reality is confined to sensible things" (τὰ δ' ὄντα ὑπέλαβον εἶναι τὰ αἰσθητὰ μόνον) (*Metaphysics* 1010a2–3). After having concluded the interpretation and explanation of these authors, Aristotle affirms that "we must prove to them and convince them that there is a kind of nature that is not moved" (ἀκίνητός τις φύσις) (1010a34). Such a recommendation, applied to a philosopher that spoke about an immutable being, would have sounded odd. In *On the Heavens* 298b15–24, Aristotle attributes the same thesis to the followers of Melissus and Parmenides.[4]

In book B of *Metaphysics*, Aristotle thinks that it is necessary to investigate this aporia: "This too is a question which demands inquiry: should we hold that only sensible substances

---

[2] Verdenius (*Parmenides*, p. 2) affirms that in making reasoning the guide of his inquiries, Parmenides is the first Greek thinker who satisfies Plato's principle of "proceeding through argument." There is only one objection to this observation: why should we consider as platonic a principle initially formulated and implemented by Parmenides? It is true, however, that Plato (and Socrates, as shown in *Crito* 46b) insists on this methodological principle in many passages (*Republic* 351a, 475a, 534c; *Sophist* 253b).

[3] Cherniss (*Criticism*) will be invoked immediately to disqualify the testimony of Aristotle. So remarks Tarán (*Parmenides*, p. 291), who asserts that "Aristotle's testimony concerning Parmenides is of no positive value." In the specific case at hand, I should warn that we cannot resort to Cherniss's authority, since there is no explicit pronouncement about these texts in his works.

[4] The more angry protest against the Aristotelian claim, according to which Parmenides only admitted the existence of the sensible realities, is in Simplicius, *On the Heavens* 558.12. On this issue, see Solana (*Logos*, pp. 131–134, 198–199).

exist (πότερον τὰς αἰσθητὰς οὐσίας εἶναι μόνον), or that there are other besides" (ἢ καὶ παρὰ ταύτας ἄλλας)? (995b13, 997a34, 1059a38). In a different passage and context, he comes back to the question and affirms that "some believe that there is nothing of this kind besides sensible things (παρὰ τὰ αἰσθητὰ οἱ μὲν οὐκ οἴονται εἶναι οὐδὲν τοιοῦτον), while others believe in eternal entities more numerous and more real than sensible things" (id. 1028b18). The Pythagoreans, Plato, Speusippus, and Xenocrates are included in the second group, but Aristotle never includes Parmenides among them.[5]

Even starting from Cherniss's analyses (*Criticism,* p. 347) and accepting that Aristotle uses the doctrines of his predecessors and changes them to benefit himself, we should have to explain the antithetic behavior of Aristotle in two different questions: on the one hand, he affirms that Parmenides was the first to conceive the notion of cause of movement (*Metaphysics* 984b3). On the other hand, if we suppose that Parmenides conceived the existence of an immovable being, it would be necessary to explain why in this case Aristotle does not recognize such a contribution, and maintains in addition that the Parmenidean thesis was the opposite, that is, that only the sensible world exists.

With these points in mind as the main guidelines for my argumentation, I would like to state, from the very beginning, my conviction that the interpretation of Parmenides' ἀλήθεια, that is to say, the first part of the goddess's speech (in principle, the lines of fr. 1.28 to fr. 8.50), depends largely on being capable of specifying which is its starting point.

I will begin the discussion by taking an article by Owen ("Plato and Parmenides," 272) as a pretext. This well-known scholar, after conjecturing that Parmenides was the discoverer of the atemporal eternity, affirms that the poem begins

[5] In his commentary on *Metaphysics*, Ross asserts that the philosophers of the first group are the Presocratics and refers to 1002a8: "This is why the vulgar and the earlier thinkers supposed that substance and Being are Body (τὴν οὐσίαν καὶ τὸ ὂν ᾤοντο τὸ σῶμα εἶναι), and everything else the modifications of Body; and hence also that the first principles of bodies are the first principles of existing things (τὰς ἀρχὰς τὰς τῶν σωμάτων τῶν ὄντων εἶναι ἀρχάς)."

"perplexingly enough, without specifying what the discussion is about, what the subject of his argument is." Owen talks about perplexity in relation to the problem of the subject in lines 2.3 and 2.5. But those lines are not the beginning of the poem, and therefore it would be inexact to affirm that Parmenides starts without specifying what the subject of his discussion is.

We can appreciate a remarkable didactic intentionality throughout the whole poem, most of all in the fragments of its first part. Thus, after the student's trip, the ceremony of reception on the part of the goddess consists of two parts: first, the words of welcome (fr. 1.24–28), and then, the presentation of the work program (fr. 1.28–32). The goddess addresses the young man on familiar terms and maintains the same kind of treatment during the lesson.

In the presentation of the program, we have the first terminological clue of the theoretical content. It would be about truth (ἀλήθεια) and opinions (δόξαι), both terms being of epistemic, and not ontological, content.

Following this formal act, the class begins in fragment 2. The goddess speaks and the student must listen with care (fr. 2.1). The goddess maintains direct language in second the person (fr. 2.1, 2.6, 2.7, 6.3, 7.2, 8.8. 8.50, 8.60, 8.61), and she sometimes orders (fr. 2.1, 6.2, 7.5, 8.52) and sometimes prohibits (fr. 7.2, 8.7–8). This treatment is maintained in the second half as well.

After line 2.1, the beginning itself comes in line 2.2 rather than in line 2.3. The issue that would occupy the goddess during the first part is what she has denominated the truth (line 1.29), and that part concludes explicitly in line 8.50, when the goddess warns that the first part of the program, the discourse on truth (ἀλήθεια), is over, and the second part, the opinions of mortals (δόξαι), is about to start.

Thus, Parmenides starts the first part in 2.2 without any perplexity. The goddess begins her speech talking about the two sole ways of study. She refers to the activity of understanding, namely thinking (νοῆσαι). It is not just about conceivable ways, but about ways of understanding, that is, logical or aprioristic ways, different from those of sensible activity.

It is crucial to bear this beginning in mind to see that Parmenides does not begin with existence. He begins, by contrast, with what is announced in line 2.2, ways (ὁδοί), rather than landscapes or territories (φύσις or whatever). He talks about investigation or study (διζήσιος), and the study is just restricted to the field of understanding, or thinking (νοῆσαι), not to that of senses.

Because of this starting point, we should consider the Parmenidean claim an original one, since no former philosopher had clearly set the beginning on such an area. The Milesian philosophers began on the scene of φύσις, while Parmenides proposes—and this is his innovation—not a theory about physics, but a new area for investigation. The question of knowledge is the first and even more important issue. The theory about nature would be in second place.

If we affirm that Parmenides begins with the existence,[6] or that "he wants to reason about whatever it is that can be a subject" (Owen, "Plato and Parmenides," 272), we do not emphasize sufficiently the difference between Parmenides and other thinkers. This approach seems to suggest that while Thales is speaking about water or Anaximander about ἄπειρον as principles of the φύσις, Parmenides would place this principle in τὸ ἐόν. This approach is confusing, because Parmenides is not in the same area and is not concerned about an identical problem. Τὸ ἐόν, or existence, does not constitute a starting point for Parmenides, though it is an essential element in his argument.

The great Parmenidean innovation has two basic components: first, the field of φύσις moves to λόγος, knowledge; and second, once this field, which had already been addressed, in a somewhat erratic way, by thinkers like Xenophanes or

[6] Tarán (*Parmenides,* p. 37) asserts that the starting point is the existence expressed by a verb. He adds: "Let it be stated once and for all that the different idioms which Parmenides uses to express being and non-being are synonymous." For Tarán, to distinguish between the use of the participle and infinitive, for example, as some scholars do, is to obliterate the fact that for Parmenides there is only absolute Being, although the language, the meter, and the necessity of referring to the phenomenal world in order to deny its existence, forced him sometimes to use expressions like "the things which are not" (line 7.1).

Heraclitus,[7] is established, he proposes the thesis that we should discern two modalities of knowledge, the *alethic* (apodictic) and the *doxastic*. This issue is essential to establishing the problem of the beginning.[8]

The goddess, certainly taking into account the change of field,[9] draws attention to the two only ways of inquiry (line 2.2), which are named in lines 3 and 5 and which we briefly summarize in the two expressions "is necessarily" and "is not necessarily." I use the term "expressions," not "statements," for to be statements there should be a subject or the verb εἶναι should be used in the impersonal sense,[10] which does not seem acceptable from a grammatical standpoint.

Both expressions have a common part ("*necessarily*") and an individual one (ἔστι/οὐκ ἔστι). We are again faced with a crucial issue. If they are indeed expressions of existence (by the presence of ἔστι, whose existential value seems to me undeniable), we cannot ignore, as some scholars[11] do, the modal expressions linked to the verb ἔστι by the coordinate conjunction καί.

---

[7] Fragment 1 of Heraclitus, which, as everyone knows, is the beginning of the book, is also of clear epistemological orientation, although its treatment of λόγος is different from that of Parmenides.

[8] Tarán (*Parmenides,* p. 33), when analyzing fr. 2, puts aside the crucial line 2 and claims that "it is necessary to begin with an analysis of lines 3 and 5, for they contain the starting point of Parmenides' philosophy and it is due to the misunderstanding of them that many misinterpretations of Parmenides' thought have arisen."

[9] In this issue, apart from fr. 1.28–30, it is crucial to fr. 2.2 (Solana, *Logos,* p. 47).

[10] Tarán (*Parmenides,* p. 36) considers *esti* in lines 3 and 5 as impersonal. Fränkel (*Poesía,* p. 333 n13) affirms the same, that *esti* is impersonal. However, the question is not if *esti* is impersonal (Tarán and Fränkel agree on that) or not, but whether such expression (*esti*) constitutes a statement, in which case we should be able to determine what the subject is. Otherwise, we must be able to provide an explanation of that particular grammatical fact. It is clear that the impersonal use of a verb does not imply the absence of an impersonal subject.

[11] O'Brien (*Parménide,* p. 16) writes these verses as follows: "«est», et aussi: il n'est pas possible de ne pas être" (verse 3) and "«n'est pas», et aussi: il est nécessaire de ne pas être" (verse 5). Tarán (*Parmenides,* p. 32), for his part, translates verse 3 as "exists" and "it is not possible not to exist" and verse 5 in a similar way: "exists-not" and "not to exist is necessary." Bernabé and Pérez de Tudela (*Parménides,* p. 23) translate: "el uno, el de que 'es' y no es posible que no sea" (line 2.3) y "el otro, el de que 'no es' y que es preciso que no sea (line 2.5)."

Thus, assuming that ἔστι and the modal expression constitute a unity, that the verb ἔστι has existential sense and that the expression is not a statement, we can conclude that Parmenides, by means of the expressions in lines 2.3 and 2.5, is naming the contents of the two ways announced in line 2.2.

Therefore the content of these two ways should be that of the necessary existences and the necessary nonexistences, if we emphasize the existential ἔστι plus the modal expression, or that of the necessary affirmations and necessary negations, if we emphasize the specific part of both ways (affirmation ἔστι and negation οὐκ ἔστι). Those two nuances, the ontological and the logical, are not differentiated in the poem, and, for this reason, we must explain the explicit indistinction between ontology and logic.

What is the critical issue? Keeping in mind the Parmenidean advice about judging by means of reason, we should conclude that, if ontology is in the second part of the poem, because Parmenides only admits the existence of sensible things, the first part should be understood in a logical and epistemological sense, as a propaedeutic, prior to the development of physical theory.

The ontological bias of the interpretations of the poem is due to the massive presence of the verb εἶναι in its various flexive forms and, most of all, the substantivated participle (τὸ ἐόν). Of course, a text containing a few terms related to plants does not automatically equal a treatise on Botany. The same is true of the Parmenidean poem.

Calogero (*Logica Antica,* pp. 64–65) asserts that the indistinction between the ontological, logical and linguistic fields is a constitutive feature of the archaic mentality, evidenced in Heraclitus in a clearer and more typical form than in Parmenides; he also speaks of "archaic triunity of ontological, logical, and linguistic areas."[12] Considering the development of logic, Calogero (p. 153) concludes that the history of Western logic is in this sense

[12] There is no doubt that certain elements of culture and human life are in fact united. That occurred, for instance, in the early Greek period, where poetry, music and dance constituted an indissoluble unity. In everyday life, verbal language is intimately connected with gesture (body language). Under no circumstances can we infer from such a practice a confusion or indistinction in the concepts, unless

the history of the efforts to release thought from Parmenidean servitude.

In order to understand the indistinction of those areas, we must keep in mind that the philosophical vocabulary was not yet set at that time, let alone did the separation among disciplines we are used to nowadays exist universally. There was not an independent reflection about each of the issues in any way. However, in Parmenides, there is a clear awareness of the need of an adequate articulation (we could also say cohesion or coexistence) between being (εἶναι), saying (λέγειν), and thinking (νοεῖν). That is exactly the task. The three terms are not confused in the poem, although there is no specific treatment pointing out the differences among them.

So there are two critical elements in fr. 2 that allow us to interpret the beginning of the first part of the Parmenidean poem as an inquiry in the field of the logic. The first, line 2.1, talks about ways of research for thought. The second, the phrases that refer to such ways, put us on the scene of necessity and not merely on that of existence.

However, why call these ways necessary existences or inexistences instead of talking about necessary truths or falsehoods, as is usual in the field of logic?[13] What sense should be given to the expressions "is necessarily"/"is not necessarily"?

The notion of necessity is what allows us to separate the nature of the ἀλήθεια from that of the δόξα. We cannot say, "What does not exist, exists" (fr. 7.1), but we can say, "Atoms do not exist." The first statement cannot be formulated without contradiction—it is necessarily false—whereas we can formulate the latter and, in doing so, we can be right or wrong. Such a difference in the concept of existence is undoubtedly of great importance, to an extent that we cannot affirm that the starting

we can provide arguments for proving such confusion. Also Hoffmann (*Sprache*, p. 11) speaks of "Drei-Einigkeit von Seiendem, Gedachtem und Gesprochenem."

[13] It is needless to say that logic, at the time of its birth, was not yet a formal logic in a strict sense. We cannot demand such a condition even of the Aristotelian *Organon*. As Aubenque ("Aristote," pp. 620–690) states, Aristotle never reached the idea of a formal logic, which would involve a strict separation between the form of speech and its contents, as modern logicians understand it.

point (if we take as a starting point 2.3 and 2.5) is the existence, because it is clear that the judgments of purely factual existence are excluded from the contents of the Parmenidean ways.

Hence, in my opinion, it is not acceptable to assert that Parmenides considers the notions of possibility of being, reality and necessity as coextensive, as Gómez-Lobo (Parménides, p. 89) does. This confusion results from merely understanding the content of the ways on the basis of the affirmation (ἔστι) and negation (οὐκ ἔστι), without taking the modal expressions into account.

Up to this point, it could be said that the theme of the ways is necessary existence, and therefore, ontology would be at the forefront. This assertion would be acceptable if the discussion were about just one way. But it is about two; thus, it is necessary to assert that what really is at the forefront is the necessary existence as well as necessary inexistence, which moves us away from ontology to logic. Indeed, we might believe that with the phrase "necessary existence," Parmenides is affirming the existence of necessary being, but how could a necessary nonexistence be understood? It seems to me that such an expression could only be understood in terms of a contradiction or an absurdity.[14] If we accept this for the "necessary nonexistence"—and in my opinion, we are forced to do so, for otherwise we would have to say that Parmenides affirms the nonexistence of some necessary being—I see no reason not to accept that Parmenides, by using the term "necessary existence," is referring to a tautology.

Moreover, it should be stressed that the proximity between reality and truth is a constant in the history of philosophy and in everyday language. Depending on which term we accentuate, we are located in ontology or epistemology. Philosophers also speak about the truth of the thing, that is to say, the ontological truth. However, conceptual clarity in the analysis of the poem requires that we speak about truth only in the case that, besides the thing we speak about, there is some statement on the thing itself.

Parmenides is unequivocal on that issue. The problematic questions in the poem are resolved within the triad

[14] Solana, *Logos*, p. 53n77.

"being-saying-thinking," and that framework is widely attested in the Parmenidean verses.

The first of the two ways described, improperly called way of truth, "is the way of persuasion (for persuasion accompanies truth)," and the second is "a way that does not teach anything." If we bear in mind that among the propositions whose truth value is determined, some are always true (tautology) and others always false (absurd), we can establish a correspondence between both groups and the two ways. That means that Parmenides was the first to discover the existence of necessary propositions, characteristic of a new discourse, the logical discourse, clearly distinct from the speech of the physicists. That new universe of discourse, reserved exclusively for thought, is made up of two elements, the necessary affirmation and the necessary negation.[15]

A discourse taking as its subject nonexistence would necessarily be an empty discourse. Only tautology would be possible: "Non-being is not." Non-being cannot be known nor can statements be made about it, and therefore the second way cannot teach anything. Statements such as "non-being has *x* property" could never be formulated, because we can say or think nothing about what does not exist.

That is why I have spoken (*Logos,* pp. 51, 58) of *existential necessity*, because the truth is necessarily truth about something that exists, a necessary precondition for any true statement. That existential necessity is based on the election of τὸ ἐόν as the subject of the Parmenidean proposal and also on the affirmation that τὸ μή ἐόν is unknowable and inexpressible. From that perspective, what does not exist is not cognoscible nor expressible.[16]

---

[15] According to Calogero, archaic awareness tended to feel embodied in the "is" (the true and the real) and in the "is not" (the false and the non-existent) (*Logica Antica,* p. 115). This statement does not seem to me an adequate explanation, since it is obvious that, in some cases, the truth is on the side of the affirmation, others, the negation, as it may be seen in the poem itself.

[16] Owen ("Eleatic Questions," p. 72 n44) argues that the Parmenidean requirement that we cannot talk about the non-existent is wrong. He replies: "We can, of course: mermaids, for instance." In the context of the poem and the entire scientific language, Owen's response is invalid, because Parmenides would reply that mermaids are not real (they do not exist), but fictional beings and, consequently, the discourse on mermaids would not take part in scientific language.

Once the domain of inquiry is established (the necessary existence or the necessary truth), the second step in the ἀλήθεια is the establishment of tautological statements (axioms, principles) and contradictions corresponding to the two mentioned ways in fr. 2. First, the tautology (T): "what is, is" (ἐὸν ἔμμεναι) (fr. 6.1); and second, the contradiction (C): "what is not, is" (εἶναι μὴ ἐόντα) (fr. 7.1). About the tautology it is said that "it is necessary (χρή) to say and think that T," that is, it is stated that it is a proposition necessarily true, whereas about contradiction, it is said that "never will C be valid," that it is a necessarily false proposition.

How are these kinds of statements built? By taking a single meaning and forming the subject and predicate based on it. "Whatever exists, exists" is as good an example as "whoever speaks, speaks" or "man is man." The same could be said of "whatever does not exist, does not exist" or "whoever is not a man, is not a man."

These considerations might seem trivial, except for the fact that Parmenides was the first to write and meditate on them, and also the fact that they are the only particular statements written by Parmenides that are formed with the verb *be* (εἶναι, τὸ ἐόν). And there is still one more important problem, since according to Parmenides, what we consider a trivial truth is disregarded again and again by Greek physicists who talk about φύσις, men and gods. In other words, according to him, there are philosophers who explicitly affirm that the non-being is, and others who, even if not explicitly, build their theories in such a way that makes it possible to infer the existence of the non-being from them. The allusion is obviously directed toward philosophers like Heraclitus (who could be referred to in fr. 6.8) or the Milesians and, in general, toward those who talk about change.

These statements are necessarily true or false because of the meaning of the terms. For this reason, I prefer to use the phrase *analytical necessity*, because we can determine the truth-value of these statements through the analysis of language. The lines 6.1–2 and 7.1 are sharp formulations on the part of Parmenides about what a tautology is, as a necessary truth, what a contradiction is, and the idea that a contradiction, which is a necessary falsehood, becomes a tautology when negation is applied to it.[17]

There are only two ways: one of them allows us to build an account, the other does not. If we read the Poem from an ontological perspective, we cannot give any explanation of this fact. Indeed, only by putting the logical perspective in the foreground, can we emphasize the negation way. Without it, the contradiction would not be possible, and in such a case, the proof itself would not be possible either. If the test proof were not possible, the scientific debates would not be possible either. The non-being notion (τὸ μὴ ἐόν) is a constant reference in the proof in fr. 8. From a purely ontological perspective, such a presence would not be justified; without the non-being, the logical principles cannot be formulated, nor can the logical error of the ἄκριτα φῦλα be shown.

The third step in the logical outline of Parmenides is that of the deduction of theorems, the account in fr. 8 built by using the established axioms.

Perhaps the notion that more strongly allows us to understand the priority of the logic against the ontology in fr. 8 is again the notion of necessity, as affirmed by three different formulations: the mythical (Dike, Anauke, Moira), the metaphorical (limit, chains), and the theoretical. The latter is expressed by the terms of necessity (χρή, χρῆν, χρέος, χρεόν, χρεών, ἀνάγκη) and the modal terms of possibility, besides having a zero degree in the tautology, for which we have some examples in fr. 6.1, 7.1, 8.11 and 8.16.

Necessity, moreover, is the notion that links the first and the second part, for in the same way that there is a physical necessity that maintains the limits of the stars in a fixed position (fr. 10.6–7), there is a logical necessity that affects and ties some statements together (fr. 6, 7 and 8). The first statement of necessity in the poem is in fr. 1.31–32 (χρῆν), and it deals with the sensible world (δοκοῦντα), so that it, as a necessary statement, is part of truth

[17] I have tried to explain in *De Logos a Physis* (pp. 58–64) the question of why Parmenides resorts to the verb εἶναι to formulate the tautology and the contradiction.

(ἀλήθεια) and, as long as it is related to the sensible world, also part of physics. Consequently, the difference between the ἀλήθεια and the δόξα statements is determined by their analytical or empirical nature. In other words, there are not two ontological worlds or areas matching the *alethic* and the *doxastic* statements. The ἀνάγκη that maintains the course of the stars fixedly (fr. 10.6–7) is a physical force, while what makes us accept the statement "the sensible things had to have real existence pervading all things completely" (fr. 1.31–32) is the logical necessity, attached to a proof that takes the impossibility of non-being as a premise, that is, the impossibility of a universe in which there is a void together with being. Both statements are justified in a different way: in the first, we depend on observation; in the second, we resolve through rational examination.

Between these two examples, other necessary statements are formulated, either in zero degree (ἔστιν ἢ οὐκ ἔστιν) or relying on all three types of the mentioned expressions, all of which can be explained in terms of modality, but not implying the existence of a necessary being. The same goes with the metaphorical notions of "chains and bounds." Limits cannot be physical, since time and space have been excluded, and since, by logical demand, infinity is one of the attributes of ἐόν (ἀτέλεστον) (fr. 8.4). Therefore, they can just allude to logical necessity,[18] namely, to the necessity of the discourse that forces predication on the infinity and nongenerability of τὸ ἐόν because of its own internal laws. Thus, for example, the text that affirms that the Moira forced the being to "be whole and immovable" (fr. 8.37–38) would be the same as saying "It is necessary that the being is whole and immovable"; when it is said that "Justice did not allow to come into being or to perish" (fr. 8.13–14), we must understand "it is not possible for the being to be born or to perish."

[18] So it is admitted by Tarán (*Parmenides*, pp. 117, 151) and Cordero (*Deux Chemins*, p. 190). For Verdenius (*Parmenides*, p. 101), the goddess as *Ananke* is both the logical force of the demonstration and the cosmic necessity, and as *Dike*, determines both what can be thought and what can be.

Therefore, except for fr. 10.6–7, necessity always has logical sense, no matter if the particular statements refer to τὸ ἐόν, τὰ ὄντα or τὰ δοκοῦντα.

Bearing in mind the reiterative Aristotelian assertion, according to which Parmenides only recognizes the existence of sensible substances, and that this Aristotelian information is only refuted by those who, like Simplicius, intend to depict Parmenides as a predecessor of Plato, I think we can interpret the first part of the goddess's speech as an outline of a logical system with a minimum material burden, the existence (τὸ ἐόν) plus the supplemental deductively derived (theorems) of nongenerability and completeness. These predicates would have the range of requirements a priori to think about the φύσις. These theorems have two important implications for Greek thought after Parmenides: a new manner (not contradictory) to think about change, and denial of the void.[19]

With regard to a similar debate, that of atemporal eternity, Tarán ("Perpetual," 211) claims that "Plato—and Parmenides too, if he did grasp the notion of atemporal eternity—discovered this notion because of his metaphysics, because he saw that atemporality is the necessary consequence of postulating unchangeable entities. And there is no evidence—nor any reason for supposing—that it was reflection on tenseless statements that led him to postulate the existence of eternal ideas." In short, Tarán asserts that the Greek philosophers went from metaphysics to logic, and never the other way round. Such an assertion is consistent with his thesis that Parmenides starts from existence to build the ontology.[20]

---

[19] The most obvious consequences of the Parmenidean logic in physical theories were drawn by Anaxágoras (fr. 17) and Empedocles (fr. 8), when they explained birth and death as mixture and separation.

[20] Owen ("Plato and Parmenides," 288) asserts, and I share his view, that "to be tensed or tenseless is a property of statements and not of things, and that paradoxes come from confusing this distinction; just as they come from trying to manufacture necessary beings out of the logical necessity that attaches to certain statements." Tarán ("Perpetual," 212), by contrast, insists that Parmenides, although using timeless statements, is not aware of their properties. Parmenides' concern is to deny any kind of change to his immutable Being. According to Tarán, this doctrine entails the atemporality of such an entity, but this does not mean that Parmenides saw the necessary connection between change and time.

Whether the discussion is about atemporal statements or about necessary statements, atemporality and necessity being two properties of logical statements, it seems to me undeniable, first, that Parmenides used them rigorously, and second, that he distinguished two well-defined epistemic areas, the *aletheia* and the *doxa*. If so, it does not appear that such a distinction could have been carried out without a clear reflection on the language, taking it in all its variety as λόγος (λέγειν), ὄνομα (ὀνομάζειν), μῦθος and ἔπος.

Against those who understand the concepts of atemporality or necessity to be inevitably associated with a suprasensible entity (an immutable and necessary being), I would like to add two final notes. First, I remind them of the aforementioned Aristotelian thesis that Parmenides only admits the existence of sensible substances. The second is better expressed through the following words from Nagel (*Logic,* p. 102): "If philosophers propose to supply a foundation for logical principles by reading them as formulations of immutable and necessary structures of everything that is or could be, I know of no method for proving them in error. I believe, nevertheless, that it is possible to dispense with such interpretations without impairing our understanding of the nature and power of logic."

# Bibliography


Aubenque, Pierre. "Aristote et le Lycée." In Brice Parain, ed., *Histoire de la Philosophie, I: Orient, Antiquité, Moyen Age* (pp. 620–690). Encyclopédie de la Pléiade. Paris: Gallimard, 1969.

Bernabé, Alberto. *Parménides. Poema. Fragmentos y Tradición Textual.* Introduction to the original text and commentary by Jorge Pérez de Tudela. Epilogue by Néstor-Luis Cordero. Madrid: Ediciones Istmo, 2007.

Calogero, Guido. *Storia della Logica Antica.* Bari: Laterza, 1967.

Cherniss, Harold. *Aristotle's Criticism of Presocratic Philosophy.* Baltimore: John Hopkins Press, 1944, 1964. Reprinted, New York: Octagon Books, 1983.

Cordero, Néstor-Luis. *Les Deux Chemins de Parménide. Édition Critique, Traduction, Études et Bibliographie.* Bruxelles-Paris: J. Vrin-Éditions Ousia, 1984, 1997.

_____. *By Being, It Is: The Thesis of Parmenides.* Las Vegas: Parmenides Publishing, 2004.

Cornford, Francis M. *Platón y Parménides.* Translation to Spanish by Francisco Giménez. Madrid: Visor, 1989.

Fränkel, Hermann. *Poesía y Filosofía de la Grecia Arcaica.* Madrid: Visor, 1993.

Gómez-Lobo, Alfonso. *Parménides.* Buenos Aires: Editorial Charcas, 1985.

Hoffmann, Ernst. *Die Sprache und die Archaische Logik.* Tübingen: Mohr, 1925.

Mourelatos, Alexander P. D., ed. *The Presocratics: A Collection of Critical Essays.* New York: Anchor Books, 1974.

Nagel, Ernest. *Logic without Metaphysics and Other Essays in the Philosophy of Science.* Glencoe: Free Press, 1956.

O'Brien, Denis. *Études sur Parménide* I. Paris: J. Vrin, 1987.

Owen, G. E. L. "Eleatic Questions." *Classical Quarterly* 10 (1960): 84–102. Reprinted in R. E. Allen and David J. Furley, eds., *Studies in Presocratic Philosophy, Vol. 2: Eleatics and Pluralists* (pp. 48–81). London: Routledge & Kegan Paul, 1975.

_____. "Plato and Parmenides on Timeless Present." *The Monist* 50 (1966): 317–340. Reprinted in A. P. D. Mourelatos, ed., *The Presocratics: A*

*Collection of Critical Essays* (pp. 271–292). New York: Anchor Books, 1974.

Solana Dueso, José. *De Logos a Physis: Estudio sobre el Poema de Parménides.* Zaragoza: Mira Editores, 2006.

Tarán, Leonardo. *Parmenides: A Text with Translation, Commentary, and Critical Essays.* Princeton: Princeton University Press, 1965, 1971.

_____. "Perpetual Duration and Atemporal Eternity in Parmenides and Plato." *The Monist* 62 (1979): 43–53. Reprinted in L. Tarán, *Collected Papers (1962–1999)* (pp. 204–217). Leiden: Brill, 2001.

Verdenius, Willem J. *Parmenides: Some Comments on His Poem.* Amsterdam: Hakkert, 1964.

_____. "Der Logosbgriff bei Heraklit und Parmenides." *Phronesis* 12, 2 (1967): 99–117.

Vernant, Jean-Pierre. *Mito y Pensamiento en la Grecia Antigua.* Barcelona: Ariel, 1983, 1992.

# Parmenidean Dualisms

Panagiotis Thanassas

## Summary

The poem of Parmenides is systematically composed of dual structures. The part of Aletheia establishes an opposition between Being and Non-Being, but also an "identity" between Being and Thinking; the part of Doxa attempts to give an account of the relation between the two forms of Light and Night; finally, it is the duality of the two parts of the poem themselves that poses the question of their own relation. I attempt to explore the character and role of these dualisms, and especially their impact on the traditional perception of Parmenides as a rigorous "monist."

For the last two centuries, a specter has been haunting Parmenides, his poem and the research on it. It is the specter of "monism," i.e., the philosophical view that "exactly one thing exists."[1] The term "monism" appears for the first time in the 18th century, as a way of denoting a philosophical position that denies the Cartesian dichotomy between *res cogitans* and *res extensa*—a dichotomy which, for its part, offered the prospect of a philosophical "dualism." In the course of time, however, the concept of monism transcended these narrow semantic limits and came to denote every philosophical position that insists on an indestructible unity of reality (be this the unity of a variety of beings, a single principle that rules over them, or even a solitary existing substance). In the context of this

[1] We adopt here the formulation of Barnes ("Eleatic One," p. 2); cf. also that of Mourelatos: "all things are one thing" ("Alternatives," p. 4).

semantic amplification, monism could henceforth be attributed to earlier philosophers, the first of them being Parmenides. I do not consider such anachronisms problematic in themselves. I believe, on the contrary, that hermeneutically performed dialogues between philosophers that have lived in different times are a fundamental component of any history of philosophy that would remain part of philosophy proper, rather than reducing itself to a philologizing doxography.

The problem with "monism," therefore, is not its anachronistic association with Parmenides, but its use as a philosophical "label"—as a notion with a conceptual content considered so self-evident that its elucidation is deemed redundant. Such labels have the effect of inhibiting the very impulse that drives philosophical activity. They seem to name solutions to problems in such a way that the problems themselves cease to occupy us, and no longer call for inquiry. As Hans-Georg Gadamer has shown, understanding is nothing but a dialogic procedure, in which the interpreter states a question to which his subject-matter is expected to provide an answer. In this dialogue between interpreter and subject-matter, the question always remains crucial, even more important than the answer itself.[2] What is then the character, the quality and the significance of those questions, with respect to the answers of which Plato is labeled as an idealist but Aristotle as a realist, Democritus as a materialist and Thales as a hylozoist, Kant (together with Hegel!) as an idealist, Heidegger (together with Sartre!) as an existentialist? The Stalinist categorization of philosophers into "reactionary idealists" and "progressive materialists," which remained the starting point and conclusion of philosophical interrogation in Eastern Europe for the longer part of the 20th century, is nothing but an intensified form of this kind of history of philosophy.

It is worth noting, however, that Parmenides has not only been considered an apostle of monism, but also a pioneer of dualism—e.g., by Burnet, who entitled the chapter of his his-

---

[2] See Gadamer on "the hermeneutic priority of the question" (*Truth*, pp. 356–371).

tory dedicated to the Doxa "The Dualist Cosmology" (p. 185).[3] The basic scheme dominating the interpretation of Parmenides speaks of a monistic Aletheia and of a dualistic Doxa. What I will attempt in this presentation is an inquiry into the legitimacy, the character and the function of the notions of monism and dualism, intending to show the restrictions of this scheme and to demonstrate the polymorphous content of both notions. Concerning monism, this has already been to some extent achieved. In the first part of my presentation, I will attempt to evaluate this extant discussion of monism and to articulate my own proposal largely in its terms (I). Then, I will try to present and describe dualistic structures in the Aletheia (II) and in the Doxa (III). In the closing part (IV), I will outline the relation between ontological and cosmological dualisms and finally ask if and in what sense we could maintain that monism, dualism and pluralism belong together and determine each other in Parmenidean philosophy.

## I. Monism?

The first thinker who assigned to Parmenides a monistic position was none other than Plato. As is well known, in the dialogue *Parmenides* the persona of young Socrates addresses the old Eleatic by summarizing his doctrine as follows: σὺ μὲν γὰρ ἐν τοῖς ποιήμασιν ἓν φῄς εἶναι τὸ πᾶν (128a–b). In the *Sophist*, yet another person expected to be knowledgeable about the philosophy of "the father Parmenides," the Eleatic Stranger, includes him among those who maintain the position ἓν τὸ πᾶν.[4] It is worth dwelling on the content and the significance of this position here ascribed to Parmenides, and especially on the notion of totality denoted by πᾶν. We all know that this word has a collective and a distributive meaning ("all" and "each," respectively). In both cases, unity and multiplicity are present, with the unity ruling in the collective and the multiplicity ruling in the distributive meaning: "all"

[3] When writing Aletheia and Doxa in capitals, I want to denote only the two parts of the poem (as divided at 8.49–50) and not their special content or their possible polymorphy.

[4] See *Sophist* 244b: ἓν τὸ πᾶν λεγόντων. Cf. also *Sophist* 242d, *Theaetetus* 180e.

represents a totality that is constituted on account of its own unity, while "each" stresses the multiplicity of the individual units belonging to the unity.

The reasons for which Plato summed up Parmenidean philosophy in the position "all is one" are apparently related to his intention to schematically expose his two most important predecessors, Heraclitus and Parmenides, as rivals in an antithesis that could be mediated only through his own philosophy, and in particular through the "hypothesis of Forms." If, however, the preceding observations have some import, if unity is already present in the concept of πᾶν, if each πᾶν is πᾶν only to the extent that it is also a ἕν, then the phrase ἓν τὸ πᾶν proves to be scarcely more than a tautology. If, on the other hand, unity makes sense only as unity of a multiplicity, then rejecting multiplicity annuls the conceptual content of unity as well. In other words: If the phrase ἓν τὸ πᾶν intends to be something more than a tautology, it becomes meaningless. Its adaptation to the view that "all things are one thing" is simply absurd.

It is precisely these deadlocks or, if you want, this exceptional dialectical force of the word πᾶν, that have led to the long and interesting discussion on the character of Parmenidean monism carried out in the last decades. The initiation of this undertaking is considered to be a text by Barnes on the "Eleatic One," which denied that Parmenides favored a "real monism" in the sense that "exactly one thing exists" (p. 2). As in many other areas of research on Parmenides, the important stimulus here emanated from Mourelatos, who made clear that the philosophical position conveyed in the poem does not imply this kind of monism (*Route*, pp. 130–133). On the work of Mourelatos was also based Curd's interpretation of Parmenides' doctrine as a case not of "numerical," but of "predicational monism": "each thing that is can be only one thing; it can hold only the one predicate that indicates what it is, and must hold it in a particularly strong way."[5] Curd thus frees Parmenides from

[5] Curd (*Legacy*, p. 66). For some interesting reservations raised by Mourelatos against this parallel interpretation, see his "Parmenides and the Pluralists."

the obtuse monism usually ascribed to him and rehabilitates pluralism as compatible with his theoretical enterprise: "it is possible for there to be a numerical plurality of entities each of which is predicationally one."[6] In a recent, very interesting essay, Rapp explores a further possibility of "predicational monism" that goes beyond what he calls Curd's "essentialism": "it is the word 'to be' itself and only this word that [. . .] can exclusively be predicated of everything that is" ("Eleatischer Monismus," pp. 303, 292). According to this version, reality consists of a plurality of entities, and the only task and topic of ontology is to confirm the Being of each one of them. This predicational-ontological monism, which certainly accommodates the typical Paremenidean monolectics, is not only compatible with ontic pluralism, but also presupposes it.

Are there hints of such a position in the text of Parmenides? My answer is affirmative, and in this point the possibility explored by Rapp meets with my own hermeneutic approach presented some years ago. That interpretation was initiated (though not determined) by a new reading of the notoriously difficult last verses of the proem. The better attested reading πάντα περ ὄντα in 1.32 remains there unsatisfactory and inadequate, so long as it yields the meaning: "what appears is everything." Evidently, such a complete and utter dominance of appearances would never have been proclaimed "acceptable" (δοκίμως) by the goddess.[7] I therefore propose to understand the participle ὄντα here not as a copula, but in an "absolutive" syntactic construction and to attribute to it the entire ontological weight of the verb "to be" as it is encountered in other

[6] Curd (*Legacy*, p. 5). —Cordero's notion of a "linguistic" monism (*By Being*, p. 176) also points in a similar direction, although he seems to disregard that the "oneness detectable in Parmenides" is not "only [. . .] linguistic," but also noetic.

[7] This was, however, the reading of Owen ("Eleatic," p. 88), Guthrie (*HGP*, p. 9), Curd (*Legacy*, p. 113), and many other adherents of περ ὄντα, who therefore see in the last two lines of the proemium not a transition to ontological truth but rather a description of erroneous *doxa*.

parts of Parmenides' poem: "all that appears *is*."[8] The word δοκοῦντα thus denotes here the totality of "appearing things" of our world. In respect to this manifold, and in the sense of the predicational-ontological monism depicted above, the only predicate appropriate within ontology is that these appearances "are beings," or simply that they "are." Ontological monism makes sense only on the basis of ontic pluralism, that is, on the basis of the reality of a manifold of beings. Parmenides is interested in ontology, not in henology.

## II. Ontological Dualisms

The truth of Parmenides, his ontological affirmation of the Being of entities, advances through a series of binary structures. I would like to stress the verb "advances" because, despite the persistence of interpretations describing Parmenides' philosophy as one of immobility and rigidity, Aletheia takes place as an inquiry (δίζησις) and is explicitly acquired along a road or path, remaining thus permanently "on the route." Strictly speaking, there are two different routes presented by the goddess "for thinking":

---

[8] More on this point in Thanassas, *Fahrt* (pp. 36–41) and *Cosmos* (pp. 23–26). Under this interpretation, the complete translation of the verses 1.31–32 would read:

> "But nevertheless these you shall learn as well, how appearing things should be accepted: all of them altogether as beings."

The crucial point in the grammar here is that the participle ὄντα holds no predicate; πάντα is not a predicate, but simply replaces δοκοῦντα. It is only Mourelatos and Owens that seem to have read the expression in this way. Mourelatos, whose contribution to establishing the version περ ὄντα was decisive, translates: "just being all of them altogether" (*Route,* p. 216), or "if only all of them were in every way" ("Pluralists," p. 125); Owens's gloss is: "all indeed beings," "all indeed existent" ("Eleatic," p. 385). In the same article on "The Physical World of Parmenides," a masterpiece of Parmenides studies that remains neglected, Owens stresses that for Parmenides "all sensible things have being, far more being than the ordinary mentality is willing to concede to any one of them. [. . .] any denial of the reality of the physical world would do away with the reality of being, and its reduction to an illusionary status would make being likewise an illusion. The one stable being and the multiple and changing perceptible world are the same thing, as known respectively through reasoning and through sensation" (p. 395).

> The one [route thinks][9] that Is and that it is impossible not-to-be (2.3).
> The other [route thinks] that Is-not and that it is necessary not-to-be (2.5).

In other parts of the poem, the two routes are presented in the monolectic form ἔστιν ἢ οὐκ ἔστιν; here, however, they appear accompanied by the modal complements "impossible not-to-be" and "necessary not-to-be." The role and the force of these complements have been amply discussed in the last decades. Owen's attempt to establish at this point a third, middle way, according to which "the subject *can* but need not exist,"[10] has undergone extensive and definitive refutations. The last of them is contained in a paper by O'Brien, which offers an excellent analysis of the contradictory character of the two routes and of the role of the modals in defining them.[11] For the sake of the discussion, however, I would like to mention another recent reconstruction, which in my eyes appears to be hopelessly wrong. It can be found in a dissertation by Meijer, who splits up (and eventually shuts down) the first route, by separating ἔστι from the modal οὐκ ἔστι μὴ εἶναι. In 2.3, he attempts to make a clear distinction between a way A, along which "Being is," and a way B, along which "not-being is not" (Meijer, p. 125). He thus overlooks the fact that A *must* imply B and vice versa. He even goes so far as to call these two ways "contradictory" (p. 127)! In view of this zenith of confusion, I would propose the following formalization of the ontological crossroads presented in fr. 2:

> 2.3: A and necessarily ¬(¬A)
> 2.5: ¬A and necessarily ¬A

[9] For the advantages of supplementing "thinks" rather than the usual "says," see Cordero (*By Being*, p. 42).

[10] Owen ("Eleatic," p. 91); cf. also: "the question 'Does it exist?' has to be answered sometimes yes and sometimes no," (p. 91n1).

[11] O'Brien ("Parmenides," pp. 31–32); see also the argumentation already presented by Thanassas (*Fahrt*, pp. 72–80). O'Brien alike denies that Parmenides' argument is "to be found in a syllogism" and stresses rightly that 2.6–8 does not entail a conclusion, but functions rather "as a way of ensuring that we make the right choice" between the two routes previously illustrated.

The two routes stand thus in a contradictory relation and they form a complete disjunction. By her assurance that there are "only" two routes, the goddess wishes to deny any possible "middle way." The alternative between 2.3 and 2.5 is an exhaustive one. The second of these routes is categorically rejected as παναπευθέα, a road "without any tidings,"[12] and its inadequacy is due to two reasons: Non-Being cannot be known, and it cannot be expressed. Should we thus forget this second route immediately after its rejection? Why does the goddess present this route, and why, even after its categorical rejection, does she constantly remind us of it[13] and of the Non-Being "discovered" along this way?[14] It was the poem of Parmenides that for the first time made Non-Being a subject of philosophical analysis. Was the goddess somehow hoisting with her own petard, when she introduced the "temptation" of Non-Being and prepared the grounds for Gorgias' treatise "On Non-Being"?

Every understanding and every knowledge is understanding and knowledge of something *as* something; this As effects the determination of the object of understanding, involving simultaneously—explicit or not—a distinction from other possibilities of determination and ultimately their rejection. As something to be thought of, Parmenidean Being is firstly distinguished from sensual δοκεῖν, but this distinction delineates the noetic field in general, and not specifically Being. In order to comprehend entities in their Being, this Being has to be opposed to the only

---

12 Following a translation proposed by Mourelatos (*Route,* pp. 23–24).

13 See 6.2, 8.11, 8.16, 9.4.

14 The route of οὐκ ἔστι is not utterly nugatory, and it should not be identified with the Non-Being (or "Nothing," μηδέν) that dominates on this way. Concerning Non-Being/Nothing, Parmenides maintains that "Nothing is not" (6.2), whereas the route itself is simply "without any tidings" (2.6). Mansfeld's complaints ("1.7 expresses something that stands in clear contradiction to 1.2: *one* of the two roots can *not* be thought of," *Offenbarung,* p. 57) are thus unfounded. In 2.7 Parmenides characterizes as unknowable not the route itself, but μὴ ἐόν. And in 2.6 he does not claim that the route cannot be thought of, but only that it does not convey any knowledge, and that it is hence improper to truth. In stressing this, I do not overlook the fact that in 8.17 it is the route that is characterized as ἀνόητος. I propose that this inconceivability should be ascribed to Non-Being and not to the very route itself. This problem does not emerge if we understand this ἀνόητον in the active sense of "not thinking" (as Hölscher proposed, *Parmenides,* p. 21).

contrasting possibility: that of Non-Being. Only the explicit denial of Non-Being provides Being with its determination. The κρίσις in favor of Being (8.15) presupposes its διάκρισις from Non-Being. It is not accidental, therefore, that the route of Being is stated in the form "Is and it is impossible not-to-be." This route entails the possibility of Non-Being as an essential component and consists effectively in its negation. The truth lies in the persistent reflection upon this Non-Being and in its resolute negation. Being is conceivable only as "not Non-Being," its determination needs Non-Being as its other and opposite. As for the second route, this is equally important for the crossroads: We are constantly asked to think of it, in order to avoid the permanently lurking danger of falling into Nothing. Being and Nothing belong together, and they are both present on both routes. The difference lies in the role they play on each route: the first route is presided over by Being, while in the second Non-Being is the master and Being remains inferior and renounced. This second route is not presented only to be dismissed and forgotten. On the contrary, we ought constantly to hold its possibility in mind—though as a route "without any tidings," for in its "heart" resides Non-Being, the unknowable and inexpressible.

We could thus describe the ontological crossroads as a double pair, as a double manifestation of the basic antithesis between Being and Non-Being, or as a duality of dualities. The first route consists in a relation between Being and Non-Being in which the first is affirmed and the second denied, whereas the second route presents an affirmation of Non-Being and of its necessity, that is, a denial of Being. Each route is a relation between Being and Non-Being as contradictories, and the crossroads itself is the relation between both routes. It is not true, consequently, that Parmenides "stopped at mere Being," as Hegel has claimed.[15] In the poem we might even detect a kind of *bound dialectic* between Being and Non-Being. The other of Being is included in its determination, although this inclusion is not the departure of a conceptual movement and progress (as for example in Hegel's *Science of Logic*). The relation between Being and Non-Being in Parmenides remains an invention of Thinking, within which

[15] See his criticism of the "Eleatics" in the *Encyclopaedia* (§ 86, Addition).

Non-Being ultimately remains a phantom: it never appears, for it *cannot* appear. The goddess invokes only its possibility, and precisely to steer our attention to what remains the only object of Thinking: Being.

Apart from the dualism of the routes and of the two ontological categories present on both, the section on Aletheia contains one more dual structure, which does not have the form of an antagonistic opposition, but rather that of an identity: the relation between Being and Thinking. It is the allergy against another misleading and confusing label, "idealism," that has caused numerous unnecessary discussions based on the typical, widespread assumption that "Parmenides cannot have been an idealist." Facing this unreflective assertion, it is necessary to pose two questions right at the outset:

a. *Why* can't Parmenides have been an idealist?
b. *What* is idealism?

This might prove a successful strategy for transforming an unfruitful discourse about a label into a philosophical discussion. Then we might open up for the insight that the intended paradox in fr. 4, where the goddess calls us to "see through the νόος how absent beings are firmly present to it," is clear evidence that νοεῖν and νόος are conceived by Parmenides not as instances of sense perception, but in direct opposition to it.[16] Νοεῖν means not "to know" but "to think," and this is why the second route can be an essential object of νοεῖν (2.5) but not a source of any knowledge whatsoever (2.7). And we might even realize that the traditional reading of the notorious fr. 3 remains the most compelling one:

Thinking and Being are the same.

[16] This was in fact the position of the immensely misunderstood essay of v. Fritz, who explicitly recognized in the poem of Parmenides "the most important turning-point [. . .] in the development of the concept of *nous*" in early Greek philosophy (p. 43).

In a balanced, exhaustive and, in my eyes, philologically definitive analysis, J. Wiesner has shown that although a "complete and total rejection of Zeller's explanation [. . .] cannot be justified" solely on the basis of grammar, the traditional view is nonetheless preferable to the perplexities and the ambiguities that arise from Zeller's constructions.[17] The suggestion of the philologist Wiesner that we understand the identity of fr. 3 as an "equivalence of concepts related to one another" coincides here with Heidegger's understanding of the "sameness" as a "belonging together" of Being and Thinking.[18]

As we saw, Being emerges only within the activity of Thinking; and this, having rejected the possibility of thinking and expressing Non-Being (2.7–8), turns ultimately towards Being und relies on it: "for without Being [. . .] you will not find Thinking" (8.35–36). Being is founded upon Thinking, because otherwise it cannot be grasped; and Thinking is founded upon Being (it is ἕνεκεν τοῦ εἶναι, 8.34), for otherwise it could not free itself from the senses and establish its own subject and legitimacy. This "identity" between Being and Thinking is not the outcome of some syllogistic procedure, but becomes manifest from the very beginning of the ontological survey: each of them emerges exclusively *via* the other. To be sure, τὸ αὐτό does not denote a mathematical identity, in which either term can be replaced with the other—for this would deprive them both of their distinctive character. The kind of link between Being and Thinking is specified in fr. 3 by the double force of τε καί, which suggests an interaction, a *mutual connection and reciprocal reference*, the necessity of a *reciprocal mediation*.

17 See Wiesner (*Parmenides*, pp. 139–149). Giancola's recent paper ("Parmenides' B3," 2001) presents persuasive arguments against Zeller's reading, but results unfortunately in a "religious-mystical" interpretation. —It has not been observed that Zeller's reading replaces the traditional identity with a one-sided dependence between Being and Thinking that leads to ambiguities: "Only that can be thought which can be" (³1869, p. 470), or "only that can be which can be thought" (²1856, p. 398). When assigned to the goddess herself, this very ambiguity should be reason enough for rejecting Zeller's reading.

18 See *Was heisst. . .* (p. 147) and *Identität* (p. 18).

## III. Cosmological Dualism

The dualistic structure of Light and Night in the Doxa has often been remarked upon and underlined. The mere assertion, however, that "the Doxa is dualistic" does not further our understanding of this longer part of Parmenides' poem. First of all, we should recognize that "the" Doxa exists as a simple unity only in a merely quantitative sense, denoting the section of the poem that begins at 8.50. However, as I have tried to show elsewhere, this part "is not a homogeneous unity, but rather a complex in which *several and distinct interests, intents and purposes* are pursued."[19] Their common denominator is their subject-matter: phenomenality as such, or the manifold of the world of appearance, which they approach from different perspectives. None of theses perspectives is "false"; they are altogether true, for they fulfill in different ways the task of "learning" and "understanding" proclaimed by the goddess (1.28, 8.51).

The duality of Light and Night structures the Doxa throughout. The two basic interests of the goddess here are first the disclosure of the "deceitful" mortal opinions, and then the presentation of her own, valid cosmological system. The first of these issues is announced by the adjective ἀπατηλός, the second by the participle ἐοικώς, which does not yet mean "probable," but "appearing" and "appropriate, fitting." The goddess thus contrasts her own cosmological system, which describes the appearances in an "appropriate" way, with the misleading cosmological system rooted in mortal opinions. Both systems are based on the same duality, that of Light and Night. But while the human conjectures rely on a complete and irrevocable separation and a strict isolation of these forms, the appropriate cosmology proclaims their synthesis. According to the mortals, Light and Night exclude one another; they remain in a

---

[19] See Thanassas (*Fahrt,* pp. 157–205; *Cosmos,* pp. 61–84). Meanwhile, a similar differentiation has been proposed during the Buenos Aires Symposium by N.-L. Cordero and M. Pulpito, and previously also by Graham ("Responses," pp. 168–169) and Lesher ("Knowledge," p. 240). Needless to say: the distinction I have been proposing in the last twelve years is not one between "good" and "bad" *doxa,* but rather between two different, but equally "good" claims raised within Doxa; in Kantian terms, these claims could be labeled as "critique" and "doctrine."

permanent, irreversible opposition, which Curd has aptly called "enantiomorphism" (pp. 104–110). Curd also rightly stresses that "it is not plurality itself but opposition that is at the root of the problem," and concludes: "If only Light and Night were genuine entities rather than interdefined opposites, Parmenides' cosmology would give an account of the world as experienced [. . .] that would pass tests based on the fundamental κρίσις, 'is or is not'" (pp. 110, 116). But this, I believe, is exactly what happens subsequently in the Doxa! According to the mortals, the forms remain "apart from one another" (χωρὶς ἀπ' ἀλλήλων), "contrariwise" (ἀντία) and "opposite" (τἀντία) to each other; or, as stated in a notoriously misleading phrase of 8.54a, no unity between the two forms is deemed necessary. The exclamation following ("here they have gone astray," 8.54b) expresses the core of the goddess's criticism: what is needed is unity of the two forms! Her own system, presented from 8.60 onwards, is the system of the mixture of both forms, which now appear as inextricably intertwined complementary entities that build up "together" (ὁμοῦ) the worldly arrangement (διάκοσμος).

The Doxa entails thus not one but two different dualisms: the deceitful dualism of segregation and the appropriate one of mixture. But why is mixture appropriate? In short, because it is compatible with the truth of Being. Light and Night are here "both equal, since Nothing partakes in neither" (9.4). This equality could not be maintained in the system of segregation, which seems to have some severe, fatal ontological implications. Led astray by their senses, the mortals believe that only what presents itself in Light is existent and knowable, while the dark and invisible, eluding sight and knowledge, is ultimately treated by them as not-being. Of course, humans do not reflect on Being and Non-Being as such. They only follow a tacit, hidden ontology, wherein Being and Non-Being are *illegitimately* represented by Light and Night. Humans thus lapse into a sensualist fallacy; they carry out a separation "according to the appearance" (8.55), in which they rend the world apart and create *caesurae.* But cosmological dualism is acceptable only to the extent that it accounts for ontic pluralism in a way compatible with the ontological monism of Being.

One of the confusions that arise in the context of the discussions on "the" *doxa* pertains to its relation to the so called "third way" portrayed in the part of Aletheia (6.4–9, 7.3–5 and 8.38–41). Reinhardt's discovery of this "third way" has been essential to the understanding of the structure and the argument of the poem, but its identification with "the" *doxa* has proven to be an obstacle for a productive discussion.[20] The third way cannot be identical with "the" *doxa*, because "the" *doxa* does not exist. The third way is in fact only related to a specific attitude presented within the section of Doxa. The keyword for establishing this connection is "mortals."[21] The third way is the ontological evaluation and condemnation only of the deceptive *doxa*, which in the Aletheia section is shown to be an impassable, ontologically impossible way. The notion of a third way does not for its part contradict the assertion in fr. 2 that there are "only two routes for thinking." The ontological crossroads presented there was certainly not a real alternative, but the insight into an insoluble contradiction and the enforcement and steady affirmation of the only real possibility: the truth of Being. The third way is also no real way, no real route, no real path at all. But it is nonetheless different from the second "route of inquiry" in one crucial respect; the third way does not affirm Non-Being, but rather remains ontologically blind, noetically handicapped, without any insight into the crossroads. Mortals who are "two-headed" (6.5) obviously have no head at all—at least not a head capable of distinguishing the two ontological routes, of performing the essential κρίσις (8.15) and remaining "firmly" (4.1) on the true one. The "third way" is not a way, but an impasse; it is the rejection or the negligence of the ontological dualism.[22]

---

[20] See Reinhardt's *Parmenides* (p. 69; translation in Mourelatos's *Pre-Socratics*, p. 303): "*doxa* [. . .] is nothing but the third way of inquiry."

[21] See 1.30, 6.5, 8.39, 8.51, 8.61.

[22] O'Brien denies the existence of a distinct third way, by pointing out that this alleged third way is rejected in 7.1–2 for the same reasons that lead to the rejection of the second route, that of Non-Being (O'Brien, pp. 46–47, 74, 95, and passim). But the route rejected in 7.1–2 *is* the second route! The third way is introduced only in 7.3 by the word μηδέ, which means "nor" and brings up a new subject of discussion. —Although I very much sympathize with the proposals concerning the lacuna in 6.3 to drop the traditional εἴργω in favor of a verb of

## IV. A Conclusion

As we have seen, dual structures are present throughout the poem. The ontological dualism presents Being and Non-Being as two opposed ontological categories that exclude each other; it presents a crossroads of two concurring routes that leave no place for other ontological possibilities, but jointly force the affirmation of the first of them. This mutual exclusion, a mark and an indicator of ontological truth, becomes in the Doxa the primary source of error as soon as it is applied to the cosmological categories of Light and Night. Cosmic segregation cannot compensate the failure to perform the ontological κρίσις; indeed, such segregation in fact prevents that κρίσις, for it implicitly confuses ontology with cosmology, Night with Non-Being. The ontological condemnation of this doxastic confusion can be presented as the "third way" of human aberration. The cosmological correction of that schism is subsequently supplied by the system of the goddess, who shows that while ontological intermingling was fatal, mixture is essential for a cosmology compatible with ontological truth.

Ontological monism in the Aletheia is possible only on the ground of the dual structure and the antithesis between Being and Non-Being. But it also presupposes the ontic pluralism of the δοκοῦντα, of the multiplicity of appearances. The notion of numerical monism is completely incongruent with the letter and the spirit of the poem. To the question "how many things exist," Parmenides has a clear, natural answer: many, very many![23] Parmenides was a numeric pluralist, as is shown not only by the plurality of appearances (δοκοῦντα) in 1.32, but also by the plurality of "absent beings" made present to νόος (4.1), or by the

positive meaning like ἄρξει (Cordero, "Chemins," pp. 21–24), ἄρξω (Nehamas, pp. 102–106) or something similar, I do not agree that this modification implies abolishing the notion of a "third way" established by Reinhardt. Indeed, I believe that the question of the missing verb is completely independent of the question of the number of routes.

[23] Barnes, on the contrary, remained ultimately aporetic: "it is not the case that Parmenides was a monist. I do not assert that he was a pluralist [. . .] As far as we know, the question of how many items the universe contains did not concern him" ("Eleatic One," pp. 20–21). But even if this was not a question explicitly raised by Parmenides, his philosophy nonetheless presupposes a certain perspective or position regarding this matter; and the same should be the case for his interpreters.

plurality of entities qua beings that "hold together" (4.2)[24] and "keep close" to each other (8.25). All these entities are indeed equally "full of Being" (8.24) in a way that does not permit one of them to participate in Being any more than another (8.47–48). Ontic pluralism is thus the ground of an ontological survey which operates with a dual scheme in order to lead to the monism of Being. This monism takes place on the basis of a further dual structure, that of Being and Thinking, which for its part does not represent an opposition but an identity. The truth of Being thus requires plurality (of entities or appearances), an oppositional duality (of Being and Non-Being), identicative duality (of Being and Thinking) and compatibility with cosmological duality (Light and Night equally participating in Being).

There remains, however, a further, deeper duality, which we have not yet touched upon: the very duality of the two parts of the poem, or the duality of ontology and cosmology. This duality has often been treated as a defect, if not as a scandal. But questioning the legitimacy of this duality is as forceful as questioning the legitimacy of Aristotle's double attempt to establish not only ontology, but also physics (in the broad sense, including zoology, astronomy, etc.). Seen from this perspective, the question of why Parmenides "added" Doxa to the Aletheia becomes obsolete. The two parts of the poem are both true, offering different responses to different questions. The first part inquires into the Being of appearances, the second into the mode in which they appear. The two inquiries are autonomous and complementary, and they cannot be reduced to one another. The only issue arising here is that of their compatibility, which is clearly assured in 9.4: Neither of the two forms operative in the "appropriate" cosmology is contaminated with Non-Being; their interplay and mixture do not endanger ontological truth.

[24] See also Owens ("World," pp. 387–388): "The fragment [4] envisages a multiplicity of things, each of which may be called 'a being.'" Similarly Asclepius, many centuries ago: οἴεται ὁ Παρμενίδης πλῆθος ἐν τοῖς οὖσι (*In Met.*, p. 202).

This is the only "mediation" between the two parts necessary for the consistency of the whole. As for the transition from human, traditional cosmology to ontology, this transition is effected in the poem by means of an anonymous goddess, i.e., by means of the Divine. This, however, is not an answer to the question "how philosophy arises," but only the articulation of that question, which will remain unanswered in the history of philosophy to follow. Philosophy still remains ungrounded.[25]

[25] This text was prepared in the Summer Semester 2007 at the Philosophical Seminar of the University of Heidelberg, during a sabbatical leave with a scholarship funded by the Alexander von Humboldt Foundation. I would like to thank the Seminar and its director at that time Prof. Jens Halfwassen for the excellent working conditions, the Humboldt Foundation for the generous support, and Kenneth Knies for help in smoothing out the prose for this final version.

## Bibliography


Allen, Reginald E. and Furley, David J., eds. *Studies in Presocratic Philosophy, Vol. II: The Eleatics and the Pluralists.* London: Routledge, 1975.

Austin, Scott. *Parmenides: Being, Bounds, and Logic.* New Haven: Yale University Press, 1986.

Barnes, Jonathan. "Parmenides and the Eleatic One." *Archiv für Geschichte der Philosophie* 61 (1979): 1–21.

Bodnár, Istvan M. "Reason and Revelation in Parmenides." *Doxa* 17 (1989): 61–67.

Buchheim, Thomas. *Die Vorsokratiker. Ein philosophisches Porträt.* München: Beck 1994.

Burnet, John. *Early Greek Philosophy.* London: Adam & Charles Black, 1892; 4th Edition, 1930.

Cordero, Néstor-Luis. *By Being, It Is. The Thesis of Parmenides.* Las Vegas: Parmenides Publishing, 2004.

_____. "Les deux chemins de Parménide dans les fragments 6 et 7." *Phronesis* 24 (1979): 1–32.

Curd, Patricia. *The Legacy of Parmenides. Eleatic Monism and Later Presocratic Thought.* Princeton: Princeton University Press, 1998. Reprinted with new introduction, Las Vegas: Parmenides Publishing, 2004.

Finkelberg, Aryeh. "Being, Truth and Opinion in Parmenides." *Archiv für Geschichte der Philosophie* 81 (1999): 233–248.

Fritz, Kurt v. "*Nous, Noein*, and their Derivatives in Pre-Socratic Philosophy." *Classical Philology* 40 (1945): 223–242; 41 (1946): 12–34. Reprinted in A. P. D. Mourelatos, ed., *The Pre-Socratics. A Collection of Critical Essays.* New York: Anchor Books, 1974. 2nd Edition printed by Princeton: Princeton University Press, 1993: 23–95.

Gadamer, Hans-Georg. *Truth and Method.* Translation revised by Joel Weinsheimer and Donald G. Marshall. English Edition: London, New York: Continuum, 1975; 2nd Edition, 1989.

Giancola, Donna M. "Toward a Radical Reinterpretation of Parmenides' B3." *Journal of Philosophical Research* 26 (2001): 635–653.

Graham, Daniel W. "Empedocles and Anaxagoras: Responses to Parmenides." In Anthony A. Long, ed., *The Cambridge Companion to Early Greek Philosophy.* Cambridge: Cambridge University Press, 1999: 159–180.

Guthrie, William K. C. *A History of Greek Philosophy*, Vol. II. Cambridge: Cambridge University Press, 1965.

Heidegger, Martin. *Identität und Differenz*. Pfullingen: Neske, 1957.

_____. *Was heisst Denken?* Tübingen: Niemeyer, 1954.

Hölscher, Uvo. *Parmenides. Vom Wesen des Seienden*. Frankfurt am Main: Suhrkamp, 1969; 2nd Edition, 1986.

Kahn, Charles H. "The Thesis of Parmenides." *The Review of Metaphysics* 22 (1969): 700–724.

Lesher, James H. "Early Interest in Knowledge." In Anthony A. Long, ed., *The Cambridge Companion to Early Greek Philosophy*. Cambridge: Cambridge University Press, 1999: 225–249.

Mansfeld, Jaap. *Die Offenbarung des Parmenides und die menschliche Welt*. Assen: Van Gorcum, 1964.

Meijer, Pieter A. *Parmenides Beyond the Gates. The Divine Revelation on Being, Thinking and the Doxa*. Amsterdam: Gieben, 1997.

Mourelatos, Alexander P. D. "Parmenides and the Pluralists." *Apeiron: A Journal for Ancient Philosophy and Science* 32 (1999): 117–129.

_____. "Some Alternatives in Interpreting Parmenides." *The Monist* 62 (1979): 3–14.

_____. *The Route of Parmenides*. Revised and Expanded Edition, Las Vegas: Parmenides Publishing, 2008.

_____, ed. The Pre-Socratics. A Collection of Critical Essays. New York: Anchor Books, 1974. Reprinted, Princeton: Princeton University Press, 2nd Edition, 1993.

Nehamas, Alexander. "On Parmenides' Three Ways of Inquiry." *Deucalion* (Athens) 33/34 (1981): 97–111.

O'Brien, Denis. "Parmenides and Plato on What Is Not." In Maria Kardaun and Joke Spruyt, eds., *The Winged Chariot: Collected Essays on Plato and Platonism in Honour of L. M. de Rijk*. Leiden: Brill, 2000: 19–104.

Owen, G. E. L. "Eleatic Questions," *Classical Quarterly* 10 (1960): 84–102.

Owens, Joseph. "The Physical World of Parmenides." In J. Reginald O'Donnell, ed., *Essays in Honour of A. C. Pegis*. Leiden: Brill, 1974: 378–395.

Rapp, Christof. "Eleatischer Monismus." In Georg Rechenauer, ed., *Frühgriechisches Denken*. Göttingen: Vandenhoeck & Ruprecht, 2005: 290–315.

Reinhardt, Karl. *Parmenides und die Geschichte der griechischen Philosophie.* Frankfurt: Klostermann, 4th Edition, 1985. Partial translation reprinted in A. P. D. Mourelatos, ed. *The Pre-Socratics. A Collection of Critical Essays.* New York: Anchor Books, 1974. Reprinted, Princeton: Princeton University Press, 2nd Edition, 1993: 293–311.

Robbiano, Chiara. *Becoming Being. On Parmenides' Transformative Philosophy.* Sankt Augustin: Academia Verlag, 2006.

Skirry, Justin. "The Numerical Monist Interpretation of Parmenides." *The Southern Journal of Philosophy* 39 (2001): 403–417.

Stokes, Michael C. *One and Many in Presocratic Philosophy.* Washington, D.C.: Center for Hellenic Studies, 1971.

Thanassas, Panagiotis. *Die erste "zweite Fahrt." Sein des Seienden und Erscheinen der Welt bei Parmenides.* München: Wilhelm Fink, 1997.

_____. *Parmenides, Cosmos, and Being. A Philosophical Interpretation.* Milwaukee: Marquette University Press, 2007.

_____. "How Many *Doxai* Are There in Parmenides?" *Rhizai* 3 (2006): 199–218.

Wiesner, Jürgen. *Parmenides. Der Beginn der Aletheia. Untersuchungen zu B2-B3-B6.* Berlin/New York: de Gruyter, 1996.

Zeller, Eduard. *Die Philosophie der Griechen in ihrer geschichtlichen Entwicklung,* Erster Teil. 2nd edition, Tübingen: Fues, 1856; 3rd edition, Leipzig: Fues, 1869; 6th edition, Leipzig: Reisland, 1919.

# Part II: Parmenides in the Tradition and Cognate Themes

# Persuasion and Deception in Gorgias' *Encomium to Helen*. About the Powers and Limits of λόγος

Esteban Bieda

**Summary**

In this paper I will show that even when Gorgias, in his *Encomium to Helen*, says that λόγος is a "powerful sovereign" (δυνάστης μέγας)—a sovereign capable of doing the most divine actions—it still depends, however, on the person who utters it. Although Gorgias insists on separating speech from reality, he does not do the same thing regarding speech and the particular man who pronounces it.

Gorgias' *Encomium to Helen [EH]* (DK B 11) constitutes a rhetorical exercise that tries to take account of all the possible causes that could have led Helen to travel along with Paris to Troy. Since the intention of Gorgias is, against certain "traditional" versions of the facts, to exempt Helen from responsibility, the text analyzes meticulously each of the reasons that may have caused the journey to the city of Priam. The third of these causes is speech (λόγος). In this article, I will try to show that even when the sophist makes a "powerful sovereign" out of λόγος, a sovereign capable of doing the most divine actions, it depends, however, on the person who utters it. Although Gorgias insists on separating speech from reality[1] he does not do the same thing regarding speech and the particular man who pronounces it.

[1] See Gorgias, *On not being* § 83–86.

# I

The third cause considered by Gorgias in the *EH* consists in an external agent that moved Helen; in this case, different from the previous ones, the agent is not physical but symbolical: persuasion through words (§§ 8–14). Persuasive λόγος is closely related to its capacity for deceiving: "if it was the λόγος that persuaded <her>, and the one that deceived her soul (τὴν ψυχὴν ἀπατήσας), then not even in this case is it hard to speak in defense and drive away the cause" (§ 8). According to Gorgias, λόγος has a great power, a capacity that, driven through persuasion, can deceive the soul, can make the soul err and be mistaken.[2] The appearance of ἀπάτη in the middle of the treatment of λόγος brings up what plenty of specialists have emphasized: Gorgias' inheritance of poetic tradition.[3] What seems more attractive about poetry, "λόγος with measure," is its capacity to deceive.[4] This deceiving, different from physical strength, is much more effective because it makes the persuaded one act on his or her own account believing that he or she is doing the right thing.[5]

The first thing to be noticed is that even when Gorgias talks about λόγος as something independent of the speaker, the fact is that behind it we find, in this particular case, Paris himself. Although λόγος is considered a "powerful sovereign" (δυνάστης

---

[2] The verb used by Gorgias is "ἀπατάω." The first transitive values refer to "deceiving" or "cheating" and the passive uses mean "to be mistaken or self-deceived"; see Liddell-Scott-Jones (LSJ) s.v. About the archaic and classical uses of the verb "ἀπατάω" and the substantive "ἀπάτη," see Mario Untersteiner, *I Sofisti* (Torino: Giulio Einaudi, 1949), pp. 125–170; and W. J. Verdenius, "Gorgias' Doctrine of Deception" in G. B. Kerferd, ed., *The Sophists and Their Legacy* (Wiesbaden: Steiner, 1981), pp. 116–128.

[3] See v.g. Untersteiner, op. cit., Verdenius, op. cit., Jacqueline De Romilly, "Gorgias et le pouvoir de la poésie," in *Journal of Hellenic Studies* 93 (1973), 155–162; and Giuseppe Mazzara, *Gorgia: La Retorica del Verosimile* (Sankt Augustin: Academia Verlag, 1999).

[4] See Gorgias DK B 23. About poetry as a deceiving device and the tradition Gorgias joins, it is possible to track different authors, chronologically prior and posteriors to Gorgias, which agree with him in this matter: see v.g. Homer, *Iliad* II, 485; Hesiod, *Theogony* 27–28; Pindar, *Olympics* I 28–33 and *Nemea* VII 23–24; Plato, *Protagoras* 338e–339a; Isocrates XII, 18. For the role of poetry in the *Encomium* see especially De Romilly, op. cit.

[5] See Plato, *Philebus* 58a.

μέγας),[6] we must note that behind it, supporting it, we find the one who makes it possible: the speaker. This is linked directly to the translation of the clause "λόγοις πεισθεῖσα": it does not mean "persuaded *by* <the agency of> words" but "persuaded *with* words." In § 7, with the analysis of violence (βία), Gorgias inaugurates a new way of expressing the causes: if so far we had *causal* datives, we now find *instrumental* datives dependent on passive aorist participles. If my assumption is correct, "βίᾳ ἁρπασθεῖσα" means "kidnapped *with* violence" and "λόγοις πεισθεῖσα" means "persuaded *with* words."

It has been discussed whether the dative can be used to express the agency (when the agent is a thing, not a person) of a passive verb or participle. Even when we do not think this is possible,[7] some Greek grammars consider it: when the agent is a person, the agency is expressed by the preposition ὑπό with the genitive; but if the agent is a thing, not a person, the dative without preposition may express it. This would let us translate the clause "λόγοις πεισθεῖσα" as "persuaded *by* <the agency of> words" and, by doing that, reject the reference to the speaker: if we translate "persuaded *by* <the agency of> words," we can say that the persuasive power belongs to λόγος itself, "powerful sovereign," independent of the speaker. Humbert[8] presents three syntactical uses for the dative and the agency is not one of them: the interest (indirect object of the verb), the instrumental and the locative (§§ 472–495). He says that when the dative seems to mean agency it is, in fact, either the *instrument* of the action or that *in the interest of which* the action is done (§ 172).

[6] Even when the substantive "δυνάστης" is usually translated "master" or "ruler," the root δυν- (present also in the verb δύναμαι and the substantive δύναμις) refers to the semantics of "power." If we translate "δυνάστης" as "*souverain*" [Barbara Cassin, *L'effet Sophistique* (Paris: Gallimard, 1995)], "master" (Verdenius, op. cit.), "signore" (Mazzara, op. cit.) or "soberano" [Antoni P. Angordans, *Sofistas: Testimonios y Fragmentos* with Introduction, Spanish Translation, and Notes (Barcelona: Bruguera, 1985)], we must not overlook that we are dealing with a master who specifically has "power."

[7] In what sense can a "thing" be *stricto sensu* an "agent" if it is not personified (which means that it is not a thing anymore) or used by someone (which means that it is in fact the instrument of that someone)?

[8] Jean Humbert, *Syntaxe Grecque* (Paris: Klincksieck, 1972).

Smyth[9] says something similar: even when the dative seems to mean agency in some particular cases, this may occur when the verb's tense is perfect or pluperfect (our participles in the *EH* are aorist); nevertheless, he concludes that the main use of the dative is interest, not agency.[10] This is why, in my opinion, if we have either a "thing-agent" or an instrument, in both cases it is necessary to recover the one that moves the "agent-thing" or uses the instrument.

On the other hand, if we translate "λόγοις πεισθεῖσα" as "persuaded *by <the agency of>* words," we should do the same, given the special care taken by Gorgias in the κόσμος of the *Encomium,* with "βίᾳ ἁρπασθεῖσα," formally equivalent. We should read, then, "kidnapped *by <the agency of>* violence." Someone could say that this is plausible since we are dealing with a personified Βία. But if this is so, if Gorgias is talking about a personified Βία, why did he not put it together with the other personified forces of nature? Why did he not place it alongside Necessity (Ἀνάγκη), Fortune (Τύχη), and the gods as a part of the first cause in § 6? He did not do that because βία is not, as well as λόγος, independent of the person who may use them as instruments.

Besides the formal reasons I just gave, someone could object that we are making no more than an instrument out of Gorgian λόγος; and this may be a plausible objection since λόγος is presented by the sophist as something capable of completing the most divine works (θειότατα ἔργα ἀποτελεῖ, § 8). Besides that, Gorgias introduces λόγος in § 8 using active participles (πείσας and ἀπατήσας) which may imply that it is in fact an agent. I think that while active, λόγος is also an instrument. The paragraphs dedicated to it in the *EH* (§§ 8–14) must be understood in two different but complementary senses: in one sense (i) Gorgias presents the *formal* and *general* capacities and characteristics of λόγος: its capacity to complete divine works, of deceiving, of bewitching. But, in another sense (ii) λόγος is

[9] Herbert W. Smyth, *A Greek Grammar for Colleges* (New York: American Book Company, 1920).

[10] "The notion of agency does not belong to the dative, but it is a natural inference that the person interested is the agent," (§ 1488); see also §§ 1755–1758.

not something so autonomous as to materialize the capacities it has; this means it cannot, by itself, direct its powers and capacities to a certain aim. It needs the speaker to provide the precise *intentions* that λόγος does not have *per se*. After (i) describing the general powers of λόγος, Gorgias (ii) refers those powers to the specific case of Helen where *someone* (Paris) used it to convince *another someone* (Helen) to do *something specific* (travel to Troy). The "powerful sovereign" does not have the concrete intentions which can aim its capacities toward a specific end. These intentions can be supplied only by the speaker. This is why, in a certain manner, speech is the *agent* of the action since it makes another person act in a certain way; but at the same, time it is the *instrument* of the person who uses it to persuade in that specific way and not in another.

## II

We have already touched upon Gorgias' inheritance of poetic tradition. The innovation introduced by the sophist in this respect is mentioned by De Romilly: *"En effet, ces pouvoirs du poète, ou plutôt de la poésie, ne sont jamais, dans tout ces textes* <sc. previous to Gorgias>, *présentés comme une fin en soi, et moins encore comme un moyen."*[11] Gorgias finds in this natural capacity of poetry a weapon that, when used skillfully, ends up being something poetry never was: a τέχνη that would eventually be called "rhetoric."[12] Unlike the inspired rhapsodist or the chant of the Muses, he who dominates Gorgian λόγος does not need divine participation and can make discretional use of its powers. The speaker is, once more, fundamental if the power of deceiving λόγος is to be materialized in a certain manner: the Muses that speak lies disguised as truths (*Theogony* 27–28) are no longer relevant for a particular man with particular intentions.

Poetry, then, makes the soul suffer (πάσχειν) a certain passion (πάθος) because of the fortune of the characters involved in the poem. The power of the charm (ἡ δύναμις τῆς ἐπῳδῆς)

[11] De Romilly, op. cit., p. 158.

[12] *"La place semble donc prête pour Gorgias, pour un homme qui va dire que, ce que la poésie peut faire, la parole rhétorique peut le faire également"* (De Romilly, op. cit., p. 160).

consists in seducing, persuading and, in short, transforming (μεθίστημι) the soul by means of a spell that makes something different out of it, something different from what it was before hearing the charm. All this converges into the following conclusion: "therefore, what cause impedes, certainly, that chants entered in Helen—even when she was not young—as if she was kidnapped with violence?" (§ 12).[13] The power of λόγος is compared with the power of the βία presented in § 7. By putting λόγος and βία on the same level—βία that, as discussed above, supposes an agent capable of practicing it—Gorgias implies again that behind speech must be a man whose intentions "activate" its powers in a certain manner. Because of this, the conclusion that follows must be analyzed carefully: "so, the λόγος that persuaded the soul forced (ἠνάγκασε) it to obey what was said and to agree with what was done. Therefore, he who persuaded, since he forced, commits injustice, but she who was persuaded, since she was forced by means of speech, is defamed in vain" (§ 12).[14] Even when Gorgias says that it was λόγος which persuaded Helen, he immediately adds that the one who persuaded, Paris, is the one who commits injustice against the one forced and persuaded, Helen, who suffers it. Someone might say that since the passive participle "πείσας" is masculine, it may be ascribed to "λόγος." But what sense would it make to say that λόγος committed, by itself, injustice towards Helen? Things do not have morality because they do not have intentions or wishes; only a man, the speaker, can be judged. A scalpel is not evil or virtuous whether it is used to kill or to perform an operation.

If, as Gorgias says, λόγος is a φάρμακον for the soul, we need someone capable of prescribing such a drug, someone aware of the effects it may cause in the person who takes it. Acting under the influence of such a drug, the action of Menelaus' wife could not have been a result of her own free will, will trapped

---

13 The Greek text I follow for this first part of § 12 corresponds to Untersteiner's edition (for the justification of each variant see his notes): τίς οὖν αἰτία κωλύει καὶ τὴν Ἑλένην ὕμνο<υ>ς <εἰσ>ελθεῖν ὁμοίως ἂν οὐ νέαν οὖσαν ὥσπερ εἰ [βιατήριον] βίᾳ ἡρπάσθη;

14 For "κακῶς ἀκούειν" see LSJ s.v. ἀκούω and its use with a modal adverb.

by the muzzle of Alexander's words. The persuaded one had the misfortune of being persuaded; she can not be judged for falling into the claws of speech for the same reason that a person under the influence of a sleeping pill can not be judged for falling asleep. Helen's misfortune was that she listened to Paris, being in the worst place at the worst time: the "powerful sovereign" is infallible once it is heard. The misfortune does not consist, then, in the fact that the φάρμακον worked: once you take the sleeping pill, the effects are necessary. Rather, the problem here is that Helen did not know that in her glass, mixed with the wine, there was a drug, a terrible and powerful drug, a drug that would lead her to her ruin, a drug called "λόγος," a drug whose father was the guest of her husband, a guest known as Alexander or Paris, son of the king of Troy.

# Thought as Perception: Aristotle's Criticism of Parmenides in *Metaphysics* IV, 5

María Elena Díaz


## Summary

This article analyzes the reasons for the inclusion of Parmenides in the list of physicists who strayed away from the conception of phenomena contemplated in Aristotle's support of the principle of non-contradiction in *Metaphysics* IV, 5, and the partial appropriation of the perceptual model of thinking present in Parmenidean developments. In this passage of *Metaphysics,* Aristotle mentions the verses that form part of fragment B16, where thought is explained in terms of a perception understood as a physical alteration. Aristotelian opposition to such conception of perception and thought is radical. In B3, however, there also appears a thinking scheme which involves capturing processes similar to perception, only that in this case, Aristotle appears to act both as critic and as heir of the Eleatic philosopher in his explanation of the capturing process of the simple objects of thought.


In two passages of *On the Soul* III, 3 and *Metaphysics* IV, 5, 1009b22–25, which are, to a certain extent, parallel, Aristotle criticizes those who, according to his views, had considered that thought consists of a physiological activity that comprehends its object analogically to the act of perception. Parmenides' verses that are part of fragment DK B16 are quoted in the last passage. This idea of intellect as a changing element dependent upon the body differs from that in DK B3, which involves a type of comprehension of being that is constantly true and that only leaves room for the absence of capturing processes. It is precisely in light of this difference that B16 was placed in the way of δόξα and B3 in the way of truth.

Interpretation of fragment 16 gives rise to two different hermeneutical problems: one in connection with the meaning of the fragment within the Parmenidean poem, and another with reference to the Aristotelian reading of said fragment. This presentation will focus on the second problem, connecting *Metaphysics* IV, 5 with Theophrastus' reading of those verses in *On Sensation* 1–3. While Aristotle certainly recognizes the Parmenidean theory of being and non-being, he places these ideas within the group of philosophers who strayed away from the consideration of sensible things. In accordance with the reading I support, Aristotelian criticism comes down to the conceptualization of thought in similar terms to perception; therefore, even assuming that B16 represents a criticism by Parmenides of the way of thinking of any mortal men, Aristotle would believe that thought, while wrong, cannot operate that way. On the other hand, I will defend that the conception of thought as infallible apprehension of being, present in B3, provoked on the part of Aristotle both a critique and a partial appropriation. However, it is not taken into account in the context of Metaphysics IV, 5 because—though it generates analogous problems for the explanation of error—rather than relying on the mobility of the object and the subject (as B16 does), it supposes, on the contrary, stability."

## The inclusion of Parmenides among the Physicists in *Metaphysics* IV, 5

Aristotle does not ignore the Parmenidean doctrine about being and not being, which in fact he mentions in *Metaphysics* XIV, 2, 1089a4 = DK B7. Its inclusion in the list of Physicists can be explained by the support of the Eleatic philosopher for a conception of the nature of thought that would lead to the impossibility of explaining error, which would give rise to a series of unacceptable consequences connected with perception and thought, apart from the problematic truth of all opinions.

Parmenides is mentioned in *Metaphysics* IV, 5 as part of a group of thinkers that also includes Empedocles, Anaxagoras, and Homer. They, as stated by Aristotle, would have also arrived through a way of thinking different from that followed by the Sophists, to the denial of the principle of non-contradiction based on the observation of change.[1]

Regarding the verses in fragment B16, Aristotle only affirms that Parmenides expresses himself in the same way as Empedocles.[2] Both fragments by Empedocles support two theses:

1. "For wisdom increases in men according to what is before them."[3]
2. "So far as their nature changed, so far to them always, came changed thoughts into mind."[4]

The Aristotelian reading of these fragments confers them a conception of thought as perception, understanding the latter as an alteration produced like an object. Based on this, it could be inferred that all phenomena are true.[5] According to Aristotle, Empedocles would have settled an equation between ἕξις (understood as physical disposition) and φρόνησις.[6]

The Parmenidean verses mentioned by Aristotle are the following:

ὡς γὰρ ἑκάστοτ᾽ ἔχει κρᾶσιν μελέων πολυκάμπτων,
τὼς νόος ἀνθρώποισι παρίσταται· τὸ γὰρ αὐτό
ἔστιν ὅπερ φρονέει μελέων φύσις ἀνθρώποισιν
καὶ πᾶσιν καὶ παντί· τὸ γὰρ πλέον ἐστὶ νόημα.

---

[1] Aristotle introduces a distinction between Physicists and Sophists. The latter have only talked for the pleasure of it and, therefore, could not be persuaded as the former, who are in a genuine *aporia*, and are to be forced instead (1009a18).

[2] Καὶ Παρμενίδης δὲ ἀποφαίνεται τὸν αὐτὸν τρόπον· (*Metaphysics* IV, 5, 1009b21–22).

[3] πρὸς παρεὸν γὰρ μῆτις ἐναύξεται ἀνθρώποισιν (1009b18–19).

[4] ὅσσον ‹ δ'› ἀλλοῖοι μετέφυν, τόσον ἄρ σφισιν αἰεὶ καὶ τὸ φρονεῖν ἀλλοῖα παρίστατο (1009b20–21).

[5] ταύτην δ' εἶναι ἀλλοίωσιν, τὸ φαινόμενον κατὰ τὴν αἴσθησιν ἐξ ἀνάγκης ἀληθὲς εἶναί φασιν· (*Metaphysics* IV, 5, 1009b13–15).

[6] καὶ Ἐμπεδοκλῆς μεταβάλλοντας τὴν ἕξιν μεταβάλλειν φησὶ τὴν φρόνησιν· (*Metaphysics* IV, 5, 1009b17–18).

The passage can be translated in many ways, as it can be noticed in the different versions described below. The problematic elements are the subject of ἔχει in line 22, the reference to τὸ αὐτό in line 23, the relationship between ὅπερ and φρονέει in line 24, the translation of μελέων in lines 22 and 24, and the choice between ἕκαστος and εκάστοτ' in line 22.[7]

Based on Cassin and Narcy, the choice that better describes the aim of the Aristotelian quotation is to consider ὅπερ as nominative, to keep the reading of ἑκάστοτ' of Ross's edition and thus to conclude that the subject of ἔχει in line 22 is νόος:

"For like on each occasion the mixture of motion members is kept, in this way, intellect is present. For it is the same what it thinks in each and every one of men: the nature of the members; for what predominates is what it thinks."

In this way, there is evidence of the idea emphasized by Aristotle about the concept of thought as similar to a perception that, at the same time, implies a physical alteration. Commentators frequently tend to locate the fragment in the way of δόξα, and, in this way, Tarán even stated that Aristotle's mistake was to ascribe to Parmenides the opinion of mortal men.[8] I believe that this thought does not represent the position of the philosopher from Stagira; instead, I think that he intended to point out in a functional way consistent with his argumentative line, that in the text of the Parmenidean poem thought is described in perceptual terms, irrespective of whether the problem lies in a conception of the philosopher from Elea, or a criticism of the way of thinking of mortal men. In both cases, his reasoning might be criticized, for the error of most men would not be thinking in such a "physical" way because, as stated by Aristotle, thinking is not possible in those terms (and, as will be seen below, neither is perceiving). Let us remember that the purpose of *Metaphysics* IV, 5 is to refute the opinion of those who arrived at the denial of the principle of non-contradiction

[7] Cf. Barbara Cassin and Michel Narcy, *La Décision du sens: le livre Gamma de la "Métaphysique" d'Aristote*, introduction, établissement du texte, traduction et commentaire (Paris: J. Vrin, 1989), p. 236.
[8] Leonardo Tarán, *Parmenides* (Princeton: Princeton University Press, 1965), p. 253.

from the observation of phenomena. In order to refute their ideas, Aristotle resorts to the distinction between the potential and the actual being, as well as to the existence of entities that do not experience constant change, thus assuring the stability of the object of thought and its independence from the object of perception.

According to Aristotle, the criticism to the mentioned position relies on the ideas that thought is dependent upon physical abilities to the same extent as perception, and that the process of thought is, therefore, limited to the capturing of like by like.[9] On the other hand, this position includes another simplification referred to the very same nature of the αἴσθησις, conceived as an alteration (ἀλλοίωσις) of the body. Thus, if thought is identified with perception and the latter with a physical alteration, when interchanging the terms it is found that thought would ultimately be defined as a sort of physical alteration.

The basic problem that both Aristotle and his master noticed in the perceptual model is the impossibility to successfully account for error. In this way, every thought would either be true or would not be considered thought at all, which leads to the impossibility of thinking falsely. In principle, for those who support the identification between perception and thought, Aristotle observes two basic choices: either that whatever seems is true, or that error is in contact with the unlike. The last option is to be discarded, since it would imply an explanation of the truth isolated from the explanation of error, to which Aristotle expresses his disagreement through an opinion that carries wider consensus: "error as well as knowledge in respect to contraries is one and the same."[10] Ross points out that Aristotle is criticizing those who consider the difference between knowledge and error as a distinction among different objects, specifying that it is rather a difference in the relationship established with the objects than concerning the objects themselves.[11]

[9] In these terms, the question is set in a parallel passage in *On the Soul* III 3.

[10] In *On the Soul* III 3, Aristotle does not provide more specific opinions on the matter. However, this is further dealt with in *Metaphysics*.

[11] Cf. David Ross, *Aristotle De Anima* (Oxford: Oxford Clarendon Press, 1961), pp. 284–285.

## Theophrastus' comment

It is Theophrastus who offers a comment on this matter, although the context of analysis of the quotation is different from that of Aristotle's. In his treatise on sensation, he divides the opinions of previous philosophers in two groups: those who explain sensation in terms of knowing of like by like, and those who explain it in terms of knowing the unlike.[12] According to Theophrastus, Parmenides, Empedocles, and Plato belong to the first group; Anaxagoras and Heraclitus belong to the second. Before the reproduction of the same quotation of *Metaphysics* IV, 5, he comments that Parmenides stated that knowledge is produced based on the predominance of the cold or the hot. The purest thought, he continues, would be that deriving from the hot, even though it would also imply a certain proportion. The explanation of the latter would be, as affirmed by Theophrastus, the aim of the fragment. After quoting the Parmenidean verses, he concludes that Parmenides believed that perception and thinking are the same.[13] Theophrastus' perspective could help interpret the Parmenidean position as capable of accounting for true and erred thoughts. I believe that it is necessary to have in mind that in the Parmenidean poem there is a double register of the vocabulary of understanding since it is said that it is only possible to understand the being, but the mortal man who illegitimately mixes being and not being is then referred to as a "wandering intellect."

## Critics to the understanding of αἴσθησις and νόησις as alteration

As it will be explained latter on this presentation, Aristotle denies that thinking constitutes a physical alteration because of the difficulties that said conception would represent regarding the possibility of explaining error.[14] But he also refuses to characterize

[12] In *On the Soul,* Aristotle attributes to ancient philosophers the opinion that sensation implies capturing like by like. (*DA* III, 3, 427a26).

[13] τὸ γὰρ αἰσθάνεσθαι καὶ τὸ φρονεῖν ὡς ταὐτὸ λέγει (*On Sensation* 4, 1).

[14] In *On the Soul* III 3, for those who support the identification between perception and thinking in terms of physical alteration, Aristotle sees two basic choices: either that whatever seems is true, or that error is in contact with the

the αἴσθησις itself in terms of alteration (ἀλλοίωσις). To explain this clearly: the term ἀλλοίωσις has, in the Aristotelian line of thought, a technical sense of change according to the category of quality (κίνησις κατὰ τὸ ποιόν, *Categories* 14, 15b12) as well as a wide sense, suggested by the etymology of the term, of future and faith which would characterize the process leading to a different state (ἀλλοῖος).[15] It is clear that Aristotle considered the possibility that αἴσθησις is an alteration in terms of a serious problem, since it presents several treatments of the question. With certain caution in its characterization, we find that in *On the Motion of Animals* and *On Dreams,* he affirms that αἴσθησις is "a certain alteration" (ἀλλοίωσις τις).[16] Nevertheless, in *On the Soul,* he corrects the considerations about this matter included in said treaties stating that either it is not an alteration or it is a different kind of it (417b7). This idea forces us to consider "ἀλλοίωσις" in a wider sense that should include the changes toward the updating of one's own nature (*On the Soul* II, 5, 417b6–7). Finally, in the same text, he denies that αἴσθησις is ἀλλοίωσις (*On the Soul* III, 7, 431a6). For Aristotle, perception is, in fact, the updating of a second potentiality, analogous to the state of one who has developed a knowledge of grammar, and not a first potentiality, similar to the situation of one who, even if capable of acquiring said kind of knowledge, has not yet acquired it, and therefore needs to undergo another process first so as to move from power to action.[17]

Therefore, any common element between both functions of the soul that Aristotle may recognize would imply neither the

unlike. The last option is to be discarded, since it would imply an explanation of the truth isolated from the explanation of error, to which Aristotle expresses his disagreement through an opinion that carries wider consensus: "error as well as knowledge in respect to contraries is one and the same."

[15] Cf. Victor Caston, "Pourquoi Aristote a besoin de l'imagination?" *Les Études Philosophiques* 1 (1997), p. 19.

[16] Cf. *On the Motion of Animals* 7, 701b16 and *On Dreams* 2, 459b4.

[17] The difference between first potency and action, and second potency and action is developed by Aristotle in *On the Soul* II 4, as a sort of expansion of his classic treatment of the distinction between power/action in *Metaphysics* V, 12 and, more widely, in book IX of the same work.

extension to the νόησις of a strong dependence nor a limitation to the physiological process.

## Partial appropriation of the idea of *nóesis* as capturing something that is

In order to prove such appropriation, I will analyze two key passages: chapter six, Book III of *On the Soul*, and chapter ten of Book nine of *Metaphysics*.[18] The first of them starts with a division between the operation of the intellect, which consists in providing unity to different elements to produce a composition, and the process of thinking about indivisible objects (III, 6, 430a25–b6). In the first case, we find a choice between true/false, while, according to Aristotle, in the second case, περὶ ἃ οὐκ ἔστι τὸ ψεῦδος (430a26–27), or, in other words, that they are always true, as he asserts in the parallel passage of *Metaphysics* IX, 10.[19]

---

[18] In my presentation, I will not take into account *On interpretation* 1, 16a8–18, because dealing with the same problematic as in *On the Soul* III, 6 and *Metaphysics* IX, 10 is controversial. Berti, for instance, considers that this is not about the same discussion nor, consequently, the same type of separated objects (Enrico Berti, "Reconsidérations sur l'intellection del 'indivisibles' selon Aristote, *De anima* III, 6," in Cristina Viano *Corps et âme. Sur le De Anima d'Aristote* (Paris: Vrin, 1996), pp. 391–404.

[19] Throughout the chapter, Aristotle makes a distinction between indivisible objects by quantity, by shape, and causal indivisible objects. I will not deal with the description of the first group; I focus on the last two groups about which critical dissent has been shown. Regarding its identification, there are three possibilities:

1) The first motionless force
2) Concepts such as nouns and verbs that take part in predication
3) The essences

The possibility that Aristotle may be alluding to the first motionless force is supported in a specific reading of χωριστόν in line 430b26. There, Aristotle explains the understanding of the causes, and divides the treatment of the subject into the understanding of causes that present contraries and those that do not. As for the latter, he asserts: "But if there is anything that has no contrary, then it knows itself and is actually and possesses independent existence" (*On the Soul* III, 6, 430b24–26), in opposition to those who see a reference to separation between the first motionless force and the rest of the universe in this term. Berti, on the other hand, states that this interpretation is Neo-Platonic, since for Aristotle the first force is not the object of understanding but of a proof of existence (cf. *Metaphysics* XII, 6 and 7), inclining toward the identification of indivisible objects with essences.

Regarding the way in which knowledge of indivisible objects takes place, in *Metaphysics* IX, 10, after affirming that the truth about the combined is not expressed in the same way as about the separated, Aristotle points out the following with regard to the latter:

"Contact and assertion are true (assertion not being the same as affirmation), and ignorance is non-contact. For it is not possible to be in error regarding the question what a thing is, save in an accidental sense." (*Metaphysics* IX, 10, 1051b24–26)

In this passage, he refers to the understanding of the separated with the verb θιγγάνω, "touch," as if in this case understanding would work in an analogous way as perception. The same verb appears in *Metaphysics* XII, 7, 1072b20–21, where Aristotle asserts that "the intellect touches the intelligible, so that the intellect and the intelligible come to be identical."[20] How should we interpret the use of this verb of perception with respect to understanding? Romeyer differentiates two basic ways of doing it: 1) a Platonic interpretation, in which understanding would be touch/fusion without intermediaries and linked to the use of the verb ἅπτεσθαι in connection with the access of the non-hypothetical principle in *Republic* VI, 511b4 and 7; and 2) a more faithful reading of the Aristotelian thought, which emphasizes the metaphorical use of the sense of touch with respect to a kind of understanding that does not meet the requirements of sensitive perception.[21] The sense of the analogy lies in the fact that, in the same way as the sense of touch is in the closest position with respect to its object, the single object of understanding is in the closest position with respect to the intellect. The limit of the analogy is that the object of understanding is not external as in the case of the sense of touch, and

[20] Soon afterward, he goes on to say: "For that which is capable of receiving the object of thought, i.e., the essence, is thought. But it is active when it possesses this object. Therefore the possession rather than the receptivity is the divine element which thought seems to contain, and the act of contemplation is what is most pleasant and best."

[21] Gilbert Romeyer Dherbey, "La construction de la théorie aristotélicienne du sentir" in Cristina Viano *Corps et âme. Sur le De Anima d'Aristote* (Paris: Vrin, 1996), pp. 127–148.

it is not possible to strictly speak of "contact," since intellect and understanding have no matter.

Against the classical interpretation that Aristotle maintained toward some kind of instantaneous intellectual intuitionism, Berti has recently suggested that Aristotle affirmed that understanding of indivisible objects covers a time unit that would not necessarily be an instant, but a period of time in which the intellect is thinking of nothing else; in other words, a sole act that consists of only one understanding that has no other object. Let us remember that in *On the Soul*, when Aristotle describes the intellective ability, he draws a parallel with perception settling significant differences and not limiting it to enumerating similarities. His first approach to intellective analysis in *On the Soul* III, 4 is an analogy of the relationship between the sensitive and the sensitive ability, and the intelligible with the intellective ability. However, Aristotle's interest in preserving a qualitative difference can be immediately observed, for, as soon as it is formulated, he promptly sets limits to the analogy. It is possible to find a potentiality both in the sensitive and intellective abilities with respect to the understanding of its objects. This fact was conceptualized by Aristotle in terms of impassiveness (ἀπάθεια, 429a29). It is precisely the ἀπάθεια that allows him to point out significant differences between perception and understanding. Since the latter does not depend directly on a physical organ, it is not subject to the limitations which are typical of sensation. The senses, which do not exist without the body, are physically affected when perceiving a strongly sense-oriented object, like a loud sound or an intense color. The intellect, on the other hand, intensifies its own capacity toward "strongly intelligible" objects. This is possible due to the Aristotelian conception of the dynamics of knowledge, which shows a sort of circular structure, with its starting point in a fact considered amazing and its culmination in causal and universal knowledge that helps explain that same phenomenon, toward which the certainly amazing thing would now be that it may not happen that way (cf. *Metaphysics* I, 2). Thus, it is the "strongly intelligible" (i.e., the universal and the causal), that actually makes it possible to know particular phenomena.

## Conclusions

In *Metaphysics* IV, 5, Aristotle attempts to allege the underlying stability and order of sensitive things against those who proved themselves to be unable to notice it. In order to do so, he needs to resort to a conception of perception which, on the one hand, should have an objective pole in things themselves and, on the other, should offer the possibility of perceiving and thinking about said things in a reliable way. Otherwise, those who seek the truth end up discrediting it and indirectly supporting the Sophistic theses, the refutation of which is Aristotle's main objective in this chapter.

The Aristotelian criticism of his predecessors has been very much criticized, particularly after the publication of Cherniss's work.[22] In the issue at hand, the philosopher establishes a close relationship between disparate philosophies, including even representatives of Sophistics, focused on the aim of his line of argument in favor of the principle of non-contradiction. When dealing with these thinkers, he does not show interest in the interpretation of their texts, but in what they have contributed to the problems that arouse his own philosophical interest. In connection with the difference between perception and thought, he sharply notices that there appears no clear distinction among the pioneers of philosophical thought and points out the consequences of that lack of distinction.

However, we have also seen that Aristotle insists on establishing a significant difference between those who, committed with the challenge of knowledge and based on the consideration of phenomena, have presented the validity of the principle of non-contradiction as a serious problem, and those who did so just to generate controversy for the sole purpose of arguing and not of attaining truth (λόγου χάριν, *Metaphysics* IV, 5, 1009a21). Parmenides would not be included in the list of Sophists but on

22 Harold Cherniss, *Aristotle's Criticism of Presocratic Philosophy* (Baltimore: Johns Hopkins Press, 1935).

the list of philosophers who attempted to solve serious problems concerning what is and the way of understanding it. For that reason he mentions the close relationship between perception and thought as a factor to be taken into account, and he even adopts this formula in part in connection with the capturing of indivisible objects. As far as the latter are concerned, and in parallel with Parmenides, thought captures something that is and is infallible. However, regarding the rest of the exercise of thought, since the perceptual model focuses on passivity and receptivity, it is not sufficient to account both for error and truth.

Therefore, we can observe that Aristotle's opposition to the perceptual model of thought should be understood as a rejection of said model as a *general* structure able to account for the different modalities of human thought. But when analyzing in detail the several functions of the intellective ability, he will get close to a certain extent to the criticized position when he acknowledges that, in the process of capturing simple objects, the intellect operates in a similar fashion to perception. It is evident that this approach should not be interpreted as an assimilation or reduction of the rejected position, since while establishing several analogies between perception and understanding, at the same time, he points out its differences. Unlike the Sophistic theses, the Parmenidean verses are included among those Aristotle considers that "have developed before us the powers of thought."[23]

[23] This is how Aristotle refers to the contribution of his predecessors in *Metaphysics* II, 1, 993b13–14.

# The Father and the Sophist: Platonic Parricide in the *Statesman*

Gabriel Livov


## Summary

Through a certain approach to Plato's philosophical parricide, I try to prove the strong political significance of the *Statesman* as a metaphorical and theoretical space of criticism of the Parmenidean principles of the *Republic*.

I intend to shed light on a well-known metaphor that Plato uses to illustrate the controversy he engages in against Parmenides, his Philosophical Father. The motif of Father Parmenides' crime appears as a superb key to the interpretation of the reformulation process Plato undertakes in his late dialogues, clearly in the *Sophist*, but also in the *Statesman*. I take both dialogues as a methodological, conceptual and dramatic unity, and my general argumentative operation implies projecting the refined logics and ontology of the *Sophist* onto its practical counterpart, a revised version of the standard Platonic politics of the *Republic* that is exposed in the *Statesman*. I will explore some political analogies and concepts closely related to the metaphoric system of parricide, which will work as a vehicle to understand the Platonic criticism of Parmenidean metaphysico-political unity and, at the same time, as significant evidence of the self-criticism of the *Republic's* Parmenidean homogeneity.


In this paper, I aim to illuminate a well-known metaphor that Plato deploys to illustrate the controversy he engages in against Parmenides, his Philosophical Father. The motif of Father Parmenides' crime appears as a superb key to the interpretation of the reformulation process Plato undertakes in his late dialogues, clearly in the *Sophist*, but also in the *Statesman*. I take both dialogues as a methodological, conceptual and dramatic unity, and my general argumentative operation implies projecting the refined logics and ontology of the *Sophist* onto its practical counterpart, a revised version of the standard Platonic politics of the *Republic* that is exposed in the *Statesman*. I will explore some political analogies and concepts closely related to the metaphoric system of parricide, which will work as a vehicle to understand the Platonic criticism of Parmenidean metaphysico-political unity and, at the same time, as significant evidence of the self-criticism of the *Republic*'s Parmenidean homogeneity.

## 1. Parmenicide

> I have another still more pressing request: [. . .] that you will not think I am turning into a sort of parricide. [. . .] We shall find it necessary in self-defense to put to the question the pronouncement of father Parmenides, and establish by main force that what is not, in some respect has being, and conversely that what is, in a way is not. (*Sophist* 241d)[1]

The *Sophist*'s conversation, during which the parricide takes place, is conducted by a nameless Stranger from Elea. It is this Stranger who, before going on to the refutation, introduces the metaphor of parricide quoted above.

It seems necessary to specify the meaning and reach of the *parmenicide*, since it is a topic so widely discussed. What is the philosophical point of this crime hinted at under the guise of murdering a father? I suggest viewing the Platonic parricide as a complex act that is made up of three closely related moments: the *transgression of a precept*, the *negation of a concept* and the *reformulation of a method*.

The *transgression of a precept* relates to the strict prohibition that Parmenides' Goddess imposed prohibiting any possible

---

[1] "We must now dare to lay unfilial hands on that pronouncement, or else if some scruple holds us back, drop the matter entirely" (*Sophist* 242a). Translation by F. M. Cornford, *Plato's Theory of Knowledge* (London: Routledge, 1935).

exploration of the way of non-being, conceived as unthinkable and unnameable.[2] While the father from Elea claimed that non-being cannot be thought of, expressed or be, Plato's Stranger will walk the path of non-being in order to try to justify its entity (as a Form of Otherness) as well as the possibility of being thought of and expressed through language.[3]

The *conceptual negation* involves the rejection of the Parmenidean conception of being (τὸ ἐόν), specifically the attribute of homogeneity. For Parmenides, τὸ ἐόν does not know of interstices, gaps or points of interruption, its cohesion is absolute, "since non-being, which would prevent it from attaining homogeneity, does not exist" (8.46).[4] According to Plato's Stranger, being, discourse and thought demand another approximation that does not aim at a perfect and round identity, but rather at the difference, combination and mixture underlying all entities, words and concepts.[5]

The *reformulation of a method* is bound to the refined exploration that Plato tuned up in the *Sophist*, aimed at defining a matrix of comprehension of being in terms of the mixture (σύμμειξις) and combination (συμπλοκή) of certain supreme genres. By virtue of its interdiction of non-being, the demanding Parmenidean program of ontological research did not admit the possibility of any mixture whatsoever—since every mixture always meant some kind of non-being with which being would mix—; in correspondence, the characterization of τὸ ἐόν is conducted as

---

2 "Never shall this be proved—that things that are not, are; but do thou, in thy inquiry, hold back thy thought from this way" (quoted in *Sophist* 237a [translation of the *Sophist* by F. M. Cornford, op. cit.]). "It has already been decided, of necessity, that one remains unthinkable and unnameable (since it is not the true way) and that the other exists and is genuine." (fr. 8, vv. 15–18 [from now on: 8.15–18] [translation of Parmenides' poem by N.-L. Cordero, *By Being, It is: The Thesis of Parmenides* (Las Vegas: Parmenides Publishing, 2004)]).

3 "You see, then, that in our disobedience to Parmenides we have trespassed far beyond the limits of his prohibition. [. . .] In pushing forward our quest, we have shown him results in a field which he forbade us even to explore" (*Sophist* 258d [Cornford's translation, slightly revised]).

4 Parmenides presents a conceptual metaphor that compares being to a sphere: "it is everywhere finished, like the mass of a well-rounded sphere, completely equidistant from the centre, here or there" (fr. 8, quoted in *Sophist* 244e).

5 Cf. *Sophist* 260a–b.

an analytical deduction of necessary attributes. Through the philosophical rehabilitation of a relative concept of non-being, Plato rehearses an outline of synthetic ontology, an ontology of synthesis whose expression is encoded in the combining mixture of being and non-being as structure of discourse, thought and reality.[6]

In the next sections, I expect to test the political scope of the *parmenicide*, under the triple assumption that 2) it constitutes the sacrifice that founds for dialectic the *possibility to confront its main enemy (the hydra-headed sophist)*, 3) it points at a *new (immanent) modality of political legitimacy* in compliance with the theoretical needs of the times, and 4) it enables a *new (textile) paradigm of political comprehension*.

## 2. The hydra-headed sophist

> We must begin by investigating the nature of discourse and thinking and appearance, in order that we may then make out their combination with non-being and so prove that falsity exists, and by that proof pin down the sophist there, if he is amenable to capture, or else let him go and pursue our search in some other kind. (*Sophist* 260e–261a)[7]

In this statement, the killing of Parmenides betrays clear political motivations, insofar as its aim is to determine the profile of the main enemy of Platonic dialectic. The perpetration of parricide becomes functional to the search for the sophist: to prove the existence of what is not is the key to characterize the region of falsehood, where these impostors and conjurers hide.

The emergence of such an elusive and resistant adversary indicates a fundamental change within the conceptual space of Parmenides' poem. Plato's times are marked by the breach that the sophistic dagger introduced into the well-rounded sphere of Parmenidean τὸ ἐόν, which opened a time and space characterized by the division between being, thinking, and saying, where the

[6] Cf. *Sophist* 257a; 259a.

[7] Cornford's translation, slightly revised.

persuasion of discourse is freed from the mortgage of truth; thought has cut its bonds with a state of affairs that aimed at restricting it; and words have become privileged, reality-producing devices.

I understand that the sophist is the symptom and, at the same time, the cause of the crisis of Parmenidean political semiology, to the extent that it produces an irreversible interference in the Eleatic mediation between opinion (δόξα) and truth (ἀλήθεια). Parmenides dealt with the problem of erratic opinion and the battle of perspectives among two-headed mortals, but even so he ensured the presence of the goddess's Persuasion to lead them to agreement under the sign of truth.[8] As a mortal, Parmenides could not conceive of himself as apart from the struggle for imposing meaning,[9] but the rhetorical surplus of Parmenides' discourse was guaranteed by a theological transcendence that grounded both trust and truth (πίστις ἀληθής *pistis alethēs*, 8.28) and made possible the power of conviction (πίστιος ἰσχύς, 8.12).

However, in the course of the fifth century, the foundations that anchored the circulation of signs to a solid and unshakable basis lose both legitimacy and effectiveness. Due to the fall of the theological warrant, Parmenides' semantico-political code cannot hold erratic intellects anymore, and the loss of unity and stability in the regulatory system of signs carries the crisis of the Eleatic community of communication.

The result is a decentralized semiology that annihilates the paternal monolingual cannons. The sophistic destruction of the system of truth—through the reduction of all knowledge to a war of opinions and perspectives—wrecks the bases of Parmenidean mediation and breaks the onto-theological balance that backed Eleatic politics.

Simultaneously, we do not face subjects who, despite being erratic, allow themselves to be convinced by divine words and who agree to head towards the communal domain of truth. The

[8] "This is the way of persuasion, since it accompanies the truth" (2.3–4).

[9] According to the words the Goddess addresses to him, she reveals a "polemical proof" (πολύδηρις ἔλεγχος, 7.5); at the end of fr. 8 she will contact him with a probable cosmic order "so that no viewpoint of mortals will prevail over you" (8.61).

relatively normal two-headed individuals have now degenerated into appalling monstrosities. According to the parricide Stranger, the enemy of truth appears now as a multi-headed creature: "the sophist of many heads" (ὁ πολυκέφαλος σοφιστής).[10] In the *Statesman* proper he refers to "the chorus of all the sophists that deal with the affairs of the cities" and to "a race mixed out of all sorts," misshapen specimen that "quickly exchange their looks and capacity with one another."[11]

To carry out the hunt for the sophist, Platonic dialectic understands the sacrifice of the father from Elea as a crime that responds to historical demands and implies the emergence of an enemy who cannot be understood under its categories anymore. Only by killing the Father can a philosophical thought of non-being be founded, with the objective of thus getting a selection criterion of rivals in order to exclude the sophists' discourses.

This polemico-political interpretation receives a metaphorical confirmation in the Platonic text. Faced with Theaetetus' uneasiness about the path that apparently must be walked to corner the sophist, the Stranger comforts him as follows:

> A man should be of good courage, Theaetetus, if he can make only a little headway at each step. If he loses heart then, what will he do in another case where he cannot advance at all or even perhaps loses ground? Such a faint heart, as the proverb says, will never take a city. And now that we have surmounted the barrier you speak of, we may have already taken the highest wall and the rest may be easier to capture.[12]

In a state of tension because of the persistent invasion of an enemy who is to be evicted from the dialogical acropolis, the inquiry gains a high tone of politicity. To define the sophist and to banish him to the realm of falsehood implies reconquering the city-State,

[10] *Sophist* 240c: "Our hydra-headed sophist has forced us against our will to admit that non-being has some sort of being" [Cornford's translation, slightly revised].

[11] *Statesman* 291a–c, S. Benardete's translation, op. cit., slightly revised.

[12] *Sophist* 261b–c, Cornford's translation, slightly revised.

expelling the impostor who entrenched himself behind the walls of non-being and ensuring the governability of dialectical space.

## 3. Politics in the age of immanence

> Law, the king of all, of mortals and immortals, leads them, making just what is most violent with arm supreme. (Pindar, fr. 169, vv. 1–4)[13]

> Law, despot of men, often constrains us against nature. (Hippias)[14]

The emergence of such an elusive and resistant adversary indicates a fundamental shift from the times of Parmenides' poem. We could take the two quoted statements above to approach this difference: what happened between Pindar and Hippias? How can this temporal mutation be characterized?

The well-known fragment of Pindar testifies the universal reach of a Law that is capitalized and which extends its rule across all areas of reality: within this onto-theo-nomocrace, political concepts are not cut autonomously from ontological, cosmological and theological considerations, but rather belong to the same realm. Physics, cosmology and politics become dependent upon the same all-embracing theological justification. Parmenides' trip to the Goddess, under the guidance of the Daughters of the Sun, is backed by Themis and Dike. The preface appears to be inhabited by divinities in charge of enforcing the cosmic laws (the keys of night and day are kept by Dike, "prodigal in punishments"), and it is goddess Dike herself who neither allows being to generate nor to corrupt itself.[15]

[13] Translation by H. Lloyd-Jones, "Pindar, fr. 169," *Harvard Studies in Classical Philology*, Vol. 76 (1972), 45–56.

[14] Plato, *Protagoras* 337d [translation by W. R. M. Lamb, *Plato in Twelve Volumes*, Vol. 3 (Cambridge, MA: Harvard University Press, 1967)].

[15] The transcendent basis of the political is shown with meridian clarity by Heraclitus: "for all human laws are under wardship [τρέφονται] to one, the divine (law); for it rules as far as it wills and protects all (laws) and prevails over (them)" (DK B 114). I follow A. P. D. Mourelatos's translation, which emphasizes the metaphorical pastoral nexus implicit in the verb τρέφειν ("Heraclitus, fr. 114," *The American Journal of Philology*, Vol. 86, No. 3 (1965), 258–266, 263–264).

However, in the course of the fifth century BCE, a decisive mutation takes place that could be understood as a process of progressive desacralization and autonomization of the political with regard to its theological and ontological grounds. This epochal change is crystallized in Hippias' rewriting of Pindar. Law is not the sovereign of both mortal and immortal anymore, but rather it only imposes its coercion on men, and it does so in a way that opposes nature. In the line of thought that started with the Protagoric dissolving of reality into its human measuring criteria, and with the Gorgean praise of language as supreme producer of being, the sophistic movement extends to the political a process of denaturalization and desacralization that precipitated the corruption of the onto-theological foundations of authority.

In Plato's *Statesman* (269c–274e), the same Stranger who killed Parmenides in the *Sophist* tells a myth that can be read as expressing this transformation. According to the myth—a *collage* of traditional cosmological motives structured in two phases separated by a cataclysm—the Universe and human life were originally under the direct tutorship of the gods, according to a cosmology described in terms of shepherds and flocks: the Universe is grazed directly by god Kronos with the help of other minor divinities, each in charge of herding a different portion of reality. A harmonious order imposed on all animal breeds, each governed by a deity, made war (πόλεμος), and inner conflicts (στάσις) impossible (271e), so there were no political regimes (271e).

Plato appeals to the pastoral analogy in order to show the immediate and personal modality divine rule adopts in these primordial times. In the age of Kronos, human beings did not have to worry about anything because "a god was himself in charge and grazed them, just as human beings now, being another more divine animal, graze different genera inferior to themselves."[16]

At a given time, Kronos and his helpers give up on this cosmic grazing and there is a cataclysm by which the world starts to

[16] *Statesman* 271e, translation by S. Benardete, *Plato's* Statesman (Chicago: University of Chicago Press, 1984).

turn in the opposite direction, left to its own course and domain. Doomed to immanence, although aided by certain gifts given by Olympic gods such as Prometheus and Hephaestus, human beings organize themselves autonomously, they secure their food and get to attending to their own affairs (274c–e).

In the light of this myth, the murder of Father Parmenides is shown as a historical need, as the condition of possibility to think about politics in times of autonomy and desacralization. Once we have admitted the corruption of the onto-theological foundations of power, the search for the political way in its specificity demands the sacrifice of the father figure that symbolizes a whole mechanism of transcendent legitimation.

## 4. Weaving the city-State

I will now focus on how the pastoral metaphor is substituted for a textile model (under the impression that this change of metaphor in the *Statesman* implies a change in the paradigm of comprehension of politics) and on how it is closely related to the crime of Father Parmenides.

In the *Statesman*, the Stranger from Elea subjects the pastoral analogy to a strict critical test in order to prove its effectiveness to think of the definition of the ruler in its specificity. The visitor anchors the process of dichotomic division in a traditional metaphor within Greek political comprehension, the definition of the command-obedience relation through the semantic field of herding. Thus politics is a technique of common breed or herd-nurture (261e) that is applied on tame (264a) and solid ground flocks (264d), made up of pedestrian animals (264e) without horns (265c) and which are defined as bipeds (267c).

This definition of politics as grazing and of the politician as shepherd is a dialectic formalization of an analogy that the Socrates of the *Republic* had used widely when it came to modelling the ideal city-State. The demands of absolute unity and homogeneity—two traits that would already enable us to understand *Kallípolis* as the political transposition of Parmenidean being—is symbolically allowed through herding metaphors: the State guardians are dogs that protect a flock, the enemies of the people are similar to wolves, and the rulers are called city shepherds.[17]

The *Republic* is politically inscribed within the metaphoric system of grazing. In terms of the aforementioned myth of the *Statesman*, the philosopher shepherds translating Ideas into actual politics recall the same immediate, all-inclusive and transcendent modality of government as the divine shepherds of Kronos' times.

The Stranger's critical metaphorology refutes the old pastoral transcendent way of power legitimation and points at two inescapable theoretical drawbacks to the use of herding metaphors in politics: their theological burden and their tyrannical implications. The difference in nature between the power-holder and the power-subject is evident: in the same way as the sheep shepherd is a man, the shepherd of men is a god. Therefore, the metaphor cannot work in the realm of immanence and it appears to be only appropriate to allow a theocratic system in which the human specificities of that power would be blurred. The metaphor also blurs the specific modality of political relationships of command. The flock follows its shepherd without conflicts and it would seem that this type of automatic, non-reflective, and not agreed-on submission—unidirectional and total, overlapping with the absolute rule of the tyrant—cannot account for political obedience.[18]

In times of the divine neglect of the cosmic rudder, we have to admit that the problem of defining the sophist and the philosopher-king is no longer solved by drawing divided lines between opinion and truth. The Stranger has to specifically determine that which for both the Parmenides of the poem and the Socrates of the *Republic* was sanctioned by transcendent warrants. The distinction between philosopher-politician and sophist can no longer be dealt with in pastoral terms because, as

[17] Cf. *Republic* 440d, 451d; 415e, 416a, 565d–566a; 343a–b, 345b–e; etc.

[18] *Pol.* 274e–275a. For a wider exposition of this perspective, I refer to G. Livov, "Triple Aproximación a la Metáfora Política del Apacentamiento de Platón [Triple approach to Plato's Metaphor of Political Herding]," in N. Andrade, ed., *Estrategias Discursivas en la Grecia Antigua* (Buenos Aires: Eudeba, 2009), pp. 105–158; cf. section 3: "Metaforología Crítica del Apacentamiento").

it is made clear in the *Sophist*, they resemble each other as "the dog to the wolf—the fiercest of animals to the tamest."[19]

The adequacy of the textile paradigm to describe the figure of the statesman consists in accounting for a complex activity with a multiplicity of rival figures. Because it suggests a specific criterion that manages to detach the real politician from those who compete against him to care for public affairs, false claimants happened to be in the same situation as those who deal with spinning, carding or knitting and those who produce textile tools, in case it would occur to them to challenge the royal weaver for the main responsibility of the creation of the fabric.[20]

The textile city-State of the *Statesman* blends together different kinds of souls (*Pol.* 309a–b; 311c), overthrowing in this way the myth of the metals in the *Republic*, a "noble lie" that was meant to avoid mixture in the social body (*Rep.* 415a–c; 434a–c) and that served the purpose of making the flock participate in a "community of pleasure and pain" as a unique homogeneous body (*Rep.* 462a–464b). The domain of politics can no longer be thought of in terms of a spherical field without any cracks, a well-rounded unique and homogeneous surface, but it should rather be understood as the fruit of an architectonic labor of intertwining that works within a complex and heterogeneous political reality.

The new system of political comprehension that the Stranger from Elea presents in the *Statesman* shows the signs of parricide insofar as it adopts the art of weaving, whose paradigm is built on the notions of mixture and combination, as its fundamental political metaphor. The parricide allows Plato to admit that politics in the times of difference interweaves different kinds of souls, makes up webs of intersubjective relationships from a diversity that is not to be suppressed, and combines different sciences, which coordinate their efforts in the pursuit of the common good. Weaving sciences and souls allows building a political community to which we can no longer demand a flock-like homogeneity.

---

19 *Soph.* 231a.
20 *Pol.* 289c–d.

## 5. Final remarks

In the paragraphs above, I tried to prove the strong political significance of the *Statesman* as a metaphorical and theoretical space for criticism and revision of the Parmenidean principles of the *Republic*.

However, from the perspective of the development of Plato's political thought, it is to be pointed out that the *Statesman* involves a metaphoric and theoretical movement that is not continued in subsequent texts. In effect, while in this dialogue politics starts precisely when the theological rule of the divine shepherds ends, the latest Platonic political dialogues explicitly restore the pastoral metaphor from a theocratic point of view. In the pastoral myth presented in *Critias* 109b–d, the gods Hephaestus and Athena, in charge of grazing old Athenians, "put into their minds the order of government."[21] According to the *Laws* 713d–e, Kronos ordered that some minor divinities were in charge of herding human beings, providing them with peace, shame, good legislation and good disposition towards the law.

This metaphorical verification receives an ulterior confirmation if one considers Magnesia's penal code, definitely opposed to any form of parricide: "and if a man could be slain more than once, most justly would he who in a fit of passion has slain his father undergo many deaths" (*Laws* IX 869b).[22] It is not a coincidence that the same dialogue that represents a return to political theology—in which human rules come from divine sources and where god is the measure for all things[23]—is the one that suggests the worst of sentences for the parricidal Stranger who articulated the defense of a textile immanence.

However, Platonic criminology considers a fundamental extenuating circumstance that could favour the Stranger from Elea—and may exonerate Plato himself—and which implies a reduction of the sentence only if the father who is about to die forgives his murderous offspring.[24] In view of this situation, would Parmenides have forgiven Plato? Most scholars answer

---

21 B. Jowett's translation, op. cit.
22 B. Jowett's translation, op. cit.
23 Cf. *Laws* 716c.
24 Cf. *Laws* 869a.

affirmatively to this question, holding an ironic reading of parricide: Plato says to have killed the Father when in truth he does not want to kill him but, on the contrary, he wants to revive him, defend his name and demand his legacy against the sophistic creature's claims.

Or it may be said that it is a "Platonic crime" in the same way we usually speak about a "Platonic love": parricide would then be an ideal crime, without shedding blood, carried out by a Stranger without either an identity or concrete features, with good intentions, whom the victim forgives in the instant prior to his death.

Considering the metaphoric evidence presented, it becomes appropriate to assign the *Statesman* a theoretical space with its own irreducible density. Thus, it is a dialogue that performs a fecund, new and radical self-critical rehearsal that deserves a specific consideration and can neither be reduced to a mere propedeutic antechamber for the *Laws* nor to a transitional stage of indecision in Plato's own thought.

At this point the correspondence between logics, metaphysics and politics through the counterpoint *Sophist/Statesman* becomes evident, both dialogues led by the Visiting Parricide. The metaphysical, gnoseological and logical sophistication of the *Sophist* demands taking the combination and the mixture seriously, something unthinkable from the Eleatic purism of the *Republic*, which aimed at absolute concord. In the same way that the *Sophist* suggested understanding concepts, words and objects in their reciprocal interminglings, the textile paradigm of the *Statesman* demands thinking of the city-State as the place of articulation of an irreducible social heterogeneity in a time when theological warrants fall short. It is necessary to abandon the Parmenidean principles of politics if we do not want to renounce thinking the complexity of a society that seems to have gone through a fundamental epochal threshold and which can no longer be illustrated by archaic images of lost homogeneity.

# “Thinking That I Did Something . . .”: Apollodorus and Diotima’s Teaching[1]

Ezequiel Ludueña


## Summary

My paper deals with the interpretation of the meaning of the famous Ladder of Love in Plato’s *Symposium*. Through a study of the formulas ἀγάλματα ἀρετῆς (222a4) and εἴδωλα ἀρετῆς (212a4), I intend to demonstrate that two different kinds of ποίησις can be pointed out in Plato’s dialogue: a true ποίησις, identical with the supreme θεωρία; and a fake one, practiced by everyone who has not yet experienced Beauty itself. The former produces ἀγάλματα, while the later can only produce εἴδωλα.


## I - Before and after philosophy: Apollodorus’ “conversion”

As is well known, the *Symposium* opens with a brief prologue that presents us with the narrator of the work. Moreover, the entire work is presented as a generous answer given by Apollodorus—the narrator—to a group of businessmen interested in the matter. Apollodorus is a young disciple of Socrates who also appears in the *Apology*[2] and the *Phaedo*.[3]

Apollodorus reproduces to the businessmen the same answer he had given to Glaucon when Glaucon asked him about the time when a symposium was celebrated in honor of Agaton’s first poetic victory on the Leneas of 416 BCE. The answer reproduces

[1] I am grateful to Pablo Maurette and Laura Duberti for kindly helping me out with the translation of this paper.

[2] *Apology*, 34a; 38b.

[3] *Phaedo*, 117d.

essentially the story Aristodemus told Apollodorus about that symposium. But before Apollodorus starts the story once again, Plato makes him reveal to us some details about himself. Apollodorus tells us that for almost three years now he has been looking for Socrates' company in order to always know what Socrates says or does (εἰδέναι ὅτι ἂν λέγῃ ἢ πράττῃ).[4] That is, he is not just interested in Socrates' λόγοι but also in his πρᾶξις. Having made the acquaintance of Socrates is described by him as a kind of revelation: "Before this time I wandered about wherever it might chance, thinking that I did something (οἰόμενος τὶ ποιεῖν), but being, in truth, a most miserable wretch, not less than you are now, who believe that you ought to do anything rather than practice the love of wisdom (οἰόμενος δεῖν πάντα μᾶλλον πράττειν ἢ φιλοσοφεῖν)."[5]

Before meeting Socrates he *thought* he was doing something, whereas, *actually*, it seems now to him, he was doing nothing. This statement—which Plato thought expressed a sort of revelation to Apollodorus—suggests the idea of philosophy understood as ποίησις and πρᾶξις. It may seem trivial to indicate this, but perhaps one would expect that at the time of defining what that revelation consisted in, Apollodorus would appeal to a more common notion in order to define Socrates' view of philosophy; something like: "I thought I *knew* something . . . ." That would have been indeed far more natural. After all, Socrates seems to have said that there is no difference between ethics and epistemology. It is noteworthy to point out the fact that that particular expression ("I thought I was *doing* something") was not written at random[6]: Apollodorus uses that very same expression only a few lines below, just before he starts telling the story. After his "conversion" he can only stand philosophical discussions because "whenever I hear your discussions about wealthy men and great proprietors, I am weighed down with grief, and pity you, who,

---

[4] *Symposium*, 172c6.

[5] *Symposium*, 173a1–3. I avail myself of the fine version of Percy Bysshe Shelley: Plato, *The* Symposium, translated by P. B. Shelley, edited and introduced by D. K. O'Connor (South Bend: St. Augustine's Press, 2002).

[6] As nothing that was written by Plato's quill.

doing nothing (οὐδὲν ποιοῦντες), believe that you are doing something (ὅτι οἴεσθε τὶ ποιεῖν)."[7]

Clearly, Apollodorus has a fixed idea about the difference between his early nonphilosophical life and his present state after meeting Socrates; and that difference finds its expression in the lines just quoted. This notion, of course, is not new. It is just another way of putting the well known intellectualism of Socratic and Platonic ethics.

But at this point, we must ask ourselves a question. Is philosophy said—albeit implicitly—to be a kind of ποίησις, or just the realization that a man can do nothing at all? Whatever our answer might be, that answer appears to state what is the essence of philosophy according to the very first page of the *Symposium*. In order to answer the question, it might be helpful to review—having Apollodorus' insistent testimony in mind—the λόγος of Diotima, the ultimate source[8] of Socrates' wisdom (and consequently that of Apollodorus). Besides, if it turns out that philosophy is in fact a kind of ποίησις, we may find some specification about the nature of this ποίησις. It might also be that the meaning of Apollodorus' words is that there are two kinds of ποίησις, a real one (the one philosophy strives to attain) and a fake one, an illusory one which common people believe to be ποίησις.

## II - Ποίησις and θεωρία in Diotima's speech

According to Diotima's famous definition of ἔρως—τόκος ἐν καλῷ[9]—it is not a matter of discussion that there is some kind of active process involved. Besides, Diotima herself points out that procreative activity, inwardly impelled by an everlasting ἔρως for immortality in any of its modes—a desire that always aims at leaving something new in the place of the old destined to die—is in fact the engine leading to every human activity: "Do you believe (οἴει) that Alcestis would have died in the place of Admetus, or Achilles for the revenge of Patroclus, or Codrus

[7] *Symposium*, 173c5–d1.
[8] Whether fictional or not.
[9] *Symposium*, 206b7–8.

for the kingdom of his posterity, if they had not believed (μὴ οἰομένους) that the immortal memory of their actions, which we now cherish, would have remained after their death? Far otherwise; all such deeds are done (πάντες πάντα ποιοῦσιν) for the sake of ever-living virtue (ἀρετῆς), and this immortal glory which they have obtained; and inasmuch as any one is of an excellent nature, so much the more is he impelled to attain this reward. For they love (ἐρῶσιν) what is immortal."[10]

It seems that everyone accomplishes all sorts of deeds and even sacrifices just for the sake of ἀρετή. The truth, however, is that ἀρετή is a means to achieve immortality through a perennial fame, through memory and respect. That is why, in fact, everything happens for the sake not of ἀρετή, but of φιλοτιμία.

That ἀρετή that everyone seeks but only a few attain is, then, practiced only in order to attain fame. Until here we have reached a high level along the scale of ἔρως, but nonetheless an ordinary height. The young Socrates can be initiated in the lesser mysteries of ἔρως, inasmuch as they include a revelation only relative to a common way of fulfilling the ἔρως. That is the common ποίησις of the common people, even if only the few reach the end of the path. The product of that ποίησις is not true ἀρετή, as it turns out from the last words of Diotima. The true initiated in matters of love ascends above this common practice within which ἀρετή is just a means. He does not seek for the immortality offered by fame. He needs a more intense immortality. Accordingly, a different kind of *doing* is required. The true lover goes from physical procreation, passing through engendering λόγοι and ways of lives, to reach a level where he can realize that there is beauty in knowledge. However that is not the end of the ascent. Only when he can behold Beauty itself, instead of things that are beautiful, he shall reach the end of the ascent. Only then perfect θεωρία shall suddenly happen: "'Such a life as this, my dear Socrates,' exclaimed the stranger prophetess, 'spent in the contemplation of the beautiful (θεωμένῳ αὐτὸ τὸ καλόν), is the life for men to live.'"[11]

10 *Symposium*, 208d2–208e1.
11 *Symposium*, 211d1–3.

## III - Apollodorus' ποίησις and Diotima's θεωρία

If from these heights we now return to those words uttered by Apollodorus, we find it difficult to reconcile his words with the last words of Diotima,[12] at least at first sight. It was his insight—as noted before—that the way of philosophy implies a certain kind of *doing*—a πρᾶξις and ποίησις.

From this point of view, one might think that Apollodorus has not yet fully comprehended Diotima's teaching, because, *prima facie*, what could be most opposite to that supreme and absolute θεωρία than that exhortation of Apollodorus to a true πρᾶξις and ποίησις? An obvious (albeit vague) answer could be given at once, namely the already mentioned intellectual character of Platonic ethics. But all the same, one might ask the following question. According to Diotima, that intense desire for procreation and for immortality—such that urges us to do, to ascend any number of steps—does not culminate in the inaction and passivity of θεωρία? He who attains the contemplation of true Beauty shall not be dragged into some sort of drowsy quietism, given that he has obtained what he has so strong longed for?[13] Now, if we stop in front of this kind of ἀπορία, we risk to forget the reason why he who looks for Beauty actually looks for it. Diotima, however, assessed that ἔρως was an ἔρως of beauty inasmuch as only in beauty some sort of procreation can take place. Now if we grant to these words all the weight they merit, and if we then read again Diotima's last words, maybe we shall find the reason Apollodorus uses those exact words. As a matter of fact, once we attain the supreme contemplation—explains Diotima—we shall not be still and enter the numbness of an ecstatic experience. Procreation and ποίησις—the means that

[12] We say with the *last* words of Diotima, i.e., with the end of the ascent, for one could say that Apollodorus in what concerns Diotima's teaching has not yet reached the final steps that lead to the crucial ἐποπτεία.

[13] This traditional understanding of contemplation is expressed, e.g., by Brochard: ". . . la contemplation purement intellectuelle est toujours aux yeux de Platon la forme la plus parfaite de la vie. L'amour est un conducteur qui nous amène jusqu'à ce terme suprême, mais quand nous y parvenons son rôle est achevé. Il n'a plus qu'à se retirer pour faire place à ce qui est plus noble et plus divin que lui, l'intuition pure de la raison," Victor Brochard, *Études de Philosophie Ancienne et de Philosophie Moderne* (Paris: J. Vrin, 1926), p. 80.

led us to θεωρία—shall not stop there, as if there they could find their own negation. However, our fruits will be of a different kind. Once that instance has been reached, virtues will be engendered, but not fake ones; our offspring will not be εἴδωλα ἀρετῆς[14] anymore, but true ἀρετή.

According to a famous passage of the *Sophist*,[15] an εἴδωλον can be an εἰκών—if it conserves the essential symmetry of the model—or a φάντασμα—if it corrupts that symmetry. Plato does not present there the εἴδωλον as something negative in itself. A few lines later in that same dialogue, we are told that the sophist's λόγοι are like φαντάσματα ἐν τοῖς λόγοις.[16] But then—not caring about his own taxonomy, as he usually does—Plato speaks of those λόγοι simply as εἴδωλα λεγόμενα.[17] The reason is that already the fact that the λόγος as an image points to certain degradation, one necessary to every μίμεσις as such. On the other hand, leaving out the *Sophist*, and, as Kerényi[18] correctly observes, the very word εἴδωλον implies a definitive negative connotation. Homer describes the shadows of the dead as εἴδωλα.[19] There seems to be a certain superficiality in the word, almost as if the similitude were situated on a surface that retains the characters of an empty identity, an identity that resembles the very nothingness and which, notwithstanding, should be identical to something. Εἴδωλα are also the images gods produce to deceive men.[20]

Later in the *Symposium*, we hear of εἰκόνες, of similes, at the beginning of Alcibiades' eulogy of Socrates.[21] But almost at the same time, precisely as one of those similes, the word ἄγαλμα appears.[22] We cannot find this word in the *Sophist*. Ἄγαλμα has a profound meaning. The word—before meaning "statue of a god"

---

14 *Symposium*, 212a4.
15 Cf. *Sophist*, 235b–236e.
16 *Sophist*, 234e1–2.
17 *Sophist*, 234c5–6.
18 Cf. Karl Kerényi, *Scritti Italiani* (Napoli: Guida Editori, 1993), pp. 83–97.
19 Cf. *Iliad* XXIII, 72; *Odyssey*, XI, 475; XXIV, 14.
20 Cf. *Iliad* V, 451; *Odyssey*, IV, 476.
21 *Symposium*, 215a5.
22 *Symposium*, 215b3.

or "holy image"—signifies "glory" and "delight."[23] It derives from ἀγάλλω (to glorify, to exalt) and ἀγάλλομαι (to rejoice exceedingly) and it engenders ἀγαλλίασις (great joy), a word that in the vulgate of the *New Testament* is rendered as *exultatio*. Socrates bears something like ἀγάλματα, holy, delightful images—not εἴδωλα. Thus, in Kerényi's opinion, the surface of the ἄγαλμα is not merely superficial; it launches one into another dimension: the dimension of the joy that identifies itself with its source. Presence and transcendence are ineluctably united in this word, whose very religious meaning opposes it to the idea of εἴδωλον, a plain, empty surface.

Maybe the εἴδωλα ἀρετῆς produced by everyone who has not yet experienced the very Beauty itself should be opposed to these ἀγάλματα that Socrates seems to shelter within himself. Then we should speak—as Alcibiades does—of ἀγάλματα ἀρετῆς[24]—of a virtue practiced in the joy of θεωρία. And maybe then we could see in that very opposition the cipher of another opposition, the one Apollodorus refers to, namely that between a state in which one *thinks* to do something and the certainty of true ποίησις. The first one would produce εἴδωλα, whereas the second would bring forth ἀγάλματα, true virtues.

Having reached this point, we should also conclude that Apollodorus' words follow Diotima's teaching rightly, and that true θεωρία is real ποίησις, and true philosophy is not true θεωρία if it is not, at the same time, true ποίησις. We cannot only talk about a ποίησις that seeks θεωρία, but also about a more real ποίησις, founded upon a supreme θεωρία.

[23] Cf. Liddell-Scott-Jones (LSJ), *A Greek-English Lexicon* (Oxford: Oxford University Press, 1996), p. 5.

[24] *Symposium*, 222a4.

# Megaric Philosophy Between Socrates' Influence and Parmenides' Ghost

Claudia T. Mársico

## Summary

The theoretical origins of Megaric philosophy have been discussed at length. The ancient sources refer to the influence of Socratism and Eleatism on Euclid, but some more recent studies deny that his last current of thought had any importance in the formation of the Megaric theses. This article studies the disadvantages of this proposal and sets out to show that it is necessary to consider the Eleatic influence. In order to support this point, it examines some aspects of Euclid's position and their connections with Parmenidean philosophy. Then, three doctrines of later authors associated with the Megaric line (Eubulides, Diodorus Cronus, and Stilpo) are examined in order to show the presence of Eleatic approaches and its persistence and relevance for the theoretical identity of the group.

The Socratic philosophers have for a long time received the attribute of "minors." Because of this minority, anyone who observes the few conserved testimonies feels that he is going into the house of the poor relatives of Greek philosophy. They have often been considered a gang of weak thinkers that became a bit famous because they were students or companions of real philosophers—the golden group consisting of Socrates, Plato and Aristotle. These real philosophers are supposed to construct their theories including the complete rejection of their theoretical adversaries, who, because of their incompetence, their perversion or both, cannot cast a shadow over them.

Despite changes in the approach to classic antiquity during the last decades, the custom to begin works dedicated to "minor" authors with some excuses remains. In a certain sense, we could say that the judgment that closes the introduction of the traditional work of H. Kitto is intact: "I have tried not to idealize, though I deal with the great men rather than the little ones, and with philosophers rather than rogues. It is from the mountain-tops that one gets the views: and rogues are much the same everywhere—though the Greek rogue seems rarely to have been dull as well as wicked."[1] The risks of this perspective are clear: we confine ourselves to the selection of tradition, which usually do not agree with the judgments of the ancients themselves, who are less inclined to this "mountaineering" practiced by the critics.

In the case of the Socratics, this situation is extreme, because their texts are almost completely lost. Thus, the scornful view about these authors, sketched like rather eccentric figures who propose anti-intuitive theses, contrasts severely with the theoretical connections that can be observed when we study their works in dialogue with other currents of thought. If we do so, the importance of their positions in the intellectual field of the classical age becomes manifest. This is our "excuse."

In what follows, I will not concentrate on the relation between Megarics and their contemporaries and heirs, but on the connections between them and their predecessors, in order to review the problem of the Eleatic origin of this doctrine. The relevance of this point becomes manifest when we ask about the identity of the Megaric group and the Socratics in general.

---

The problem regarding the origin of the Megaric group refers to Euclid. The traditional historiography maintained that his position combined Socratism and Eleatism. Diogenes Laertius says that "Euclid practiced the beliefs of Parmenides,"[2]

[1] Humphrey D. Kitto, *The Greeks* (Harmondsworth: Penguin, 1951), p. 11.

[2] Diogenes Laertius, II.106 (= Filósofos socráticos, *Testimonios y fragmentos. I. Megáricos y Cirenaicos*, Introducción, traducción y notas de Claudia Mársico

and the same association between Euclid and Parmenides is also outlined explicitly by Aristocles.[3] This double origin gave rise to the theoretical nucleus exposed by Diogenes: "the good is one, although it is called by many names: sometimes good sense, other divinity, other intelligence, etc. Also he <sc. Euclid> rejected the opposite of good, saying that it does not exist." Traditionally it was considered that this passage contains three basic theses that characterize the position of Euclid: 1) the good is one; 2) language multiplies and attributes many names to this unity; 3) the opposite of good does not exist; therefore, reality and good are the same. From the link between these theses arose the identification of being, good and one (ὄν, ἀγαθόν, ἕν), i.e., a synthesis of the Eleatic and Socratic lines. We could see, according to Zeller, the reduction of Socratism by the Eleatic influence, or an integration of both lines, which implied an ethical transformation of the Parmenidean ὄν and an ontological transformation of the Socratic perspective. H. von Arnim, P. Natorp, W. Nestle, L. Robin, G. Field, among others, support positions like this. More recently Rankin, Canto, and Dorion adopted this interpretation.[4]

This way of reading was soon interrupted by the work of Karl von Fritz in 1931, who denied the relation between Eleatism and Megarism, showing that the Megaric theses derive from the

---

(Buenos Aires: Losada, 2010) [= *FS*], 83; Gabriele Giannantoni, *Socrates et Socraticorum Reliquiae* (Napoli: Bibliopolis, 1990) [= *SSR*], II.A.30).

[3] *On Philosophy*, 2 (= Eusebius, *Preparation for the Gospel*, XIV.17.1, p. 756 b–c; *FS*, 302; *SSR*, II.O.26).

[4] Eduard Zeller, *Die Philosophie der Griechen in ihrer geschichtlichen Entwicklung* (Leipzig: Reisland, 1923), pp. II.1.251ff; Hans von Arnim, *Leben und Werke des Dio von Prusa* (Berlin: K. Barr &J. Asmussen, 1898), pp. 21ff; P. Natorp, *Pauly's Real-Encyclopädie*, Sup. VI.1, s.v. *Eukleides* (Stuttgart: Druckenmüller, 1907), coll. 1001ff; Wilhelm Nestle, *Die Sokratiker in Auswahl* (Jena: Diederichs, 1922), pp. 40ff..; Leon Robin, *La pensée grecque et les origines de l'esprit scientifique*, (Paris: Albin Michel, 1973; 1st edition, Paris: La Rennaissance due Livre, 1923), p. 205; Guy C. Field, *Plato and his Contemporaries: A Study in Fourth Century Life and Thought* (3rd Edition, London: Methuen, 1967), pp. 169ff.; Herbert D. Rankin, *Anthisthenes (sic) Sokratikos* (Amsterdam: Hakkert, 1983), pp. 190ff.; Platon, *Euthydème*, Introduction, traduction et notes par M. Canto (Paris: Garnier-Flammarion, 1989), pp. 57–58; Aristote, *Refutations sophistiques*, Introduction, traduction et notes par A. Dorion (Paris: Vrin, 1995), pp. 54.

Socratic notion of the good.[5] The studies of Guthrie and Döring develop, with different emphasis, this exegetical way.[6] In turn, Giannantoni concludes "[. . .] it is possible to conjecture by the content of Euclid's works and their titles, that we are in front of a type of literary activity completely 'Socratic' and nothing induce us to suppose some study about ontological or metaphysical problems in the field of the Eleatic tradition."[7] Nevertheless, what does it mean to strictly emphasize the Socratic mark? Since this thesis is usually associated with the denial of unity regarding the Megaric group and the supposition that common aspects are a projection of later doxography, do we not run the risk of circularity? That is, we deny a metaphysical dimension in Euclid's proposal, but as soon as these treatments are undeniable in other authors, like Diodorus or Stilpo, we deduce that the group does not have theoretical cohesion. Instead, although the Megaric group is not a school in the strict sense, I propose that it is necessary to consider the Eleatic influence as we try to understand the basic points of his position.

We have already said, regarding Diogenes' testimony, that Euclid seems to have maintained that language multiplies the unity as in the example about virtue in Diogenes Laertius VII.161 (*FS*, 86 = *SSR*, II.A.32). It is said that it is one, but receives many names. This is the ground for a great part of the Megaric activity: it is necessary to construct arguments in order to show, through paradoxes, the incoherencies in language, and, therefore, the inconvenience to use it as a medium to grasp reality. In any case, we could say, the Megarics interpret the idea about "to take refuge in language," proposed by Plato in *Phaedo* 99d5, as an easy way to get lost.

This opposition between unity and multiplicity allows a reference to Parmenides' poem, in which we find an explicit mention of the problems of adequacy between language and

5 Karl von Fritz, *Pauly's Real-Encyclopädie*, Sup. V, s.v. Megariker (Stuttgart: Druckenmüller, 1931), coll. 707ff.

6 William K. Guthrie, *A History of Greek Philosophy*, Volume III: *The Fifth-Century Enlightenment* (Cambridge: Cambridge University Press, 1971), pp. 489ff.; Klaus Döring, *Die Megariker: Kommentierte Sammlung der Testimonien* (Amsterdam: Grüner, 1972), pp. 82ff.

7 *SSR*, IV, p. 51.

reality. Thus in 28B8.52, Parmenides speaks of the "deceptive order of my words" (κόσμον ἐμῶν ἐπέων ἀπατηλόν), that mark the beginning of the second part of the poem concerning the opinions of the mortals. Indeed, the goddess judges it necessary to know that "they resolved to name two Forms" in order to name the appearances and that in this point "they have gone astray" (28B8.53ff.). At least in this aspect, it is manifest that the Megarics adopted a Parmenidean perspective. Equally clear is the critique of the way in which the human language expresses reality in 28B19. There, he says: "men bestowed a name to give its mark to each thing." Here we have an association between multiplicity and arbitrariness. For this reason, we can doubt the capacity of language to grasp reality. This idea will reappear among the Megarics.

---

Strictly speaking, the philosophy of Parmenides gradually became a theoretical frame regarding which, to a large extent, the later tradition defined itself. This is clear in the Gorgianic system, constructed as the rejection of the Parmenidean proposal, as well as in Antisthenes' position, which equally derives from the Eleatic scheme, or in Platonic philosophy, which ends in tragedy, through parricide. In these last two cases, we find Socratic authors who adopt ontological tenets to answer the "Socratic question." We can add to this context doxographical testimonies like that of Aristocles, already mentioned, where he affirms that the Megarics maintained "that being is one and nothing else exists, neither is generated, nor destroyed, nor moves under any circumstances." The philosophy of Parmenides must have seemed to Euclid a good theoretical matrix to explain theses about the Good and the unity of virtue, which are associated with the historical Socrates.

Despite these objections, let us suppose that the position of Euclid can be interpreted in strictly ethical terms, without an ontological dimension. If so, the activity of Euclid's disciples revealed that they felt the necessity to add this aspect, and therefore they finally approached Eleatism. Let us look at three examples. Eubulides, Euclid's direct disciple, is known as the author of a series of dialectic arguments, like the Sorites and the Horned, among others. In the first case, he deals with the vagueness of certain terms like "many" or "few." Diogenes Laertius says about this: "this is not the case that two are few but three are not also. It is not the case these are and four are not also. And so on up to ten. And two are few, therefore ten are also."[8] This is an antecedent regarding important tenets of contemporary logic. Indeed, Eubulides attracted attention to the impossibility of determining the notion of a pile and thus to the faults that affect the information of the senses. As Aspasius says: "among sensible things none of them can be grasped accurately, but in general and in an approximate way."[9] In the case of the Horned—"what you have not lost you still have. But you have not lost horns. So you still have horns,"[10]—Eubulides distrusts the effectiveness of the deduction, because it could lead to believe in the existence of something clearly non-existent, as the horns in this example. The view that arises from Eubulides' arguments shows that the frame of Parmenidean thought is present: mortals are mistaken when they use names, so linguistics can lead to error.

---

The position of Diodorus Cronus shows a Parmenidean inspiration as well. Among his doctrines, several of which illustrate my thesis, let us take two cases. He associates reality and intelligible level in a way that places the sensible things thoroughly separate. This option gives rise to the problem regarding the explanation of the physical level. Nevertheless, in the same way Parmenides has an explanatory device for the many in the last part of the poem, as has Diodoro. He talks about a kind of atomism, with several consequences in his doctrine.[11] This thesis could have already been present in the Euclidian position.

[8] Diogenes Laertius, VII 82 (= *FS*, 170).

[9] Aspasius, *Commentary in Aristotle's* Ethics, 56.32–57.3 (= *FS*, 167).

[10] Seneca, *Letters*, 49.8 (= *FS*, 184).

[11] Stricltly speaking, the sources outline these bodies as *amerê*, "without parts." This seems a lexical terminological alternative for the traditional *átomos*. Surely, the change in the denomination implies a doctrinal difference. Indeed, the Diodorean thought stresses the pure simplicity of these elements and not only the impossibility of further division.

Indeed, it has been noticed that when Plato mentions the Friends of Forms, in *Sophist*, 246 b–c, he says that they "crumble <the bodies> in small pieces," which could be a reference to the doctrine of the indivisibles. If we accept that this could be a veiled mention of the Megarics, it would reveal, as early as Euclid's time, that they explain the sensible level with a kind of atomism. If so, this is in association with the structure of certain dialectic arguments, like the Sorites, as already mentioned.

Some authors have pointed out that this thesis contradicts the Megaric monism, and therefore it would be just a dialectic hypothesis, that is, something that is not accepted by Diodorus.[12] Nevertheless, this thesis does not affect intelligible entities, the real ones. It is just an explanatory device for the sensible level, in the same way that, in the final verses of B8, Parmenides begins with a reasonable explanation about the many. Furthermore, within the framework of the discussions on inference,[13] this thesis is mentioned as an example of true proposition, so it would be really absurd if it were a dialectic hypothesis in which Diodorus did not believe.

Moreover, this kind of doctrine is the base of Diodorean developments like the impossibility of present movement. The sources transmit the idea that it can be said that something has moved, but it is impossible to say that something is moving, adding that this idea agrees with Eleatic thesis.[14] Diodorus says: what exists must be in a place, but what is in a place is quiet, so that its movement is impossible. This surely reminds us of Zenonian arguments.[15] It is worth noting that this is not just a logical ruse, but an idea based on a theoretical system that supposes the thesis of the indivisibles. From this framework, the Megarics deduce that language does not constitute a reliable representation of reality. On the contrary, whole sectors of the

[12] See, among recent interpretations, Döring (*Die Megariker*), p. 129.

[13] See Sextus Empirius, *Outlines of Pyrrhonism*, II.110–1 (= *FS*, 232; *SSR*, II.F.19).

[14] See, for instance, Sextus Empiricus, *Against the Professors*, X.48 (= *FS*, 224; *SSR*, II.F.12).

[15] Sextus connects Diodorus with Parmenides and Melissus. See Döring (*Die Megariker*), pp. 129–131, and Robert Muller, *Les Megariques: Fragments et témoignages* (Paris: J. Vrin, 1985), pp. 137–141.

structure of language, like the number and tense systems, do not have a correlation with real entities.

---

As a third example, let us turn briefly to Stilpo of Megara. Diogenes Laertius says about him that he rejected Platonic Forms and affirmed that "when somebody says 'man', he does not mention anybody, because neither he says this one nor that one. Then, why would he be mentioning more this man than that one? Therefore, this one is never mentioned."[16] In spite of the brevity of this testimony, which only adds the example of "vegetable," it is possible to suggest a parallel between Stilpo's argument and the Third Man argument attributed to Polixenus. Polixenus is often associated with the Megaric movement. He said that Plato's theory of participation supposes that man exists through participation in the Idea, but that this situation cannot apply to the Man himself, because he *is* the Idea; nor can it apply to the individuals. Therefore, a third man must exist who is neither the Man nor the Idea.[17] There is no explanation of the reason why the individual cannot participate in the eidetical sphere, but it is possible that the argument of Stilpo regarding the lack of correlation between the individual and the Idea has been an assumption of the argument of Polixenus. The approaches are only superficially different: while Polixenus says that the particular man does not participate in the Idea, Stilpo, conversely, says that Ideas are associated with universal names, so they are useless for mentioning particular entities. This is coherent with Platonic passages like *Republic* X 596a, where it is said that there are Ideas for all for which we have a name. It is worth noting that this testimony about Polixenus appears in a work against Diodorus—surely Diodorus Cronus—and this emphasizes the idea that the Megaric group has certain theoretical constants that give it cohesion. Furthermore, this cohesion is based on topics directly related to Eleatism.

---

[16] Diogenes Laertius, II 119 (= *FS*, 303; *SSR*, II.O.27).

[17] Alexander of Aphrodisias, *On Aristotle's* Metaphysics, 84.16–21 (= *FS*, 132; *SSR*, II.T.10).

---

This brief series of examples can be expanded. It shows clearly that the theoretical framework of the Megaric group studies the relation between language and reality in a way that agrees with the Parmenidean—or Eleatic in general—approach. This is the point of departure for a revision on the links between Megarism and Eleatism, and, therefore, shows the Megaric philosophy as a theoretical space animated by the figure of Parmenides. Parmenides is, as Plato says, venerable and awesome, and his influence is alive, although changed, in later philosophy, especially among the Megaric group through its suspicion and its denunciation of the deceptive order of words.

# Plato's *Sophist* on Negation and Not-Being

Fabián Mié

## Summary

This brief paper develops an interpretation of Plato's theory of negation understood as an answer to Parmenides' paradoxes concerning not-being. First, I consider some aspects that result from an analysis of *Sophist* 257b–259d, formulating some general theses which I then go on to unfold in more detail in the following section. Finally, I show what exactly Plato's so-called overcoming of the Eleatic problem related to negation and falsehood is; and I outline some of the main semantic and metaphysical consequences that are entailed by this overcoming.

## 1. Plato's relocation of "not" as a solution to Parmenides' problem

At the end of the passage in Plato's *Sophist* that is dedicated to the analysis of the combination between the greatest kinds emerges the thesis according to which the not-being must be firmly established as something that is not and, like every idea, as something which has its own nature. This may be the main result of the investigation that was meant to examine the problems of the Parmenidean *dictum*, expressed in the only possible way that fragment 2 of the Poem declares viable, the one in which being is and not-being is not (fr. 2.3). This same way—Parmenides' Way of Truth in the Poem—had also been clearly judged in the dialogue at 241d7 as paradoxically not viable, since Parmenides' theory did not allow us to explain one of our most elementary comprehensive abilities, the one that permits us to work with the negation and to admit the possibility of the falsehood. Plato's idea is that if not-being were not accepted, falsehood would not be possible (237a3–4; 241a9–b3).

The postulation of the idea of not-being as a necessary condition to justify some of our basic linguistic practices as well as the use of negative predicates and the meaning of false statements constitutes, therefore, a first relevant topic of the *Sophist*. A second one, on which I will also focus in this paper, is an ontological one. It lies namely in the formulation of some metaphysical central tools which introduce clearly anti-Eleatic features in our ontology. The main metaphysical tool of Plato's *Sophist* consists in accepting not-being in its only admissible sense, that is to say, as *difference* (255b3–4, c8–10, d1), and rejecting the ontological monism that Plato considers directly associated with an erroneous semantic that, in the end, does not account for predication and in which there only exist *names* that would apparently name the only reality of its correlate.

## 2. Naming and negating

Let us now characterize in a loose way some of the main theses that emerge from the aforementioned passage (*Sophist* 257d–259d).

(i) Parmenides' thesis arises from a basic misconception of the primary function of language, which he reduces to naming something. In this way, the sophistic thesis about the impossibility of falsehood, which Plato discusses in the *Sophist*, must be understood as a consequence of Parmenidean exclusion of the "not" from its original place in language, namely in the predicative statement, and of the erroneous Eleatic assimilation of the function of the negative particle to a negation of the subject-name. Such assimilation, in turn, gives rise to expressions like "not-being," in which "being" appears as the name of an object. The Eleatic rejection of the "not" is, at the same time, a consequence of comprehending the statements wrongly as if its function were the mere *nominal identification* of a single or atomic object. Therefore, the Parmenidean rejection of "not" as a meaningful function of language is based on and, at the same time implies, a theory of names, which involves the supposition that names are doing his complete linguistic work in language without any logical relation to other linguistic functions.

(ii) Taking loosely Tugendhat's[1] reconstruction of the argument that Plato would attribute to Parmenides, we obtain the following:

(1) "*s* thinks/says that *x is not*"

equals Parmenides in

(2) "*s* thinks/says (the) *nothing*";

(2) implies that the negation operates as negation of the object. Besides, according to the perceptual model, applied to the epistemic operations of thinking/saying, Parmenides would clarify (2) in terms of

(3) "*s does not* think/say,"

from which we can infer that (2) is impossible or unacceptable. Parmenides takes the function of "not" in (1) according to the objectual or nominal sense of the negation of something, of a being. And he does this in the following way: whoever thinks/says that something *is not*, thinks/says the *not-being*, since to think/say *what is not* equals to think/say that *something is nothing* (fragment 8, 10; fr. 6.2), which in the end is at the same time absurd, because of (3). In this way, not-being is introduced as the absurd specter to which we should commit ourselves if we accepted the negation in our linguistic uses mentioned in (1). Thereafter, the prohibited Way of not-being commits the following absurdity:

(4) "*s* thinks/says the *not-being*,"

[1] Tugendhat, "Das Sein," pp. 36–66, 48f.

where the completive grammatical form of the sentence through which "not" in the predicative part of the statement would be introduced in (1) has disappeared, being replaced in (4) by the nominalized use of the negation.

If we accepted (1), we should admit (4) to explain the supposition of (2). (4) clarifies that the "nothing" of (2) means "not-being." The "not" would lead us, then, to negate the act of thinking/saying, as in (3). And (3) would be taken by Parmenides as a thought (*act*) without thought (*content*), that is, as a meaningless thought containing a senseless expression—the negative particle—which does not refer to some being in the world. Parmenides develops such analysis under the *perceptual* model through which he would understand thinking and saying. Under the powerful influence of this model, thinking or saying something negatively qualified would equal "seeing without seeing anything," which implies the elimination of the visual act and the corresponding act of thought as a consequence of having accepted the negation of the content by not having excluded, at the beginning, the use of "not" as a deceptive resource of human language.

If the previous reconstruction of the Parmenidean rejection of negation is right, we can claim to have a plausible explanation of Plato's criticism of Parmenides' odd and strict philosophical thesis about being, according to which whatever we think of, necessarily is. The monistic thesis, along with which being is the only possible thing, was read by Plato as a consequence of the only form that is accepted by Parmenides as a possible correlate of thinking/saying, that is, a simple and absolute unified object, without any logical relation to any other thing. Parmenides' metaphysics was for Plato a coherent but paradoxical result of the prohibition of the "not" as a non-sense and deceptive expression.

(iii) To Parmenides, admitting not-being would imply nonsensical terms with the semantic form of "the not-real." He arrives at this thesis as a consequence of incorrectly placing the "not," conceiving it as if this particle would make a backward movement that would cancel the one made through the mere denomination of something.

(iv) Plato correctly transfers the "not" to the predicative expression. The Platonic negation now does not make such expressions as "the not-real," but operates on the assertive place of a statement, that is to say, on the predicate, allowing to make sentences in which what is said about something is not the case and avoiding, thanks to the change of the position of "not," that which is being negated would equal zero.

(v) In addition, through the negation we can discover "what it is" as long as the propositional function of "not" articulates the subject in its own *how*, and this requires, consequently, a new theory of language, which the *Sophist* develops by appealing to the combination of being and not-being and clarifying that "what it is" is expressed through the propositional form ". . . *is* . . ." or ". . . *is not* . . .," wherein "is" is used in an incomplete sense.[2]

## 3. The parts of otherness

The form of otherness and its parts, a controversial doctrine that the *Sophist* introduces in 258d5–259d7, is postulated to explain that everything that is *is—. . . and is not—. . .* Let us examine it briefly:

(i) 258e6–259a2: The Parmenidean theory of an *absolute or nominal not-being* (238c9–12), understood as contrary (258b3) to the absolute being, has been discarded some time ago in the dialogue (237b), because it entails a complete non-sense (259a1). Instead, the theory of the

[2] Frede, *Prädikation;* Brown, "Being," pp. 49–70.

combination of the greatest kinds allows the Stranger from Elea to establish the *reality* of not-being (259a2), understood as what supports the predication of something different from what the subject really is.

(ii) 259a4–b1: The contribution of the theory of the greatest kinds to the Platonic explanation of the negation is stated there in the following way:

(a) Being and difference go through all the kinds and they interrelate with each other (259a4–6), in so far as everything that is delimits their identity differentiating themselves from a multiplicity of other things in which this thing does not participate. Besides, what is not delimits everything that is different from the properties which constitute the identity of something. Consequently, what is not draws up the boundaries of the group of properties, which are equally real among themselves, but different from those in which a specific object participates.

(b) Insofar as the not-being participates of being, it *is*; but, since its own nature consists in delimiting everything that is different from what constitutes the specific identity of a thing, the not-being is not the *same* as what a thing really is, but precisely different from it. *The reality of not-being consists in that it is not* (259a6–b1). To make this possible, not-being does not have to be understood in an absolute way, but as something which *participates of being* (258e6–7).

(iii) 259b1–6: The apparently paradoxical identity of not-being is solved if we take into account that being is not, too, since "what it is" is not, for Plato, something undifferentiated. The bare fact that something *is*, does not entail that what is lacks relationships with different properties. In other words, the apparent paradoxical *identity* of the Platonic being, which bears the *difference*, is explained because "being," just as "not-being," is not for Plato the sign of an object. The nominal grammatical form, "the being," does not seem to have deceived Plato, tempting him to postulate an object as "the reality" *apart from* the real objects. "Being" and "not-being" do not have a nominal sense; the sentences in which they appear mean the identity and the difference, respectively. That is why, everything that is *is—. . . and is not—. . .* "Being" and "not-being" mean neither specific classes, like "man" or "horse," nor its contraries, but they constitute the *formal structure* through which every specific determination is possible.[3] "Being" and "not-being" are signs of the *combination among ideas that constitute the reality of each object.* For this reason, the being of something includes explicitly or tacitly its difference with regard to other things whose definitional properties are different from the ones that constitute the own identity of the object (259b2–5).

(iv) 255c12–13: The *things which are* are *identical* or *different*, that is to say, "what it is" is always *articulated* whether in an affirmative way with the properties that constitute its identity, or in a negative way with those other properties from which it differentiates. Here, identity and difference are the *formal structures* that *go through* every relationship among ideas *making them possible*, that is to say, making possible the determination of each entity via its participation in ideas. Something participates of the identity in so far as it takes part of those forms that determine its sameness. But the identity, the same as the difference, is not one more form of the same type of which an object participates in the definition of its sameness. Identity and difference are not specific kinds, but ideas that *formally* structure the determination of any object. Negation is explained, then, through this structural form by which Socrates' sameness, in fact, delimits a scope of the incompatible

[3] Gill, "Method," section 5.2.

properties and different predicates that are *not* said of it with truth.[4]

(v) Plato claims that the nature of otherness is divided in "parts" (257c5–258c5, 258d5–e3),[5] which is coherent with the *formality* of this idea, since the parts of the difference are delimited as those which *are not* the same as those that a certain thing participates in. Each part of not-being has, in this way, a positive reality, since what is not—. . . means only what is not *F, G, H,* so long as these properties do not constitute the sameness of *x*. However, as what is not is merely a property that is found in an *antithetical* relationship (258b1–4), that is to say, it is *incompatible* with the ones that are the *same* in relation to *x*, the properties that are *other* in relation to the ones that are said to be of *x* with truth are not, themselves, less real (258a9, b2, c3, e2–3). In fact, the negative predicates do not introduce *not-objects,* something *contrary* to a Parmenidean *absolute-being* (258b3), but the parts of not-being are the correlates of the negation applied to the assertive function of a statement that predicates certain things of *x*.[6]

## 4. The negation explained in the metaphysical terms of identity and difference

Furthermore, the Platonic solution to the Parmenidean problems of not-being and falsehood through a clarification of the use of "not" is sufficiently general so as to give space not only to contradictory predicates but also to contrary predicates. The contradictory ones are those which can be characterized as members of two statements which, being mutually inconsistent, do not leave room for a third statement that includes a predicate inconsistent with both previous statements. This is the case of the logically exhaustive antithesis, but scarcely informative, between "big" and "not big." On the other hand, contrary predicates are those that belong

[4] For further details on this interpretation, see my book, *Dialéctica,* pp. 47–100.
[5] Owen, "Not-Being," pp. 223–267, 232ff.; Lee, "Negation," 267–303.
[6] Szaif, *Wahrheit,* pp. 436ff., 446–453.

to sentences which can give room to a third statement including a third predicate that is inconsistent with the two initially opposite predicates. This is the case of the antithesis between "white" and "black." There is a mutual relationship of opposition in antithetical terms between what is and what is not (258b1).

Plato thinks that the restricted interweaving of the greatest kinds assures the participation between specific forms, and he assumes that this doctrine also allows us to justify the primary predicative function of the language (259e4–6), saving it from its annihilation. The diagnosis that motivates Plato's therapy of "not," manifests that if we do exclude the combination among forms, which is useful for giving account of our operation with the negation, we will be deprived of the language (260a8–9). This, in turn, supposes a frontal rejection to reduce the linguistic functions to naming, as well as to vindicate naming as the primary linguistic function.

Finally, the *Sophist* maintains that identification comes specifically through a method of division, which aims to fix the complex definition of a thing by means of genus and differentiae. Such a theory of definition implies a claim according to which identification entails the articulation of the multiplicity that is comprised within the inner structure of each entity. In this way, the form of the difference plays, in the end, the role of a necessary presupposition, to explain not only *predication* but also *identification*.

Translated by Marcela Leiva

# Bibliography


Brown, Lesley. "Being in the *Sophist*: A Syntactical Inquiry." *In Oxford Studies in Ancient Philosophy* 4 (1986): 49–70.

Diels, Hermann, and Walther Kranz. *Die Fragmente der Vorsokratiker*, 3 Volumes. Berlin: Weidmann, 1903. 6th edition with final editing and revisions by W. Kranz, 1952. Editions after the 6th are mainly reprints with little or no change. References are to the 1992[18] Edition.

Duke, E. A., W. F. Hicken, W. S. M. Nicoll, D. B. Robinson, J. C. G. Strachan, eds., *Platonis Opera*. Tomus I. Tetralogias I–II continens. Recognoverunt brevique adnotatione critica instruxerunt. Oxford Classical Texts. Oxford: Oxford University Press, 1995.

Frede, Michael. *Prädikation und Existenzaussage. Platons Gebrauch von „... ist ..." und „... ist nicht ..." im* Sophistes. Göttingen: Vandenhoeck & Ruprecht, 1967.

Gill, Mary Louise. "Method and Metaphysics in Plato's *Sophist* and *Statesman*." In Edward N. Zalta, ed., *The Stanford Encyclopedia of Philosophy* (Fall 2008 Edition). Available online: http://plato.stanford.edu/archives/fall2008/entries/plato-sophstate/.

Heidegger, Martin. *Platon:* Sophistes. Gesamtausgabe II. Abteilung, Bd. 19. Edited by I. Schüssler. Frankfurt am Main: Klostermann, 1992.

Lee, E. N. "Plato on Negation and Not-Being in the *Sophist*." In *The Philosophical Review* 81 (1972): 267–303.

Mié, Fabián. *Dialéctica, Predicación y Metafísica en Platón. Investigaciones sobre el* Sofista *y los diálogos tardíos.* Córdoba: Ediciones del Copista, 2004.

Owen, G. E. L. "Plato on Not-Being." In Gregory Vlastos, ed., *Plato I. Metaphysics and Epistemology. A Collection of Critical Essays* (pp. 223–267). Garden City: Doubleday & Anchor, 1971.

Ryle, Gilbert. "Letters and Syllables in Plato." In *The Philosophical Review* 69 (1960): 431–452.

Szaif, Jan. *Platons Begriff der Wahrheit.* Freiburg im Breisgau/München: Alber, 1998[3].

Tugendhat, Ernst. "Das Sein und das Nichts." In *Philosophische Aufsätze* (pp. 36–66). Frankfurt am Main: Suhrkamp, 1992.

# Parmenides and His Precursors

## A Borgesian Reading of Cordero's Parmenides

Lucas Soares


### Summary

In this paper I focus primarily on Cordero's Parmenides and the basic nucleus of the reading in his most recent book—*By Being, It is* (2004)—on Parmenides' "venerable," "profound," and "enigmatic" philosophical thesis. Secondly, I undertake a Borgesian reading of the Parmenides that arises from this book. In other words, a reading of a reading.


Borges writes at the beginning of his short essay "Pascal's Sphere" that "it may be that universal history is the history of a handful of metaphors."[1] If we apply this phrase to the history of philosophy, it could be said that it is the history of a handful of concepts (namely, being, nothingness, becoming, truth, opinion). It is a matter of thinking of the history of philosophy not under any criteria of author or era, but from a series of basic concepts that have been and continue to be resignified throughout history by different philosophers. If the history of philosophy is the history of a few concepts, of all the concepts that make up a glossary of philosophy there is one that holds a privileged and fundamental place, the first letter in the philosophy alphabet: the concept of being. Its creator (because philosophy, as Deleuze and Guattari

---

[1] Jorge L. Borges, "La Esfera de Pascal," in J. L. Borges, *Otras Inquisiciones, Obras Completas,* Vol. II (Buenos Aires: Emecé, 1989), p. 14.

argue, "is the discipline that consists of *creating* concepts"[2] was Parmenides of Elea. From Parmenides to Heidegger, everything revolves around the nascent philosophical adventure of being that starts the former's Poem. Fragment 5 of the Poem frames the history of philosophy perfectly, when the goddess states that "it is the same for me from what place I should begin, for to that place I shall come back again." The road of the history of philosophy is, like Parmenidean truth, circular, and regressive: it begins with being and returns to being. The starting part is the same as the arrival point. It is Heidegger's "step back": "Only when we return with thinking to what has already been thought are we at the service of what is to be thought. For us, the conversation with the history of thought is no longer a matter of elevation, but a step back."[3] Because in philosophy, by going back one advances. To advance thus means returning to the fact of being. That is, returning to Parmenides' thesis. From here the paternal place that Parmenides holds in the history of philosophy is related to his being the father of the concept of being. Perhaps this was what Plato meant when he spoke in the *Sophist* of the "father" Parmenides,[4] of a "venerable and fearsome"[5] father, whose philosophy holds for him a highly "profound and enigmatic"[6] nature, where the "venerable" and "fearsome" entity may not be as much Parmenides as his thesis, the fact of being, for which he is no more than a medium. Despite the numerous parricides—starting with Plato—to which Parmenides was subjected, that paternal place that he holds to this day becomes patent in view of the unavoidable modernity of the object of his study: the fact of being.

But how to find Parmenides among so many Parmenideses? Especially when, as Cordero writes, "if there is a pre-Socratic author of whom the interpreter must distrust entirely the opinion

[2] Deleuze, Gilles, and Félix Guattari, *¿Qué es la filosofía?* (Barcelona: Anagrama, 1993), pp. 11, 85.

[3] Martin Heidegger, *Identidad y Diferencia* (Barcelona: Anthropos, 1988), pp. 97, 111.

[4] Plato, *Sophist* 241d.

[5] Plato, *Theaetetus* 183e.

[6] Plato, *Theaetetus* 184e.

of ancient commentators, it is Parmenides."[7] There is Plato's Parmenides, a strange hybrid of ideas taken from Parmenides himself plus elements of Zeno and Melissus; Aristotle's Parmenides, who denies the reality of movement, a fundamental postulate of physics; and the Parmenides of other ancient philosophers such as Plutarch, Sextus Empiricus and Simplicius, not to mention other Parmenideses forged in the context of modern and contemporary philosophy, such as Hegel's "idealist" Parmenides, for whom the identity between thinking and being encloses "the fundamental thinking of Parmenides," to the extent that true philosophy begins with him;[8] the Parmenides of Nietzsche, the least Greek of all in his philosophy of the tragic era, that of cold and petrifying logical abstractions;[9] Heidegger's Parmenides, in whose fragments the posterior forgetting of being still does not resonate, but rather the "dawn of deconcealment (ἀλήθεια) of being" as presence;[10] Popper's "cosmological" Parmenides;[11] the Parmenides of "inseparability of the truth faced with the multiplicity of opinions" proposed by Gadamer;[12] and lastly the Parmenides of Badiou, who subscribes to the fusion between the subjective authority of the poem and the "mathematical interruptions."[13] What can be done in order to not lose oneself amid all these Parmenideses conceived by ancient, modern and contemporary commentators? In this paper, I would like to focus primarily on one of many readings of Parmenides which, in the face of such a diversity of points of view, looks critically at this web of comments that in most cases, since we

[7] Néstor-Luis Cordero, *Siendo, Se Es: La Tesis de Parménides* (Buenos Aires: Biblos, 2005), pp. 183–184. English Edition: *By Being, It Is: The Thesis of Parmenides* (Las Vegas: Parmenides Publishing, 2004), p. 160.

[8] Georg W. F. Hegel, *Lecciones sobre la Historia de la Filosofía*, Vol. I (México: Fondo de Cultura Económica, 1955), pp. 234–235.

[9] Friedrich Nietzsche, *La Filosofía en la Época Trágica de los Griegos* (Buenos Aires: Los libros de Orfeo), pp. 34–44.

[10] Martin Heidegger, "Moira (Parménides VIII, 34–41)," in M. Heidegger, *Conferencias y Artículos* (Barcelona: Ediciones del Serbal, 1994), p. 215.

[11] Karl R. Popper, *El Mundo de Parménides. Ensayos sobre la Ilustración Presocrática* (Barcelona: Paidós, 1999).

[12] Hans G. Gadamer, "Parménides y las *Dóxai Brotòn*," in H. G. Gadamer, *El inicio de la filosofía occidental* (Barcelona: Paidós, 1995), p. 109.

[13] Alain Badiou, "El Recurso Filosófico al Poema," in A. Badiou, *Condiciones* (México: Siglo XXI, 2003), pp. 84–86.

are not talking about philosophy "historians," were made with the intention of backing up the commentators' own philosophical ideas or purely out of a fondness for erudition. I am referring to Cordero's reading in his most recent book on Parmenides: *By Being, It Is* (*Siendo, se es*).[14] Here we can read his definitive settling of accounts with Parmenides' "venerable," "profound," and "enigmatic" philosophical thesis. Secondly, I intend to undertake a Borgesian reading of the Parmenides arising from this book. In other words, a reading of a reading.

We know that the history of the transmission of ancient sources is, fundamentally, a long history of copies and recopies, a set of Russian dolls, such as Plato's masterly staging when he takes to the extreme the dramatic-philosophical use of the indirect style in dialogues such as *Symposium* and *Parmenides*, where the interference that affects the original telling of events becomes infuriating. I say this because there is, beforehand, a tragic starting point in relation to the state of the text of Parmenides' Poem, which can be extended to the quotations which, in this arch of textual references from Plato to Simplicius, are preserved from the pre-Socratic philosophers. How to reconstruct the authentic meaning of a text written in the late sixth century BCE that is known to be irremediably lost? As in tragedy, it is the attempt to reconstitute a lost order that knowledge is consumed, even when this order is never the same again. In spite of this tragic outcome, the most important thing, as always, is found in the journey, in the attempt to reconstitute a text that is as close as possible to the lost original. Because each attempt to reconstitute these nineteen incomplete quotations from Parmenides' Poem produces a *new version* of the poem and, above all, of its principal thesis. We are far from managing to reconstruct the original meaning of its ideas. But at least we can, from each interpreter's review of the manuscript sources of the Poem, distinguish an "approximate image." Whether we like it or not, with the pre-Socratics it is always a matter of an approximate image. Our knowledge of Parmenides is at stake precisely in every attempt to reconstitute an irremediably lost poem. And the most surprising aspect is

14 Cordero, *Siendo* and *By Being*.

that in each *reconstitution* the Poem opens up and continues to open up new paths of thought.

What paths are opened up by Cordero's new reconstitution of the Poem? Let us resume in general the main points of his reading. Firstly, it is a Parmenides that, without clear affiliations with preceding philosophical thought, subscribes a rigorously dichotomous philosophy, structured around a thesis that expresses an obvious and fundamental truth: the fact of being. It is this "fact of being" that allows there to be "things which are." The Archimedean point of Parmenides' philosophical thesis assumes a fact that is *prior* to the adoption of a determined constitutive ἀρχή of things. A basic fact overlooked in earlier philosophy: that "there are" things, which implies the recognition that "there is, what is being." According to Cordero, the fundamental thesis of Parmenides' philosophy lies in this theoretical point of view that confirms the "fact of being."

Secondly, focus is placed on Parmenides in the light of the abusive presence of the verb "to be" in his Poem. Cordero's Parmenides philosophically exploits a linguistic fact, a "syntactic anomaly" (to use his term) concerning the Greek language. He takes advantage of the plasticity of the verb "to be" in Greek. A first way is characterized by the starkness of the verb "to be" in the present tense, third person singular: "is" (ἔστιν), the conjugated form preferred by Parmenides, and nothing that implies any type of objectification of the stark "fact of being." This is a starkness that ἔστιν produces in the subject, a kind of product—argues Cordero—extracted analytically from the predicate. His reading does not dodge the issue of the subject of Parmenides' thesis, that is, the subject of the "is." In other words, to make a subject explicit would have distracted attention from the "fact of being," which is precisely what Parmenides wants to emphasize. Cordero's reading of the subject of ἔστιν thus moves away from classical conceptions (which either resorted to an implicit conceptual subject traced in the rest of the Poem or ruled out any possible subject). Cordero takes the middle ground: while not denying that there is a subject, he considers that this should not be extrapolated from other passages, but rather, as mentioned, should be gathered analytically from the signification of the ἔστιν. From the conjugated form "is" the subject is clarified ontologically, and is no other than "[that which is] being," as expressed in the Poem in the present participle of the verb to be (ἐόν, translated by Cordero as the Spanish gerund "siendo" ["being"]), or through the infinitive εἶναι. The "is" refers to a "to be being." Hence "by being, it is." Cordero's translation-interpretation of Parmenides' thesis reads: "Nobody can deny that what is, is being (ἐὸν ἔστιν)."[15]

This is a Parmenides that is defined, thirdly, by the absolutization of his original thesis, that is, by the necessary, absolute, and unique character he confers on the fact of being. We should not be surprised that Cordero's book carries the title *Parmenides' Thesis* and not *Parmenides' Thesis and its Negation*. The reason is simple. The negation of the thesis assumes—and by assuming reaffirms—the thesis itself. Or the reverse. The impossibility of negating the thesis demonstrates the validity of the thesis. The negation represented by the second route of not being is, in this respect, secondary and derived from the thesis or *primary* affirmation. Here Cordero pins down his reading: the negation of the thesis is impossible, because any negation of the fact of being must start from an understanding of the notion of the fact of being.

Fourthly, Cordero's Parmenides assumes a literal reading of the Poem, respecting above all its dichotomous logic. A Parmenides that alone takes responsibility for two "unique" (μοῦναι) routes of investigation, rather than three. Nor does his reading dodge the prickly issue of the number of routes. And this is important, because for some time it appeared that the fate of Parmenides' thinking was decided from the question of the number of routes in the Poem, as if anyone who wished to penetrate Parmenidean philosophy had to take on board the recent and burdensome inheritance of the routes question. By this I do not mean that the issue is a minor or banal one, but that it has taken on an exclusive prominence (especially since the last century) which has ultimately obscured other important areas of Parmenidean thought. Even so, Cordero has something to say about the "philological tragedy" surrounding this matter. If there is a wrong route in Parmenides' Poem it can only be the second

[15] Cordero, *Siendo*, p. 69; *By Being*, p. 52.

(i.e., the negation of the thesis). For Cordero this question is a closed case, because *all* the theoretical Parmenidean model rests on a rigorously dichotomous base (day-night, being-not being, truth-opinion), dominated by the principle of non-contradiction and excluded third.[16] Hence to hypostatize a "third" route has for him neither a theoretical nor practical basis. Let us say it is a problem of philosophical economy, as Aristotle said in that lethal passage in *Metaphysics* when he criticized the unnecessary duplication of reality that the Platonic theory of Ideas assumed: "as if someone, wanting to count, thought that he could not do so for there being few things, and yet, then counted them after increasing their number."[17] Gadamer, another philosopher who does not subscribe to the hypothesis of a third route, even declared ironically in a work titled "Parmenides and being": "Evidently Parmenides did not foresee the great wisdom of 19th century philosophers, capable of also finding in his text what is not there."[18]

In short, Cordero's reading shows us a Parmenides who subscribes to a fundamentally ontological philosophy: the first to be analytical about the "fact of being." This does not detract from the fact that this thesis throws up consequences on the gnoseological, logical and physical plane. Unlike interpreters in the English-speaking sphere, it is not an analytical line that predominates in his reading. Because Cordero is not interested in reducing Parmenides' philosophy to empty, formal models, under which "routes" are limited to expressing abstract principles applicable to any content. Although he clarifies that the principle of non-contradiction constitutes the basis of the thesis or route to the truth, there is less insistence on the logical Parmenides

16 There is a footnote in the book repeated twice which is worth highlighting: "An impartial observer would say that this question [of number of routes] is irrelevant, as when Parmenides presents the two possibilities in fragment 2 he says that they represent the 'unique' (μοῦναι) ways of investigation. There are only two 'unique' ways." (Cordero, *Siendo*, p. 116; *By Being*, p. 98). Since this tends to be overlooked, in Cordero's reading it takes on the form of a clear and distinct truth.

17 Aristotle, *Metaphysics* XIII, 4, 1078b34–36.

18 Hans G. Gadamer, "Parménides y el Ser," in H. G. Gadamer, *El inicio de la filosofía occidental* (Barcelona: Paidós, 1995), p. 124.

as "founder" of the three basic principles (of identity, non-contradiction and excluded third) systemized later.

Thus far is what I consider the basic nucleus of Cordero's Parmenides. Anyone who works in the area of ancient philosophy knows only too well that to reach a *way of reading* which carries the hallmark of an interpreter requires years of work and research, readings, rereadings and revisions. It is philosophy, recalling Bergson's phrase, as the result of a unique original intuition that then demands thirty or forty years to think it and translate it into concepts. But beyond the basic concepts mentioned, Cordero's reading reveals, in a general sense, the mark of Borges. Cordero's Parmenides implies, in my view, a reading hypothesis from which other hypotheses arise which ultimately form a *reading system*. A broad framework of understanding which makes it possible to discover throughout the book a network of underlying relationships. A reading device that, through the exegesis of the philosopher in question, makes it possible to read pre- and post-Parmenidean literature under a new light.

And it is here that Borges comes into play, because I believe that Cordero's reading of Parmenides employs an idea that Borges illustrates in a masterly style in his essay "Kafka and his precursors." In this celebrated essay, Borges recognizes the *preconfigurations* of the Kafka tone in texts from diverse literatures and periods. He records, for example, echoes of Kafka in Zeno's paradoxes against movement and in the religious parables of Kierkegaard's writing. In all the texts he enumerates, Borges recognizes, to a lesser or greater degree, the idiosyncrasy of Kafka. The thesis his essay rests on is simple: "The fact is that each writer *creates* his precursors. His work modifies our conception of the past, how it has to modify the future."[19] The same, I believe, can be applied to the figure of Parmenides and to the reading system proposed by Cordero. To reiterate: a system which, taking Parmenides as its center of reference, makes it possible to read backwards and forwards, thus resignifying pre- and post-Parmenidean literature. Because Parmenides' philosophical work modifies our conception of the

[19] Jorge L. Borges, "Kafka y sus Precursores," in J. L. Borges, *Otras Inquisiciones, Obras Completas,* Vol II (Buenos Aires: Emecé, 1990), p. 90.

past and the future. A kind of *Parmenides' thesis and its precursors.* What is stimulating about this Borgesian idea applied to the case of Parmenides is that it allows us to measure his philosophical work not only as a break with posterior philosophy but also as a resignification of our philosophical reading of the past. Read under this light, the break that Parmenides makes in the history of philosophy implies not only that the philosophy forged after his appearance can no longer be the same as what came before, but also—and this is the interesting part—that what came before can no longer be abstracted from his conceptual prism. Following this Borgesian idea which I believe can be seen to operate in Cordero's reading, we would have echoes of Parmenides in the Homeric-Hesiodic epic. For example: something of the deceiving and enchanting discourse of the "opinions of the mortals" in the sirens' song that Odysseus manages to resist by tying himself to the mast of his ship; something of the philosophical ἀγών between truth and opinion in the Muses of Hesiod; and something of the Parmenidean philosophical grammar in the Homeric signification of the verb "to be" as a synonym of "to live," "to breathe," "to exist" or "to be present." But echoes of Parmenides can also be heard in later philosophy, especially if we observe the fate that later awaited the "journey" or "path" narrative in the history of philosophy. This is a topic that Parmenides borrows from the mythical-religious world to retranslate it in a philosophical-poetic key. Following the Borgesian proposal, there may be clear echoes of the Parmenidean philosophical method or path in the pedagogical-political journey the prisoner undertakes in the Platonic allegory of the cave, in the erotic initiation of *Symposium* under the guide of another woman, Diotima; thus, as in Cartesian arguments of dream and malign genius, conceptual characters that attack, in the opinion of mortals, the straight path of knowledge or, in Cartesian terms, its refounding on the Archimedean point of the *cogito.*

Under this Borgesian reading device implicit in Cordero's reading, it is possible to illuminate the drifts of Parmenidean thought in the subsequent philosophy and, above all, the incomprehension it was often the object of: why Gorgias decides to penetrate and explore the second route prohibited by Parmenides, or why, in more general terms, the Sophistic takes on the task of deconstructing the Parmenidean trilogy of being-thinking-saying; why Plato in the *Sophist* undertakes the mission of *making more flexible* the absolute conception of the Parmenidean being which, from being so rigid and extreme, turned inoperable for his purpose of justifying the existence of images and false λόγος. Not to mention the issue of retroactive application to Parmenides of Platonic models, which obscure instead of clarify and even, arguably, *Platonize* the philosophy of Parmenides. An example of this can be found in the construction in the *Sophist* of an Eleatic "school," or the attribution of the "monist" label through which Parmenides made his triumphant entrance into the philosophy books, as well as the significations of λόγος and δόξα in Parmenides and in pre- and post-Parmenidean literature, fundamental for ceasing to read in him the alternative "sense versus reason" or the Platonic distinction between "being" and "appearing."[20]

Paraphrasing a phrase from the essay "The Pascal Sphere," I said at the start that perhaps it is now time to think of the history of philosophy as the history of a handful of concepts, among which that of "being" coined by Parmenides stands out. In an essay on poetry, Borges states that in the east neither literature nor philosophy were studied historically. "The history of philosophy is studied as if saying Aristotle argues with Bergson, Plato with Hume, all at once."[21] Without saying so explicitly, I believe that Cordero follows this Borgesian idea to the letter, in signaling as a conceptual framework of his reading that the classic philosophers "were conversing with ideas, not real people."[22] Philosophy as a perpetual dialogue between ideas, transcending the characters that formulate them. A dialogue route from a handful of concepts. This route—and no other—was for Borges in another text called "The Beginning," whose characters are Socrates and Parmenides, the "not impossible route to reach a truth."[23]

---

20 Gadamer, "Ser," p. 119.

21 Jorge L. Borges, "La Poesía," in J. L. Borges, *Siete noches*, *Obras completas*, Vol. III (Buenos Aires: Emecé, 1990), p. 265.

22 Cordero, *Siendo*, p. 14; *By Being*, p. x.

23 Jorge L. Borges, "El Principio," in *Atlas*, *Obras Completas*, Vol. III (Buenos Aires: Emecé, 1989), p. 415.

# Aristotle on the Semantic Unity of Parmenidean Being

Pilar Spangenberg

**Summary**

This article presents a reading of Aristotle's criticism of the Parmenidean thesis about the unity of being at *Physics* I, 2–3. I intend to show that Aristotle reduces the Parmenidean denial of the multiplicity of beings to the denial of the categories, and that this reading of Parmenidean monism determines the logical character of the strategy Aristotle utilizes against it. I argue that *Metaphysics G* represents a clue for understanding this strategy against Parmenides: in both cases the refutation must be radical in order to preserve the very possibility of science and language.

κτενεῖν νιν τοὺς τεκόντας ἦν λόγος
Sophocles, *Oedipus Tyrannus* 1180

Unlike his master, Aristotle does not have a filial relationship with earlier philosophers. On the contrary, he assumes the role of a severe and fair father who, faced with their philosophical mumblings, points out wise moves and corrects deviations. This paper attempts to show that Parmenides is to physics what sophists are to metaphysics: he represents the most feared son, who must be killed in order to survive.

Despite the texts offered by the tradition started by Plato, the fragments of Parmenides' Poem do not refer to the affirmation of a monism understood in terms of dissolution of all things into one.[1] In the presentation of the σήματα of ἐόν it is actually stated that it is total (8.4), homogeneous, and one (8.5–6) and, as a result, it has been established that the predication of unity is almost marginal in Parmenides.[2] Nevertheless, Aristotle often ascribes to Parmenides the theory that all things are one: πάντα ἕν.[3] I will attempt to explain, on the one hand, Aristotle's understanding of Parmenidean monism as it is dealt with in *Physics* I. And, based on such analysis, I will try to account for the strategy undertaken to combat the Eleatic. In order to throw light on the texts in *Physics* I and Aristotle's strategy, I will also make reference to some passages of *Metaphysics* IV, where the argumentative engineering employed shows significant similarities with *Physics* I, 2–3.

In the first book of *Physics*, Aristotle analyzes the principles of physical entities and, in chapter 2, he refers to the need to establish the number of existing principles.[4] Although in the dialectic analysis of his predecessors' doctrines regarding the number of principles Aristotle studies and refutes different philosophers, it is to monists that he pays most attention. Chapters 2 and 3 provide a long refutation to the monistic theory, a fact that leads us to question the reason why the monistic figure has such a vital role. I believe that *Metaphysics* IV gives us a clue to answer this question: both there and here, the possibility to demonstrate the first and most solid principle is denied. Thus, when undertaking the science of being in *Metaphysics* IV, the refutation of the opponent who denies the principle of non-contradiction (PNC) represents the opportunity to settle the first and most important

---

[1] Cordero states that "the only oneness detectable in Parmenides is linguistic; the singular replaces the plural; reflection upon *on* replaces reflection upon *onta*." See Néstor-Luis Cordero, *By Being, It is: The Thesis of Parmenides* (Las Vegas: Parmenides Publishing, 2004), p. 176.

[2] See Karl Reinhardt, *Parmenides und die Geschichte der Griechischen Philosophie* (Frankfurt: Vittorio Klostermann, 1916), p. 108, taken up by Cordero (*Siendo,* p. 101; *By Being,* p. 83).

[3] Thus, in *Parmenides*, Socrates ascribes to the Eleatic the thesis by which "the all is one" whereas in the *Sophist* he ascribes to him the thesis by which "each and all is one" (242d).

[4] The fact that Aristotle primarily refers to the number of principles and not to what those principles are, shows a fundamental question as regards the scope of Aristotle's *Physics*.

ontological principle. I consider that in this case, the monist's role is similar to that of the opponent of the PNC in *Metaphysics* IV, 4–6. In *Physics*, the monist opposes the most important principle of this science: that natural things are subject to change (κίνεσις, 185a12–13). Strictly speaking, monists undermine the possibility of any science, for they oppose the possibility of principles in themselves: no principle would exist if there is only one entity, for this would imply the existence of at least two things: the principle of the entity and the entity to which the principle belongs. Thus, by stating that being is one and motionless, the Eleatics, on the one hand, hinder the possibility of any principle and, on the other, deny the fundamental principle of physics: change.[5] For that reason, Aristotle states that their study is not about nature, since it is not incumbent on a particular science to shed light on its own principles (184b26–185a3).[6] However, he finds it appropriate to say something in that respect, for such analysis "is of interest for Philosophy" (185a20).[7] Thus, we can see that in *Physics* I, 2 as well as in *Metaphysics* IV what is at stake is a fundamental principle pertaining to the science in question, and that, as a consequence, it does not allow proof within the context of such science. Therefore, the refutation of its opponents will imply, for Aristotle, the opportunity to establish the basis of those sciences. In both cases, the theory of the opponent goes against the very possibility of science (of ontology, on the one hand; of physics, on the other).

---

[5] If, as ascribed by the doxographers, Parmenides' Poem is titled "*On Nature*," Aristotle would be directly suggesting that the Eleatic did not even refer to what his object of study would be.

[6] And Aristotle says: "It is the task of another science, or of a science common to all, to investigate the assumptions or principles of sciences." Much has been discussed about what this "science common to all" would be: some, like David Ross, *Aristotle's Physics: A Revised Text with Introduction and Commentary* (Oxford: Oxford Clarendon Press, 1936), p. 461, believe that Aristotle is making reference to the primary philosophy, i.e., metaphysics; others, like Wieland, think that he is talking about dialectics (134). See Wolfgang Wieland, *Die Aristotelische Physik* (Göttingen: Vandenhoeck & Ruprecht, 1970), p. 134.

[7] On the basis of such statements, it is evident that, for Aristotle, the φυσική ἐπιστήμη is not based on determining the physical principles, but on a philosophical analysis aiming at setting up the criteria by which it will be possible to postulate the principles of physical realities.

Aristotle asserts that monists formulate a paradoxical thesis like Heraclitus', and like those who affirm that "being is a unique man" (under which Protagoras would be concealed);[8] all these theses are formulated for the sake of mere discussion. Discussing them is like refuting an eristic argument (λόγον ἐριστικόν, 185a5–12). The comparison with Heraclitus (186a5 and 185b10) and Protagoras also makes direct reference to *Metaphysics* IV in that both thinkers are at the forefront of those who opposed the PNC, and are often said to "talk for the pleasure of it" (1009a16–22). There it is possible to identify several adversaries under the guise of the opponent of the principle that can be classified as those who argue for the pleasure of it and those who have fallen into an aporia as from the consideration of the sensible (ultimately, for being unable to explain motion).[9] With respect to the first group, he refers to sophists and specifically to Protagoras (1007b22; 1009b1ff.); among the physicists, he mentions Parmenides (1009b22). Consequently, in the context of the ontological book *Metaphysics,* the Eleatic receives a "physical treatment" while in the context of *Physics*, he paradoxically gets an "ontological treatment." Both in *Physics* and in *Metaphysics* IV, physicists seem to have made a mistake and, in this sense, they could be persuaded with regard to the truth of the principles.[10] But in *Physics*, Parmenides is distinguished from the rest, firstly because based on the aforementioned monism, he denies the possibility of physical science; and, secondly, because, like sophists in *Metaphysics* IV, he argues for the sake of discussion and develops eristic arguments. The parallel between the treatment given to the sophist in *Metaphysics* IV and to Parmenides in *Physics* I is not a coincidence: in the contexts of *Physics*, Parmenides is placed among those who support a total indetermination of being. In *Metaphysics* IV he makes explicit that the monist thesis

[8] Charlton says that it is "perhaps a solipsistic extension of Protagorean doubt." W. Charlton, *Aristotle's Physics* I, II (Oxford: Oxford Clarendon Press, 1970), p. 54.

[9] On the adversary typology in *Metaphysics* IV, see Barbara Cassin and Michel Narcy, *La Décision du Sens* (Paris: Vrin, 1989), pp. 56–57.

[10] The chart including those who have dealt with the number of principles is included in this chapter, whereas the dialectical treatment of their theses begins in chapter 4.

implies denial of the PNC: "If contradictories are all simultaneously true of the same thing, it is plain that everything will be one" (1007b18–19). Thus, the denial of the principle involves monism. And monism involves the denial of the PNC: "If all things are one in account, like raiment and apparel, they will find themselves in the position of Heraclitus. The being of good and the being of bad, of good and not good, will be the same, so that good and not good, man and horse, will be the same" (185b19–24). Thus, in the context of *Physics*, Parmenides plays a role equivalent to that of the sophist's in *Metaphysics*: he is the opponent of change, first principle of physics.

Another sign of the parallel is that in *Metaphysics* IV Aristotle states that asking for a demonstration of the PNC constitutes ignorance, and that no error is possible in connection with it and, similarly, in *Physics* he states that the reality of motion is clear by ἐπαγωγή (a term that here acquires the sense of experience rather than of logical reasoning, 185a12–14).[11] In other words, in both cases what is threatened is evidence.[12] However, in both texts there is a line of argument that refutes the opponent of the principle, for we have already seen that there is no science without refutation of these radical positions.

Let us consider the main criticism to prove how the multiplicity of entities is reduced to the multiplicity of the senses of being by Aristotle (the newly established step from physics to logic). The argument starts by formulating his own thesis: "The most pertinent way to begin will be to point out what do they mean (πῶς λέγουσιν) those who assert that all things are one. For

---

[11] On this subject, see Marcelo Boeri, "Aristóteles contra Parménides: el problema del cambio y la posibilidad de una ciencia física," *Tópicos: Revista de Filosofía* 30, 2 (2006), 45–68.

[12] Aristotle says: "That nature exists, it would be absurd to try to prove; for it is obvious that there are many things of this kind, and to prove what is obvious by what is not is the mark of a man who is unable to distinguish what is self-evident from what is not. To inquire therefore whether Being is one in this sense would be like arguing against any other position maintained for the sake of argument [. . .] or like refuting a merely contentious argument—a description which applies to the arguments both of Melissus and of Parmenides: their premises are false and their conclusions do not follow [. . .]. We must take for granted that the things that exist by nature are, either all or some of them, in motion which is indeed made plain by ἐπαγωγή" (193a3–6).

being is said in many senses (πολλαχῶς λέγεται τὸ ὄν, 185a21)." This anticipates the way in which Aristotle primarily conceives Parmenides' monism: a denial of *the multiplicity of the senses of being*. Thus, criticism will be conducted from the analysis of the concepts of "being" and "one." Hence, from the statement "being is one," Aristotle will examine, in the first place, what "being" means and, in the second place, what "one" means.

Aristotle starts by studying what monists understand by "being." He believes that "being" and "one" have only one meaning for Parmenides, who gives to such terms an absolute sense (ἁπλῶς, 186a24). If everything that is is one single thing, monists could consider that all things (τὰ πάντα) are identified with substance or quality or quantity, on the one hand, and with a particular substance (like one man or one horse) or quality (like pale, or hot), on the other. None of these possibilities can be affirmed, for if substance and quantity and quality are, then, whether these exist independently of each other or not, being will be many; and, if everything is quantity or quality, then being is multiple, because none can subsist without substance, and that involves at least two categories. This criticism is clearly based on his own theory of the categories.

In the second place, Aristotle applies a semantic analysis to "one." Like "being," "one" is used in many senses since it means (a) a continuous; or (b) an indivisible; or (c) that two things have the same definition. Aristotle performs a *reductio ad absurdum* by proving that "all" cannot be "one" in none of these three senses: (a) if "one" is one in the sense of continuous, it is many, for the continuous is (potentially) divisible *ad infinitum*;[13] (b) if it is indivisible, nothing would have quantity or quality (because it

[13] Here, Aristotle does not seem to be entirely fair with Melissus and Parmenides. They could reply that while "all" remains as a unity and its parts are not separated, only "all" exists, not its parts. According to Aristotle himself, parts potentially exist, but this is the same as affirming that they *could* exist separately. But, on the other hand, that possibility is explicitly denied by Parmenides, for, in order to separate them, it would be necessary to divide "is" from "what is," and such a thing could only be carried out by introducing "what is not" as a dividing means. However, since the existence of the "not being" is not possible for Eleatic thinking, the parts are impossible. See David Bostock, *Space, Time, Matter, and Form: Essays on Aristotle's* Physics (Oxford: Oxford University Press, 2006), p. 104.

presupposes another thing: substance), and so the "one" will not be infinite nor limited, for though the limit is indivisible, the limited is not; (c) if it is "one" by having the same definition, as we have seen, we should go back to the doctrine that Aristotle ascribes to Heraclitus in *Metaphysics* IV by which it is possible to affirm the contradictories at the same time with truth: if two things have the same definition, it is because they are the same. If it is all the things at the same time, it is not (185b19–24).

In the context of this analysis of unity, Aristotle makes reference to the realm of language when he mentions the perplexity of ancient thinkers in view of the possibility that something can be "one" (a subject) and "many" (the predications) at the same time, as shown by the λόγος. He states that, in order to solve this problem at the language level, some, like Lycophron, were led to omit "is" for fear that if they added it they would be making the "one" be "many."[14] To overcome this aporia, Aristotle resorts to the ideas of power and act. In *Metaphysics* IV, in parallel, this distinction solved the problem of φύσις (because it allowed defeating the aporias of motion); here, it solved the problem of predication (the possibility of λόγος).[15]

In chapter 3, he addresses more critiques to Parmenides. Aristotle repeats that the Eleatic begins from false premises and that his arguments do not follow (186a23–24). The false premise from which Parmenides starts implies that "being" is one (this has already been examined and refuted in chapter 2). His conclusions do not follow, because if there are only white things, says Aristotle, and if "white" has a single meaning, nonetheless it will be two things: the being of white and that of the thing of which "white" is predicated. "White" has to manifest itself in something, for it is a characteristic or determination of a οὐσία. On the basis of this theory, it is evident how the many different senses of "is" appear again.

Some scholars have considered that, at this stage, the Aristotelian arguments against monism imply a break. Further

[14] Aristotle seems to face the same opponent mentioned by Plato in *Sophist* 244b–245d.

[15] Regarding the ideas of power and act and their importance when explaining motion cf. *Physics* II.

on (from 186a32 to 187a11), no proper names appear. Aristotle then avoids technical language and adopts more simple linguistic schemes, since terms like οὐσία, ποιόν, and ποσόν are not mentioned.[16] That is why it has been understood that these arguments try to be based on Parmenides' premises without risking his own (Aristotelian) categories of thought; but this is not absolutely so. These last arguments are strictly logical (understanding "logic" in a broad sense determined by the plurality of significations of λόγος in Greek) and aims at showing that Parmenides' theory is untenable from the point of view of predication and definition. The Aristotelian thought and terminology about being reappears, but this time it is deduced from the critiques he addresses to the Eleatic thesis.

Now, I have presented an overview of the interpretations and criticisms made of Parmenidean being in *Physics* and we saw that Aristotle confronts Parmenides by analyzing the senses of being. The logical nature of the interpretation and criticism of the unity of the Parmenidean being has lead some scholars to criticize it. Cherniss, for example, understands that Aristotle confuses logic and physics when dealing with Parmenides' thought. This confusion would arise from the dependence of physics with regard to logic.[17] In my opinion, this interpretation implies ignoring the mediating role of semantics between logic and ontology in Aristotle's thought.

However, in order to deal with this idea, it is first necessary to establish what "physics" and "logic" mean. Clearly, Aristotle's physics constitutes a meta-investigation which does not mainly seek to determine what the specific principles of physical objects are, but to present a hypothesis about the characteristics of any theory of motion.[18] In this sense, it involves the development of an ontology of the entities that have in themselves the principle of

---

[16] D. E. Gershenson and D. A. Greenberg, "Aristotle Confronts the Eleatic Two Arguments on 'The One,'" *Phronesis* 7 (1962), 137–150.

[17] Harold Cherniss, *La Crítica Aristotélica a la Filosofía Presocrática* (México D.F.: Universidad Nacional Autónoma de México, 1991), p. 97.

[18] David Bostock emphasizes the meta-investigational nature of this book (*Space*, p. 4). For a complete discussion on the nature of the Aristotelian *Physics* see Lambros Couloubaritsis, *La Psysique d'Aristote. L'avènement de la Science Phsysique* (2nd edition: Bruxelles: Editions OUSIA, 1997), pp. 17–48.

motion and rest.[19] And all that is connected with the understanding of physics in a broad sense. So, in the first place regarding logic, it is known that its separation from ontology is fictitious in Aristotle. His great ontological texts show the semantics of being. This implies that the criticism of the Eleatic philosopher that is based on a semantic analysis does not involve a reduction of the Parmenidean being into a merely logical being, but to a metaphysical commitment consisting of finding the opening of "being" to the world (or, in the case of Aristotle's Parmenides, the closure), and a methodological commitment that involves the analysis of the senses of being as a privileged procedure of philosophy. Thus, logic and physics are intercepted in ontology.

Secondly, Aristotle does not ignore the difference between logic and physics. In fact, in *Metaphysics* I, Aristotle states that Parmenides "conceived of the unity as one in definition (κατὰ τὸν λόγον)." This formulation, asserts Aristotle, is more interesting than that of all other monistic thinkers[20] for "Parmenides seems in places to speak with more insight. For, claiming that, besides the existent, nothing non-existent exists, he thinks that by necessity one thing exists, viz. the existent and nothing else" (986b18 et seq.). And, in *On the Heavens,* the Parmenidean One is characterized in similar terms, affirming that Eleatics do not think in terms of physics, for the supporters were the first who realized that knowledge requires the existence of immutable substances. But as they only considered that sensible objects existed, they applied to them the arguments concerning the objects of thought (298b14–24).[21] Therefore, it is clear that here Aristotle does something similar to what was done in *Metaphysics* IV, where he takes advantage of his adversary's weapon, the *lógos,* and uses it against him. On the basis of the identity between logic and

[19] Boeri, "Aristóteles," p. 57.

[20] He mentions Xenophanes and Melissus, who, he affirms, are more "rustic."

[21] "They (Melissus and Parmenides), however, had no idea of any form of "being" other than the substance of things perceived; and when they saw, what no one previously had seen, that there could be no knowledge or wisdom without some such unchanging entities, they naturally transferred what was true of them to things perceived." (*On the Heavens,* 298b21–24). Cherniss, *Crítica,* p. 84 holds that Aristotle infers this explanation from a literal interpretation of Plato's *Parmenides* 135 b–c.

physics assumed by Eleatics, as attributed in *Metaphysics* I and *On the Heavens*, a logical-semantic analysis will be enough to dismiss Parmenidean thinking from the field of physics.

Finally, the fact that Aristotle uses his own language when formulating the thesis ascribed to Parmenides would not be a vice from the Aristotelian viewpoint, but would rather show for him the limits of a thought that, from his perspective, cannot be but translated into a language that, at the same time, invalidates it in its own formulation. Nevertheless, with regard to Parmenides Aristotle is not as cold as when, for example, he criticizes Plato. Aubenque has shown how some sort of dissatisfaction can be perceived in Aristotle's text when he confronts the sophist, and this explains the harsh treatment received by this adversary.[22] This may be due to the fact that he is totally conscious that it is impossible to strictly refute his adversary, who would remain impassive towards Aristotelian criticism. In my opinion, Aristotle's harshness towards Parmenides in this context is due to the same matrix: a refutation in the strict sense of the Eleatic thinker is not possible because, from Aristotle's point of view, Parmenides subtracts himself even from language, for it necessarily implies "many." The possibility of a sophistic or Parmenidean λόγος would then dissolve the λόγος itself and, with it, the possibility of any science. Then, the battle against them must be a matter of life and death.

[22] Pierre Aubenque, *Le Problème de l'être chez Aristote* (Paris: Quadrige, 1966), p. 94.

# Index Locorum

# General Index

# Index of Greek Terms Discussed

• ALSO AVAILABLE FROM PARMENIDES PUBLISHING •

## PRE-SOCRATICS

***By Being, It Is:*** *The Thesis of Parmenides* by Néstor-Luis Cordero

***To Think Like God:*** *Pythagoras and Parmenides. The Origins of Philosophy.* Scholarly and fully annotated edition by Arnold Hermann

***The Illustrated to Think Like God:*** *Pythagoras and Parmenides. The Origins of Philosophy* by Arnold Hermann with over 200 full color illustrations

***The Legacy of Parmenides:*** *Eleatic Monism and Later Presocratic Thought* by Patricia Curd

***Parmenides and the History of Dialectic:*** *Three Essays* by Scott Austin

***Parmenides, Venerable and Awesome:*** *Proceedings of the International Symposium* edited by Néstor-Luis Cordero

***The Route of Parmenides:*** *Revised and Expanded Edition, With a New Introduction, Three Supplemental Essays, and an Essay by Gregory Vlastos*, by Alexander P. D. Mourelatos

***The Fragments of Parmenides:*** *A Critical Text with Introduction and Translation, the Ancient* Testimonia *and a Commentary* by A. H. Coxon. Revised and Expanded Edition edited with new Translations by Richard McKirahan and a new Preface by Malcolm Schofield

## PLATO

***God and Forms in Plato*** by Richard D. Mohr

***Image and Paradigm in Plato's* Sophist** by David Ambuel

***Interpreting Plato's Dialogues*** by J. Angelo Corlett

***One Book, the Whole Universe:*** *Plato's* Timaeus *Today* edited by Richard D. Mohr and Barbara M. Sattler

***The Philosopher in Plato's* Statesman** by Mitchell Miller

***Platonic Patterns:*** *A Collection of Studies* by Holger Thesleff

***Plato's Late Ontology:*** *A Riddle Resolved* by Kenneth M. Sayre

***Plato's* Parmenides:** *Text, Translation & Introductory Essay* by Arnold Hermann. Translation in collaboration with Sylvana Chrysakopoulou with a Foreword by Douglas Hedley

***Plato's Universe*** by Gregory Vlastos

## ARISTOTLE

***One and Many in Aristotle's* Metaphysics**—*Volume I: Books Alpha-Delta* by Edward C. Halper

***One and Many in Aristotle's* Metaphysics**—*Volume 2: The Central Books* by Edward C. Halper

## HELLENISTIC PHILOSOPHY

***A Life Worthy of the Gods:*** *The Materialist Psychology of Epicurus* by David Konstan

## ETHICS

***Sentience and Sensibility:*** *A Conversation about Moral Philosophy* by Matthew R. Silliman

## AUDIOBOOKS

***The Iliad*** (unabridged) by Stanley Lombardo

***The Odyssey*** (unabridged) by Stanley Lombardo

***The Essential Homer*** by Stanley Lombardo

***The Essential Iliad*** by Stanley Lombardo

## FORTHCOMING

***Aristotle's* Physics *VII.3*:** *What is Alteration? Proceedings of the International ESAP-HYELE Conference* edited by Stefano Maso, Carlo Natali, and Gerhard Seel

***Plotinus the Platonist:*** *A Comparative Account of Plato and Plotinus. Their Mysticism, Epistemology, Metaphysics, and Ethics* by David J. Yount

***Presocratics and Plato:*** *A Festschrift in Honor of Charles Kahn* edited by Richard Patterson, Vassilis Karasmanis, and Arnold Hermann

***Ennead IV.8:*** *On the Soul's Descent into Body. Translation, with an Introduction and Commentary* by Barry Fleet

The above will be the first volume in our new series

***THE ENNEADS OF PLOTINUS:***

*Translations with Introductions and Philosophical Commentaries on Individual Treatises.*

Series edited by John M. Dillon and Andrew Smith